*The Hidden Law*

# THE HIDDEN LAW

*The Poetry of W. H. Auden*

Anthony Hecht

HARVARD UNIVERSITY PRESS
Cambridge, Massachusetts
London, England

10  9  8  7  6  5  4  3  2

Pages 465–467 constitute an extension of the copyright page.

This book is printed on acid-free paper, and its binding
materials have been chosen for strength and durability.

Library of Congress Cataloging-in-Publication Data

Hecht, Anthony, 1923–
   The hidden law : the poetry of W. H. Auden / Anthony Hecht.
      p.     cm.
   Includes index.
   ISBN 0-674-39006-7 (alk. paper) (cloth)
   ISBN 0-674-39007-5 (pbk.)
   1. Auden, W. H. (Wystan Hugh), 1907–1973—Criticism and
interpretation.     I. Title.
PR6001.U4Z73 1993
811'.52—dc20                                    92-25497
                                                    CIP

To the memory of my brother, Roger,
and of Timothy S. Healy, S.J.

# Contents

# *Preface*

In an essay on La Fontaine, Paul Valéry astutely comments, "What is more misleading than those truthful men who confine themselves to telling us what they saw, just as we might have seen it ourselves? What do I care for what can be seen? One of the most responsible men I ever knew, and with the most methodical habits of thought, ordinarily gave the impression of complete frivolity: a second nature cloaked him in nonsense. Our mind and our body are alike in this: they wrap in mystery and hide from themselves what they feel is most important; they mark and protect it by the depth at which they place it. Everything that counts is well veiled; witnesses and documents obscure it; acts and works are expressly made to disguise it." I have not the least doubt that Auden would have approved of these views, and would have known perfectly well that his own work was a resounding instance of their truth. Poetry has long been thought of as a sort of code, and more than that, a shibboleth: a device to prevent any invasion of the domain of occult knowledge and understanding by those who are deemed unworthy. And poets exhibit varying degrees or strategies of reticence.

At the same time, no poet would desire to be so exclusive as to divorce himself entirely from all his readers, and each poet must have an audience, no care how small, in mind. This makes of the critic, for better or worse, a kind of code-breaker, a *soi-disant* Champollion whose sustaining energy derives from the conviction, not always justified, that he has rent the veil and seen to the heart of the mystery.

I have had the pleasure of reading Auden's poetry for all my mature life. I first discovered it at the age of eighteen, when Auden, who was sixteen years my senior, was already famous and settled in America. I had always reserved for his work, through varying stages of opinion about it, the sort of instinctive respect one pays to an elder, and though the interval between our ages necessarily remained the same sixteen-year interval throughout our lives, it became increasingly less significant as we both grew older. And now I am shocked to discover that by a bewildering accident of fate I am older than Auden ever lived to be, and have grown, at least in years, to be his senior. That very fact, along with his penetrating gaze from the photographic portrait on the cover of the Vintage International Edition of the *Collected Poems,* has alerted me to the singular (and plural) dangers of presumption, both of youth and of age. And so have his poems, which both invite the intrusive scrutiny of the cryptographer and deny him access.

In offering this book to the public I can claim no privileged intimacy with the poet or special knowledge of his ideas. I have wanted simply to set down my own by no means settled views of his work. And if at times I sound as if I had decisively broken the code-barrier, I have always tried to remember that my own views have changed as much as Auden's over the years. In fact, I suspect that I may have changed my views more often and decisively than he, for it may be claimed that certain strands of his thought remain fixed through all the phases of his career. For example, his embrace of certain doctrines of psychology, Freudian, Lawrentian, and other varieties, concerning the dangers attendant upon the suppression of instinctual feelings, were to survive in theological guise as a fierce repudiation of the Manichaean heresy and a principled disdain for the Albigensians and Cathars. In someone less thoughtful, less principled and conscious than Auden, this might be taken as little more than a series of rationalizations for self-indulgence, a sybaritic defiance of puritanism. And while there is no way to prove that it was not, I am confident in my belief that it wasn't. There is very little, if anything, in the way of "abandon" in his work, and he inclined, quietly but firmly, to disapprove of some of the more celebrated work of the fifties and sixties which promoted and expressed a reckless anti-intellectual libertinism. The dialectical oppositions of Plato (representing a sublimated and discarnate mental life) and Rousseau (representing raw, instinctual antinomian willfulness) figure importantly and often in his work. He would have strongly endorsed Valéry's declaration: "I like those lovers of poetry who venerate the goddess with too much lucidity to dedicate to her the slackness of their thought and the relaxation of their reason. They know well that she does not exact the *sacrifizio dell' Intelletto.*"

No enterprise such as mine could have been undertaken without the distinguished work of others who preceded me. Some of these critics I must have read almost as carefully, if not as often, as I read Auden himself; and I am probably only partly aware of the full burden of my indebtedness to them. But so much was I truly aware of it that, for the most part, I tried not to look at their books as I was writing my own, except in cases where I found myself puzzled or in doubt. So when the reader finds that, without any expression of gratitude, I have belatedly offered an explication that greatly resembles those of earlier critics, apart from the slender possibility that critics may sometimes arrive at similar interpretations without consultation with one another I must claim that the work of some few but eminent ones has so much by now become a part of my general sense of Auden's work that I can no longer distinguish between aperçus of my own and their early, persuasive instruction. Of these the most important must include Monroe K. Spears, who enjoyed the unique benefit of Auden's cooperation in writing his magisterial work, *The Poetry of W. H. Auden: The Disenchanted Island,* which surely remains the most commanding conspectus of Auden's rich and varied career. I am probably almost equally indebted to John Fuller, whose *Reader's Guide to W. H. Auden* undertakes to offer critical comment on each and every one of Auden's poems and plays. I have relied in ways that are explicit and acknowledged on the diligent research of Humphrey Carpenter, whose careful biography of Auden was blamed, when it first appeared, for perhaps revealing too much about the poet, but which has in the course of time lost its small *frisson* of scandal and has proved to have been written in a spirit of genuine respect and admiration. And it goes not without saying that my debt to Edward Mendelson, like that of any careful reader or scholar of Auden today and henceforward, must be incalculable. His editorial supervision of the publication of Auden's *oeuvre* would alone be grounds for indebtedness, including as it does the *Selected Poems, Collected Poems, The English Auden,* and the volume of *Plays, 1928–1938* of the projected *The Complete Works of W. H. Auden,* which Princeton University Press has undertaken to publish under Professor Mendelson's editorship. To this must be added his exemplary volume of critical analysis, *Early Auden,* in which all of Auden's writing prior to his arrival in the United States is examined with punctilious care. Insofar as I have ventured to differ from him on one or two small points, this was never without complete respect and great admiration for his work.

More warmly and personally still, I wish to thank Daniel Albright and J. D. McClatchy, who read through the entire manuscript (but for the final, as of that time unwritten, chapter) in one of its very late incarnations, and gave me unstintingly the full benefit of their very wise counsel. They are, of course, not to be held accountable for follies of my own, insinuated into the text after it had passed beyond their scrutiny, nor for those other occasions on which I rashly ignored their tactful hints. I have profited beyond any possible accounting from their careful, detailed, informed advice and their invaluable encouragement.

I must list one other scholar, this one whose name is not yet well known. David Mason wrote his as yet unpublished dissertation on Auden's longer poems partly under my supervision for his doctoral degree at the University of Rochester. Both his researches and his acuity taught me a good deal I would not myself have discovered; I want to express here my deep and sincere gratitude for his help.

In addition, I am greatly indebted for help, information, or insights of one sort or another, to the following: Alan Ansen, Joseph Brodsky, Ashley Brown, Ted Danforth, Samuel Hynes, Nicholas Jenkins, Bernard Knox, Elias Mengel, the Right Reverend Hays H. Rockwell, Jon Stallworthy, and William H. Whyte. I owe special thanks to Joan Reuss, who typed the manuscript of this book through a number of revisions without ever evincing anything but a friendly cheerfulness. I acknowledge with great gratitude and considerable chagrin the enormous labors of Katya Rice, who went through the manuscript with meticulous care and saved me from more clumsiness and error than anyone but the nameless compositor—may he keep his peace—shall ever know. And I owe a huge debt to Jennifer Snodgrass, not alone for her scrupulous editing but for subtle, persuasive, and invaluable suggestions. She did so after having first proposed that I write a book of perhaps a hundred and twenty pages, and remained undismayed by what she got instead.

It is, of course, my hope that the reader will not be dismayed, either, by the bulk of what is here set down. When one hundred and twenty pages' worth was first proposed to me, I was uncertain and dimly alarmed that I might not have enough to say. But I hope that the reader will be persuaded that everything I have written was engendered and sustained by a prolonged sense of excitement and discovery. And it was sustained as well by the encouragement of my beloved wife and youngest son.

I have completed this book on the last day of 1991, on the threshold of my seventieth year. It has given me great delight, and my feeling for its subject is one of undiluted gratitude.

A. H.

The Hidden Law does not deny
Our laws of probability,
But takes the atom and the star
And human beings as they are,
And answers nothing when we lie.

It is the only reason why
No government can codify,
And verbal definitions mar
        The Hidden Law.

Its utter patience will not try
To stop us if we want to die:
When we escape It in a car,
When we forget It in a bar,
These are the ways we're punished by
        The Hidden Law.

# I. Everything That Counts Is Well Veiled: *Poems*

The foreword to W. H. Auden's *Collected Shorter Poems, 1927–1957* begins, "In 1944, when I first assembled my shorter pieces, I arranged them in the alphabetical order of their first lines. This may have been a silly thing to do, but I had a reason. At the age of thirty-seven I was still too young to have any sure sense of the direction in which I was moving, and I did not wish critics to waste their time, and mislead readers, making guesses about it which would almost certainly turn out to be wrong. Today, nearing sixty [the copyright date of this volume is 1966], I believe I know myself and my poetic intentions better and, if anybody wants to look at my writings from an historical perspective, I have no objection."

"Silly" is a curious word to describe Auden's radical reordering and revision of his poetry (as well as some prose) in the volume of 1945 called *The Collected Poetry of W. H. Auden*. There was something astonishing, reckless, and defiant about that volume. And if the poet was concerned about "critics" who were trying to trace or to predict the direction and movement his poetry had taken or was to take, it seems reasonable to suppose that one of these critics was Randall Jarrell, who, having been from the first one of Auden's warmest and most enthusiastic admirers and outright imitators, in 1941 published an essay called "Changes of Attitude and Rhetoric in Auden's Poetry," which opens, "In the first part of this article I want to analyze the general position Auden makes for himself in his early poems, and to show how the very different attitude of the later poems developed from it; in the second part I shall describe the language of the early poems and the rhetoric of the late, and try to show why one developed from the other." The "anatomy" Jarrell proceeds to offer is not merely historical or morphological; it vibrates with rising hostility as it advances. This is by no means the first index of Jarrell's disaffection, nor the last. Also in 1941 he published a brief review of the *New Year Letter*, which says,

In 1931 Pope's ghost said to me, "Ten years from now the leading young poet of the time will publish, in *The Atlantic Monthly,* a didactic epistle of about nine hundred tetrameter couplets." I answered absently, "you're a fool"; and who on this earth would have thought him anything else? But he was right: the decline and fall of modernist poetry—if so big a swallow, and a good deal of warm weather, make a summer—were nearer than anyone could have believed . . . The poem is not quite first-rate. It lacks the necessary finality of presentation; it is at a remove; the urgency and reality have been diluted. Evil is talked about but not brought home; there is a faint sugary smell of *tout comprendre [c']est tout pardonner:* everything is going to be all right in the end. When one remembers his earliest poetry at its best, one feels unreasonably homesick for the fleshpots of Egypt.

By the time (1945) Jarrell got around to writing the essay called "Freud to Paul: The Stages of Auden's Ideology," his patience had worn very thin indeed. And he was still engaged in examining the evolution, or changes, of the *ideas* in Auden's poetry. Others had also expressed reservations and dissents about the later poetry, but Jarrell's attack, coming after his early adulation, was a dramatic turnabout that struck Auden with personal force. It was therefore at least in part to scotch the kind of intellectual autopsy Jarrell was performing with such surgical gusto that Auden came up with the rather eccentric but also ingenious and mechanical means of randomly reordering a large segment of his work.

The revision was more than the purely alphabetical reordering. The poems were divided into a section called "Poems" and another called "Songs and Other Musical Pieces." The reasons for this division are not always plain, and sometimes are frankly obscure. Certainly Auden wrote "songs," and verses either that were written for a composer or that he envisioned as fit for musical setting. He also wrote poems that were frankly imitative of popular songs, of blues, ballads, and the sort of Broadway musical lyrics that Cole Porter or Rodgers and Hart had made familiar. But mixed in with these, usually lighter, verses were such poems as "Look, stranger, on this island now," which has little in common with the songs, as well as "Jumbled in one common box," "Dear, though the night is gone," and "Lay your sleeping head, my love." The assemblage of such diverse lyrics under a separate heading is odd and not easy to explain, except as a further means of obfuscation.

In addition, there is a section devoted entirely to the prose piece titled "Depravity: A Sermon," which careful readers have recognized as the absolutely unaltered text of the Vicar's sermon at the end of *The Dog Beneath the Skin*. The stage directions which preceded that sermon read,

> The Vicar *rises to his feet. He delivers the following sermon: beginning in his usual pulpit manner, but quickly becoming more excited, more histrionic, more daring in his gestures and poses. The final passage is wailed rather than spoken. Tears pour down his cheeks, saliva runs from his mouth: He has worked himself up into an hysterical frenzy.*

The text which follows, and which begins, "What was the weather on Eternity's worst day?" is clearly meant (in the context of the play) to represent the cheapest kind of pietistic evangelism, a sacerdotal defense of bourgeois values, a canting, self-hypnotic doomsaying whose theatrical purpose is to be comically satiric. But in the collection of poems it is preceded by a note that reads,

> *I can only hope that this piece will seem meaningless to those who are not professing Christians, and that those who are, and consequently know that it is precisely in their religious life that the worst effects of the Fall are manifested, will not misinterpret it as simple anticlericalism which always implies a flattery of the laity.*
>
> *It is concerned with two temptations: the constant tendency of the spiritual life to degenerate into an aesthetic performance; and the fatal ease with which Conscience, i.e., the voice of God, is replaced by "my conscience," i.e., the Super-Ego which, as a writer in* Punch *remarked some years ago, "is very genteel," and holds one variant or another of the Dualist heresy.*

(One would like to know how Auden would have reconciled the rather high tone of this note with the passage in the 1964 essay "The Protestant Mystics," in which, writing of "the Vision of God," he states, "There is, as one can see in the writings of men like George Herbert, Lancelot Andrewes, Charles Williams, a characteristic Anglican style of piety . . . At its best, it shows spiritual good manners, a quality no less valuable in the religious life than in the social life, though, of course, not the ultimate criterion in either"—which *also* sounds pretty genteel.)

Auden had made changes, some of them important, in individual poems: a whole stanza was omitted from "September 1, 1939," and a crucial line that Orwell had made callous fun of was altered in "Spain." *Paid on Both Sides* was omitted *in toto*. Of *The Orators* only "Letter to a Wound" was included, along with a couple of the six odes with which it concluded. In other words, a muddying of the waters of sequence was accomplished in that volume in a very thoroughgoing way. And the effect of this was implicitly to ask of the reader that each poem be appraised, as it were, on its own merits, in isolation, as an individual work, and without regard to its place in any larger scheme of personal development or growth. And this is, in the long run, the way we really do read most poetry: poem by poem. It is held neither for nor against Dryden *as a poet* that he began as a defender and admirer of Cromwell and ended as a Catholic. His poems are not valued as being either better or worse for such changes.

Nor is Auden the first to have looked back upon his own literary past and regretted some of it, and even to have attempted to alter it. Very many poets revise—and suppress. Eliot rather interestingly changed from lower- to upper-case *j* in the word "Jew" in several poems. And he tried so successfully to erase the publication of *After Strange Gods* that there are now college and university libraries that do not possess a copy of that work, and readers of Eliot who are only dimly aware that he wrote it. Lowell was an even more relentless reviser of his work; some of his poems are almost unrecognizable when we encounter them in their second or third incarnations. And the *Variorum* Yeats is a monument to tinkering. Curiously, for all the alterations and modifications Auden continued to make in his poems, he nevertheless is reported by Alan Ansen to have said (in 1947), "I decided not to do any correcting of the earlier syllabic pieces. After all they're all in print. I shouldn't go back on them. That was a detestable habit of George Moore's—he kept revising his works."

We all, of course, are accomplished revisionists of our histories by the familiar mechanism of repression that shapes our dreams and memories. Auden was fascinated not only by the agile ways of the unconscious but by the keenly conscious ways we contrive to present ourselves to the world (as well as to ourselves) in a, for the most part, favorable light. He was always interested in the modes, the styles, the disguises, of biography and autobiography, and the ways we find—either dangerous or amusing—of distorting the views of our lives. This interest of his shows itself in his ambivalent attitude towards the records and recording of his own life. While appearing to be flatly opposed to biographies of writers, which he called "always superfluous, and usually in bad taste," and while requesting that all his friends destroy all the letters from him they had received, he was often delighted by the biographies (and autobiographies) of other writers, an avid reader of their letters, and in a review ("As It Seemed to Us" in *Forewords and Afterwords*) of memoirs by Evelyn Waugh and Leonard Woolf, he volunteers some unusual and interesting information about himself. He took particular delight in Nigel Denis' remarkable work, *Cards of Identity,* which presents, under the rubric of fictive "case histories," the account by one Father Golden Orfe of an English monastery peopled entirely by former Communists, now converts to the Roman Catholic faith, who are committed to the writing of autobiographical confessions, which, if deemed not to be in line with the orthodoxy of their new faith, are "purged" in much the same way that obtained in the Soviet Union under Stalin. It also contains another "case history," this one of totally garbled sexual identity.

> When I was being pubescent, both my parents were killed in a railway accident . . . I passed into the care of a minor aunt. At least, I think she was an aunt, though I remember calling her Nunk. I am unsure because it was at this time that I began to treasure the words which were my father's only bequest to me. "Always remember," he had said, "that there is no such thing as pure male and pure female. Some wear skirts and some wear pants, but this is only convention. Every man is stuffed with womanly characteristics, every woman is fraught with man. The gap between the powder-puff and the cavalry moustache appears wide but is merely a hair's breadth. I tell you this so that when you grow up and find yourself behaving oddly, as I trust you will, you will know that it is quite apropos. After all, think of dogs."

Of this 1955 book Auden commented, "I have read no novel published during the last fifteen years with greater pleasure and admiration." The delight of the mature man must have required an important eclipse of memory, for, as Carpenter reports, in 1971 "Auden recalled that one of the last times he saw his father before Dr. Auden joined the R.A.M.C. was when his parents put on fancy dress for a party: 'She had on his clothes and a false moustache, and he was wearing hers . . . I suppose they thought it would amuse me. I was terrified.' John Auden [an elder brother] says that this incident in fact happened in 1912, when Wystan was five." In what seems startlingly like the fulfillment of an Oedipal fantasy, Auden would one day write, for *The Rake's Progress,* a libretto in which the hero marries a bearded lady. As if this were not telling enough in itself, the part of Baba, the bearded lady, is scored for a male voice, recalling perhaps first the shiftings of gender roles in quite a few of Shakespeare's plays, including *As You Like It* and *Twelfth Night*. In his *Stravinsky: Chronicle of a Friendship, 1948–1971,* Robert Craft reports (March 21, 1968), "I.S. [Igor Stravinsky] likes the male Baba vocally ('voyce of unpaved Eunuch,' as Cloten says in *Cymbeline*), and the sound *is* good, except for an alarmingly clamant bark on the A in *alt.* 'After all,' I.S. remarks, 'the opera takes place in the age of Farinelli [one of the most extraordinary male soprano singers who ever lived, 1705–1782], when operatic sex-swapping was conventional.' True, but in the period of tonight's staging, universal transvestism constitutes a stronger justification for the switch."

A further light may perhaps be thrown on this puzzle concerning sexual identity by two axioms about personal Edens in an essay called "Dingley Dell and The Fleet," in *The Dyer's Hand.* Auden specifies that in such an Eden "there is no distinction between the objective and the subjective. What a person appears to others to be is identical with what he is to himself. His name and his clothes are as much *his* as his body, so that, if he changes them, he turns into someone else." He also writes, "Three kinds of erotic life are possible, though any particular dream Eden need contain only one." The first of these, and the only one to concern us at this point, is the "polymorphous-perverse promiscuous sexuality of childhood." This sexual ambiguity, which figures in a number of poems, also appears in an account by Harold Norse *(Memoirs of a Bastard Angel)* of a comic but edgy spat between Auden and Chester Kallman that took place in a subway train as "the passengers stared in disbelief."

> WYSTAN:  I am *not* your father, I'm your *mother!*
> CHESTER:  You're *not* my mother! I'm *your* mother!
> WYSTAN:  No, you've got it all wrong. I'm *your* mother!
> CHESTER:  You're not! You're my *father!*
> WYSTAN (screaming): But you've *got* a father. I'm your bloody mother and that's that, darling! You've been looking for a mother since the age of four!

This "adoption of roles," whether by our own choice or at the behest of another, was a serious concern of Auden as a poet throughout his career, expressing itself in his early poetry through the figure of the spy or enemy agent, a figure whose disguise was all but impenetrable, as well as in the assertion, in *The Age of Anxiety,* that "human beings are, necessarily, actors who cannot become something before they have pretended to be it;

and they can be divided, not into the hypocritical and the sincere, but into the sane who know they are acting and the mad who do not." And in Alan Ansen's *Table Talk,* his record of Auden's conversations, there appears Auden's declaration, "You know, *Tristan* should really be done by two 'lizzies.' They eat each other up, try to replace the world. Isolde is the English Mistress, Tristan the Hockey Mistress." Auden was also to write (in the essay "The Greeks and Us"),

> Whenever a married couple divorce because having ceased to be a divine image to each other, they cannot endure the thought of having to love a real person no better than themselves, they are acting under the spell of the Tristan myth. Whenever a man says to himself "I must be getting old. I haven't had sex for a week. What would my friends say if they knew," he is re-enacting the myth of Don Juan. It is significant also . . . that the instances in real life which conform most closely to the original pattern of both myths are not, in either case, heterosexual; the Tristan and Isolde one actually meets are a Lesbian couple, the Don Juan a pederast.

And we are reminded of what an important role *Tristan* played in the young Auden's relationship with his mother. "When he was eight she taught him the words and music of the love-potion scene from Wagner's *Tristan and Isolde,* and together they sang this intensely erotic duet, Wystan taking the part of Isolde," Carpenter reports, adding, "She was, Wystan said as he looked back at this, sometimes 'very odd indeed.'" And in a suppressed poem, appearing in *The English Auden* with a first line that reads "The month was April, the year," Auden presents a dream sequence, a technique he employed in a number of poems. In this one the governing metaphor, as in "The Hunting of the Snark," to which Auden's poem bears an interesting resemblance, is that of a sea journey, the voyage of a ship named *Wystan Auden Esquire,* which the poet visits in the incarnation of a sea gull. "The Captain," summarizes Edward Mendelson, "who proves to be a woman with the formidable traits of Auden's mother, stands for his will. The mate, who looks and sounds like Auden's father, acts on the will's commands." The poem is a lighthearted and generally comic allegory, though in the final stanza the captain-mother turns fiercely upon the poet: "'Saboteur, spy', she hissed, / 'I've got you.' The musket spoke," whereupon "I got up, and on the verandah / The table was laid for tea."

No one would have known better than Auden how convenient was that waking up into another world, or how ominous was that cry of "Saboteur, spy," which, in this poem of 1933, echoes the 1931 prologue to *The Orators:*

> The band roars 'Coward, Coward', in his human fever,
> The giantess shuffles nearer, cries 'Deceiver'.

And that awakening also bears upon one of the most persistent themes and puzzles of Auden's career: his revisionism. It is a topic raised in his very first work, the "charade" called *Paid on Both Sides.* This is, in many ways, an unsatisfactory work, containing, among other things, nearly impenetrable speeches in the manner of the densest verse of Hopkins:

> Not from this life, not from this life is any
> To keep; sleep, day and play would not help there
> Dangerous to new ghost; new ghost learns from many
> Learns from old termers what death is, where.

The charade / play is about the endless, repetitive mechanism and cycle of revenge ("I and the public know / What all schoolchildren learn, / Those to whom evil is done / Do evil in return"). But in the course of this very early work there is a dream sequence in which the protagonist, John Nower (does his surname place an emphasis on the immediate present, on negativism, or on hidden knowledge? "Nower" is listed as an obsolete form of "nowhere" in the *OED*), "*kills his own past* and then with the help of a comic healer—the first of many in Auden's poetry—emerges reconciled and renewed," as Edward Mendelson explains, though my emphasis is added. But as contrasted with the suppressed poem of 1933, in this play when the hero awakens he is not saved; he dies.

I would want the revisionist element in Auden to be understood in the broadest sense—indeed, in the very sense Harold Bloom asserts regarding all poets and their edgy relationships to their literary ancestors whom they revise. Auden revised not only his predecessors but himself as well, and this seems to me a fairly common human practice, when in fact it does not become central to the analogous and more dramatic act of religious conversion. And since such a conversion, though moderated and slow and less dramatic than some (he mocked at the "television" conversion of Malcolm Muggeridge), was a feature of his life that alienated many of his early admirers—Jarrell, who was an ardent liberal secularist, among them—that conversion must have seemed to Auden both risky and pivotal.

But it was only the most conspicuous part of an evolution of thought and style that had gone on virtually from the first.

Jarrell tries to give an account of this development in a brisk, and therefore necessarily blurred, summary that describes Auden circa 1930 as

> unable or unwilling to accept the values and authority, the general world picture of the late-capitalist society in which he finds himself . . . Auden synthesizes (more or less as the digestive organs synthesize enzymes) his own order from a number of sources: (1) Marx—Communism in general. (2) Freud and Groddeck: in general, the risky and nonscientific, but fertile and imaginative, side of modern psychology. (3) A cluster of related sources: the folk, the blood, intuition, religion and mysticism, fairy tales, parables, and so forth—this group includes a number of semi-Fascist elements. (4) The sciences, biology particularly: these seem to be available to him because they have been only partially assimilated by capitalist culture, and because, like mathematics, they are practically incapable of being corrupted by it. (5) All sorts of boyish sources of value: flying, polar exploration, mountain climbing, fighting, the thrilling side of science, public-school life, sports, big-scale practical jokes, "the spies' career," etc. (6) Homosexuality: if the ordinary sexual values are taken as negative and rejected, this can be accepted as a source of positive revolutionary values.
>
> Auden is able to set up a We (whom he identifies himself with— rejection loves company) in opposition to the enemy They . . . We are Love; They are hate and all the terrible perversions of love . . . We are health; They are disease . . . We are Life. They are Death.

This is the beginning of what must be called a diatribe, which both in its economy of compression and in its diagnostic statements seems to me seriously misleading. Apart from compression (by which I mean that Jarrell is writing about a large variety of Auden's work composed over a number of years, work that is much less "of a kind" than he allows) and misleading statements, there are two other kinds of faults in Jarrell's summary. The first is that it rather airily proceeds to describe Auden's work as a body of doctrine and a disembodied group of ideas. From this fault derives a second, which is that in fact Auden's "ideas" were neither so clear-cut nor so homogeneous and neatly separable as Jarrell wants us to believe. No one was more suspicious of a doctrinaire, inflexible, unthinking position than Auden himself, and he needed no Jarrell to lecture him on this topic. Jarrell's account leaves out too much, and of what it does include, makes a tidy schematization of those themes in Auden's work which were constantly changing.

More usefully, and with more scrupulosity, Jarrell proceeds to characterize the language of Auden's early poetry. Again he errs in implying that it is all of a kind. But his observations in this area are astute, and he specifies some twenty-six linguistic traits of the early poems, of which some of the most important are the following:

(1) The frequent omission of articles and demonstrative adjectives. (2) The frequent omission of subjects—especially *I, you, he*, etc. . . . (4) The frequent omission of coordinate conjunctions, subordinating conjunctions, conjunctive adverbs, etc. Even prepositions are sometimes omitted. (5) The frequent omission of relative pronouns . . . (8) Unusual punctuation; a decided underpunctuation is common . . . (11) Constant parataxis, often ungrammatical. In these poems Auden is willing to stretch or break most rules of grammar and syntax . . . (13) A sort of portmanteau construction—common to the Elizabethans—in which a qualifying phrase may refer both to what comes before and to what comes after . . . (17) The use of normally uncoordinate elements as coordinates . . . (20) Frequent ambiguity—usually effective, sometimes merely confusing.

These "mannerisms" are ones Jarrell purports to admire, and which he speaks of as characterizing "a peculiar language," in contrast to what he will reprehend as a later "rhetoric." This opposition between language and rhetoric seems to me just as misleading as the neat polarization of We and They. But he proceeds to identify what he regards as some of the unpalatable faults of the later rhetoric. One of these is what he calls "the Orator's Favorite: a surprisingly abstract word is put into a concrete 'poetic' context. The consistent use of this device is one of the things that has got Auden's poetry attacked as relaxed or abstract." Another "rhetorical" device is the "juxtaposition of disparate coordinates," which looks suspiciously like one of the elements (17) of "language" that merited praise in the early poetry. One of the most vivid and successful modes of the juxtaposition of uncoordinated details that Auden used throughout his poetic career was that of deliberate anachronism, almost an invention of his own. This "juxtaposition of disparate coordinates" may have at least partly derived from Baudelaire's doctrine of correspondences. The French poet was an early literary hero of Auden's, and Allen Tate has described the Baudelairean theory thus: "Baudelaire's Theory of Correspondences—that an idea out of one class of experience may be dressed up in the vocabulary of another—is at once the backbone of modernist poetic diction and the character which distinguished it from both the English tradition and free verse."

In the midst of these cavils, Jarrell isolates for discussion an important device of Auden's; but though he identifies it, he misses its serious purpose. He observes, "Auden fairly early began to use words like *lovely, marvelous, wonderful, lucky, wicked* (words that are all weight and no 'presentation'; that are all attitude of subject and no description of object; that approach as a limit the semanticists' *meaningless emotional noises*) in a peculiarly sophisticated sense." The verbal device he points to is worth noting, and can, I think, properly be identified not as a blemish ("all attitude of subject and no description of object") but as a "nanny's" or "mother's" voice, which, in the arch manner of adult with child, undertakes to characterize the world in simplistic terms, and to divide experience into good things and bad, into We and They, into what "our sort" value and what "their sort" indulge in. It is didactic in character but ironic in purpose, since it invites us to consider how all such neat divisions are false. Jarrell then returns to "incongruity," inflated into the alarming and cumbersome "Bureaucratization of Perspective by Incongruity," which, he declares, Auden has mechanized into a metaphor-producing engine, that turns out a Freud who is a "*climate, weather. The provinces* of Yeats's body revolted; *the squares of his mind were empty, / Silence invaded the suburbs, / The current of his feeling failed.* Matthew Arnold is a *dark disordered city,* completely equipped with *square, boulevard, slum, prison, forum, haphazard alleys,* etc."

But the "incongruities" so deplored here are no more than elaborations (and, in my view, highly imaginative and original ones) of the "use of normally uncoordinate elements as coordinates" that Jarrell admired in the earlier part of his essay. In the particular cases Jarrell is deploring, Auden is establishing a relationship between the individual and his environment, as well as his society; a relationship fundamental to the *paysage moralisé* that was useful to him, and which also bore upon his "revisionist" attitude towards Freud. As he wrote in his journal of 1929, "Freud's error is the limitation of neurosis to the individual. The neurosis involves all society."

But rather than continue to worry the categories and demurrals of Jarrell, let me set forth some categories of my own, simpler and more generalized than his, but, I hope I can claim, more to the point. I propose that from the very first Auden had two identifiable styles in operation, two styles which sometimes he was able to merge into a third and hybrid one, no less successful for its mongrel nature than its interesting parents. Of these three, the first is the most personal, and often is a love poem, though framed in the most obscure and hermetic language.

The love poem always involves a not wholly assimilable mixture of strategies and motives. If, as is most often the case, it is addressed to a particular person, it ought, in the interests of the sincerity of its passion, to be read by that person alone; but since it is a "published" work, either printed or circulated in manuscript, there is in its publication, if not a violation of the intimacy it purports to convey, at least the use of the intimacy as a pretext for public and observed behavior. Now public and observed behavior is just what love comes to in the ceremony of marriage; and there are, consequently, many famous and admired nuptial poems, which involve no complication of motive. But Auden was already a reader and reciter of Shakespeare's sonnets when he was an undergraduate, as Stephen Spender tells us; and the sonnets present all manner of problems as regards their delicacy, since they were published, so far as we know, without Shakespeare's authorization. The sonnets employ many of the Petrarchan conventions of the day, standing some on their heads, flouting others altogether ("My mistress' eyes are nothing like the sun"), but there are enough surprising particulars here and there to have encouraged a lot of "scholars" to weave a story out of them with very precise, and sometimes shocking, incidents. As a love poet, Auden had a duty to some sort of fidelity to the facts or nature of his relationship as well as to the public circumstances of a written poem intended for publication. So if these poems can be called "confessional," one must immediately add that the confessions are hedged about with all sorts of misgivings and doubts, and protected by a sometimes opaque screen of difficult verbal constructions. To the degree that love poems are not "conventional," they invite from the reader a prurient interest in circumstances and feelings of the most private sort. And if the love is of a kind looked upon uncharitably by society in general, a good deal of covert communication may be called for. Housman, whom Auden also admired and quoted, expressed his feelings for young men by imitating the spareness as well as the moods of bitterness and resignation of certain classical poets, and since his most

famous book of poems was published not long before World War I, it
aroused in the general public during that war a keen sympathy for men
whose lives were cut short in the flower of their youth. The poems,
enjoying this fortuitous historical appearance in print, were thought
irreproachable, not suspected of any indelicacy, and their classical stoicism
seemed to confirm some widely shared feelings of the times about the
sacrificed lives of young men.

Many early poems of Auden's, and the love poems in particular, are
composed in what seems a sort of code. It has been claimed before, and
with justice, that all poetry is a kind of code. In this it is pridefully elitist,
inviting the comprehension only of those who are skilled in its ways and
its evasions. This elitist quality can be greatly magnified by the use of
special languages, the employment of an arcane vocabulary, the use of
names of places and persons that might be known only to a select few, a
suggestion of dramatic fragments formed into a collage that only initiates
could recognize or interpret. There are details in the Shakespeare sonnets
("For why should others' false adultrate eyes / Give salutation to my
sportive blood?") that seem to refer to an unspecified drama, a context
unexplained because expected to be understood, either by one solitary
reader or else by a very few. Yvor Winters furiously condemns in Eliot's
poetry what he calls making "reference to a non-existent plot." Throughout his career Auden will do much the same, even inventing words
("soodling" has found its way into the Supplement of the *OED;* according
to Toby Litt, Worcester College, Oxford, in *The W. H. Auden Society
Newsletter,* no. 4, Auden's wish to be included in the *OED* has been
granted at least 724 times), but also introducing the names of sex partners,
and the vocabulary of private and fictitious worlds he shared with only a
few friends in poems that are ostensibly addressed to a general public. (In
a poem there is also, of course, a code of which the poet himself is
unaware; but that need not concern us here.)

What one immediately notices about many of the early poems is the
abstraction and generalization of their language. Consider these three
fragments:

> Love by ambition
> Of definition
> Suffers partition
> And cannot go
> From yes to no

A neutralizing peace
And an average disgrace
Are honour to discover
For later other

Upon this line between adventure
Prolong the meeting out of good nature
Obvious in each agreeable feature.

John Fuller and Robert Graves have both suggested that the rather forbidding music of such lines, their brevity and their abstraction, is indebted to the work of Laura Riding, and this may be true. But the first of these fragments belongs to a poem which, if I understand it, exactly opposes the polarities of We and They, good and bad, that Jarrell so much insisted on as elements of the early work.

Love by ambition
Of definition
Suffers partition
And cannot go
From yes to no
For no is not love, no is no
The shutting of a door
The tightening jaw
A conscious sorrow,
And saying yes
Turns love into success
Views from the rail
Of land and happiness,
Assured of all
The sofas creak
And were this all, love were
But cheek to cheek
And dear to dear.

Voices explain
Love's pleasure and love's pain
Still tap the knee
And cannot disagree
Hushed for aggression
Of full confession

Likeness to likeness
Of each old weakness;
Love is not there
Love has moved to another chair.
Aware already
Of who stands next
And is not vexed
And is not giddy
Leaves the North in place
With a good grace
And would not gather
Another to another
Designs his own unhappiness
Foretells his own death and is faithless.

This poem appears, with differing divisions and differently punctuated, in *Poems,* Auden's first book published in America, in *The Collected Poetry of W. H. Auden* of 1945, in the *Collected Shorter Poems, 1927–1957,* and in *The English Auden.* In its earliest appearances it was without a title but was later called "Too Dear, Too Vague." In *The English Auden* a break is introduced between the twenty-eighth and twenty-ninth lines, i.e., after "Love has moved to another chair," yet though I have no way of determining whether or not this conformed with the poem's first periodical appearance, the break at that point seems to me, as it must have seemed to Auden himself, a mistake.

The poem presents some plain problems of interpretation. Its first section or strophe has been described as an account of the difficulty of defining so mysterious, ambiguous, and, one may add, polymorphous a thing as love. Our attempts at definition lead us straight into the irreconcilable oppositions of "yes" and "no," identified by John Fuller as reciprocated and unreciprocated love. This does not seem to me satisfactory, or to fit comfortably with the rest of the poem. I will risk taking a hint from the March 1929 version that appears in *The English Auden,* which puts a colon at the end of the fifth line, after "From yes to no," and suggest that the tone of the remaining lines of the first section is deliberately satiric. In other words, the poem is asserting that society itself, in laying down its codes and mores, has so defined love as to make it either acceptable or unacceptable. These definitions invite rehearsed responses, clichés, simpleminded, heedless acceptances and denials. "Approved" love is described in the popular song, "cheek to cheek" and "dear to dear." It is conceived of as something that, once it takes the right track, "turns . . . into success," a panorama of bliss such as a tourist views luxuriously from the windows of a train, and a private room where the sofas creak under the strain of sexual athletics. And "were this all," things would be as simple as the songs suggest and as the tyranny of society demands.

But the rest of the poem proceeds to declare that things are not so simple, that love is more mysterious than society allows, that society's attempt to define it is to treat it like a sick patient with a familiar malady. It is put through all the diagnostic tests, its reflexes are examined, and there is a general consensus that it will turn out to be some "old weakness." This is all a mistaken procedure because whatever is being examined is not love. The only love society recognizes and endows with "success" is monogamous and as enduring as marriage vows. It is therefore implicitly heterosexual. The love that society is unable to recognize is "faithless," "foretells [its] own death," and "designs [its] own unhappiness," because it is disapproved of and must be covert, brief, and promiscuous. The "North" is very probably one of the four "poles of the dynamic psyche" that D. H. Lawrence speaks of in the chapter "The Birth of Sex" in *Fantasia of the Unconscious,* as John Fuller has suggested. Lawrence writes very movingly of this revolutionary change in the human body and psyche, saying, "A child knows the abyss of forlornness. But an adolescent alone knows the strange pain of growing into his isolation of individuality." He also writes of this period in human development, "Now mother and father inevitably give way before masters and mistresses, brothers and sisters yield to friends . . . A child before puberty has playmates. After puberty he has friends and enemies . . . The father and mother bonds now relax . . . It is the hour of the stranger. Let the stranger now enter the soul." It hardly needs pointing out how important to almost all Auden's early writing is the idea of the stranger, and how that idea is mixed up with the notion of sexual emancipation.

"Love by ambition," though expressing "subversive" sentiments, and perhaps obscure for that reason, is not a personal poem and presupposes no particular addressee or beloved. Such an intimate mode of dramatic speech appears in "From the very first coming down," which, though much commented on, is by no means free of obscurity. Not least of its puzzles arise from rash and unexpected changes of tense. (The 1945 *Collected Poems* contains the deviant fourth line "You certainly remained . . .")

From the very first coming down
Into a new valley with a frown
Because of the sun and a lost way,
You certainly remain: to-day
I, crouching behind a sheep-pen, heard
Travel across a sudden bird,
Cry out against the storm, and found
The year's arc a completed round
And love's worn circuit re-begun,
Endless with no dissenting turn.
Shall see, shall pass, as we have seen
The swallow on the tile, spring's green
Preliminary shiver, passed
A solitary truck, the last
Of shunting in the Autumn. But now
To interrupt the homely brow,
Thought warmed to evening through and through
Your letter comes, speaking as you,
Speaking of much but not to come.

Nor speech is close nor fingers numb,
If love not seldom has received
An unjust answer, was deceived.
I, decent with the seasons, move
Different or with a different love,
Nor question overmuch the nod,
The stone smile of this country god
That never was more reticent,
Always afraid to say more than it meant.

There is a sort of consensus about this poem on the part of the commentators, but this may be due to the fact that so much has been left undiscussed. There is at least a mild disagreement about who it is that does the "coming down" in the first line, and the poet has very deliberately avoided being clear about this; he could easily have said "From my first coming down" or "From your first coming down" if he had cared to, and without damage to the poem's rhythm. The ambiguity that seems to be courted in that first line continues with a "frown" induced by the sun *and* a lost way. The causes are both outward and inward, and suggest the discomfort and anxiety entailed in the journey into a new valley, the crossing of a frontier or border into a new world of experience. Here, in this new world, "you certainly remain." This claim will seem to be contradicted by the poem's conclusion; but we may reinterpret it in retrospect to mean that the speaker has never forgotten, and still feels the effect of, that first appearance.

The speaker ("to-day" as distinct from the time of the first coming down) crouches behind a sheep-pen, presumably because of the storm, but also because the rural setting will serve as part of the natural and seasonal machinery of the poem, harnessed to imply that everything that has happened is part of an ordained and natural sequence. The "sudden bird" that cries out against the storm is prophetic of disruption, as birds commonly are in classical literature, and seems to be an avian commentator upon the dissolution and conclusion of what had once been love. By what seems a fated coincidence, that relationship appears to have terminated precisely on its anniversary, and the year's arc has been a completed round not only in calendrical and seasonal terms but also in terms of the whole repetitive cycle of love, which entails the cautious initial attraction with the fear of rejection, the more confident period of courtship, the ardent and mutual consent, and the waning and dissolution of passion. This is "love's worn circuit," which seems almost of necessity to begin in spring, the erotic season, and to move to its inevitable demise. The speaker knows the entire cycle by heart, having gone through it at least once, and knows that he "shall see, shall pass" all the signs of spring, as he and his beloved have seen them, and have passed the solitary truck, which in autumn moves households to new addresses, shunting them from where they were (unless it is the autumn itself that is being "shunted in"). But now, as the speaker, having evaded or recovered from the storm, warms his thought with the comfortable prospects of evening, its quiet, its domestic security, its interior homeliness, there comes to him "your letter," which is both personal and evasive, like this poem.

Up to this point the poem has been written with such emotional neutrality and remoteness as to suggest complete command and impassive objectivity. But after the break there follows a decided note of resentment, though this, too, is so stated as to leave moot just where and upon whom the blame is being placed. Some sort of betrayal, at the very least a violation of the trust required in love, as well as rebukes, lies, or accusations, have brought love to the end of its cycle. But they have not succeeded in inhibiting speech or the sensation of touch, life-signs that continue in "decent" (i.e., suitable or fitting) synchrony with the seasons; and the speaker, who now knows the full cost and reward, "love's pleasure and love's pain," that are entailed by "love's worn circuit," is preparing to undertake the whole enticing and dismaying cycle once again, because of the allure that it offers, even if the final cost exacted will be painful ("Before, a joy proposed, behind, a dream") and because Nature herself, or, in the person of the "country god," who is probably the phallic Priapus, *himself*, ordains that this must come to pass. The god's fear of saying more than it meant is a touching acknowledgment that while sexual attraction seems to be the initial stage of love, it may never develop beyond simple erotic feeling, and the god who presides over the spring rites, speaking through its now experienced devotee, is reluctant to appropriate the language of love for an experience to which it may only loosely apply. This scrupulosity on the part of the god, whose "stone smile" might well be a fixed amusement at the predicament of mortals, may also be a sign of how untrusting is that god of all the pretension to permanence we commonly assign to love.

Even so, there is finally something rueful about the tone with which the poem ends. Whether the speaker is seen as the helpless prisoner and instrument of a necessary cycle, or whether he has been educated to distrust the possibility of an enduring love, it is a small consolation (palatable perhaps only to the young) to attribute this to the unalterable processes of nature.

These two poems, "Love by ambition" and "From the very first coming down," are written in a voice that is essentially private. But there is a "public" voice to poems that Auden was writing at pretty much the same time. "Love by ambition" is dated March 1929, and in November of the same year Auden wrote, "It's no use raising a shout." It is a kind of "blues," imitative, Edward Mendelson suggests, of Sophie Tucker, and certainly familiar enough as a type of complaint. The nature of the complaint here covers virtually everything, including the charge that the man who speaks feels himself an obsolescent product of the evolutionary process, and yearns to return to the maternal embrace, to childhood and beyond that to some irresponsible primordial life—to that of, in Eliot's words, "an irresponsible foetus." The language of the poem involves none of the elliptical tricks, grammatical ambiguities, short circuits of syntax that so mark the "private" poems. "Public" in this accessible sense are most of the poems, early and late, that express a formal indebtedness to conventions of song or to poetic ancestors. "Get there if you can and see the land you once were proud to own" is, as has been noted, composed in the trochaic octameter couplets with catalectic closure of Tennyson's "Locksley Hall," and is indebted to Tennyson in more ways than one. Auden's poem, and perhaps Tennyson's as well, is wryly self-mocking. Both poems shift in tone from nostalgia and regret to fierce and violent outrage; both are at points slightly hysterical in ways that invite us to regard their speakers with reservations and suspicions. Both speakers are slightly paranoid. And both entertain a vision of a perfect society, Tennyson's embodied "In the Parliament of man, the Federation of the world," Auden's personified by "Lawrence, Blake and Homer Lane." Both poems point with acid comment to the failures of scientific modernity (the first quotation is from Tennyson, the second from Auden):

> There methinks would be enjoyment more than in this march of
>     mind,
> In the steamship, in the railway, in the thoughts that shake
>     mankind.

> Power-stations locked, deserted, since they drew the boiler fires;
> Pylons fallen or subsiding, trailing dead high-tension wires.

Both poems bristle with condemnations and achieve moments of nearly suicidal passion, mitigated by an invitation to suspect that neither poet is wholly serious. Both poems are full of posturing. But whereas Tennyson's is a dramatic monologue, involving a crossed love and a complex past history, Auden's is oratorical, hortatory, though exhibiting as full a range of mocking tones as Tennyson's. And though a "public" poem, spoken by a young man to the young men of his own generation, it is nevertheless laden with little private jokes and references to be understood only by the initiate.

> These were boon companions who devised the legends for our
>     tombs,
> These who have betrayed us nicely while we took them to our
>     rooms.

> Newman, Ciddy, Plato, Fronny, Pascal, Bowdler, Baudelaire,
> Doctor Frommer, Mrs. Allom, Freud, the Baron, and Flaubert.

This litany of betrayers is tauntingly composed of "public" and "private" names. Freud, about whose significance Auden was to revise his judgment a number of times, is here among the culprits because, according to the 1929 journal, "The error of Freud and most psychologists is making pleasure a negative thing, progress towards a state of rest . . . Freud you see really believes that pleasure is immoral, i.e., happiness is displeasing to God." (Carpenter reports of Auden that "near the end of his life he remarked to a friend that it was odd that Freud died of cancer of the jaw—'Who'd have thought he was a liar?'" Carpenter considers it an example of the poet's continued faith in Groddeck's theory of symptoms and causes. To me Auden said sometime around 1950 that Freud died of cancer of the mouth [*sic*] because he had uttered "blasphemy" in writing *Moses and Monotheism.*) Of the "private" names, Fronny, who gave his name to a lately recovered play of Auden's, and who figures as Francis in Isherwood's *Christopher and His Kind,* is one Francis Turville-Petre, an English homosexual who introduced Isherwood to "boy bars" in Berlin. We may assume that the general reader was not expected to know this; but we may also wonder whether there may not have been a hidden challenge to the future invited by such intimate details: could it be that the poet was saying secretly to himself, "If my work is taken seriously enough there will be the probers, the detectives, the analysts, to comb through and document every last word of it. I shall try to defy them, but it may all come out in the end"? Several pages could, not unprofitably, be devoted to why each of those names, public and private, appears on the poet's list of traitors, but if we contrast them, as Auden clearly wants us to, with the poem's heroes, Lawrence, Blake, and Homer Lane, they may be seen as advocates of repression or sublimation and thus as evaders of instinctive feeling. Isherwood characterizes the Lane doctrine, as received through John Layard, this way: "There is only one sin: disobedience to the inner law of our own nature. This disobedience is the fault of those who teach us, as children, to control God (our desires) instead of giving him room to grow."

The poem ends in tones of exhortation, mixed with contempt, and suggests that our whole future may be regarded as the ultimate wager.

> Shut up talking, charming in the best suits to be had in town,
> Lecturing on navigation while the ship is going down.
>
> Drop those priggish ways for ever, stop behaving like a stone:
> Throw the bath-chairs right away, and learn to leave ourselves
> alone.

If we really want to live, we'd better start at once to try;
If we don't, it doesn't matter, but we'd better start to die.

Along with the urgency there is the implied contempt for the thinker as opposed to the doer in the line "Lecturing on navigation while the ship is going down," a contempt that also appears in other Auden poems, particularly in "'O where are you going?' said reader to rider." Learning "to leave ourselves alone" is an injunction against masturbation—not, we may presume, on Biblical grounds, but because it is an unsatisfactory substitute for or deflection of sexual union of any kind whatever. "If we really want to live" has by the end of the poem taken on vaguely doctrinal meaning; "to live" means according to impulse, instinct, id, in defiant rebellion against superego, authority, the "old gang," our repressed and suppressing elders. But if the poem exhorts its readers to action, and if it seems to divide society into good and bad, it cannot be said that "We" are good and "They" are bad, as Jarrell suggests. It is "we" after all who, if we do not start to try, had better start to die at the poem's end: we are so situated as potentially to be either impotent and infected or active and healthy. Moreover, just before the end some questions are asked.

Have things gone too far already? Are we done for? Must we
    wait
Hearing doom's approaching footsteps regular down miles of
    straight;

Run the whole night through in gumboots, stumble on and gasp
    for breath,
Terrors drawing close and closer, winter landscape, fox's death;

Or, in friendly fireside circle, sit and listen for the crash
Meaning that the mob has realized something's up, and start to
    smash;

Engine-drivers with their oil-cans, factory girls in overalls
Blowing sky-high monster stores, destroying intellectuals?

(The first of these couplets is only one of several passages of Auden's that might have inspired Empson's "Just a Smack at Auden.")
    There are a number of puzzles here, not least of them having to do with grammar and syntax. If "mob" is singular, should not "start" be "starts"? Or, since "start" is plural, are readers to understand that "we" start to smash, in sympathetic harmony with the "mob"? And is the general

destruction of monster stores and intellectuals, undertaken by engine-drivers and factory girls, something "we" approve of or something which endangers us? Are we, "in friendly fireside circle" sitting and listening, the inert, inactive source of the whole problem? These are not the only puzzles in the lines, but they will do to show that probably both consciously and unconsciously Auden was far from neat in his division of the enemies and the friends.

This poem is one I have designated as public, and it is at least less hermetic than the ones cited earlier. But its inclusion of names known only to a few, and its, as I would claim, highly ambivalent moral stance, put it in a mediating position and lend it a greater power and honesty than any poem which was flatly and unambiguously polemical. It was almost a technique of Auden's to interfuse the public with the private domain, and to write of one in terms of the other. This was partly an application of medical-diagnostic theories to society. But Auden was also, as Samuel Hynes has shown, a member of a generation that felt profoundly betrayed by its elders, the "leaders" who had presided over the debacle of the Great War and the unsatisfactory peace that followed. The disillusionment that began even while the war was in progress, and that raged like an infection long afterwards, is hard to exaggerate, but its pervasiveness has been conveyed not only by Hynes but also by Paul Fussell in *The Great War and Modern Memory* and, especially as regards the defiant and rebellious younger generation, by Martin Green in *Children of the Sun.*

A poem like "Let History Be My Judge" is intricately both private and public. Its very title suggests its public aspect, though it must be noted that the title was a late embellishment, appearing for the first time in the 1945 collection, where, as in its original appearance in Auden's first book, the poem was mispunctuated. Initially, it appears to be about the imperial occupation of a colonial dependency which is exhibiting political unrest. It seems to be spoken by a public administrator who is dutifully checking off all the points of emergency precautions that according to regulations must be taken should any hint of an uprising present itself.

> We made all possible preparations,
> Drew up a list of firms,
> Constantly revised our calculations
> And allotted the farms,
>
> Issued all the orders expedient
> In this kind of case:

> Most, as was expected, were obedient,
> Though there were murmurs, of course;
>
> Chiefly against our exercising
> Our old right to abuse:
> Even some sort of attempt at rising
> But these were mere boys.
>
> For never serious misgiving
> Occurred to anyone,
> Since there could be no question of living
> If we did not win.

However, as the poem progresses, we come to realize that the speaker, a representative of the "law-and-order" establishment, easily enough recognizable as any spokesman for an authoritarian government, is also and at the same time a representative of the older generation. An antagonism of generations is evoked, which pits fathers, with their wealth, power, seniority, and privilege, against sons, with their subordinate weakness. The father/son conflict is, of course, not only the more familiar one in several senses of the word, but perhaps the more ancient, and certainly the more inward, since all fathers were once sons. And by this implied extension of the poem's basic metaphoric structure, an enormous mythic dimension, involving both Oedipus and Prometheus, is hinted at.

The most riddling (in the old oracular sense) stanzas in the poem come near the end.

> The generally accepted view teaches
> That there was no excuse,
> Though in the light of recent researches
> Many would find the cause
>
> In a not uncommon form of terror;
> Others, still more astute,
> Point to possibilities of error
> At the very start.

It seems to me that these stanzas, by their deliberate ambiguities, prevent us from reading the poem as though it were plain who were the villains and who the heroes. Who are we to believe are the holders of "the generally accepted view"? Is it those who agree with the speaker, or those who oppose him? Do the holders of that view believe "there was no excuse" for the imposition of special precautionary and repressive measures, or for the acts of rebellion? Is the "not uncommon form of terror" a rebellious political act on the part of subordinates, or a sensation familiar to rulers who are always subject to threats of potential insurrection? And if there is a suspicion of "possibilities of error / At the very start," does this mean that there is something wrong with the genetic system? With traditional society? Or is something being hinted at about the Fall from grace in the Garden of Eden? It would not be wrong to find orthodox religious ideas and even language in Auden's early poems, no matter how secular they seem initially to be.

Consider, for example, this celebrated, and later suppressed, sonnet.

> Sir, no man's enemy, forgiving all
> But will his negative inversion, be prodigal:
> Send to us power and light, a sovereign touch
> Curing the intolerable neural itch,
> The exhaustion of weaning, the liar's quinsy,
> And the distortions of ingrown virginity.
> Prohibit sharply the rehearsed response
> And gradually correct the coward's stance;
> Cover in time with beams those in retreat
> That, spotted, they turn though the reverse were great;
> Publish each healer that in city lives
> Or country houses at the end of drives;
> Harrow the house of the dead; look shining at
> New styles of architecture, a change of heart.

In the foreword, partly quoted earlier, to the 1927–57 *Collected Shorter Poems,* Auden wrote, "Some poems which I wrote and, unfortunately, published, I have thrown out because they were dishonest, or bad-mannered, or boring. A dishonest poem is one which expresses, no matter how well, feelings or beliefs which its author never felt or entertained. For example, I once expressed a desire for 'New styles of architecture'; but I have never liked modern architecture. I prefer *old* styles, and one must be honest even about one's prejudices."

Whatever a "dishonest poem" may be, this comes very near to being dishonest prose. At the very least, it is disingenuous. Auden knew perfectly well that many poems express "feelings or beliefs which its author never felt or entertained." Not only is there a large body of poetry which expresses sentiments projected onto imaginary, created characters, and of which the author patently disapproves, but Auden himself had done so, and would continue to do so after this foreword was written.

The salutation "Sir," with which the poem begins, may seem an oddly distant and impersonal way of addressing the Deity, which is certainly what is here intended; but Auden has a pious and respectful precedent in a sonnet based on the text of Jeremiah 12 by Hopkins: "Thou art indeed just, Lord, if I contend / With thee; but, sir, so what I plead is just." The word "sir" appears to derive from the word "sire," applied to kings and also meaning "father," as both Hopkins and Auden are likely to have known. Auden's sonnet is written in slant-rhyme couplets, after the fashion of Wilfred Owen, and its first two lines invite deliberate confusions by the omission of normal punctuation; one would have expected "his negative inversion" to be set off by commas. But that would merely be one way of reading the second line. If we assume that the poet desired a slight pause at the end of the first line, and was addressing God as able to forgive all sins, then "will" in the next line may be read in the hortatory mood, and "but will" can mean "simply exert the divine will." And what is to be willed is man's "negative inversion." This is probably not what Auden meant, but it is certainly a permissible way of reading these lines. And we still have to deal with the puzzle of "negative inversion," which looks curiously like a double negative. Are there positive inversions, as opposed to negative ones? Most modern readings interpret "negative inversion" as standing in apposition to "will," and maintain that man's stubborn will is his only unforgivable fault; hence the desired commas mentioned above. If man's will is his unpardonable fault, in what way may it be called a "negative inversion"? "Inversion," of course, has an explicit sexual meaning, often confused (by Freud, among others) with straightforward homosexuality, but specifically distinguished from it. The OED proposes that "homosexuality refers to sexual activity or the desire for such activity between two members of the same sex, while the criterion of inversion is a personality in which a person's thinking, feeling, and acting are typical of the opposite sex." If Auden had this distinction in mind, he may have wanted to distinguish effeminate behavior (negative inversion) from homosexuality, and to suggest that the former is "willed" while the latter is a condition to which people are born. "Will" in the language of psychologists and philosophers was used conventionally in opposition to "impulse," and was so used in the doctrines of Lane and Layard that Auden so enthusiastically embraced as a young man, doctrines which gave passionate endorsement to impulse over will. Yet in a poem addressed to the Deity we cannot reject the notion that "will," when it is man's and not God's, may be a theological sin, the source of the first act of disobedience and the cause of all mortal misery. And Auden would have been perfectly aware of this meaning. What his poem does is to allow us to entertain these many irreconcilable readings one after another, without the hope of clear resolution. In any case, if "will" is man's active sin of disobedience and selfishness, "negative inversion" becomes very difficult to interpret.

Furthermore, if the poem begins with theological terms, it shifts quickly to psychological ones, and the two sorts of language do not consort comfortably together. After the generalized petition of the opening two lines, the remainder of the sonnet is a catalogue of specific prayers and enumerated requests. "Power and light" sounds dangerously like the commercial product of a utilities company. The "sovereign touch," of course, was a royal gift purporting to cure scrofula, the "King's Evil." In Auden's poem we may presume that the monarch is God, and that the illness is inward, an affliction of the nervous system, rather than outward. "The exhaustion of weaning" is a subject that reappears in much of Auden's early work, and sometimes takes the form of very bitter and uncharitable attitudes towards mothers, who are not infrequently represented as forcing their sons into playing roles the sons have no desire to play. The mothers of *Paid on Both Sides* are the continuators, if not the instigators, of the feud; a mother is the deceitful figure at the top of *F6* towards which Michael Ransom strives; and it is the mother, as giantess, who turns upon her son in the prologue to *The Orators*. Mothers are usually seen as tyrannous, and as requiring their sons to enact their fantasies of heroic male achievement, which roles and actions have been denied to them because of their gender. Regarding "weaning": Isherwood wrote in *Lions and Shadows,* "[Auden] smoked enormously, insatiably: 'Insufficient weaning,' he explained. 'I must have something to *suck.*'"

The phrases that immediately follow, "the liar's quinsy," "the distortions of ingrown virginity," "the rehearsed response," and "the coward's stance," are all what may be called outward signs of an inward condition, and so may be thought of both as Groddeckian or Freudian symptoms or as signs of a spiritual malaise. "Ingrown virginity" must either be habitual or principled virginity, or else be the sort of fear of sex that in Auden's poem about Miss Gee he associates with cancer. It is, in any case, not unlike "the rehearsed response," which is anything but spontaneous or impulsive. The "liar's quinsy" presumably also arises out of fear; and fear, like will, seems to be a prime cause of the maladies that this petition asks to have alleviated. There follow, however, two lines which, if they are addressed to God, present some serious problems.

The lines seem to be petitioning God not merely to expose to humiliation and possibly to danger "those in retreat," but, in imagery drawn either from prisons or from warfare, to turn searchlights upon them, spotting them in their act of cowardice. The difficulty lies in the fact that earlier in the poem it was asked that God "gradually correct the coward's stance." And how are we to distinguish between the first set of cowards and the second? If the imagery is drawn, as I feel almost certain it is, from warfare, "those in retreat," once spotted, will be exposed to the hostility and the fire of both sides, and will not be likely to survive; and God is being asked to show His malevolence by exposing them to this predicament.

The last four lines, by contrast to what immediately precedes them, are decidedly benign. The healers may be found in both the city and the country, that is, they are suitably distributed through all parts of the population, rural and urban; which means that they are not exclusively available to the rich or the sophisticated. The only problem is that their identities are not widely known, and the speaker prays that what has been the privileged knowledge of who and where these healers are will become public and general knowledge. The healers, presumably, are such men as Lawrence, Blake, Homer Lane, John Layard, Groddeck, and Freud: healers of the sickness in the souls of men, ministers at once secular and spiritual.

There now appears what may be Auden's most daring touch. The harrowing of Hell (meaning, the despoiling of it by Christ, who descended into its regions to pardon and to free many good souls who had died before his birth) is a familiar Christian phrase, not out of place in a poem addressed to God, but much more conventionally religious than most of the poem's language, which almost from the first has neatly employed meanings chiefly secular, though potentially religious. Here, I think, the reverse emphasis occurs. The explicitly religious prayer may be understood as bearing secular implications: "the dead" are those in need of cure by healers, the cure is psychological; "the dead" are like the living dead of *The Waste Land,* a poem Auden admired extravagantly. The prayer is for their restoration to vitality.

The final line and a half, beginning "look shining at . . . ," is meant, I think, to echo the satisfaction of the Creator during and after the original

Creation, when at each stage of His labors "God *saw* that it was good." The "shining look" here is the look of divine approval, and the signs of inward regeneration are exhibited in outward manifestations of architecture, representing the inward "change of heart." All of this makes clear sense as a petition for spiritual renovation, and it is entirely irrelevant to the sense or success of the poem whether or not the poet happens to like modern architecture. He is praying for a rebirth of the spirit, which will of necessity express itself in all of mankind's arts, especially in its most societal and communal one, architecture. Furthermore, it may be claimed that the entire poem is based upon the suppressed metaphor of rebirth, or, in more familiar, historical terms, *renaissance*. It is difficult to guess how conscious Auden himself may have been of this metaphoric germ while he was writing his poem. But clearly both the Italian and Northern Renaissance gave rise to "new styles of architecture" which constitute some of the glories of their respective nations.

What, then, was Auden's motive for dropping this poem from the published body of his work? (Although the sonnet appeared in the 1945 *Collected Poetry,* Auden did not include it in his *Collected Shorter Poems, 1927–1957* or in any *Selected Poems* issued in his lifetime.) My guess is that there must have been two reasons. The lesser of the two may concern the invitation to God to show his divine malevolence against backsliders, "those in retreat." In a poem otherwise devoted to healers and healing, this parenthetical outburst of vindictiveness is perhaps out of tone and place. More serious, I think, is the doubtful moral and religious idea of petitioning for instant, immediate, gratuitous salvation to be rendered entirely as a gift of God, and without the need of any effort, act, or faith on the part of mankind, which is to be the passive beneficiary of this unprecedented renovation. Such reasons seem more sound and serious than the one Auden offered.

Nevertheless, and in spite of its pietistic stance, the poem bears many important resemblances to the decidedly secular poems Auden was writing at around the same time. Prayer is in some ways uniquely a mode of utterance that is at once public and private. It is public insofar as it is conventionally part of communal service and ritual practice; it is an established and traditional means of commerce with divinity, and it has the sanction of churches and of ancient custom. It is private insofar as it offers each person a singular avenue of address to God, the most intimate of all possible relationships with divinity. Purely as a convention, prayer afforded Auden a way of being public and private at the same time, and a means of writing about crises that were at once societal and uniquely personal conditions of the soul.

It is also worth noting that Auden made fun of the very yearnings this poem seems to express when he came to compose *The Dance of Death*, another suppressed work. It begins with the Announcer saying,

> We present to you this evening a picture of the decline of a class, of how its members dream of a new life, but secretly desire the old, for there is death inside them. We show you that death as a dancer.

And the Chorus naively sings:

> We shall build tomorrow
> A new clean town
> With no more sorrow
> Where lovely people walk up and down.

There is also an exchange of dialogue in which the tenets of Lawrence and Layard are presented as ridiculous clichés and cheap nostrums.

> B.                                              Be true
>     To the inner self. Retire to a wood
>     The will of the blood is the only good
>     We must learn to know it.
> A.                                        I see what you mean
>     We must keep our primal integrity clean.

Plotinus fares no better than Lawrence. *A.* declares,

> You are mistaken
> . . . . .
> You won't find the truth
> In a beautiful youth
> Nor will it be found
> In tilling the ground
> For the Eternal Word
> Has no habitation
> In beast or bird
> In sea or stone
> Nor in circumstances
> Of country dances
> It abideth alone.
> He who would prove

The Primal love
Must leave behind
All love of this kind
And fly alone
To the Alone.

*The Dance of Death* is a genuinely unsatisfactory work, crude in its satiric thrusts, vulgar in its tasteless and undramatic music-hall theatricality and in much of its language. But it is of interest as a document that shows Auden mocking ideas that he seriously entertains elsewhere. The key to its chief weakness (a weakness that will infect much of Auden's dramatic work) lies in the word "ideas." Auden is not truly a dramatist, and most of his plays are didactic in one way or another. They are not so much the vehicles for ideas as insolent commentaries on or parodies of ideas. And this brief work is perhaps the weakest of them all. The ideas presented are, especially in this early work, competing ideologies, secular or religious, but so presented as to be transparently feeble, and therefore easily replaceable by one another, like auto body parts. There have been, of course, certain critics, and even fellow poets, with limited sympathy for Auden's work, who have crudely characterized him as an intellectual or ideological poet, and who imply, when they do not actually state, that the value of any particular ideology or set of ideas from which Auden draws his metaphoric and intellectual structures is pretty much the same as the value of any other one he may switch to. Auden is thus presented as an intellectual dilettante, dabbling in ideas (Marxist, psychoanalytic, Christian) without being obliged to take any of them very seriously except as a point of departure for a literary work or ground for argument. (George Orwell's famous attack smacks slightly of this view.) It is a view which serves handily in a double capacity. First, it can suggest that Auden himself doesn't really believe any one of these ideas more than any other, and is simply using them as debating points, a frivolity which relieves his readers of the burden of taking any of these ideas very seriously. Second, and particularly for those who are made deeply uncomfortable by Auden's late religious preoccupations, it serves to suggest that, quite apart from any question of Auden's personal convictions, the "ideas" themselves are still merely alternative views of life, and no one of them is to be prized above another.

Perhaps the chief interest now of *The Dance of Death* lies in the series of choruses that present a slightly jazzy, clichéd outline of the economic history of Western civilization. There is, I think, no other modern poet for whom history itself plays so important a part of his thought throughout his career. Yeats, admittedly, relied heavily at certain points in his career on a peculiar theory of history and on specific historical data, and, like Auden later, saw himself as living through a time of unique historical change which it was his mission to record and meditate upon. But while Yeats was concerned with the symbolic repetitions of historical cycles, or with the special crises and cruxes that signaled the beginning or end of an epoch, Auden, who also imposed one era upon another, especially through anachronism, confined himself chiefly to Western history (as distinct from Yeats) and roamed through it sometimes with detailed attention to its principal actors (Pascal, Marx, Freud, Herod, Pope Gregory the Great, Luther, Tamerlane, Caesar, Achilles, Montaigne, Fortunatus, Newton, and Henry James). In the vaudeville context of *The Dance of Death* what we get is a sort of *Reader's Digest* or *Cliffs Notes* version of elementary history.

> The Greeks were balanced, their art was great
> They thought out in detail the city state
> But the gap to their interior was found at Carcassonne
> So trade moved westward and they were gone.
> . . . . .
> The Romans as every schoolboy knows
> United an empire with their roman nose
> But they caught malaria and they couldn't keep accounts
> And barbarians conquered them who couldn't pronounce.
> . . . . .
> The feudal barons they did their part
> Their virtues were not of the head but the heart.
> Their ways were suited to an agricultural land
> But lending on interest they did not understand.
> . . . . .
> Luther and Calvin put in a word
> The god of your priests, they said, is absurd.
> His laws are inscrutable and depend upon grace
> So laissez-faire please for the chosen race.
>
> The bourgeois thought this splendid advice
> They cut off the head of their king in a trice
> They enclosed the common lands and laid them for sheep
> And the peasants were told they could play bo-peep.

. . . . .
They invited them into a squalid town
They put them in factories and did them down
Then they ruined each other for they didn't know how
They were making the conditions that are killing them now.

This is, certainly, a secular and economic account, for all the mention of Luther and Calvin; it is an entropic history of decline, in a skit which will close with the Chorus singing:

O Mr. Marx, you've gathered
All the material facts
You know the economic
Reasons for our acts.

Something in the nursery-rhyme-doggerel quality of this final quatrain, and perhaps in those which precede it as well, suggests that as doctrine the Marxism here is not being taken very seriously and may very well be intended to seem ridiculous. Nevertheless, and however equivocally it is presented, it is a well-known historical thesis.

History, especially as depicted by dialectical materialists, but more broadly by determinists of any kind, bears an intimate relationship to theories, especially the Darwinian theory, of evolution. Implacable or inexorable systems of development, based on superseding species, races, civilizations, genetic varieties, a strong, vigorous, youthful and adaptable one triumphing over and annihilating its predecessor, had not only a familiar resonance of the Oedipal rebellion of son against father, but the equally familiar echo of the "survival of the fittest."

But precisely because these theories presented inexorable patterns they prohibited the freedom for which Auden yearned during his early years; and the rigor of those theories led him to identify them with the rigidities of the establishment, with the "old guard," inflexible zealots, with everything despised by the subversive and innovative. And the spirit of much of Auden's early poetry is that of the naughty boy who says and does what is forbidden by his elders, especially perhaps by his parents. While sometimes these gestures of revolt are elaborate structures with covert meanings, like *The Orators,* sometimes they are simple, witty acts of impudence, such as the parody of Campion's poem:

Rose-cheekt *Lawra,* come
Sing thou smoothly with thy beawties

>            Silent musick, either other
>                Sweetly gracing . . .

Auden's version is called "Uncle Henry":

>        When the Flyin' Scot
>        fills for shootin', I go southward,
>        wisin' after coffee, leavin'
>                Lady Starkie.

>        Weady for some fun,
>        visit yearly Wome, Damascus,
>        in Mowocco look for fwesh a-
>                -musin' places.

>        Where I'll find a fwend,
>        don't you know, a charming cweature,
>        like a Gweek God and devoted:
>                how delicious!

>        All they have they bwing,
>        Abdul, Nino, Manfwed, Kosta:
>        here's to women for they bear such
>                lovely kiddies!

Campion's poem appears in his essay "Observations in the Art of Englishe Poesie," where it is offered as an instance of the application of classical meters to English poetry. Auden was a sincere admirer of Campion, but could not resist the temptation to an impertinent parody. It should perhaps be noted first of all that Auden's "Uncle Henry" would have been received with outrage by the homosexual community if it had not been written by an acknowledged homosexual. It would probably have been called demeaning and offensive. It contains, in other words, an insider's joke. And the joke it makes is rather complicated. First of all, it sets at mockery the whole traditional and hyperbolic basis of Campion's poem, its neo-Platonic equation of mortal and physical beauty with the music of the spheres, its easy and casual commerce with the transcendent, its celestial imagery marshaled in praise of a woman's beauty. She is endowed with the familiar name of Laura, the beloved of Petrarch, whose devotion to her was not confined to her life on earth. Campion's poem is lyrically musical and employs musical metaphors; and its loveliness is wittily based on the contrast between earthly and heavenly music, the latter of which is likened to the "silent musick" of the woman's beauty, which is celestial in its origin.

Auden's poem has nothing to do with music, though it keeps, roughly, to Campion's scansion. (By "roughly" I mean that Campion does not allow himself a line so metrically deviant from the trochaic base as "like a Gweek God and devoted," where "Gweek God" is a spondee). Not only does Auden's poem repudiate the transcendent and "heavenly" aspects of beauty and the consequent sublimation of love into worshipful Petrarchan reverence, but it puts women in the demeaning position of being no more than the incubators and bearers of children, with no other desirable function. The poem is about "the hunt," most heading north for grouse in Scotland, Henry heading south for boys in more heated and exotic regions. There is even a little catalogue of the names of the hunted and captured, like Don Giovanni's list. And then we come to the question raised by the title.

In the "Journal of an Airman" section of *The Orators,* Auden had ingeniously proposed, with the aid of a Mendelian genetic diagram, that we were not necessarily most intimately or directly connected with our parents:

> The true ancestral line is not necessarily a straight or continuous one. Take a simple biological analogy, black and white colour, with white recessive to black.
>
> [He presents the diagram]
>
> In the $F_3$ generation the true ancestor of the pure white is his uncle or his great-grandfather . . .
> . . . My first memories of my Uncle were like images cast on the screen of a television set, maternally induced . . . I thought I hated him but I was always eager to please him or run errands, and a word of approval from him made me happy for the rest of the day.
>
> He didn't come very often, but I can remember when I was about thirteen a letter from him coming at breakfast. "Of course I know he's very clever," my mother sniffed, and then there was a silence.
>
> It wasn't till I was sixteen and a half that he invited me to his flat. We had champagne for dinner. When I left I knew who and what he was—my real ancestor.

There is to this, of course, the transparent wish-fulfillment fantasy of the adolescent, whose imagination gives him the power to pick his own parentage or heritage. And the indulgent "uncle" is to be preferred to the inhibiting parent. The desire to short-circuit the family structure is a common and ancient one, and is the subject of myths, dreams, and folk-tales in which it turns out that the persons we regard as our parents are not really ours, but that instead we are the children of kings or heroes, persons of infinite and widely acknowledged wealth, wisdom, and power. This dream of secret and inherited power belongs to Auden's Airman, who yearns for heroism but is also afraid of it, and afraid of failure. And this is partly because, as Samuel Hynes points out, the Airman's "thoughts are primarily about the Enemy [in part, our parents] . . . The fight against the Enemy, Auden seems to conclude, cannot be fought in public: the Enemy is ourselves." But the dream of being the heir of our uncle, the genetic heir as well as other kinds of heir, is a repudiation of family life, and of the determinism that normal genetics implies; it is a claim for freedom.

In the case of this little poem, it may carry another and still more concealed meaning. While Auden did not himself have an Uncle Henry, Isherwood did, and had some interesting things to say about him in his autobiographical *Christopher and His Kind*.

> The cause of his [i.e., Christopher's] unforeseen return [to London from Berlin] was Henry Isherwood, Christopher's elder uncle. Henry was the only member of the family who could be described as wealthy; he had inherited the Isherwood estates and money when his father died in 1924. Soon after this event, Christopher had decided to become Uncle Henry's favorite nephew; and he had done so instantaneously, by making it clear to Henry that they had the same sexual nature. Henry's brothers and sisters had always known about his homosexuality and had made unkind jokes behind his back, of which he was well aware. So Henry was delighted to discover a blood relative who shared his tastes—using the slang expressions of his generation, he referred to himself as being "musical" or "so" . . . Christopher couldn't have afforded to live in Berlin without Henry's allowance.

Mention must now be made of two figures in Auden's earliest pantheon not yet discussed: Baudelaire and Hardy, who bear little resemblance to one another, though both provoked the censor's wrath. Baudelaire fascinated by virtue of his deliberate inversion of all pieties, his determination to shock the bourgeois establishment, to court the satanic in preference to the tabernacles of the masses. But there was something further. In his introduction to Isherwood's translation of Baudelaire's *Intimate Journals* Auden observes: "Random jottings though they are, most of the entries revolve around one central preoccupation of Baudelaire's, namely: What makes a man a hero." Since Auden was likewise concerned with this problem and had cast about for many kinds of heroes in his youth, carefully distinguishing between what he called the "Truly Weak Man," or False Hero, and the "Truly Strong Man," or True Hero (the distinction being based upon the need of the weak man to make a display of his daring, prompted to this by the tyrannous demands of his mother, whereas the strong man demands no notice, having conquered himself—for a long time Auden thought T. E. Lawrence a strong man, but changed his mind), Baudelaire's similar attempt to define a hero in modern terms met with his admiration. It may be pointed out that Auden's search for the meaning of heroism continued for the better part of his life. His ideas about what constitutes a hero were to change considerably, and in the course of time would find expression in—to offer only two instances—the essay (in *Secondary Worlds*) titled "The Martyr as Dramatic Hero" and the powerful poem "The Shield of Achilles." "Like most of my generation, I was obsessed by a complex of terrors and longings connected with the idea 'War,'" writes Isherwood in *Lions and Shadows*. "'War,' in this purely neurotic sense, meant The Test. The test of your courage, of your maturity, of your sexual prowess: 'Are you really a Man?' Subconsciously, I believed, I longed to be subjected to this test; but I also dreaded failure."

The "test," Isherwood goes on to say,

symbolized, in my mind, the career of the neurotic hero, The Truly Weak Man—antithesis of "the truly strong man" spoken of by the homicidal paranoiac whose statement is quoted by Bleuler [Eugen Bleuler, heterodox psychoanalyst]: "The feeling of impotence brings forth the strong words, the bold sounds to battle are emitted by the trumpet called persecution insanity. The signs of the truly strong are repose and good-will . . . the strong individuals are those who without any fuss do their duty. These have neither the time nor the occasion to throw themselves into a pose and try to be something great." "The truly strong man," calm, balanced, aware of his strength, sits drinking quietly in the bar; it is not necessary for him to try to prove to himself that he is not afraid, by joining the Foreign Legion, seeking out the most dangerous wild animals in the remotest tropical jungles, leaving his comfortable home in a snowstorm to climb the impossible glacier. In other words, the Test exists only for the Truly Weak Man: no matter whether he passes it or fails, he cannot alter his essential nature.

Edward Mendelson elaborates helpfully upon this topic in *Early Auden:*

> The Truly Strong Man, and his opposite, the Truly Weak who defies the Lords of Limit, is an idea that brings into focus Auden's divided wish for private satisfaction and public responsibility . . . The Truly Weak, Auden wrote, takes to "blind action without consideration of meaning or ends"; he pursues what Isherwood called the futile compensatory North-West Passage. In 1929 Auden began writing his relevant case-histories of Truly Weak neurosis, for example,

> > Pick a quarrel, go to war
> > Leave the hero in the bar
> > Hunt the lion, climb the peak
> > No one guesses you are weak.

> . . . Until Auden found a plausible model for what he called "the transformation of the Truly Weak Man into the Truly Strong Man" (in 1934 he thought T. E. Lawrence might serve), he was able to identify the Truly Strong only by his absence.

Hardy was admired for wholly different reasons, having to do almost exclusively with his prosodic and stanzaic invention. Hardy was one of the most experimental and original formalists of his day, creating novelties of lyric patterns beyond even the wide range of Tennyson, and resembling in this the musical acuity of Campion. Hardy even titled a poem "To a Movement in Mozart's E-Flat Symphony," as well as adapting classical forms and meters. In addition, Auden shared with Hardy a lifelong devotion to the rural landscape; and though Auden idealized the city as the model of the human and civilized community, and though he was unusually myopic, lacking altogether Hardy's keenness of ocular observation, he was deeply loyal to the kind of English countryside in which he had been brought up, and, as we have seen, he was particularly given to moralizing landscapes, and using them in symbolic ways, as Hardy did in, for example, "The Darkling Thrush."

In *Lions and Shadows* Isherwood publishes some of Auden's very earliest poems, earlier even than the poems published in the 1928 pam-

phlet called *Poems,* printed by Stephen Spender, and appearing nowhere
that I have been able to find among the various collections of Auden's
work, including *The English Auden,* which is surely the most comprehensive assemblage of his writing prior to his settlement in America. One of
the poems Isherwood prints, "The Traction Engine," is very clearly
indebted to Hardy, though it lacks Hardy's formal correctness, and it
concerns Auden's "first love," which was of industrial machinery.

> Its days are over now; no farmyard airs
> Will quiver hot above its chimney-stack; the fairs
> It dragged from green to green are not what they have been
>     In previous years.
>
> Here now it lies, unsheltered, undesired,
> Its engine rusted fast, its boiler mossed, unfired,
> Companioned by a boot-heel and an old cart-wheel,
>     In thistles attired.
>
> Unfeeling, uncaring; imaginings
> Mar not the future; no past sick memory clings,
> Yet it seems well to deserve the love we reserve
>     For animate things.

Auden captures here a gentle ruefulness about the past that was truly
Hardy's, and so expresses Hardy's kind of reverence for the nonhuman
(though as far as I know Hardy never directed that love towards a
machine). But nevertheless Auden ventures on Hardy's daring use of the
pathetic fallacy in "unfeeling, uncaring." There is a Hardy we know
behind those words. And the internal rhyme in the third line of each stanza
is a species of formal patterning the younger poet admired in the work of
his elder, and later was ingeniously to use in his own work.

# II.  The Curative Power of Love: *On This Island*

*On This Island* (New York, 1937) is an extraordinary achievement. If Auden's first book dazzled with its variety of effects, its secretiveness, virtuosity, impudence, vaudeville panache, Marxist posturing, this second volume represents a huge advance in several ways. Perhaps most important of all, the book, though simply a collection of individual poems, is cunningly planned and thematically more unified than was ever to be the case again with any of his volumes of poetry, with the obvious exceptions of the large major works like *The Age of Anxiety* or *For the Time Being.* That unity lends the book a very considerable cumulative force, sadly lost when, as time passed, Auden eliminated from his canon thirteen of its thirty-two poems.

In addition (and, in terms of its influence on other poets, of still greater importance), this book introduced with astonishing effect the absolute novelty of a new diction, a fresh idiom that was instantly recognized and characterized as Audenesque. With the earlier publication of *Poems,* brilliant as it was, the public had been able to identify Auden with the work, the views, the very language, of his most notable contemporaries: with MacNeice, Spender, Day-Lewis, in particular. The 1937 book set Auden's thumbprint on his language so strongly that it could be, and was, adopted by a number of American admirers and imitators.

The rewarded porters opening their smiles

they have come back to tomorrow's city

a journey to the vacant / Satisfaction of death

The gangling and abortive fathers

The singular protein, the abstract cell

A year ago you owned me like a chair

As it happens, these little characteristic snippets are all drawn from Randall Jarrell's first book of poems, *Blood for a Stranger* (1942), and represent precisely the linguistic manner he was so vigorously to reprehend in his hostile essays. It was not wrong for him first to imitate this manner, nor was it wrong to isolate and identify it critically. But there was something unseemly about reprehending it, especially since it served Auden so admirably.

What Jarrell exemplifies in these early poems, and then proceeds to deplore in his later criticism, is what he characterized as "the juxtaposition of disparate coordinates." Auden had lots of ways of doing this; a random sample from *On This Island* would yield:

the valley of regret

this village of the heart

your map of desolation

the last feast of isolation

Duty's conscious wrong
The Goodness carefully worn
For atonement or for luck

The pool of silence and the tower of grace

the mountains of fear

The unbreakable habits of death

A moment's consideration will indicate how close are these coinages to the traditional device of personification. And indeed the language of this book abounds with this device.

And every day there bolted from the field
Desires to which we could not yield

Gross Hunger took on more hands every day

Where fancy plays on hunger to produce
The noble robber, ideal of boys . . .

Has not your long affair with death

> Of late become increasingly more serious; Do you not find
> Him growing more attractive every day?

The tone is so decidedly Auden's that we are likely to forget that the device itself is a perfectly innocent and ancient one; and one, moreover, that was rarely better employed than by one of Auden's revered masters, Hardy. It is a device that is closely associated with allegory and parable, which were forms Auden was to employ with enormous success through his life. They were in some ways his native and habitual modes of thought, and it can be claimed that his dramatic works, from *The Ascent of F6* and *The Dog Beneath the Skin* to the libretto for *The Rake's Progress,* including along the way *The Sea and the Mirror* and *The Age of Anxiety,* are all the products of an allegorical mind.

*On This Island* begins with a prologue and closes with an epilogue, neither of which Auden valued enough to retain, but which are not only remarkable in themselves but particularly potent in terms of the roles they play, the places they hold, in this book. They are its Lords of Limit, its termini, both literally and figuratively. And their prominence in these polar positions invites attention to their importance and to the roles they are assigned. The prologue, admittedly a poem that provokes irritation by the curled, cloudy, and elusive nature of its syntax (the tracking of which is an infuriating task), is a "dragon at the gates" of this book (a phrase I borrow from Robert Bridges, used to describe the intimidating effect of "The Wreck of the Deutschland," which he placed at the beginning of his edition of Gerard Manley Hopkins' *Poems, 1876–1889*). Auden's poem is a prayer and a prophecy, and it begins with what turns out to be an illusion of simplicity.

> O love, the interest itself in thoughtless Heaven,
> Make simpler daily the beating of man's heart; within,
> There in the ring where name and image meet,
>
> Inspire them with such a longing as will make his thought
> Alive like patterns a murmuration of starlings
> Rising in joy over wolds unwittingly weave.

The simplicity is illusory because these superficially transparent lines present problems upon examination. What, for example, is the antecedent of "them" in the fourth line? The only possibility seems to be "name and image," but how can they feel "longings"? Is the "ring" a marriage ring, as has been suggested, or a prizefighting or bullfighting ring? Name and image presumably meet in a unified and rational consciousness, but there is a good deal of evidence that rational consciousness is not what is being prayed for. Indeed, something of the oxymoronic "unpremeditated art" of Shelley's skylark seems to be exhibited by those starlings in which the "thought" of man is to be made as free as "love," which is the interest itself in "thoughtless" Heaven. "Thought" in this complex construction seems to be regarded with distrust, and the prayer that the beating of man's heart should be simplified conforms to this approval of instinct over intellect.

The poem is organized (as not very much later "Spain" will be) on a triadic design of past, present, and future. It first contemplates our too "contented" dream of "uniting the dead into a splendid empire," and the deceitful comforts of idle retrospection. It then proceeds to explore the actual present from which the dream has retreated,

> Leaving the furnaces gasping in the impossible air,
> The flotsam at which Dumbarton gapes and hungers,

and remarks on how improbably our ancestors, "Affectionate people, but crude their sense of glory," would have foreseen the likes of us, their posterity who, "tall with a shadow now, inertly wait." The poem is moving to an announced, expected, virtually scheduled apotheosis which is to arrive "out of the Future into actual History." This visionary change is as radical and deep as the one prayed for in an earlier poem which was to be expressed in "New styles of architecture, a change of heart." It appears that "at this very moment" when there is no hope at home (though on the continent whole populations look to England for the rejuvenating sign),

> Some possible dream, long coiled in the ammonite's slumber
> Is uncurling, prepared to lay on our talk and kindness
> Its military silence, its surgeon's idea of pain;
>
> And out of the Future into actual History,
> As when Merlin, tamer of horses, and his lords to whom
> Stonehenge was still a thought, the Pillars passed
>
> And into the undared ocean swung north their prow,
> Drives through the night and star-concealing dawn
> For the virgin roadsteads of our hearts an unwavering keel.

Those who employ the prophetic voice have frequently cloaked them-selves in a certain handy obscurity; the book of Revelation is by no means crystal clear, and the old runes of the Anglo-Saxons that Auden admired were tormentingly opaque. Here there are problems that seem almost beyond solution, and suggest, among other things, that some key punctuation is missing. But it is still possible to venture a few tentative observations. We may take it that Merlin is invoked as be-ing himself a prophet who foretells the coming again of Arthur. The ammonite's slumber takes us back beyond both Stonehenge and Merlin to an almost ultimately remote ancestry from which the dream shall advance as it drives, like an unwavering keel (as when Merlin and his lords swung north their prow in maritime exploit), for the virgin roadsteads of our hearts.

I've been unable to trace Merlin's maritime journeys, but it may be worth noting that, according to Geoffrey of Monmouth, one of Merlin's earliest prophecies was based on the discovery of two terri-ble dragons, a White and a Red, who "grappled together in baleful combat and breathed forth fire as they panted." Merlin, even as a child, was able to decipher this confrontation as a long war between the Saxons and the Britons, which is to say, the ancestors of the English people. And it seems to me likely that an allusion to this conflict is made in a poem in the body of this book, "The chimneys are smoking," where we encounter "The contest of the Whites and the Reds for the carried thing / Divided in secret among us, a portion to each," though in Auden's poem the opponents may also be two sides in an athletic contest. But what carries most force in Auden's prologue is the sudden and unexpected employment of nautical imagery, along with the assertion that history from its paleon-tological beginnings is bent upon an undeviating course ("But it rides time like riding a river") that envisions and "drives" toward the purification of English hearts and the spiritual renovation of the English nation. In this it bears a kinship with Gerard Manley Hopkins' great poem "The Wreck of the Deutschland," from which the line above in parentheses is quoted, which also, and more consistently, employs the imagery of the sea journey, and which is also a prayer for and vision of the conversion of England.

Taken in isolation, the prologue might seem, for all its obscurity, a specimen of facile optimism, the shameless wish-fulfillment dream of a "change of heart" to be procured in this case by the not very well defined power of "love," which seems to operate with all the authority of historical determinacy. But this poem is ruefully balanced by the epilogue, which, at the end of the book, undercuts all of the optimism and most of the hope. It was courageous and honest of Auden to put the wish-dream first instead of last, as a sentimentalist might have done.

The epilogue deals only with a past and a present, venturing no comment on the future. It also deals with our ancestors, but now they are our spiritual teachers whose instructions we failed to take to heart. The poem opens with the familiar, dreary, sterile industrial landscape, "Built by the conscious-stricken, the weaponmaking, / By us." And then it asks,

> . . . But where now are They
>
> Who without reproaches shewed us what our vanity has chosen,
> Who pursued understanding with patience like a sex, had
> unlearnt
>   Our hatred, and towards the really better
>   World had turned their face?
>
> There was Nansen in the north, in the hot south Schweitzer, and
>   the neat man
> To their east who ordered Gorki to be electrified;
>   There were Freud and Groddeck at their candid studies
>   Of the mind and body of man.
>
> Nor was every author both a comforter and a liar;
> Lawrence revealed the sensations hidden by shame,
>   The sense of guilt was recorded by Kafka,
>   There was Proust on the self-regard.

If there are puzzles here, they are penetrable. Nansen, awarded the Nobel Peace Prize, was an oceanographer, an explorer of the North Polar region, and a humanitarian who supervised the relief and repatriation of prisoners of war after World War I and directed the relief of multitudes suffering from famine in Russia. Schweitzer's work in his African leper colony is well known, though he also had a career as an organist, a theologian, and a commentator on Johann Sebastian Bach. Auden admired such men not only because of some single virtue but because they were polymaths. Addressing his famous predecessor in the *Letter to Lord Byron,* he writes, "A poet, swimmer, peer, and man of action, /—It beats Roy Campbell's record by a mile." The "neat man to their east" who ordered the village of Gorki electrified was Lenin, literally bringing light to the provinces. The rest are too well known to need identification. But it may be remarked that Auden treats his heroes in a rather clubby way that we became familiar with in the Pindaric odes (especially the one to Gabriel Carritt, Captain of the Sedbergh School XV) that close *The Orators*.

> Tudor from the tram-lined town,
> Self-confident under the moor;
> Scott from the chalk-pitted horse-taming down,
> 　　And otter-smooth Kerr:
> Sure-footed MacColl from the life-hostile gabbros of Skye,
> Red-bush Abrahall, diving Gray,
> Waters from dykes of the Wash, and Fagge from the
> 　bird-singing plain.
> 　· · · · ·
> Symondson—praise him at once!—
> Our right-wing three-quarter back
> Sergy, bulwark of every defence,
> 　　Mainspring of attack:
> When aligned like a squadron of bombers they flew
> 　downfield
> Over and over again we yelled
> 'Let the ball out to Sergy!' They did, he scored, and we dance.

In the epilogue the suggestion that each of the named heroes has his specific province of instruction or correction ("There was Proust on the self-regard") makes us feel that each had been assigned his specialized task on the team. Still, and for all that, the poem reads honestly, acknowledging that these teachers are with us no more, that their teachings are largely ignored, that we find ourselves in a visionless present, where we still are engaged in wounding one another. As a bitter corrective to the prologue nothing could have served better.

Between these poetic antipodes Auden presents a brilliant variety of lyrics, no two in the same form except for a few sonnets, all of which are related in that they deal in one way or another with a manifestation of "love," either as a private passion or as a social requirement, either as a benign force or, in its perversion, hatred, as a danger and disease. In a poem beginning "Brothers, who when the sirens roar" (which was originally titled "A Communist to Others" and which began "Comrades" instead of "Brothers") he even finds room for a cheerfully blistering invective against the indolently spiritless capitalistic bourgeoisie:

A host of columbines and pathics
Who show the poor by mathematics
    In their defence
That wealth and poverty are merely
Mental pictures, so that clearly
Every tramp's a landlord really
    In mind-events.

Let fever sweat them till they tremble
Cramp rack their limbs till they resemble
    Cartoons by Goya:
Their daughters sterile be in rut,
May cancer rot their herring gut,
The circular madness on them shut,
    Or paranoia.

Their splendid people, their wiseacres,
Professors, agents, magic-makers,
    Their poets and apostles,
Their bankers and their brokers too,
And ironmasters shall turn blue
Shall fade away like morning dew
    With club-room fossils.

There is something undisguisedly good-natured about this detestation, borrowed in all likelihood from the skillful invectives of the Latin poets, if not from Ronsard and the Pléiades or Skelton or Robert Burns. It is however only one of a number of lighthearted poems that serve as leaven to some degree for poems of deep anguish and others of serious visionary import.

It is in any case very obviously a "public" poem, easily to be contrasted with other poems in the book that are unquestionably "private," though never, I think, so hermetic as were the very private references and names in Auden's earlier poems. These "private" or clearly personal poems would include "Dear, though the night is gone" and "Fish in the unruffled lakes." But there is a third, or hybrid, kind of poem in this book, a kind that Auden would go on to perfect and make brilliantly his own, though it would have behind it the resonant precedent of Arnold's "Dover Beach"—the poem in which the outer and public world impinges, imposes upon, and endangers the personal and private realm. Auden's book was published in 1937, and might well have been given the title Empson used for his 1940 book, *The Gathering Storm*, a title Churchill himself did not disdain. Such poems as this new kind starkly pose moral and ethical problems of major significance. How may one hope to enjoy, or even entertain the possibility of, personal happiness in a world filled with omens or actual instances of horror and danger? What, indeed, is the proper relationship, if any, between one's private and intimate life as a lover or a friend, and one's social and civic life as a citizen, both of a nation and of what may loosely be called Western civilization? The answers to these questions were easy if one was, on the one hand, a left-wing political activist, or, on the other, a poet in the Romantic tradition, but what if one were both? These dilemmas, like "the unmentionable odour of death," are blown through this book on a steady and ominous wind, felt in such otherwise different poems as "O what is that sound which so thrills the ear" and "Now from my window-sill I watch the night." Such a poem as "Easily, my dear, you move, easily your head" moves freely between imaginary "worlds as innocent as Beatrix Potter's" and one in which the speaker acknowledges the consciousness of

> Ten thousand of the desperate marching by
> Five feet, six feet, seven feet high:
> Hitler and Mussolini in their wooing poses
> Churchill acknowledging the voter's greeting
> Roosevelt at the microphone, Van der Lubbe laughing
>     And our first meeting.

Only the last line here returns to the personal and intimate. (The only item in that stanza that in these late days might require annotation is Marinus Van der Lubbe, a poor, half-witted Dutch Communist upon whom the Nazis contrived to blame the setting of the Reichstag Fire on February 27, 1933, which served as a pretext for their usurpation of power. Van der Lubbe was brutally executed by beheading. Such hovering violence permeates the book.) The poem then acknowledges the dangerous temptation to make the private love a drug that allows the lover to accept, to assimilate, all the public horror heedlessly:

> The voice of love saying lightly, brightly—
> 'Be Lubbe, Be Hitler, but be my good
>     Daily, nightly.'

With the merest hint of an echo of Shakespeare's "They that have power
to hurt" and its "lilies that fester," the poem continues:

> The power that corrupts, that power to excess
> The beautiful quite naturally possess:
> To them the fathers and the children turn:
> And all who long for their destruction,
> The arrogant and self-insulted, wait
>     The looked instruction.
>
> Shall idleness ring then your eyes like the pest?
> O will you unnoticed and mildly like the rest,
> Will you join the lost in their sneering circles,
> Forfeit the beautiful interest and fall
> Where the engaging face is the face of the betrayer,
>     And the pang is all?
>
> Wind shakes the tree; the mountains darken;
> And the heart repeats though we would not hearken:
> 'Yours is the choice, to whom the gods awarded
> The language of learning and the language of love,
> Crooked to move as a moneybug or a cancer
>     Or straight as a dove.'

Though the poem ends with what appears a familiar and orthodox
Christian symbol, the "Love" that presides in this poem is of a very elastic
and embracing character. It is an ecumenical Eros, to be sure. (That love
is first mentioned in the line "Lucky to Love the new pansy railway,"
whatever *that* railway might be; the line was revised to read, "Lucky to
Love the strategic railway." John Whitehead, in *The W. H. Auden Society
Newsletter,* no. 5, August 1990, reports that "'pansy' in those days was
slang—especially schoolboy slang—for 'smart', no more. I am sure that
all Auden meant was 'the new smart railway', and that his original readers
understood it that way." However, the Supplement to the *OED* offers
one citation that seems perhaps relevant: "Originally, his hair had been
mousy brown. He'd tried to pansy himself up—and failed." The word is
used here in much the same way as "to tart up" is used: that is to say, to
make a vulgar and tasteless attempt to improve one's looks or the looks
of some object.) But Eros is also a moral force, and something that seems
to play a role in public events, though only at our behest, since it has no
principles of its own.

> But love, except at our proposal,
> Will do no trick at his disposal;
> Without opinions of his own, performs
> The programme that we think of merit,
> And through our private stuff must work
>      His public spirit.

And, most dangerous of all, love is the mindless, impetuous infatuation of the most private kind that can say to the beloved, "Be Lubbe, Be Hitler, but be my good" (whatever else you may be, regardless of any moral or public values). In other words, the poem is keenly aware of the potentiality of both private and public corruption.

The incursions of the great public world into the most private aspects of our lives, an intrusion that always occurs in moments of international or national crisis and is always at least potentially present, is alluded to in the epigraph to the book, which is dedicated to Erika Mann, whom Auden married specifically to confer upon her the benefits of his English citizenship and thereby afford her an escape from Nazi Germany, where her politically oriented, anti-Nazi cabaret acts in Berlin nightclubs put her in great danger of immediate arrest. The epigraph reads,

> Since the external disorder, and extravagant lies,
> The baroque frontiers, the surrealist police;
> What can truth treasure, or heart bless,
> But a narrow strictness?

Terse and moderately clear as this quatrain may seem (there is a nice ambiguity to "since," which can mean "because of" as well as "since the coming into being of"), it ingeniously pairs "truth" and "heart" in its third line, the former being a publicly established value, the latter an inward gauge. The lines bear a family resemblance to some by Addison from his political tragedy *Cato*.

> When vice prevails, and impious men bear sway,
> The post of honour is a private station.

But Auden in this book is more subtle than Addison, and knows that the individual heart in its private station is not only as corruptible as society at large but may be the very heart of the public corruption.

It may be worth commenting at this point that Auden's most astute critics have been virtually at one in remarking that his way of making some sort of moral connection between the activity of the private heart and the health of the body politic—the correspondence between inward and outward, personal and societal illness—is based on an original sociological extension of psychosomatic theories, derived from the likes of Trigant Burrow, Groddeck, Eugen Bleuler, William McDougall, Lane, Layard, and Lawrence. This claim is not wrong, but it overlooks a long and honored literary tradition that is embodied in *Oedipus Rex* and *Hamlet*. In both those plays the sickness of the nation ("Something is rotten in the state of Denmark") is the outward sign of incestuous disease in the royal household.

Moreover, given the fairly clear evidence of Auden's use of religious language from virtually the very beginning of his career, even during his most "left-wing activist" period, it may be further observed that the "correspondence" so commonly described in psychoanalytic metaphor may with equal justice be described in religious terms. Here, for example, is such a description of the relationship of personal spiritual health to the health of society at large, in a commentary by Guy Davenport on Paul's Second Epistle to Timothy.

> The air around Jesus and Paul was full of devils. It is easy to see these for what they were: we call them viruses, bacteria, epilepsy, depression, phobias, obsessions, blindness, lameness, scleroses. And something subtler: meanness, cruelty, selfishness. We see Jesus healing both disease and the ungenerous heart, scarcely making a distinction between them, as if the wounded body and the wounded mind were the same kind of hurt crying out to heaven to be healed.
>
> Evil is in the mind, in the will. Evil is the power one person has over another, in governments, and especially in official views of virtue which conceal ill will, jealousy, and a great fear of the flesh and the world.

Sentiments not unlike these which Davenport attributes to Paul figure prominently in most of the poems in *On This Island*. Indeed, some of the poems are saved from the taint of naiveté by being allowed some theological expansions of the term "love." The birthday poem for Isherwood, "August for the people and their favourite islands," finds the two friends at the acknowledged homosexual resort of Rügen Island, and contains this stanza of unembarrassed fantasy.

> Five summers pass and now we watch
> The Baltic from a balcony: the word is love.
> Surely one fearless kiss would cure

The million fevers, a stroking brush
The insensitive refuse from the burning core.
Was there a dragon who had closed the works
While the starved city fed it with the Jews?
Then love would tame it with his trainer's look.

So facile in its curative dream is this stanza as to make us feel (especially with the benefit of historical hindsight) almost anything from irritation to fury. We would do well of course to remember that the poem (dated August 1935 in *The English Auden*) was written by a twenty-eight-year-old, who happened to be more prophetic in his political insights (as far as they are stated in this stanza) than most of the political and military leaders in Western Europe and the United States. But much of the rest of the book scrupulously avoids the blithe confidence expressed here, and is as sensitive as any poet of the era (and more sensitive than most public figures) to the true dangers that existed. If love was called upon to furnish the international cure-all, this was no more than what was being uttered in private prayer by many pious and troubled souls throughout the world.

By contrast, one of the most memorable poems in the book, and one of the most morally sensitive, is the deservedly well-known "Out on the lawn I lie in bed." In it the poet acknowledges himself as enjoying a serenity and happiness of an uncommon kind, for which he is deeply grateful. His gratitude is the more pronounced because he is supremely aware of the public dangers to the peace of Europe, and furthermore aware that he, and all those similarly blessed, would "not care to know / Where Poland draws her Eastern bow / What violence is done . . ." What is being experienced is a privileged and private happiness, ominously threatened by public disaster and sure signs of general unhappiness elsewhere in the world. The poet knows, indeed, that "Soon through the dykes of our content / The crumpling flood will force a rent," a knowledge that not only makes the present happiness the more precious but adds to it a special quality engendered by guilt at the fact of enjoyment (almost of what might be called unmerited enjoyment) in a context of misery and danger. But whatever is being experienced in this poem, for which profound gratitude is certainly being expressed, it is not an experience that could be called bliss, nor does it seem extraordinary or unusual. I fuss about this, and perhaps seem to make less of the occasion of the poem than I might, only because Edward Mendelson has identified the poem so firmly with something like a spiritual vision which Auden did in fact write about in prose many years later. In *Early Auden* Mendelson writes,

On a warm June evening in 1933 . . . Auden experienced what he later called a mystical vision, probably the only such event in his life. He characterized it as a *vision of agape,* one in which, for the first time, he knew what it meant to love his neighbor as himself. His vision revealed neither sexual intensity nor undifferentiated groups nor social revolution, nor any of the extreme personal and public ordeals he had imagined as the only possible escapes from privacy. But while it lasted his isolation dissolved.

He wrote about the vision twice. Within a few days or weeks he celebrated its mood in the poem he later entitled "A Summer Night." In 1964 he returned to it and wrote a detailed factual account in a prose essay on the varieties of mystical experience.

That essay, as Mendelson goes on to say, was written as the introduction to Anne Fremantle's anthology *The Protestant Mystics.* And in the course of his introduction Auden rather coyly adverts to "an unpublished account of an experience for the authenticity of which I can vouch," which is a pretty devious way of acknowledging it as his own—if that is indeed what he is doing, as Mendelson simply assumes. I shall not argue that point, though it is clearly debatable. Mendelson then quotes the relevant passage of Auden's about this "experience."

One fine summer night in June 1933 I was sitting on a lawn after dinner with three colleagues, two women and one man. We liked each other well enough but we were certainly not intimate friends, nor had any one of us a sexual interest in another. Incidentally, we had not drunk any alcohol. We were talking casually about everyday matters when, quite suddenly and unexpectedly, something happened. I felt myself invaded by a power which, though I consented to it, was irresistible and certainly not mine. For the first time in my life I knew exactly—because, thanks to the power, I was doing it—what it means to love one's neighbor as oneself. I was also certain, though the conversation continued to be perfectly ordinary, that my three colleagues were having the same experience. (In the case of one of them, I was able later to confirm this.) My personal feelings towards them were unchanged—they were still colleagues, not intimate friends—but I had felt their existence as themselves to be of infinite value and rejoiced in it.

I recalled with shame the many occasions on which I had been spiteful, snobbish, selfish, but the immediate joy was greater than the shame, for I knew that, so long as I was possessed by this spirit, it would be literally impossible for me deliberately to injure another human being. I also knew that the power would, of course, be withdrawn sooner or later and that, when it did, my greeds and self-regard would return. The experience lasted at its full intensity for about two hours when we said good-night to each other and went to bed. When I woke the next morning, it was still present, though weaker, and it did not vanish completely for two days or so. The memory of the experience has not prevented me from making use of others, grossly and often, but it has made it much more difficult for me to deceive myself about what I am up to when I do. And among the various factors which several years later brought me back to the Christian faith in which I had been brought up, the memory of this experience and asking myself what it could mean was one of the most crucial, though, at the time it occurred, I thought I had done with Christianity for good.

This account is both moving and modest. Auden has carefully distinguished his vision of agape from a vision of God such as appeared in other accounts in the Fremantle book he was introducing. But quite apart from questions of genuineness (Mendelson tells us that "the typescript of the essay shows minor stylistic revisions being made in the account while it was typed," but Auden could have wished to improve upon the style of someone he was quoting but whom he regarded as no stylist), almost the first thing to strike us is the great disparity between the particularity, the documentary precision, the undeniable drama, with its *invasion by a power,* of the prose account—and the total absence of all these in a poem which is resolutely secular, though clearly composed in a mood of deep gratitude. The poem seems almost to go out of its way to avoid saying that something happened *on a certain night.* Instead, it deliberately generalizes the occasion:

> Equal with colleagues in a ring,
> I sit on each calm evening,
>     Enchanted as the flowers
>
> . . . . .
> That later we, though parted then

>     May still recall these evenings when
>         Fear gave his watch no look;
>     . . . . .
>     Moreover, eyes in which I learn
>     That I am glad to look, return
>         My glances every day.

What is being described here is surely a sustained condition of serenity and happiness. There is nothing in the poem about a sudden access of power or insight, nor indeed anything explicitly religious at all. On the contrary, the poem makes a serious point of saying that "we . . . do not care to know / Where Poland draws her Eastern bow, / What violence is done." This expressly selfish luxuriance in private happiness firmly insists on being unaware of any grief that might compete for attention; and whatever this is, it is not a vision of agape.

Moreover, the prose account invites questioning on another ground. Writing of that account, Mendelson tells us that Auden's "three colleagues were a master and two matrons at the school." And one cannot fail to remark that such colleagues would have had much in common with Auden. They would have had comparable educations, would have come in all likelihood from the same social class, would have all been concerned with the general problems of education, would have been pretty much the same age. Having common concerns as they did, it is not difficult to imagine that a sense of deep mutual respect and liking would make itself felt, perhaps even quite suddenly, among them. The real test of being able to love one's neighbor would be to stand at the intersection of Broadway and Forty-second Street and undertake to love the first five, or twenty, or one hundred people who passed by.

One of the most admired yet complex poems in the volume is "Our hunting fathers told the story." Though it was written independently of the group, Monroe K. Spears helpfully informs us that it was used as the epilogue to some poems that were set to music by Benjamin Britten. So it seems useful to consider the opening piece in the sequence, "The Creatures," as it reflects upon the closing.

>     They are our past and our future: the poles between which our
>         desire unceasingly is discharged.
>
>     A desire in which love and hatred so perfectly oppose
>         themselves that we cannot voluntarily move; but await the
>         extraordinary compulsion of the deluge and the earthquake.

Their affections and indifferences have been a guide to all
reformers and tyrants.

Their appearances amid our dreams of machinery have brought
a vision of nude and fabulous epochs.

O Pride so hostile to our Charity.

But what their pride has retained, we may by charity more
generously recover.

(It might be worth noting how oddly suited is this prologue, as well as the
concluding epilogue, to intelligible musical setting—a fault that Auden
would learn to repair when he came to writing arias for setting by
Stravinsky.) The "creatures" of this poem are our past in the double sense
that a) we have evolved from them by the accidents and fate of evolution,
and b) in Biblical terms we were once as innocent and free from sin as
they remain. They are our future because it is their innocence that we hope
to attain in one way or another. Auden's punctuation being characteristically ambiguous here, we cannot tell whether the antecedent of "the
poles" is "they" (the creatures) or "our past and our future." I will assume
it is the second, because our "desire" is unceasingly discharged between
wanting to be as blameless and free as we were in a natural state and
wanting to be as free and untroubled by passion as we shall be in the
"blessed" state. Our bestial qualities and supernatural yearnings are so
perfectly matched that it would take an act of God to move us towards
one pole or another; these acts of God can be disasters which will bring
out in us either our natural ruthlessness or our compassion and goodness.
But the freedom of "the creatures" from ordinary human guilt or loyalty
has served reformers (who point to this kind of freedom as immoral and
tell us not to act like beasts) and tyrants (who can make good use of the
heartlessness of men). "Our dreams of machinery" are the dreams in
which we imagine creating our own man-made paradise, through complete control of our environment, but the appearances of "the creatures"
amid our dreams remind us of both the paradise of primitivism and of
Eden. "They" can be proud without sin, a condition we can never attain,
for which we must compensate with "charity." The poem, actually a set
of prose statements, was set by Britten, though the text is of a seemingly
prohibitive density that Auden would take pains to avoid when he came
to writing opera libretti, and it obviously presents some problems of
interpretation even as it lies on the printed page. But if my tentative

observations are allowed, they will reflect in important ways on the more famous epilogue to the sequence.

> Our hunting fathers told the story
>   Of the sadness of the creatures,
> Pitied the limits and the lack
>   Set in their finished features;
> Saw in the lion's intolerant look,
> Behind the quarry's dying glare,
> Love raging for the personal glory
>   That reason's gift would add,
> The liberal appetite and power,
>   The rightness of a god.
>
> Who nurtured in that fine tradition
>   Predicted the result,
> Guessed love by nature suited to
>   The intricate ways of guilt?
> That human ligaments could so
> His southern gestures modify,
> And make it his mature ambition
>   To think no thought but ours,
> To hunger, work illegally,
>   And be anonymous?

Our "hunting fathers" are not simply grouse-shooting country squires of the immediate past or even a century ago; they are our ancestors whom we can trace back to the beginnings of civilization—predators, admittedly, but not therefore to be faulted, since God gave mankind "dominion over the fish of the sea, and over the fowls of the air, and over every living thing that moveth upon the earth," commanding him to "replenish the earth and subdue it." Our hunting fathers have hunted not for sport but for food; in this they bear a clear resemblance to predatory beasts, such as the lion; but they are to be distinguished from the beasts by the faculty of reason, and it was Aristotle who defined man as a rational animal. Our hunting fathers were by no means ill at ease in acknowledging their animality because they knew themselves to be the very apex of Creation, reserved for God's last act in his formation of the world, made in his divine image, and but "a little lower than the angels." They saw themselves as a central and important link in the Great Chain of Being, whose powers

and appetites were "liberal" in the sense of "liberating," as we use the
term when we speak of the liberal arts. Mankind, in this view (which finds
its origins in both the Greek philosophers and the Bible and was taken as
a commonplace from medieval times to the end of the seventeenth
century), conceives the animal kingdom as being appropriately envious of
the gift of reason, reserved for men and bestowed by "the love that moves
the sun and the other stars." Though man can be like the lion or like its
quarry, can be either predator or victim, he has the gift of reason,
conferred by a gift of love (and is therefore, it may be inferred, capable of
salvation). This was the way men thought about themselves in relation to
the rest of creation for a very long time. Or at least it was one way of
thinking. It was given one of its earliest and most majestic expressions in
Pico della Mirandola's oration *On the Dignity of Man,* a text Auden
paraphrases in the first of the sequence called *Sonnets from China.*

But even if it was accepted as the proper way of thinking, it posed
problems. "Fine tradition" though it was, we were left to explain to
ourselves how so favored a creature ("how noble in reason, how infinite
in faculties; in form and moving how express and admirable, in action how like an angel, in apprehension how like a god: the beauty of
the world, the paragon of animals") should turn out to be no more
than "this quintessence of dust," not only unhappy in his lot, but dismayed by his animality and convulsed with guilt. There are at least
two ways to explain this, of which one, the more superficial, is the
discovery by Freud and others in fairly modern times of the mechanism
of our guilt complexes. But the other, more ancient and enduring one, and
which may be said to be "the result" of that fine tradition, is, in a sense,
part of it. It is our story of the Fall from grace in the garden. The Fall
steeped us in shame and guilt, especially as it affected the *love* expressed
in sexual relations. Milton himself made much of this. And, without its
theological trappings, so did D. H. Lawrence. And it is precisely this
Lawrence who comes to Auden's mind as he reviews Liddell Hart's
biography of T. E. Lawrence:

Different as they appear on the surface, both [T. E. Lawrence] and
his namesake, D. H. Lawrence, imply the same, that the Western
romantic conception of personal love is a neurotic symptom only
inflaming our loneliness, a bad answer to our real wish to be united
and rooted in life. They both say *"noli me tangere."* It is at least
doubtful, if in our convalescence sexual relations can do anything
but postpone our cure. It is quite possible that the way back to real

intimacy is through a kind of asceticism. The self must learn to be indifferent; as Lenin said, "To go hungry, work illegally and be anonymous." Lawrence's enlistment in the Air Force and Rimbaud's adoption of a trading career are essentially similar.

Comment needs to be made even on this prose before it is applied to the poem under discussion. "The Western romantic conception of personal love" that Auden finds neurotic is the one described by C. S. Lewis in *The Allegory of Love,* a tradition not merely literary (though it was that) but of feeling and the proper way of conducting oneself in terms of courtship and love. It laid enormous emphasis on self-denial and mortification as the true expression of devotion, and came to much the same thing as *Noli me tangere.* What Auden is saying in his review is that so neurotic have we all been made by the cruel and perverse sublimations this doctrine of love has imposed that we can no longer express *personal love* in any free and guiltless way. Since we cannot do that, we could at least, by embracing asceticism, express *social love,* love for our fellow human beings, adopting the anonymous ways of a social reformer Auden greatly admired, namely Lenin.

If love was conceived in the first stanza of "Our hunting fathers told the story" as divine, rational, and beneficent, in the second stanza it is warped, private, and guilt-ridden. Love (which is to say, the god Eros) becomes in the last six lines of the second stanza one of Auden's anonymous spies: an undercover agent, furtive, passing himself off as an ordinary citizen. "His southern gestures," as others have noted, are his genital reactions. He has given up his status as a god and assumed the mortal role of social reformer. There is something both theological and vaguely blasphemous in this parody of the incarnation of love as man. But the contrast between the first and second stanzas is a contrast between a transcendent love, which is scarcely physical at all, and a profane one, which is furtive, devious, and subversive.

What may be called a key poem in Auden's early work, if only because it goes through so many protean changes, is one that begins "Now from my window-sill I watch the night." In *On This Island* it is a fifteen-stanza poem; when it appears in the *Collected Shorter Poems* it is reduced to eight stanzas (in its newly truncated form it is given the title "The Watchers"), but that is only the slightest of the metamorphoses it underwent in the course of its curious career. It began, as the critics and biographers tell us, as the second part of a long poem called "A Happy New Year," the first part of which is printed in *The English Auden.* This first part, dedicated to Gerald Heard, is a dream sequence—a genre Auden clearly found congenial. It is an extended (stanzas varying between seven and eight lines, with forty-four stanzas in all) tour de force of light verse, much of it in amphibrachs. Its largely satiric thrust is ecumenically discharged in every direction of the ideological spectrum, including, I suspect, some small jokes at the poet's own expense. The tone is almost entirely farcical, and this makes what was originally its second part the more bewildering, since "Now from my window-sill" is a serious, enigmatic, and rather grim poem that bears no relation to the levity of what once preceded it. Humphrey Carpenter writes of it thus:

> In [this poem], Auden prays that his pupils at Larchfield and his other friends at Helensburgh shall be protected from whatever social or political upheaval—perhaps a revolution—may be in store. This prayer is addressed not to God but to two godlike figures who here make the first of several appearances in Auden's poetry, and whom he here describes as "Lords of Limit . . . / The influential quiet twins / From whom all property begins"; he also compares them to "erratic examiners," or "The stocky keepers of a wild estate." Their precise nature is not made clear, though they are obviously some kind of Fates. Auden very likely took them (as Samuel Hynes suggests) from the "two witnesses" in the eleventh chapter of the Book of Revelation, who are given authority over the earth; no doubt he was also thinking of D. H. Lawrence's gloss on this passage in his book *Apocalypse,* for Lawrence explained these "witnesses" as powers that "put a limit on man" and "say to him in every earthly and physical activity: thus far and no further . . . They make life possible; but they make life limited."

It seems to me worth quoting the relevant Biblical passage, Revelation 11:3–5, spoken by an angel:

> And I will give power unto my two witnesses, and they shall prophesy a thousand two hundred and threescore days, clothed in sackcloth.
> These are the two olive trees, and the two candlesticks standing before the God of the earth.
> And if any man will hurt them, fire proceedeth out of their mouth, and devoureth their enemies; and if any man will hurt them, he must in this manner be killed.

The ferocity of these verses in no way consorts with the sprightly jibes and lighthearted badinage of what was Part I of "A Happy New Year." Auden's "Lords of Limit" were to reappear in what he called in a letter "a narrative poem in alliterative verse." It is again a dream sequence; in it the poet and a Virgilian guide of his named Sampson encounter two old men. Carpenter explains that they are "'Titt and Tool,' and the dreamer [for example, the poet] recognises them as the authors of all the grim textbooks that made his schooldays a misery . . . But they are more than just archetypal pedagogues . . . They are in fact the Fate-like 'Lords of Limit' of Auden's earlier poem 'A Happy New Year.'" This poem, once thought to be lost, was published in the August 1978 issue of *Review of English Studies* under the careful editorship of Lucy McDiarmid. In the course of his Virgilian instruction of the pilgrim Auden, the figure of Sampson says,

> "Have you heard in your time of Titt and Tool?"
> And I, astonished, "Not the Text-book Twins
> Whose Algebra, Grammar, History and Stinks
> Made me weep before my voice had broken,
> Of whom we sang at the end of each term
> As we drove in the waggonnette down to the station
>     'No more extra writing school
>     No more beastly Titt and Tool'?"

They deny that they command any real authority, saying, "'We're simply the servants of a system, you know.' But it is made clear that they have great power and influence in the world, as is demonstrated in a song they now sing."

This song appears in at least three incarnations, the one of which, titled "The Witnesses," and dated ?late 1932 in *The English Auden,* is the longest. It begins with what seems to be the mountebank spiel of a soapbox orator or circus barker trying to assemble a crowd. He calls upon people from all ranks of society—dowagers, solicitors, stokers, shepherds—and commands them all to "come forward" and attend, for

> My companion here is about to tell
>     a story;
> Peter, Pontius Pilate, Paul
> Whoever you are, it concerns you all
>     and human glory.

There follows the story in the same light-verse stanza about one "Prince Alpha," who knew and did everything.

> At school his brilliance was a mystery,
> All languages, science, maths, and history
>         he knew;
> His style at cricket was simply stunning
> At rugger, soccer, hockey, running
>         and swimming too.

He thus advances from triumph to triumph, but nevertheless at a certain point he comes to a desert, breaks into tears, and declares,

> 'I thought my strength could know no stemming
> But I was foolish as a lemming;
>         for what
> Was I born, was it only to see
> I'm as tired of life as life of me?
>         let me be forgot.

> 'Children have heard of my every action
> It gives me no sort of satisfaction
>         and why?
> Let me get this as clear as I possibly can
> No, I am not the truly strong man,
>         O let me die.'

And now, in "The Witnesses," the two speakers, who before have alternated in discourse, presumably speak in chorus, beginning thus:

> What had he done to be treated thus?
> If you want to know, he'd offended us:
>         for yes,
> We guard the wells, we're handy with a gun,
> We've a very special sense of fun,
>         we curse and bless.

> You are the town, and we are the clock,
> We are the guardians of the gate in the rock,
>         the Two;
> On your left, and on your right
> In the day, and in the night
>         we are watching you.

Wiser not to ask just what has occurred
To them that disobeyed our word;
     to those
We were the whirlpool, we were the reef,
We were the formal nightmare, grief,
     And the unlucky rose.

. . . . .

The bolt is sliding in its groove,
Outside the window is the black remov-
     er's van,
And now with sudden swift emergence
Come the women in dark glasses, the hump-backed surgeons
     and the scissor-man.

This might happen any day
So be careful what you say
     or do
Be clean, be tidy, oil the lock,
Trim the garden, wind the clock:
     Remember the Two.

The bogeymen and -women in the penultimate stanza are the grown-ups of children's nightmares—"the scissor-man" is very likely a figure out of *Struwwelpeter,* which Auden knew from his childhood—and they are the enforcers of all the taboos and prohibitions that are imposed upon children. If I am right about this, it may further be surmised that "Titt and Tool," though presented as "two old men" in the dream poem from which "The Witnesses" is an extract, are in fact female and male parents, the creators of the superego, the conscience, and the givers of inhibitions. If, furthermore, Auden was "terrified" at the age of five at beholding his own parents transsexualized by costumes for a fancy-dress party, it is comprehensible that they might occur to him as "two old men." To be sure, the poem is in some sense a free fantasy, and composed in a form of nearly Gilbertian frivolity. But this may conceal its seriousness, of which the references to Revelation are certainly important ones. And certainly the poem that begins "Now from my window-sill" is, for all its mystery, a thoroughly serious work.

    "Now from my window-sill I watch the night" is set in spring, and though the first stanza makes mention of "a new imprudent year," that year is not the calendar year but the one inaugurated by spring, as the rest

of the poem will make clear. It takes place in a dormitory of the Helens-
burgh School just before ten o'clock at night, when the boys are asleep in
their beds. Just as in "Out on the lawn I lie in bed," in which "we . . . do
not care to know, / Where Poland draws her Eastern bow," here,

> . . . deaf to prophecy or China's drum
> The blood moves strangely in its moving home,
> Diverges, loops to travel further
> Than the long still shadow of the father,
> Though to the valley of regret it come.

That "long still shadow of the father" the blood is trying to evade even
at the cost of arriving at the "valley of regret," looks very much like
the admonitory figure of parental conscience, raised up to reproach
the antinomian, libertine self. And the diverging, looping course of the
blood may perhaps represent the physiological effects of sexual arousal,
a tumescence that the shadowy figure of the father would reprove. Such
a specter of rectitude is the more frightening and depressing because this
is the "season when the ice is loosened . . . And cameras at the growing wood / Are pointed; for the long lost good, / Desire like a police-dog
is unfastened." Those cameras are presumably alert for wildlife, the
world of instinctual behavior, which is our long-lost good, and upon
which our desire focuses with the precision and determination of a dog
with a highly sensitive and trained nose. But such desire and emancipation
is, for all its unquestioned value and importance, still and expressly selfish,
and therefore in need of some correction. So it is at this point that a
petitionary prayer begins, addressed to the Lords of Limit.

> O Lords of Limit, training dark and light
> And setting a tabu 'twixt left and right:
> The influential quiet twins
> From whom all property begins,
> Look leniently upon us all tonight.

As "trainers" of dark and light, as institutors of a taboo between left and
right, these Lords are presumably the makers of the moral distinctions the
blood in its journey has been trying to evade. The lines of property also
make distinctions, and they were sanctified by the Romans in the figure
of the god Terminus, "a divinity who was supposed to preside over
bounds and limits," according to Lemprière; and "bounds and limits"
were the continuing concern of Auden throughout his earliest poetry. It

is certainly plausible to conjecture that such Lords of Limit might, for Auden, have represented a taboo regarding his desires for the schoolboys who were his pupils. It may be worth pointing out that the annual festival of Terminus fell on February 23, two days after Auden's birthday, and he might well have thought the association important. The Lords are called "oldest of masters," feared by all schoolboys, never seen, yet encountered in dreams as "the stocky keepers of a wild estate." As estate keepers they preserve property, of course; but the dream continues to envision them "With guns beneath your arms, in sun and wet / At doorways posted or on ridges set . . . Whose sleepless presences endear / Our peace to us with a perpetual threat." As guardians of a wild estate from which we are presumably excluded, these figures bear a resemblance to the cherubim with flaming sword, who stand sentry at the gates of Eden, the "wild estate" in which man lived whole, integrated, and (except for one prohibition) ungoverned.

> We know you moody, silent, sensitive,
> Quick to be offended, slow to forgive,
> But to your discipline the heart
> Submits when we have fallen apart
> Into the isolated personal life.

This lapse into the isolated personal life is a lapse into selfishness and solipsism from which the heart can recover only by submission to a discipline represented by these stern figures. We, in our isolation, acknowledge that we are "sick," that we have no "invitation" to return to the "wild estate" for which we yearn, where we would be healed and made whole again. We are forced to use "the mole's device" (which is subversive, underground); we adopt the prideful "carriage / Of peacock or rat's desperate courage" in the hope of bypassing these sentinels. Their severity is deliberately contrasted with the God of the Old Testament who is "slow of anger, quick to forgive."

And now the poet turns his thoughts to the boys "who dream / Of a new bicycle or winning team." And here the petition on their behalf, on behalf, that is, of a new generation, as distinct from the general amnesty prayed for earlier ("Look leniently upon us all to-night") begins.

> On their behalf guard all the more
> This late-maturing Northern shore,
> Who to their serious season must shortly come.
>
> Give them spontaneous skill at holding rein,

At twisting dial, or at making fun,
That these may never need our craft,
Who, awkward, pasty, feeling the draught,
Have health and skill and beauty on the brain.

These guardians of boundaries would have special concern for England, which, as an island, has boundaries so explicitly defined. And we are reminded of the prologue, and its special prayer for the renovation of England. The boys now being prayed for are as yet uncorrupted by the sly mechanisms of the rat and the mole, to which we, the older generation, have been obliged to resort. The poet petitions the Lords on the boys' behalf, asking that they be given "spontaneous skill at holding rein, / At twisting dial, or at making fun," which is to say, *control* over horses and engines and, through cleverness and good-natured mockery, over others. The "spontaneous skill" is contrasted with all the deviousness with which we older ones are hopelessly infected. The poem nears its end with a passing image of a "starving visionary" who enviously observes "the carnival within our gates," that holiday of license sanctioned by law, but it concludes with a petition for continued protection, which is in fact the power of discipline.

The Lords of Limit in this poem are kindlier and more gracious than the analogous figures of "the Two" in the poem called "The Witnesses." This latter poem is dated ?late 1932 in *The English Auden,* while "Now from my window-sill" is dated February 1932 and is thus the earlier composition. This may mean that Auden did not think well of it, and decided to make fun of it by making his guardians inhumanly terrible, figures that no one would think of praying to, particularly for protection. But this is not the end of the matter. Auden adapted the larger part of the third or final section of "The Witnesses" (leaving out the summons of the auditors, the feeble narrative of Prince Alpha), omitting two full stanzas and altering others; and then he added an entirely new set of introductory stanzas in a different form, as well as an anxiety-ridden chorus in italics that asks nervous questions between the stanzas. This new poem he also titled "The Witnesses." It begins:

Young men late in the night
  Toss on their beds,
Their pillows do not comfort
  Their uneasy heads,
The lot that decides their fate

Is cast tomorrow,
One must depart and face
Danger and sorrow.

*Is it me? Is it me?*

Look in your heart and see:
There lies the answer.
Though the heart like a clever
Conjurer or dancer
Deceive you often with many
A curious sleight,
And motives like stowaways
Are found too late.

*What shall he do, whose heart*
*Chooses to depart?*

He shall against his peace
Feel his heart harden,
Envy the heavy birds
At home in a garden,
For walk he must the empty
Selfish journey
Between the needless risk
And the endless safety.

*Will he safe and sound*
*Return to his own ground?*

Clouds and lions stand
Before him dangerous,
And the hostility of dreams.
Then let him honour Us,
Lest he should be ashamed
In the hour of crisis,
In the valley of corrosion
Tarnish his brightness.

*Who are You, whose speech*
*Sounds far out of reach?*

Now this antiphon of statement and question, along with the verses that follow, in which "the Two," in an evasively Delphic way, identify themselves, and which begin "You are the town and We are the clock," constitute the final part of the opening chorus of Auden's play *The Dog Beneath the Skin*. (I've been unable to determine whether the poem was first composed as part of the play or later embedded in it. In any case, Auden was prepared to publish it as an independent poem requiring no further context.)

Apart from any other considerations, the poem continues the theme of the voyager or explorer who must cross frontiers and risk great dangers, like ancient heroes. The feeling of discomfort, loneliness, and terror that lies before him is the one expressed also in one of Auden's best-known and deservedly admired early poems, "The Wanderer." But whereas the early and brilliant lyric, with its Anglo-Saxon echoes and manner, is serious in its tone throughout, here in this choral piece the prophecies of danger are larded with nearly comic irony: "Something is going to fall like rain, / And it won't be flowers." It needs to be added that the resemblance of "The Wanderer" to these lyrics from the play is not a coincidence. "The Wanderer" first made its appearance in an earlier play called *The Fronny* (1930), an unfinished sketch for and forerunner of *The Dog Beneath the Skin*.

It may be as well at this point to address *The Dog Beneath the Skin,* which seems to me decidedly the best of the collaborations between Auden and Isherwood. It is a very lively, often truly funny, work, with a skeletal plot, but nearer in character to a revue with heterogeneous and nearly discrete scenes or vaudeville "turns." In addition to this it includes at least three lyrics that Auden was to publish independently and without reference to the play. It takes its point of origin in two widely disparate sources, which perfectly suits so mixed and mongrel a production as this play which, for convenience, critics and commentators have taken to calling *Dog-Skin*.

The first of these sources is an English folk-tale called *The Small-Tooth Dog*, a transformation tale that has been transcribed in a collection edited by Katharine Briggs and Ruth Tongue and published by the University of Chicago Press. The tale is of a merchant beset by thieves and rescued by a dog. Having driven away the attackers, the dog took the merchant to his very handsome home, dressed his wounds, and attended to him until he was well. (There are clear overtones here of the parable of the Good Samaritan.) In gratitude for being thus saved and nursed back to health, the merchant thanked the dog profusely and offered him anything he desired in the way of reward, including the most precious things he had.

Among these treasures was a fish that spoke twelve languages, a goose that laid golden eggs, and a mirror in which you could see what anyone was thinking. The dog politely refused all of these and instead requested, "Let me fetch your daughter, and take her to my house." (Overtones here of the tale of Jephthah's daughter, as well as other tales.) The merchant grieved at this but felt bound by his promise, and the girl was duly transferred to the possession of the dog. But she was unhappy and cried all the time, and when the dog asked her why, she said she was homesick and missed her father. "The dog said, 'If you will promise me that you will not stay at home more than three days I will take you there. But first of all,' he said, 'what do you call me?' 'A great, foul, small-tooth dog,' said she. 'Then,' he said, 'I will not let you go.'" She then broke out in more copious tears and undertook, with only a glimmering of wisdom, to call the dog instead "Sweet-as-a-honeycomb," whereupon, won over by her affectionate good nature, he began the journey home, carrying the girl on his back. When they reached a stile, the girl lapsed back into her formerly hostile description of "A great, foul, small-tooth dog," whereupon, to her considerable surprise, he simply turned around and carried the girl back to his own home. After a week of lamentation, the excursion was begun again, and when they came to the stile and the dog asked the girl what she called him, she summoned all her wits and replied, "Sweet-as-a-honeycomb," whereupon they climbed and passed the stile; but they came to a second, and at her impatience with this, the girl reverted to her former abusiveness, and was promptly returned to the dog's home. After another week of grieving the journey was begun again, and though two stiles were passed, the girl was about to call the dog the name he so obviously had no liking for when she saw the wounded look in the dog's eyes, and though she had gotten as far as "foul," she reversed herself and said, "Sweeter-than-a-honeycomb." At this the dog rose on his hind legs, with his forelegs pulled off his dog's head, removed his hairy coat, and stood revealed as "the handsomest young man in the world, with the finest and smallest teeth that you ever saw." They married, of course, and lived happily. "Beauty and the Beast" and "The Frog-Prince" are obviously analogous tales; but this one involves a journey, the answer to a riddle ("Is the name Sir Francis Crewe, / English, known perhaps to you?"), and a man who emerges from the skin of a dog who has behaved pretty anthropomorphically throughout.

The second major source is Dante, and especially the *Inferno,* which is also a journey narrative, with a guide, and with the sudden apparition to the pilgrim of certain of the "departed" whom he had known or known of. The *Inferno* is full of them; *Dog-Skin* has two, Sorbo Lamb and Chimp Eagle, who are "dead to the world." The journey in both the epic and the play is to an imaginary realm in which we are allowed to view how misdirected love expresses itself, and to what sterility, foolishness, and grief it leads.

> See love in its disguises and the losses of heart,
> Cats and old silver inspire heroic virtues
> And psychic fields, accidentally generated, destroy whole
>       families.

There is even a point late in the play in which Alan Norman, the protagonist-pilgrim, declares unambiguously, "Oh, I'm in hell!" And though some critics have called the fictive nations Alan and Francis visit scenes of current European cultures and references to actual historical incidents ("For example, the scene in which workers of Ostnia are executed by the king, while the queen comforts their widows, was suggested to Isherwood by the alleged behaviour of Frau Dollfuss, the wife of the Austrian chancellor during the Vienna Uprisings," we are told by Samuel Hynes), the dramatic fact is that they represent states of mind and conditions of the soul, as do the events and persons in Dante's poem. Francis, the Dog/Man, for all his absurd resemblance to Nana in J. M. Barrie's *Peter Pan,* is also a serious guide, a nonspeaking Virgil who more than once saves the pilgrim Alan Norman, particularly at the end when, by taking Norman off with him, he saves him from the stagnation of the English village of Pressan Ambo, and from the bigotry, conventionality, stupidity, chauvinism, and sanctimoniousness that its leading citizens represent. No doubt there is also a repudiation of heterosexuality in Norman's election of Francis over his betrothed, Iris Crewe. But such repudiation is modified by the fact that Iris represents everything Alan has learned to suspect or detest, while Francis at the end turns into the guide to a new sort of life, and whatever that sort may be has something to do with an emancipating love. This is made patently clear in the uncut version of the play edited by Mendelson and recently published by Princeton.

In the more familiar edition published in 1935 by Faber and Faber, the "character" and significance of Francis was certainly clouded and largely symbolic. But at the end of the uncut version, Francis has a very long speech in which, possibly even too explicitly, he addresses in turn all the leading citizens of the village and points out to each the spiritual errors of his or her ways. In this he takes on the role of a healer or lay priest or psychoanalyst (a Lane or Layard, for example), particularly in the case of Mildred Luce, who intensely hates the Germans (for whom both Auden and Isherwood had a decided partiality) because, she claims, they killed her two sons in battle. In the uncut version this turns out to be a falsehood amounting almost to delusional hysteria. Francis, in his incarnation as a dog, has lived with all these people, knows them to the bone, and has kept a diary of his observations. Mildred Luce, presumably convulsed with grief at the death of her two sons and expecting Francis to speak charitably of the Germans she so hates, says, "Traitor! I hear the infamy before you say it. That Germans should be loved. God strike you dumb." Francis then temperately but probingly replies as follows:

> Yes, Mrs. Luce. That too. Your grievance is just, but it is neither what Pressan thinks it is nor what you dare not admit to yourself. When I stayed with you as a dog (and may I take this opportunity of thanking you. You were kinder and more understanding than any of the others), when I stayed with you I thought the photographs on your bureau seemed vaguely familiar and one day when you were away, I took them to the photographer whose name was on them. He identified them at once as two young actors who had some success in juvenile leads about thirty years ago. Later I paid a visit to the village where you lived before you came to Pressan and discovered something else. You lived at home helping your mother with the house. She was poor and could not afford a maid. Were you ever married, I asked. No, they said, but there was talk at one time of an engagement to a young German cavalry officer. But you hadn't the heart to leave your mother alone.

Up to this point Francis sounds remarkably like Sherlock Holmes; but he continues,

> A doctor would say you hate the Germans because you dare not hate your mother and he would be mistaken. It is foolish and neurotic to hate anybody. What you really hate is a social system in which love is controlled by money. Won't you help us to destroy it?

A number of things need to be observed. A social system in which love is controlled by money is certainly what has kept Mildred Luce and her mother the prisoners of one another. But it is also, and much more obviously, the basis for prostitution. Auden's tolerance for prostitution, both in this play and in lyrics throughout his career right up to the very end, contradicts the revolutionary pieties just quoted; perhaps that is why they were cut, along with the fact that they run on too long. But the important point is that Francis, with his knowing penetration, his rejection of Freudian orthodoxies, his embrace of social reforms, shows himself to be a healer/revolutionary of a new kind who so infuriates Mildred Luce by this speech that she murders him. In the Faber version, a very few depart with Francis.

The love that Francis represents, and which clearly is deeply social in character, is expressed, among other ways, by the two lyrics about love that formally bracket the play and are related to it and to one another in very much the same way as the prologue and epilogue of *On This Island*. The first of these begins,

> Enter with him
> These legends, love,
> For him assume
> Each diverse form
> As legend simple
> As legend queer
> That he may do
> What these require
> Be, love, like him
> To legend true.
> When he to ease
> His heart's disease
> Must cross in sorrow
> Corrosive seas
> As dolphins go,
> As cunning fox
> Guide through the rocks,
> Tell in his ear
> The common phrase
> Required to please
> The guardians there.

What we have here is, first of all, a prayer to Love, the Virgilian guide, who, like Dante's classical poet, shall know all the right precautions, passwords, signs, that shall take the pilgrim safely through his journey. What we also have is a prologue of the kind supplied by the prologue-sonnet to *Romeo and Juliet:* a brief verse outline of the action of the play that is to follow. The "legends" that "love" is to enter with Alan Norman are the modes and appearances or versions of love, all of them false, that constitute the persons and scenes of the action of the play, and through which the pilgrim must be safely guided. The petition to Love continues,

> And when across
> The livid marsh
> Big birds pursue
> Again be true
> Between his thighs
> A pony rise
> As swift as wind
> Bear him away
> Till cries and they
> Are left behind.

This seems to present a clear parallel to the classical monster, Geryon, who bears Dante and Virgil upon his back and conveys them safely to the eighth circle of Hell in Canto XVII. The poem concludes,

> And when at last
> These dangers past
> His grown desire
> Of legends tire
> O then, love, standing
> At legend's ending,
> Claim your reward
> Submit your neck
> To the ungrateful stroke
> Of his reluctant sword
> That starting back
> His eyes may look
> Amazed as you
> Find what he wanted
> Is faithful too
> But disenchanted
> Your simplest love.

This conclusion is manifestly the most enigmatic part of the poem; but it is possible to interpret it to mean that once the pilgrim has found the simple and disenchanted love towards which Virgil-Love has been guiding him he will no longer need the guide and can reluctantly dispense with him, as Dante must dismiss Virgil at the entrance of Paradise. Whether or not this is a legitimate way of reading the ending, there can be little doubt that the poem as a whole is optimistic, encouraging, and hopeful in its prophecy, and as the prologue to a play it promises the audience a variety of thrills and dangers, all of them to be safely survived or overcome, and the object of the quest at last to be obtained.

The epilogue is shorter and less cheerful.

> Love, loath to enter
> The suffering winter
> Still willing to rejoice
> With the unbroken voice
> At the precocious charm
> Blithe in the dream
> Afraid to wake, afraid
> To doubt one term
> Of summer's perfect fraud,
> Enter and suffer
> Within the quarrel
> Be most at home,
> Among the sterile prove
> Your vigors, love.

The love that here is initially loath to enter the suffering winter is the love that does not want to face human realities and would prefer the adolescent raptures appropriate to the unbroken voice and the precocious charm. That love is being told to grow up, to awaken from its dream world of summer's perfect fraud, which denies that there is such a thing as winter, or suffering. And at the end this matured love is urged or implored to enter and to suffer among the sterile, and "prove" its vigors. In this there is a complex plea not only for healing, but for a particularly sympathetic kind of healing in which the healer must undergo the same misery and humiliation as the ones to be healed. This saintly form of self-sacrifice, already hinted at in the prologue when Love submitted his neck to the ungrateful stroke of a reluctant sword, represents a highly unorthodox mode of therapy, and an unusual character in the therapist. And it is plausible to speculate that behind the character of Francis lies not so much the reprobate figure of Francis Turville-Petre as the nearly heroic figure (at least in Auden's view at one time) of John Layard. We have a glimpse of Layard in an account by a classmate of his at the C. G. Jung Institute of Zurich, Robert Johnson, in the introduction to Layard's *The Lady of the Hare:*

> There was a vivid discussion of schizophrenia, a subject dear to Jung since it was he who first took this dreadful illness from the uncurable category. The main point of the lecturer was that schizophrenia can best be cured by the close relationship with a very feminine element in the therapist. This is rarely found in any therapist of any school—and, strangely, more likely to be found in a man than a woman! There was a long and dramatic silence after this statement as we tried to absorb the implications of this bit of information. Then the lecturer went on to say that John Layard was such a person and was the carrier of that particular gentle feminine quality . . .
>
> It was true of John Layard; he was a gentle soul, soft when allowed, strong when necessary.

In addition to the lyrics already mentioned as being either embedded in *Dog-Skin* or extracted from it after the fact and published as independent poems, there is one more: a Chorus decidedly superior to all the other Choruses, and noticeably independent of its dramatic context. Auden gave it the title "The Cultural Presupposition" when he included it in his 1945 collection of poems, and it begins, "Happy the hare at morning, for she cannot read / The Hunter's waking thoughts, lucky the leaf / Unable to predict the fall . . ." It is a meditation poem on a topic already mentioned, one which Auden had dealt with as early as "Our hunting fathers" and which he would continue to write about throughout his career. It is a distinctly Romantic topic, often to be encountered in Shelley and in Wordsworth, present in Yeats's poem "Death" and in Frost's "The Most of It," and abundantly present in the poems of Thomas Hardy: the fact that though human beings are a part of the natural order, they are also distinctly cut off from that order. And by being cut off, they are alienated from a world vaguely Edenic, at least morally innocent, and certainly lost. If at one time the compensation for this loss was the hope of salvation and of eternal happiness in the companionship of saints and angels, the loss of confidence in a heavenly estate became at the same time an increased sense of not being at home in a world where all the other creatures were mercifully free from our peculiar human anxieties. With his unique talent for historical diagnostics in axiomatic form, Auden explained the development of this human predicament in his introduction to the volume of Romantic poets, in the series of *Poets of the English Language* that he edited in collaboration with Norman Holmes Pearson (and which, for all its astonishing typographical mistakes—it omits whole stanzas from Collins, *adds* a word to Marlowe—is one of the best anthologies of its kind):

> In the age of the heroic epic the difference between gods and men is that the former are immortal and the latter must finally all die like the beasts. In the meantime, however, some men are made godlike and separated from nature by the favor of the gods, becoming heroes who do great deeds. The poet, that is, the man inspired by the gift of tongues, celebrates the hero and his acts.
>
> In the Middle Ages, the quality which man shares with God and which the creatures do not have is a will that can make free choices. What separates man from God is sin: that he can and does choose wrongly, love himself, act selfishly. The function of the poet is to exhibit the human soul tempted by competing loves, and to celebrate the ways in which she can be redeemed.
>
> In the neoclassical period, the divine human quality is reason, the capacity to recognize general laws, and the function of the poet is to celebrate the Rational City and pour scorn on its enemies.
>
> Toward the end of the eighteenth century—Rousseau is one of the first symptoms [note Auden's tendentious word]—a new answer appears. The divine element in man is now held to be neither power nor free will nor reason, but self-consciousness. Like God and unlike the rest of nature, man can say "I": his ego stands over against his self, which to the ego is part of nature. In this self he can see possibilities; he can imagine it and all things as being other than they are; he runs ahead of himself; he foresees his own death.

Auden, of course, is not commonly characterized as a Romantic, a term that, when we speak of twentieth-century poets, we incline to reserve for the likes of Dylan Thomas, Yeats, Lawrence, and perhaps a few others. But Auden's capsule history seems to me generally correct, and what it means is that twentieth-century poets are all, whether they wish to be or not, the cultural and psychological heirs of what was the formidable Romantic revolution. And this is why when Eliot was taken to task by some of his critics for not writing poetry that accorded with the austere tenets (classicist in poetry, catholic in religion, royalist in politics) that he affirmed, he simply said that he could only write the way he knew how, despite the fact that it fell short of his ideals.

A few additional comments are called for regarding *Dog-Skin*. In keeping with its vaudeville-like character and mixture of high- and lowbrow comedic resources, it borrows idioms and forms from very heterogeneous sources. There is some markedly alliterative verse, clearly meant to echo and recall Anglo-Saxon poetry; there are imitations of W. S. Gilbert; there are songs in the Broadway styles of Ira Gershwin, Noël Coward, and Cole Porter involving ingenious three-syllable rhymes:

> Who shall we send this time who shall look for him,
> Search every corner and cranny and nook for him?

There is a parody, a rather cutting one, of the liturgy of the Church of England, intoned by a Surgeon and his attendant-celebrants. Given Auden's devotion to psychosomatic theories, this mockery not only of religious institutions but of established medical procedures makes a kind of sense, but is still rather odd when we consider that both his parents were devout Anglicans and both in the medical profession. There is a Lawrentian condemnation of "sex-in-the-head" ("Take sex, for instance . . . Sometimes it's funny and sometimes it's sad, but it's always hanging about like a smell of drains. Too many ideas in their heads! To them I'm an idea, you're an idea, everything's an idea," says the Dog who is also the presiding Love in the play.) There is even a parody of the spellbinding end of *A Midsummer Night's Dream*, "Now the hungry lion roars, / And the wolf behowls the moon . . .":

> Now the ragged vagrants creep
> Into crooked holes to sleep:
> Just and unjust, worst and best,
> Change their places as they rest:
> Awkward lovers lie in fields
> Where disdainful beauty yields:
> While the splendid and the proud
> Naked stand before the crowd
> And the losing gambler gains
> And the beggar entertains:
> May sleep's healing power extend
> Through these hours to our friend.
> Unpursued by hostile force,

Traction engine, bull or horse
Or revolting succubus;
Calmly till the morning break
Let him lie, then gently wake.

These imitations, parodies, burlesques, give *Dog-Skin* a vivacity and lightness of touch and are no small part of its charm, easing whatever it may carry in the way of doctrinal burden. And while as a theater piece it is of necessity public in character, it is nevertheless not wholly free from private jokes and allusions like those that appeared in the early poems. Of these perhaps the most obvious is the name of Francis himself, borrowed from the "Fronny" of an early poem, a partially recovered play, and Isherwood's autobiography. "Cosy Corner," the homosexual brothel in the Red Light District scene of the play, is the actual name of a bar both Isherwood and Auden frequented in Berlin. Even Pressan Ambo, the village where the action of the play begins and ends, contains, as has been pointed out, a sly reference likely to be known only to the elect few: whereas "ambo" is a term for a pulpit, raised lectern, or reading stand in a church (and thus seems to indicate the pious orientation of the town itself), it is also an abbreviation for "ambosexual," or androgynous.

There are two scenes in the play that are brilliant tours de force, and, given the revue-like assemblage of the play, may be considered out of context and without regard to any plot line or narrative development. One of these is the execution scene, replete with organ and a choir which, just before the king addresses those about to die, sings, "Requiem aeternam dona et lux perpetua luceat eis," whereupon the king addresses the prisoners thus:

Gentlemen. I do not intend to keep you long; but I cannot let this opportunity slip by without saying how much I and the Queen appreciate and admire the spirit in which you have acted and how extremely sorry we both are that our little differences can only be settled in this er . . . somewhat drastic fashion.

Believe me, I sympathise with your aims from the bottom of my heart. Are we not all socialists nowadays? But as men of the world I am sure you will agree with me that order has to be maintained. In spite of everything which has happened, I do want to keep this solemn moment free from any thought of malice. If any of you have any complaint to make about your treatment, I hope you will say so now before it is too late . . . You haven't? I am very glad indeed to hear it. Before going on to the next part of the ceremony, let me conclude by wishing you Bon Voyage and every happiness in the next world.

After the choir sings, the queen addresses the wives and mothers of the prisoners who have been led away to be executed by the king himself:

Ladies (or may I call you Sisters?) On this day of national sorrow, my woman's heart bleeds for you. I too am a mother. I too have borne the pangs of childbirth and known the unutterable comfort of seeing a little curly head asleep on my breast. I too am a wife, and have lain in the strong arms of the beloved. Remember, then, in your loss, that in all you suffer, I suffer with you. And remember that Suffering is Woman's fate and Woman's glory. By suffering we are ennobled; we rise to higher things. Be comforted, therefore, and abide patiently, strong in the hope that you will meet your loved ones again in another and better world where there are no tears, no pains, no misunderstandings; where we shall all walk hand in hand from everlasting to everlasting.

—after which the Master of Ceremonies announces, "The ladies of the Court will offer the bereaved some light refreshment."

What I find so remarkable about this scene is that in its dark and nearly absurdist comedy, which at the same time is so close to political reality and campaign rhetoric, its grotesque hypocrisy, its inhumane pretenses and quasi-self-deceptions, it conspicuously resembles the scene in Eliot's *Murder in the Cathedral* in which the knights who murdered Becket offer their ludicrous apologia. Curiously, the two plays appeared in the same year, and one can only guess who influenced whom. But I will risk conjecturing that it was Eliot who was adapting the tricks of his younger fellow poet-playwright. My guess is based on the fact that nowhere else in any of his writing does Eliot come near the effect of broad farce produced in the knights' scene, nor is his dramatic irony ever again used with such easy and colloquial effect; whereas Auden will go on to employ it in familiar and characteristic ways, particularly, for example, in Herod's speech in *For the Time Being*.

The other scene of huge and terrible hilarity is the nightclub act in which the entertainer, Destructive Desmond, "dressed as a schoolboy, with inkstains on his cheeks, a crumpled eton collar, a striped cap, broken bootlaces . . . an inflamed, pugnacious face and very hairy knees," proceeds, to the unspeakable delight of a lowbrow philistine audience, to destroy a genuine Rembrandt right before their eyes. The scene succeeds as well as it does because it so accurately reflects the naked hostility which is felt for high art by a large segment of society. The scene may be largely, or even wholly, the work of Isherwood, but the entire play is a close work of collaboration, and this segment of it shimmers with that kind of social and political satire which constitutes an important strand in Auden's poetry throughout his career.

# III. Poetry Makes Nothing Happen: *Another Time*

*Another Time* (1940) appeared after what was one of the most dramatic and decisive alterations in Auden's life, and one that provoked heated commentary, much of it intensely hostile and unkind, in his native country: for Auden had come to settle—as he thought, for good—in the United States. He came here at a crucial and terrible time in England and throughout Europe. He arrived on January 26, 1939; World War II would begin on September 1. All the signs of the "gathering storm" had been crowding the headlines, and many of them had been mentioned in Auden's poems. In 1938 there had been the terrible bombing of Barcelona in a war that turned out to be the proving ground for Fascist and Communist forces. Hitler had invaded Austria, and his territorial ambitions were plainly beyond disguise when German and Italian arbitrators partitioned Czechoslovakia, awarding four thousand square miles of Czech territory (and roughly eight hundred thousand citizens) to Hungary. It was during the same year that Neville Chamberlain, the British prime minister, met with Hitler at Munich, returning with the infamous "Munich Pact," which awarded Czechoslovakia's Sudetenland to Germany in exchange for "peace in our time," an exchange few believed in, and which would have been a shameful accord in any case. The very phrase "peace in our time" indicated that a war had merely been postponed, and was virtually a public acknowledgment that England was not prepared for a war but was prepared to stall one off by the gift of part of another nation.

Under these circumstances, Auden's departure from home was regarded by some of his most vocal countrymen as something bordering on the traitorous, the cowardly. Such reactions strike me as eminently foolish, but they were nevertheless widely and loudly maintained in England, and voiced by people who obviously envied the luxury of his comparative safety in New York. Those who criticized Auden's departure from England must surely have known that had he remained he could have done nothing to advance the safety and welfare of the realm. And he might have positively endangered it, since his eyesight was so bad he could never have served in the armed forces, and if he had been recruited into other service such as the ambulance corps, he could easily have put lives in peril. Nothing speaks more clearly of the hand-in-glove relations of the Bureau of Motor Vehicles (at least the Michigan one) and the automobile industry than the granting of a driver's license to Auden around 1940, as reported in a memoir by Charles Miller. Not only would Auden have been no military use to his countrymen, but simply by remaining among them he would have put his life and his art as a poet in danger, to no particular purpose. And it needs to be added that apart from a few poems by Henry Reed, Keith Douglas, and a few others, as well as one by Eliot and one by Dylan Thomas, little war poetry came out of the Second World War besides what Auden himself wrote, first in England and then in the refuge of America.

His reasons for coming to this country have never been entirely clarified, either by him or by his several biographers. But it is reasonable to suppose that they were at least partly private, and bore upon his homosexuality, and the prospect of a life that could be lived comparatively anonymously in a foreign country where he was not well known, where he was apart from his parents, and where he could live in a city as multitudinous, and as hospitable to artists of all sexual inclinations, as New York. And indeed it was not long after his arrival that there began what was to be the most enduring personal relationship of his life, the one with Chester Kallman, to whom *Another Time* is dedicated.

Probably in the poet's view, certainly in his publishers', this was to be considered a major book, as indeed it is. Apart from volumes of selected or collected poems and the late volume *City Without Walls* (1969), it is the only book of Auden's poems that has its own index of first lines at the end. It is elaborate and sumptuous in its variety and composition, and it contains several of the most celebrated poems Auden was ever to write, including elegies for a number of the greatest figures of modern history, as though Auden had taken upon himself the responsibilities of an unofficial public laureate. The book is cunningly, as well as beautifully, arranged so that, for all its diversity of style and subject, it holds together with an almost musical integrity of interwoven themes, developments, and recapitulations.

It is divided into three sections, of which the first is called "People and Places," and I think it must have been intended as a genuine act of homage that Karl Shapiro, whose early work was strongly influenced by Auden,

called his first book of poems *Person, Place and Thing*. The second section
is called "Lighter Poems," and serves as a kind of scherzo that separates
the seriousness of the first part from the solemnity of the final section,
called "Occasional Poems." Moreover (to pursue the musical figure a bit
further), the book opens with a thematic statement in the form of a
formally intricate allegorical poem about the pilgrimage of mankind
towards "the defeat of grief," and advances towards two codas. The first
is another allegorical poem that closes the first section, in which mankind
is reconciled to its fallen condition and grateful for its human situation;
and the second is the final poem of the book, which is an epithalamion,
and a hymn of public and private concord. Between that beginning and
that end there is, of course, enough powerful discord to please the most
devout atonal enthusiast.

The dedicatory poem, almost a rune or occult vision—prophetic,
cryptic, both grim and hopeful—sets out some of the main themes of the
volume.

> Every eye must weep alone
> Till I Will be overthrown.
>
> But I Will can be removed,
> Not having sense enough
> To guard against I Know,
> But I Will can be removed.
>
> Then all I's can meet and grow,
> I Am become I Love,
> I Have Not I Am Loved,
> Then all I's can meet and grow.
>
> Till I Will be overthrown
> Every eye must weep alone.

Here we have the continuation from the previous book of the conviction that Love in one or another of its guises is supremely and
uniquely curative. It furthermore suggests that conscious knowledge
("I Know") can correct the common selfish impulse ("I Will"). But
most important, the curative Love will promote social as well as individual happiness ("Then all I's can meet and grow"), but this shall not
come about until our selfishness and self-concern are defeated. While the
poem itself is an indifferent one, the themes it articulates are important

for the ways in which they will resonate not merely throughout this book but through much of the rest of Auden's career. And they involve some distinctly moral elements that in no short time would take the form of explicitly religious ones. In any case, the little dedicatory verses emphatically link the public and private concerns Auden had written about from the first.

The first poem in the book is, suitably, a technical tour de force. It is composed in a highly intricate and, so far as I have been able to determine, entirely original stanzaic form.

> Wrapped in a yielding air, beside
>     The flower's soundless hunger,
> Close to the tree's clandestine tide,
>     Close to the bird's high fever,
>     Loud in his hope and anger,
> Erect about his skeleton,
>     Stands the expressive lover,
>     Stands the deliberate man.

The line length and rhyme scheme exhibited here and employed throughout can be outlined thus:

| | |
|---|---|
| tetrameter | *a* |
| trimeter | *b* |
| tetrameter | *a* |
| trimeter | *c* |
| trimeter | *b* |
| tetrameter | *d* |
| trimeter | *c* |
| trimeter | *d* |

In addition, the fourth line of each stanza repeats a key word of the third, and similarly the eighth repeats a key word of the seventh. I am not aware of any other poem that makes these formal demands.

Like some earlier poems, this one concerns the curious relationship of man to the rest of the natural world, which he inhabits but from which he is alienated and cut off. As distinct from the rest of nature, man is rational ("deliberate"), capable of hope as well as anger, expressive therefore of some of the qualities of the beasts, but significantly of more. The poem goes on to describe his situation in an uncomprehending and indifferent world, in which some beasts are stronger and fairer (that is, better designed for their own bestial purposes and thus, by the doctrine of "form follows function," more beautiful). Not only is man distinguished from the simpler and more efficient beasts, but his complexity involves paradoxes: with "gun and lens and bible" he is "a militant enquirer." His instruments of aggression ("gun") are balanced and opposed by his ethical and religious doctrines ("bible"), and between impulse and doctrine intervenes the attempt at scientific and neutral objectivity ("lens"). He is, in his complexity of self-contradiction, "The friend, the rash, the enemy, / The essayist, the able, / Able at times to cry." The cost to him of being "The Brothered-One, the Not Alone" is that he is also "The brothered and the hated." Perhaps that repeated "able" in the last lines of the previous stanza helps us recall Cain and Abel in these lines that immediately follow. In the fourth stanza man is shamed by his mother, subjugated by his nurse (a surrogate mother), and crippled by an obscure family inheritance which includes, as a trick of his legal father (Adam), "The tall and gorgeous tower, / Gorgeous but locked, but locked." This is the Eden from which he has been permanently exiled. But that very Eden fills his head both with desolation and with grandiose vision and love. He is ruled by the pieties of his forebears, deluded by his own hopes and longings, and capable both of murderous resentment and visionary dreams. His own paradoxical nature is represented by the figurative heraldry of the opposed lamb and tigress, while,

> Though faithless, he consider
> His dream of vaguer ages,
> Hunter and victim reconciled,
> The lion and the adder,
> The adder and the child.

It is not insignificant, in my view, that reference is made here to the vision of Isaiah 11:7–9, though Auden may also be alluding or indebted to a stanza from Yeats's poem "Those Images."

> Seek those images
> That constitute the wild,
> The lion and the virgin,
> The harlot and the child.

I would guess that these lines of Yeats are nearer to Blake than to the Bible. The final stanza of Auden's poem goes:

> Fresh loves betray him, every day
>   Over his green horizon
> A fresh deserter rides away,
>   And miles away birds mutter
>   Of ambush and of treason;
> To fresh defeats he still must move,
>   To further griefs and greater,
>   And the defeat of grief.

As an allegory of the condition of man, this is obviously susceptible of an explicitly Christian interpretation, including the rejections of love, the betrayals and "treason," the additional defeats and greater griefs before grief can be defeated. Yet the Christian aspects of the poem are borne lightly and not insisted upon; in fact, there are plenty of readings of the poem that take no account at all of this level of its meaning. Surely, however, just as in the dedicatory verse, Love, its defeats and its recovery, is a theme here; and that theme will be echoed and answered in the final poem of the book, a marriage hymn for Elisabeth Mann and Giuseppe Borgese, in which the lines occur:

> Happier savants may decide
> That this quiet wedding of
> A Borgese and a Mann
> Planted human unity;
> Hostile kingdoms of the truth
> Fighting fragments of content,
> Here were reconciled by love,
> Modern policy begun
>   On this day.

After the opening poem, the first section of the book, as its title suggests, is made up of poems largely, though not wholly, devoted to the lives or careers of individual people (including Rimbaud, Melville, Pascal, Housman, Edward Lear, Voltaire, and Matthew Arnold) as well as to "types" ("The Novelist," "The Composer") and to places (including Oxford, Dover, Brussels, Paris, and London). The section contains an impressive number of poems in sonnet form, a form Auden felt some comfort with and confidence in, since he was to use it a great deal at different points in his career, including the composition of sonnet sequences. This partiality may have something to do with his early fascination with Shakespeare's sonnets.

Perhaps the sonnets lend themselves to discussion as a group. Here, for example, is "A. E. Housman."

> No one, not even Cambridge, was to blame;
> —Blame if you like the human situation—
> Heart-injured in North London, he became
> The leading classic of his generation.
>
> Deliberately he chose the dry-as-dust,
> Kept tears like dirty postcards in a drawer;
> Food was his public love, his private lust
> Something to do with violence and the poor.
>
> In savage footnotes on unjust editions
> He timidly attacked the life he led,
> And put the money of his feelings on
>
> The uncritical relations of the dead,
> Where purely geographical divisions
> Parted the coarse hanged soldier from the don.

The commentators, John Fuller in particular, have been very helpful about this poem, which, like some others in this section, grew out of Auden's reading and reviewing around the time of composition. In this case it was a biography of Housman written by his brother, Laurence. (It may be worth noting that for all Auden's later expressed contempt for biographies of writers and artists, he read them at this time as well as later with interest and penetration.) This sonnet, about a repressed homosexual, bears comparison with the one on Lear, whose homosexual feelings were never reciprocated in any satisfactory way, so that both men, in their different ways, lived lives of almost complete self-mortification and sexual sublimation. In Housman's case, after a disastrously unpromising beginning as a student of the classics, he went on very gradually to become one of the leading classical scholars of his day, producing the definitive edition of Manilius, not because he liked the poems, which he did not, but because his first choice, a major Latin poet, had been preempted by another classicist. As Fuller points out, Auden much later (1957) made some pertinent comments on Housman that illuminate the sonnet:

> The inner life of the neurotic is always projecting itself into external symptoms which are symbolic but decipherable confessions. [Remember "the liar's quinsy, / The distortions of ingrown virginity."] The savagery of Housman's scholarly polemics, which included the

composition of annihilating rebukes before he had found the occasion and victim to deserve them, are as revealing as if he had written pornographic verse.

In 1972 Auden made some further observations about Housman, prompted by the publication of his letters, edited by Henry Maas.

> About his emotional life little needs to be said. It is now no secret that at Oxford he fell deeply in love with a fellow-undergraduate, Moses Jackson, an experience which, on his own testimony, he was never to repeat. Since Jackson was perfectly "straight," there was no question of reciprocation . . . If Housman did feel shame and guilt, this was caused not by the Bible but by classical literature. I am pretty sure that in his sexual tastes he was an anal passive. Ancient Greece and Rome were both pederastic cultures in which the adult passive homosexual was regarded as comic and contemptible.

Auden adds that Housman firmly denied being a Stoic, and quotes him to this effect. "As for pessimism, I think it almost as silly, though not as wicked, as optimism. George Eliot said she was a meliorist: I am a pejorist" (that is, someone who believes the world is steadily getting worse). Again Auden repeats his conviction that the choice of editing Manilius was based purely on the editorial problems it presented (an idea that I believe has now been disputed). But the clear point is that Housman was frustrated and disappointed at almost every turn in his career, and that to become "the leading classic of his generation" he had to pay a terrible (and legible) price. "Classic" is a fine word for Housman, of course, and it was used by Auden in at least a double sense: Housman was greatly influenced by classical poetry at its most somber, and he was widely read in and just after his time. (Auden's choice of this word would have been ridiculously confirmed by the practices of modern cut-rate bookstores, which under the label of "Classics" display their copies of Flaubert and Jane Austen and such other books as they fear will not have a wide appeal.)

There's much poignance in this sonnet, in which, while tactfully omitting to say how painfully Housman had failed to find satisfaction for his feelings in the world of the living, it is said that he "put the money of his feelings on / The uncritical relations of the dead." "Uncritical" makes them the classical "critic's" polar opposites, and they are of course also opposed by being dead. The wager implied in putting "the money of his feelings" on them was the real wager of Housman's life both as poet and as man. Who, before him, would have thought that the public would express any taste for the classical element in literature, even as Englished by Housman's adoption of classical themes and conventions? And to devote his feelings to the unfeeling dead was a terrible and costly human sacrifice, which, as it happened, paid off in terms of extraordinary poetry, of which it seems worth quoting a brief specimen.

> Crossing alone the nighted ferry
>   With the one coin for fee,
> Whom, on the wharf of Lethe waiting,
>   Count you to find? Not me.
>
> The brisk fond lackey to fetch and carry,
>   The true, sick-hearted slave,
> Expect him not in the just city
>   And free land of the grave.

Like the sonnets on Lear and Housman, Auden's sonnet on Rimbaud is about a troubled and tormented homosexual, who, in this case, abandons the meditative or "creative" life for a life of action. This election, at personal cost, of an active life, even of a criminal life, is one that enchanted Auden and figured prominently in a lot of his early poetry. It is present in the well-known epilogue to *The Orators,* "'O where are you going?' said reader to rider," in which passive and active are opposed throughout. Rimbaud served Auden's purposes as both a sexual and social subversive, the disguised and anonymous hero of slave or gun traffic in Africa who had also achieved poetic immortality by the age of seventeen. In both literature and society he was a rebel, but he is also one who sought to come to terms with his existence through renunciation (what Auden in 1932 called "Rimbaud's *declination*"), the abandonment of his youthful ambitions. In this, therefore, he resembles Housman and Lear, who, as if in obedience to the ascetic disciplines recommended by Lenin, learned "To hunger, work illegally, / And be anonymous." And like Rimbaud, Matthew Arnold, another poet memorialized in this collection, "thrust his gift in prison till it died."

There are two "generic" sonnets, "The Novelist" and "The Composer." Both are marked by a singular magnanimity and admiration for practitioners of other art forms. I say "singular" because poets are for the most part a grudging and envious lot, covetous of the wealth that a novelist can sometimes enjoy (not only from a much larger readership than any modern poet could hope for, but with the possibilities of movie and television adaptations) as well as of the celebrity and adulation enjoyed by such composers as, say, Verdi. Novels and musical compositions are in certain ways more "public" and accessible than what had become the elitist and forbidding difficulty of Modernist poetry, including some of the more hermetic of Auden's own *oeuvre*. Yet here is the appreciative sonnet "The Novelist."

> Encased in talent like a uniform,
> The rank of every poet is well known;
> They can amaze us like a thunderstorm,
> Or die so young, or live for years alone.
>
> They can dash forward like hussars: but he
> Must struggle out of his boyish gift and learn
> How to be plain and awkward, how to be
> One after whom none think it worth to turn.
>
> For, to achieve his lightest wish, he must
> Become the whole of boredom, subject to
> Vulgar complaints like love, among the Just
>
> Be just, among the filthy filthy too,
> And in his own weak person, if he can,
> Must suffer dully all the wrongs of Man.

The first quatrain of the sonnet about the novelist is about poets. Their qualities, as well as their rank (the military metaphor is present in "uniform" and later in "hussars"), are external, immediately detectable, their effects spectacular, because lyric poets must concentrate on metaphoric structures, dramatic instants, vivid items, and selected fragments of experience with which to "amaze" the reader; or else, like Chatterton or Keats, they move us by their youthful deaths (as Wordsworth observed in "Resolution and Independence"), or else they live in solitary obscurity, their art requiring only the vigor of a personal imagination. But in contrast to the traditional isolation of the poet's mind, the novelist is of necessity a civic or social creature, who must feel in his own person all the stages of growth, however ungainly, that humans are destined to go through. While there can be precocious poets, whose concern need only be for the workings of their own mental life, it is unlikely that there should be a precocious novelist, because the writer of fiction simply has to know more about the world in general and the behavior of diverse humanity as well. This is something that takes time (hence novelists, unlike poets, do not die young) and requires a profound selflessness. Not only does Auden very evidently admire that selflessness, but he identifies it at the close of his poem with a messianic sacrifice that takes upon itself to endure and experience "all the wrongs of Man." This ability to participate in all aspects of the human condition is described in terms that are little short of religious, and filled moreover with paradox. "For, to achieve his lightest wish, he must / Become the whole of boredom . . ." The duty of fiction is to engage our lively interest constantly, yet to represent the world so accurately as truly to portray a realm of boredom, routine, and monotony. There are, to be sure, more vulgar complaints than love, yet something about this poem suggests to me that there is a paradigmatic novelist lurking in Auden's mind, whether consciously or unconsciously, and that novelist is Flaubert, who famously remarked, "Madame Bovary, c'est moi." For her, certainly, and for her chronicler, love was a vulgar complaint.

"The Composer" is no less generous.

> All the others translate: the painter sketches
> A visible world to love or reject;
> Rummaging into his living, the poet fetches
> The images out that hurt and connect.
>
> From Life to Art by painstaking adaption,
> Relying on us to cover the rift;
> Only your notes are pure contraption,
> Only your song is an absolute gift.
>
> Pour out your presence, O delight, cascading
> The falls of the knee and the weirs of the spine,
> Our climate of silence and doubt invading;
>
> You alone, alone, O imaginary song,
> Are unable to say an existence is wrong,
> And pour out your forgiveness like a wine.

Perhaps the first thing that needs to be remarked is the astonishing metrical freedom exhibited here. So distinct is this from all his other sonnets (consider only the seventh, eighth, and tenth lines) that one suspects the poet imagined a musical setting for the poem. This suspicion is strengthened by the inverted word order in the eleventh line, a liberty Auden permitted himself when writing lyrics for musical setting, employed here as elsewhere not only to accommodate the rhyme but because the greatest of the Elizabethan song writers had done the same thing. Auden was to take the same liberties when writing lyrics for *The Rake's Progress*.

The painter's art (which, for the purposes of this poem, does not include nonrepresentational art) and the poet's are both referential, and suggest an equation of some sort, however disguised or stylized, between that art and the familiar, quotidian world we all inhabit. The octave of the sonnet is all based upon this mutual dependence or correspondence, a connection that separates those impure arts from the complete independence of music, which is an "absolute gift" because no one can achieve it through some portal of the real world, as one can be moved to paint by seeing a beautiful scene or person, and moved to write poetry by falling in love or condemning a war or by personal grief. The composer's notes are "pure contraption," relating to nothing but our (generally) diatonic habits and tonal or harmonic traditions. They are, supremely, nonreferential. That repetition of "alone, alone" in the twelfth line sounds rather like Ben Jonson, and again this sonnet closes in a language that is remarkably religious in character. The composer does not blame or accuse; he can only celebrate and rejoice; his music at least is free of all malice, or even of moral judgment, and is instead a blessing and a sacrament.

"Pascal" seems to me, if such a judgment is permissible, not a good poem but an extraordinary one. (Auden himself omitted it from the *Collected Shorter Poems* of 1966.) It presents us initially with what is a quasi-religious or semi-secular nativity, in which the mother, Antoinette, who was to survive only through her son's fourth year of life, experiences not the glory but only the horror that was the Virgin's, including a premonition that she would be bereft of her child, mocked by her neighbors, neutrally observed by the beasts. After the first four stanzas, which are a cruel parody of the Biblical nativity narrative, she disappears from the poem, the rest of which is devoted to its nominal subject, her son. But he, when we come to him, is viewed in a curiously selective way. Nothing of Pascal's extraordinary achievements as a mathematician or scientist is so much as hinted at. None of the specific illnesses of his childhood (his smallpox, for example, which seriously disfigured him and thus played an important role in what was to become of him) is mentioned. We learn only that "Whatever happened, he was born deserted / And lonelier than any adult . . . His misery was real." Then comes the great event; "Yet like a lucky orphan he had been discovered / And instantly adopted by a Gift . . ." This "Gift" is personified, rather like a fairy godmother, yet she turns out not to have any connection with his logical or mathematical aptitudes (which were so pronounced that his father, who wanted him to learn Greek when he was little more than an infant, refused to let him study any more geometry until he had made some advances in language; whereupon Pascal *fils* worked out some basic Euclidean postulates for himself with chalk on the nursery floor). The "Gift" turns out to be a species of conviction or self-assurance that was preparing him "Until at last, one Autumn, all was ready: / And in the night the Unexpected came." This was the startling, dramatic vision vouchsafed to him on the night of November 22, 1654. It was incandescent, it was vocal, he took notes on it insofar as he was able to after the fact (the notes are far from coherent) and wore them as an amulet for the rest of his life. And perhaps the most important part of that "rest of his life" was his ironic attack, in the *Provincial Letters,* on the Jesuit Order, Pascal himself having become a devoted and puritanical Jansenist. His epistles of attack Auden characterizes as "lucid and unfair." What seems to me important here, however, is that for all the too explicit use of paradox ("The empty was transformed into possession / The cold burst into flames . . ." etcetera), this is a poem about conversion, written at a time when the poet had shown both conscious and unconscious leanings towards religion. And as if, perhaps, to balance so "irrational" an impulse, he presents what is in fact a better poem, "Voltaire."

Reading the poem can leave no doubt about how fully Auden was able to identify with his subject.

> Cajoling, scolding, scheming, cleverest of them all,
> He'd led the other children in a holy war
> Against the infamous grown-ups; and, like a child, been sly
> And humble when there was occasion for
> The two-faced answer or the plain protective lie,
> But patient like a peasant waited for their fall.

Almost everything in Auden's early career, starting very obviously with his youthful identification of the older generation as the enemy, but also his brilliance, his wit, his adoption of subversive figures like the spy and secret agent as his heroes and protagonists, his view of himself and of his generation as reformers, all this certainly went into the writing of that stanza. The poem concludes:

> Yet, like a sentinel, he could not sleep. The night was full of
>     wrong,
> Earthquakes and executions. Soon he would be dead,
> And still all over Europe stood the horrible nurses
> Itching to boil their children. Only his verses
> Perhaps could stop them: He must go on working. Overhead
> The uncomplaining stars composed their lucid song.

If the identification Auden was able to make with his subject in the third stanza (the first one quoted above) was clear, it may be said that in the final one it is equally clear. The solitary men who view themselves as reformers get little rest, and atrocities are always being committed, superstition always resorted to as an explanation of calamity (as it was in the case of the great Lisbon Earthquake). The "horrible nurses / Itching to boil their children" had their vivid equivalents in the Europe of the 1930's. And the conviction that the writer's only weapon lies in his words and their cunning deployment—the conviction that, debarred from an active participation in social events, the writer must participate, and maintain his honor, by his literary works—this conviction was one that preoccupied Yeats in his dedicatory poem to *Responsibilities,* and one to which Auden would return and consider from a different point of view in his great elegy for Yeats. But, briefly, it may be noted here that a writer-reformer is likely to find his happiest and most effective instrument in satire; and we may recall what Auden wrote about the neoclassical poets who "celebrate the Rational City and . . . pour scorn upon its enemies." Though Auden was certainly able to write satirically, and did so superbly well from time to time, this was not his natural genre or idiom; there is something too lighthearted and kindly in his nature to permit him complete success. His decision to write poems about both Pascal and Voltaire may in part have been prompted by a review he published in the March 25, 1939, issue of *The Nation* of two books on Voltaire, one by Norman Torrey and the other by Alfred Noyes. Auden celebrates Voltaire as a true hero of democracy, classing him with Socrates and Jefferson, and in the course of his review he writes, "Democracy has three great enemies: the mystic pessimism of the unhappy, who believe that man has no free will, the mystic optimism of the romantic, who believes that the individual has absolute free will, and the mystic certainty of the perfectionist, who believes that an individual or a group can know the final truth and the absolute good. For Voltaire these beliefs were embodied, the first in Pascal, the second in Rousseau, and the last in the Catholic Church." It would be easy, and, in my view, mistaken, to read into this review, and the poem which may have been the fruit of his meditation on the books he was writing about, a crass and easy anticlericalism. Usually Auden tried to restrain his satiric hand.

Nevertheless, he gave it free rein in a poem later to be titled "Danse Macabre" but originally without title, which begins:

> It's farewell to the drawing-room's civilised cry,
> The professor's sensible whereto and why,
> The frock-coated diplomat's social aplomb,
> Now matters are settled with gas and with bomb.

The rollicking amphibrachs that drive this poem along in the rhythms of Browning's "How They Brought the Good News from Ghent to Aix" have persuaded one body of readers that the poem is trifling, and without serious import. There is also another, equally deluded body of readers who, upon meeting the first-person-singular pronoun, "I," midway through the poem, heedlessly assumes that it refers directly and unambiguously to Auden, the poem's author. And this is, to the degree that it is true at all, only fractionally true. For if the poem is satiric, it is dangerously double-edged, and the target of its satire is a reformer (which Auden certainly sometimes thought himself) but in this case a reformer so zealous as to be demented, and one whose cure for the ills of humanity is total annihilation, including his own self-destruction. The poem, in other words, is a clever reminder to reformers (including the poet himself) that tolerating an imperfect world is better than totally destroying error and everything else as well. It is a poem that satirically puts the brakes on the impulse of reformation, and it ingeniously balances that impulse as it is expressed in "Voltaire." The poem is a rebuke to the fanaticism envisioned in the last two stanzas.

> The fishes are silent deep in the sea,
> The skies are lit up like a Christmas tree,
> The star in the West shoots its warning cry:
> "Mankind is alive, but Mankind must die."
>
> So good-bye to the house with its wallpaper red,
> Good-bye to the sheets on the warm double-bed,

> Good-bye to the beautiful birds on the wall,
> It's good-bye, dear heart, good-bye to you all.

Coming as it does right after the image of the Christmas tree, that "star in the West" contradicts the star in the East that appeared at the nativity, and can either refer to the vision in Spengler's *Decline of the West* or, more simply and vaguely, be meant to distinguish itself from and oppose itself to the religious symbol of hope in redemption. In either case, the poem is an attack on fanaticism, and specifically on the fanaticism of the reformer.

The sonnet "Brussels in Winter" is wonderful in the indirection, the near furtiveness, of its feeling. It seems to present itself as complete impersonality, and to be about the impersonality of a foreign city in forbidding weather. It is also, of course, about loneliness (a feeling that occurs in not a few of Auden's poems)—here, a loneliness so deep as to render reality illusory.

> Wandering the cold streets tangled like old string,
> Coming on fountains silent in the frost,
> The city still escapes you; it has lost
> The qualities that say "I am a Thing."
>
> Only the homeless and the really humbled
> Seem to be sure exactly where they are,
> And in their misery are all assembled;
> The winter holds them like the Opera.
>
> Ridges of rich apartments rise to-night
> Where isolated windows glow like farms:
> A phrase goes packed with meaning like a van,
>
> A look contains the history of man,
> And fifty francs will earn the stranger right
> To warm the heartless city in his arms.

The city in this poem is heartless in a number of ways, being gripped by the cold of winter, being the assembly place of the homeless and the really humbled, and being like an opera stage-set, in which the pathos fails to distress us because we do not take it to be wholly real. And because it is not wholly real, "the city still escapes you." The evasiveness of the octave has the function of isolating and making more lonely the nameless "you" who observes the chilled and chilling scene. The homeless and humbled are now cruelly contrasted to the rich, who, in the darkness of the cityscape, seem to live loftily on ridges of apartments, where their isolated windows glow like the scattered farms of pure and rural peace. (It is characteristic for Auden at this period to adopt the pastoral conventions which associate the country with peace and innocence and the city with sophistication and corruption: see, for example, the poem called "The Capital" in *Another Time*.) And then, quite unexpectedly, after so ruminative a beginning, the poem in its eleventh line turns quietly dramatic. The phrase "packed with meaning like a van," the look containing "the history of man," are the furtive, spoken and body-language exchanges of a sexual pickup. They represent an argot known to the initiate, a special code by which those in the know can recognize each other, come to terms, reach an accord in this alien and forbidding setting. The poem is about an encounter with a prostitute, and so impersonal an encounter that "the stranger," for the agreed-upon price, embraces not a human being but the whole impersonal and heartless city: the homeless, the humbled, and even, in their remote isolation, the rich. The poem is about the most chilling and impersonal kind of sex. The gender of the prostitute, who is never seen as a human being, is suitably concealed.

Having made a glancing allusion to "The Capital," I think it worth adding that its opening lines,

> Quarter of pleasures where the rich are always waiting,
> Waiting expensively for miracles to happen,

bear an uncanny resemblance to the opening of a poem by Elizabeth Bishop called "A Miracle for Breakfast," which begins,

> At six o'clock we were waiting for coffee,
> waiting for coffee and the charitable crumb.

This collocation of miracles with the repetition of "waiting" from late in the first to the beginning of the second line is striking. I had first thought that Bishop was echoing Auden, whom she greatly admired; but it may well have been the other way around. The Auden poem is dated December 1938 in *Collected Poems,* and Bishop's poem appeared in the July 1937 issue of *Poetry.* Auden had earlier in his career been influenced by the work of women who were poets: both Emily Dickinson and Laura Riding had detectable effects on his early work.

The Auden poem envisions the city in general, and the capital in particular, as evil, corrupting, and a sinister temptation to the innocents from the rural outlying areas. The final stanza goes,

But the sky you illumine, your glow is visible far
Into the dark countryside, the enormous, the frozen,
Where, hinting at the forbidden like a wicked uncle,
Night after night to the farmer's children you beckon.

This image of the city as seduction or invitation to evil has a long literary history, and can be found in Virgil as well as in Goldsmith. What seems of interest here is that this traditional or conventional view of cities contrasts dramatically with Auden's more usual view, in which cities always represent the sort of civic accord and communal harmony that he posits as the image of an ideal society and desired city-state, a *civitas* or *polis* that embodies humane relationships. Such was his attitude in the early sestina (as yet unmentioned here) in *On This Island,* which closes with a prayer that "we rebuild our cities, not dream of islands." And of course later in his career, cities, even when they symbolize complete political corruption, are no longer contrasted with the putative innocence of the pastoral world, a world Auden regards for the most part as a sentimental hoax.

It may be that Brussels itself, or Auden's visit there, led to "Musée des Beaux Arts," which is certainly one of Auden's most widely anthologized poems, but it may be noted beforehand that this poem, so far as I can tell, is the only poem of Auden's based on a specific painting, and, given his poor eyesight, the surprising thing is that he should have written any at all. Auden did not count gallery-going among his leading pleasures, and while his bad feet had something to do with this, there is reason to believe he enjoyed reading art history and art criticism more than looking at the paintings themselves, and reaped a richer profit thereby; and I think this is true of the Breughel painting under consideration in this poem. Robert Craft writes, in "The Poet and the Rake" (in Spender's *Auden*),

With Auden the senses seemed to be of negligible importance, whereas with Stravinsky the affective faculties were virtually instruments of thought. Powerful observer though Auden was, he displayed little interest in the visual sense, being purblind to painting, for example, and even to "poetic" nature, for he was more concerned with the virtues of gardening than with the beauty of flowers. And whatever the acuteness of his aural sense, the idea of music appealed to him more than music itself, music with words—opera and Anglican hymns—more than Haydn quartets.

"Musée des Beaux Arts" is proportioned and divided, generally though not exactly, like a somewhat enlarged Petrarchan sonnet, with an opening section of thirteen lines followed by a closing section of eight. Auden cunningly surprises us, reversing our normal expectations of a poem as proportioned and balanced as a sonnet. Usually the octave presents a particular scene, event, rendered with a pleasing vividness and accuracy; and this is usually followed by a sestet in which what came before is meditated upon, regarded from a new or newly considered perspective. Auden reverses this and begins with a generalization about a lot of varied paintings, none of them really up for inspection.

> About suffering they were never wrong,
> The Old Masters: how well they understood
> Its human position; how it takes place
> While someone else is eating or opening a window or just
>     walking dully along.

The poem, in its brisk survey of quotidian life, in the midst of which astonishing events take place, "the miraculous birth" and "the dreadful martyrdom," adopts in its opening section a calm and distant language that is meant to be slightly shocking as it portrays the common human indifference to the reverent, passionate waiting of "the aged," to say nothing of the nativity itself, and bestows bland attention on the innocent dogs and the horse that belongs to the "torturer." Clearly the "Old Masters" that Auden is referring to here are only those who paint religious scenes, and very possibly he had Dutch and Flemish pictures in mind, though there are also Italian Renaissance paintings which exhibit indifferent or preoccupied people adjacent to dramatic religious events. As we read the opening section, we are in fact invited to provide our own catalogue of confirmation—though we would immediately realize that Auden's Old Masters could not include, say, Rubens, or even Rembrandt. The second part begins with "In Breughel's *Icarus*, for instance": that "for instance" serves to particularize and exemplify the generalities that began the poem. They seem to do so with especial success because the painting chosen as exemplum is not in fact a religious painting at all, which seems to confirm the suggestion that the Old Masters did not confine their view of the human situation to a purely religious one. There follows a specific, though by no means comprehensive, description of the details of the painting (no mention is made, for example, of the shepherd and his flock), and the poem ends

> the sun shone
> As it had to on the white legs disappearing into the green
> Water; and the expensive delicate ship that must have seen
> Something amazing, a boy falling out of the sky,
> Had somewhere to get to and sailed calmly on.

The painting, to be sure, is called *The Fall of Icarus,* and way over in its right-hand corner, made almost insignificant by their diminished size in the remote distance, the boy's two legs are just visible above the surface of the water which conceals the rest of his body. The most prominent thing in the painting is the ploughman, placed center and boldly in the foreground, along with his plough and his horse. But way over on the left, nearly concealed in a thicket, even more unnoticed than the drowning boy, lies the bald head of an unburied corpse, face up. And art historians have persuasively concluded (not least because of Breughel's iconographic habits in other works of his) that this painting, despite its name, is meant to illustrate a well-known Flemish proverb, "Es bleibt kein Pflug stehen um eines menschen willen, der stirbt," which means, "No plough comes to a standstill because a man dies." This maxim has its echo in the liturgy ("In the midst of life we are in death") and in the Gospels ("Let the dead bury their dead") but it has a plain, secular sense that can be viewed as callous, and which can be summarized in the saying that "it is the business of the living to live." It seems to me plausible that the generalized proposition with which Auden begins his poem may have been derived from a book on art history rather than from a personal inspection of this and other paintings.

The poem has enjoyed an unusual popularity, and this may well be due to the way in which the mythic or miraculous subject of the painting is subdued and domesticated to our habitual and quotidian experience. And the proverbial source of the painting, and hence of the poem, is shockingly and familiarly borne out by our routine experience of the daily news as we receive it in the papers and on television, where nearly unendurable agonies, cataclysmic misfortunes, and deaths are randomly juxtaposed with accounts of the weather, the announcements of betrothals, and movie reviews.

"Herman Melville" is an interesting but imperfect poem, exhibiting odd grammatical and syntactical lapses; there are, for example, two superfluous uses of "it" in the eighth line and a curious and inelegant sequence of clauses beginning with "but." Moreover, there is a kind of historical

or biographical (as well, it may be added, as aesthetic) deformity perpe-
trated: a deliberate reordering of the actual sequence of events. The poem
is composed as a kind of quest narrative, an ocean journey, subtly
compared to the Odyssey, in which Melville, saved from the Siren Isles,
is fortunately blown "Past the Cape Horn of sensible success / Which cries:
'This rock is Eden. Shipwreck here.'" But the initial part of the journey
(which, by Auden's allegory, is filled with the delusional grimness of
*Moby-Dick*) is simply something that must be overcome, endured, like a
"nightmare," in order to arrive at the pure and tranquil wisdom of *Billy
Budd*. There is something remarkably high-handed about this dismissal
of *Moby-Dick* as "intricate and false." That book is, of course, deeply
pessimistic and, not altogether covertly, anti-Christian. And one may
suspect at least in part that Auden's clear preference for the later *Billy
Budd* may have something to do with its manifest Christian symbolism
of the innocent young man, betrayed by the vindictive plot of someone
who envies him. *Billy Budd* is surely itself a Christian allegory, and
Melville's capacity to have written it after first passing through the
Marlovian and pagan defiance of his great novel seems, from Auden's
point of view, to make Melville's own quest into a kind of Christian
journey from doubt to faith (and one that some would say bears a
resemblance to the journey Auden himself would make). But it must also
be added that *Billy Budd* is more explicitly homosexual than *Moby-Dick,*
and the progress or journey may be an erotic quest as well. This second
possibility is veiled in the nominal sexual climate in which the poem
begins, and in which family domesticity seems to have triumphed; for
since the poem's first words are "Towards the end," it appears as though
the haven towards which Melville had journeyed was his faithful
Penelope, his wife. But this domestic note seems at odds with other tones
in the poem, for not only *Billy Budd* but the great novel of the Whale
that preceded it have been taken as talismans of homosexual taste.

Auden himself certainly believed in such talismans, and had a number
of them that served him as Arnoldian touchstones, by which he determined whether someone measured up to his aesthetic tastes (and perhaps
his sexual ones as well). Wendell Johnson, in his book on Auden, has a
note that reads: "The Trillings and Auden were friendly, but when Auden
once said that any lover of poetry must love the *Lord of the Rings* and was
told, 'Lionel Trilling doesn't like it at all,' he responded, 'Exactly.'"
Auden also regarded Bellini's *Norma* as a pretty accurate index of
anyone's musical taste and intelligence: to like it was to pass his test and

prove oneself civilized. As for the talismanic properties of *Moby-Dick,* the editors of the Newberry Edition remark that Edward Carpenter, both a socialist and a "champion of homosexual love," knew and admired the book.

The historical distortion appears at the poem's close, which, according to the poem's own time scheme, returns us to the tranquility with which it opened, and which had been attained only by passing through the turbulence of *Moby-Dick* and finding the serenity of *Billy Budd.*

> He stood upon a narrow balcony and listened:
> And all the stars above him sang as in his childhood
> "All, all is vanity," but it was not the same;
> For now the words descended like the calm of mountains—
> —Nathaniel had been shy because his love was selfish—
> But now he cried in exultation and surrender
> "The Godhead is broken like bread. We are the pieces."

> And sat down at his desk and wrote a story.

The violation of time sequence here has to do with Melville's initially enthusiastic, and possibly too demonstrative, friendship with Hawthorne, which appears to have embarrassed and distanced the latter in a way that hurt Melville greatly. But the words of his cry in the poem are adapted from a letter to Hawthorne written on November 17, 1851, well before their friendship had cooled and only just before *Moby-Dick* was completed. Melville wrote,

> Whence come you, Hawthorne? By what right do you drink from my flagon of life? And when I put it to my lips—lo, they are yours and not mine. I feel that the Godhead is broken up like bread at the Supper, and that we are the pieces. Hence this infinite fraternity of feeling.

Again Auden may have wanted to close on a specifically Christian and eucharistic note, though that "infinite fraternity of feeling" may have been what made Hawthorne edgy, thus allowing Auden to characterize his love as "selfish," that is, full of qualifications and reservations, as indeed it was. But Auden's line in quotes, and the original letter as well, are oddly ambiguous. Their apparent religious content or tenor seems to suggest that all human life is sanctified; and it is possible that Melville meant this, though it should immediately be added that such a meaning does not consort with the tenor and thrust of *Moby-Dick* itself. That novel was clearly the main topic of the letter from which Auden's quoted line was adapted; the letter also contains the sentence "I have written a wicked book, and feel spotless as the lamb," which we may perhaps interpret to mean that Melville is at ease in the conviction that no one will recognize how wicked the book actually is. In any case, there is another possible meaning to those appropriated words: we are the pieces of the Godhead which is broken up like bread because we, human beings, are all that there is of divinity: that is, there is no God. And whatever one may think of this interpretation, it is closer to *Moby-Dick* than the first one was. It might also be said to support the view of those who see Auden's early work as decidedly secular and agnostic.

I turn now to one of Auden's most admired, quoted, and anthologized poems, which he was eventually to title "Lullaby." He made at least one change in the course of time: in the last line of the second stanza, which originally went "The hermit's sensual ecstasy," the word "sensual" was changed, for no reason that I can see, to "carnal." The poem is so important a success, and so deserving of detailed scrutiny, that I want to quote the whole of it, and in its original form.

> Lay your sleeping head, my love,
> Human on my faithless arm;
> Time and fevers burn away
> Individual beauty from
> Thoughtful children, and the grave
> Proves the child ephemeral:
> But in my arms till break of day
> Let the living creature lie,
> Mortal, guilty, but to me
> The entirely beautiful.
>
> Soul and body have no bounds:
> To lovers as they lie upon
> Her tolerant enchanted slope
> In their ordinary swoon,
> Grave the vision Venus sends
> Of supernatural sympathy,
> Universal love and hope;
> While an abstract insight wakes
> Among the glaciers and the rocks
> The hermit's sensual ecstasy.

Certainty, fidelity
On the stroke of midnight pass
Like vibrations of a bell,
And fashionable madmen raise
Their pedantic boring cry:
Every farthing of the cost,
All the dreaded cards foretell,
Shall be paid, but from this night
Not a whisper, not a thought,
Not a kiss nor look be lost.

Beauty, midnight, vision dies:
Let the winds of dawn that blow
Softly round your dreaming head
Such a day of sweetness show
Eye and knocking heart may bless,
Find the mortal world enough;
Noons of dryness see you fed
By the involuntary powers,
Nights of insult let you pass
Watched by every human love.

Within the wide spectrum of love that this book and the previous one envisage, including love as mysteriously curative of both individual and social ills, the love described here is touching, vulnerable, and decently screened as regards gender. This may have been a sly and protective device, but it could just as easily be a trick Auden had learned very early from the popular song writers (to whose lyrics this poem owes nothing else). The Broadway musical writers he most admired had early learned a simple economic fact: though in the context of one of their shows the dramatic realities might demand that a particular song be sung by a man to a woman or vice versa, much could be so written as to be sexually indeterminate, and thus sung by either male or female vocalists for broadcast or recording purposes. Certainly the most popular and successful songs of our era observe this canny device, and Auden made handy use of it.

"Lullaby" has elicited a large variety of appreciative responses, of which it may be that the most emphatic and singular is Edward Mendelson's, who writes, "'Lullaby' marks another of Auden's innovations in love poetry. It is the first English poem in which a lover proclaims, in moral terms and during a shared night of love, his own faithlessness." This is a pretty bold claim, and sets one to think about the possibilities of any challengers. The only one that has occurred to me is the following, by Suckling:

> Out upon it! I have loved
>   Three whole days together;
> And am like to love three more,
>   If it prove fair weather.

Suckling's poem, of course, is cynical and lighthearted, and altogether different in tone from the almost religious solemnity with which Auden's poem ends. And on a purely mathematical level, Suckling's admission of having loved for three days makes him at best a poor runner-up to the "one-night-stand" declaration Mendelson claims to find in Auden's poem. That he should have found such a note struck in the poem could, moreover, be justified by the rather casual sexual encounter described in "Brussels in Winter." But that sonnet does not address the sexual partner, much less use the epithet "my love," a term of endearment that makes the notion of a one-night sexual encounter seem much less plausible. No doubt Mendelson's claim for the uniqueness of this poem in itself defies or makes irrelevant any quest for analogues or precedents. But I think that there *is* in fact a precedent, and a famous and important one—one which, moreover, Auden hoped his readers would detect. It is the celebrated *Vivamus, mea Lesbia, atque amemus* of Catullus, which has been put into English as follows by Charles Martin.

> Lesbia, let us live only for loving,
> and let us value at a single penny
> all the loose flap of senile busybodies!
> Suns when they set are capable of rising,
> but at the setting of our own brief light
> night is one sleep from which we never waken.
> Give me a thousand kisses, then a hundred,
> another thousand next, another hundred,
> a thousand without pause & then a hundred,
> until when we have run up our thousands
> we will cry bankrupt, hiding our assets
> from ourselves & any who would harm us,
> knowing the volume of our trade in kisses.

Most famous, of course, as a version of this poem, is Ben Jonson's:

> Come, my Celia, let us prove,
> While we may, the sport of love;
> Time will not be ours forever:
> He, at length, our good will sever.
> Spend not then his gifts in vain.
> Sunnes, that set, may rise again:
> But if once we loose this light,
> 'Tis, with us, perpetual night.
>
> . . . . .
>
> Cannot we delude the eyes
> Of a few poore houshold spyes?
> Or his easier eares beguile,
> So removed by our wile?
> 'Tis no sinne, love's fruit to steale,
> But the sweet theft to reveale:
> To be taken, to be seene,
> These have crimes accounted been.

This same figure of a single day to represent the lifespan of man is used by that very classical poet, Robert Herrick, at the end of his splendid "Corinna's Going a Maying," which is also indebted to Catullus.

> Come, let us goe, while we are in our prime;
> And take the harmlesse follie of the time.
>     We shall grow old apace, and die
>     Before we know our liberty.
>     Our life is short; and our dayes run
>     As fast away as do's the Sunne:
> And as a vapour, or a drop of rain,
> Once lost, can ne'r be found againe:
>     So when or you or I are made
>     A fable, song, or fleeting shade;
>     All love, all liking, all delight
>     Lies drown'd with us in endless night.
> Then while time serves, and we are but decaying;
> Come, my *Corinna*, come, let's go a Maying.

Although Auden certainly enlarges upon, and departs from, his paradigm of the Latin poem, there are crucial points of resemblance (and it may be added that Jonson also takes liberties with his Catullan model). The most important resemblance clearly concerns the notion of the human lifespan as comparable to a single day, a notion which makes a mockery of the whole idea of fidelity. In this Catullus was setting a precedent for a whole retinue of "invitations to love," in which the brevity of human life, and our fragile mortality (Marvell's "To His Coy Mistress" is only one illustrious example), play central roles. What Auden does is to equate fidelity and life itself, since both are of necessity brief.

His very first stanza, ostensibly addressed to a sleeping beloved, reminds him, and us, the readers who overhear, of what in the second line is called the speaker's "faithless arm," but which is elaborated into the physical decay of all mortals: "Time and fevers burn away / Individual beauty from / Thoughtful children, and the grave / Proves the child ephemeral." The figure of the child lends special force and poignance to the premise of life's (and love's) brevity. Indeed, the whole first stanza, in King Lear's phrase, "smells of mortality."

Mendelson finds himself puzzled by the first line of the second stanza, "Soul and body have no bounds." But surely what Auden means is that the power of love proves the falsity of the "dualistic heresy": that there is in fact no distinction between soul and body, that they are similarly blessed, and completely at one with each other. So "grave" indeed (with only the slightest overtone of the cemetery, but chiefly with the burden of "solemn" or "serious") is the "vision" Venus sends that it entails not only "supernatural sympathy" (the blessing and accord of the divine) but "universal love and hope." This is a notion we have encountered before in Auden's poems: it is a vision of society healed and rendered wholesome by the powers of love. (We shall meet with it again, in "September 1, 1939.") So universal (and therefore undeniable) is this vision that it provokes "an abstract insight" and "wakes / Among the glaciers and the rocks / The hermit's sensual ecstasy." The landscape is significantly forbidding (the antecedent of "the granite wastes" that allure "saints-to-be" in the later poem "In Praise of Limestone"), but what is being described here is the physical temptations of the desert saints, and perhaps of St. Anthony in particular, whose sexual longings and torments were recounted in a life of the saint by Athanasius, Bishop of Alexandria, and depicted vividly and variously in many paintings by Hieronymus Bosch, as well as in a few by Sasetta. It may be assumed that the "abstract insight" is the initial response to sacred accounts of a love that, as John Donne asserted in "The Ecstasy," must be expressed through the body.

> Love's mysteries in souls do grow,
>     But yet the body is his book.

The hermit, even if he starts with Scripture, comes at last, instead of at first, like the rest of us, to the Venereal "vision."

If, in the third stanza, both certainty and fidelity "pass" on the stroke of midnight, this is, I would argue, on the precedent of Catullus, no more than a commentary on mortality. The "fashionable madmen" and their "pedantic boring cry" are the Auden equivalents of "all the loose flap of senile busybodies" in Martin's version of the Latin poem, and what Jonson identifies as "a few poor houshold spyes." These are the envious moralists, full of their tiresome homilies and rectitude, saying "You'll be sorry!" "Every farthing of the cost" is Auden's brilliant way of retaining the strong fiduciary and banking metaphor that Catullus so wittily employs at the end of his poem. Strict accounts are to be kept by both the Latin poet and his English follower.

But the final stanza changes the tone of the poem (as by this time we might have come to expect of Auden) into a prayer. And it is a prayer of blessing. The three preceding stanzas have dealt in turn with "beauty," "vision," and "midnight," in that order. They are summed up in the first line of the last stanza, and their mutability is again insisted upon. This formal patterning might well remind us of the structure of Thomas Nashe's "In a Time of Pestilence," with its individual stanzas that take up in turn "Riches," "Beauty," "Strength," and "Wit," demonstrating how each one is mutable and vulnerable to the omnipotent powers of death. But the five lines that immediately follow the first one of Auden's final stanza depart from the Latin model, as well as contradict the claims of that first line, along with all the other claims of infidelity that have been scattered through the poem. These lines anticipate a waking without any consequent diminution of loving, and thereby deny some of the metaphoric premises of the earlier stanzas. Finding "the mortal world enough" is part of the blessing which no longer hopes for or needs "supernatural sympathy," a sympathy which in any case only provided a "vision" of what love could do and be like. That love is now about to wake incarnate. In the concluding lines of the prayer I think we may ascribe that "insult" once again to Catullus, who closes with a recollection of the envious and hostile, resentful of the pleasures of the amorous. But notice the paired and opposed "noons" and "nights": they assert that love will survive the original metaphor that had called for the closure of love and life together with the coming of "midnight." The prayer, for all its noticeable obscurity (what or who are "the involuntary powers"?), is nevertheless a prayer of blessing for the beloved both in hours of waking and in hours of sleeping, through the whole round and circuit of the twenty-four-hour day.

*Another Time* opened with a poem ("Wrapped in a yielding air") that was a parable or allegory of man, and its first section ends with another, "Underneath the leaves of life." But this is more than simply a meditation on the human condition, though it is surely that; and it is, moreover, a meditation deeply colored by at least the external trappings of religious tradition. It is also—and this should not surprise us, given the recurrence of its theme throughout *On This Island*—a poem in which love appears to sanctify a fallen world and to unite creatures into a single family.

> Underneath the leaves of life,
> Green on the prodigious tree,
>   In a trance of grief
> Stand the fallen man and wife:
> Far away the single stag
> Banished to a lonely crag
> Gazes placid out to sea,
> And from thickets round about
> Breeding animals look in
>   On Duality,
> And the birds fly in and out
>   Of the world of man.

The poem begins in the world after the expulsion from the Garden of Eden, in which, by the sin of disobedience, mankind has divorced himself from what had once been a united and harmonious fellowship with the world of creatures. For this reason the stag is far away, "banished" because he has suddenly become the quarry rather than the companion of our common father who, in compensation for the curse entailed by his fall, is given dominion over all the creatures, and thus is transformed into the hunter of "Our hunting fathers told the story." The breeding animals, who, along with mankind, have been cursed with mortality, have nevertheless been spared a particularly painful and tormenting human dilemma: that of being a spiritual creature as well as part of the animal kingdom, and thus inhabiting the border region of "Duality." All human anxiety arises from this predicament, which the creatures, in their innocence, are spared.

> Down in order from the ridge,
> Bayonets glittering in the sun,
>   Soldiers who will judge
> Wind towards the little bridge:
> Even politicians speak
> Truths of value to the weak,
> Necessary acts are done
> By the ill and the unjust;
> But the Judgment and the Smile,
>   Though these two-in-one
> See creation as they must,
>   None shall reconcile.

This must be one of the earliest employments of what was to become a brilliant and characteristic device of dramatic anachronism used by Auden through a large body of his work. The consequences of the Fall appear in the second stanza in all their modern proliferations, with armed troops invading a pastoral setting, while those with political power abuse it in the old familiar ways. Mankind, once judged by God, is now judged by his own members who have aggressively become soldiers; the wisdom of politicians is the wisdom of accommodation, the only possible wisdom of value to the weak. ("Politics," as our elected officials never cease to tell us, "is the art of the possible.") The world of "Necessity" is no longer the world of Grace, and so "necessary acts" are the pragmatic solutions to insoluble problems, performed, in a human society, by the ill and the unjust, who are invariably governed by ill-concealed self-interest. "The Judgment and the Smile," carefully personified and awarded upper-case initials, like allegorical figures in the poems of Marvell and Pope, are the dual aspects of Divinity, which created man and the rest of creation out of love, but which first judged him after his act of disobedience and shall judge him again at the end. These two aspects of divine power were not divided before the Fall, but they have been so since. And human intelligence is baffled by the tandem forces of Wrath and Love. The Judgment and the Smile are two-in-one because they are twin aspects of Divinity and see creation *sub specie aeternitatis,* which is beyond human comprehension.

> Bordering our middle earth
> Kingdoms of the Short and Tall,
>   Rivals for our faith,

Stir up envy from our birth:
So the giant who storms the sky
In an angry wish to die
Wakes the hero in us all,
While the tiny with their power
To divide and hide and flee,
  When our fortunes fall
Tempt to a belief on our
  Immortality.

The "middle earth" here is not an early borrowing from Tolkien but is identified in the *OED* as "the earth, as placed between heaven and hell, or as supposed to occupy the center of the universe—sometimes applied to the real world in contradistinction to fairyland." The phrase figures also in one of the works Auden declared most influenced him, Langland's *The Vision of Piers Ploughman,* which presents a dream image of Middle-Earth, a compound of Eden and the classical *locus amoenus,* or place of delight, usually a garden. In our real world, then, where no easy solutions obtain, there is a further breach of unity, another "Duality" beyond the split of "the Judgment and the Smile," and beyond the separation of mankind from the rest of creation. This is represented in rather Swiftian terms by the "Kingdoms of the Short and Tall," again given upper-case status as allegorically significant. They represent the only two possible ways that mankind can view the human lot: with defiance or submission. The "giant" who storms the sky, a Promethean hero of defiant and Pyrrhic victories, may be likened also to Icarus, to all the hubristic sins, and to the kingdom of the birds (as well as, more covertly, to "the stork-legged heaven-reachers" of the first poem in Auden's first book). By way of contrast, "the tiny" are ant-like, and their "power" is the puny one of mere survival, which tempts them to embrace the heresy that they will not die.

Lovers running each to each
Feel such timid dreams catch fire
  Blazing as they touch,
Learn what love alone can teach:
Happy on a tousled bed
Praise Blake's acumen who said:
"One thing only we require
Of each other; we must see

In another's lineaments
  Gratified desire,"
That is our humanity;
  Nothing else contents.

In this stanza, the timid dreams (of immortality) of the tiny in the previous stanza "catch fire" when lovers rush to embrace each other, since love seems to confer the illusion that both parties are immortal. But this is indeed an illusion, and love's proper function (and its compensation for the losses entailed in the Fall) consists in Blake's anti-Puritanical doctrine of mutual sexual gratification, in shared and reciprocal satisfaction, which is the nearest we shall come to heaven or immortality. It furnishes contentment, the ability to accept our human lot, without envy or resentment.

Nowhere else could I have known
Than, beloved, in your eyes
  What we have to learn,
That we love ourselves alone:
All our terrors burned away
We can learn at last to say:
"All our knowledge comes to this,
That existence is enough,
That in savage solitude
  Or the play of love
Every living creature is
  Woman, Man, and Child."

This last stanza is certainly the most problematic and difficult of all. But it concludes what had begun as a large allegory about the fate and state of all mankind with the most personal statement about love, addressed to a beloved presence who had not before been taken account of in the poem. It contains two short passages that seem familiarly to recur in other parts of this same book. "We love ourselves alone" is remarkably like the lines in "September 1, 1939" that read,

For the error bred in the bone
Of each woman and each man
Craves what it cannot have,
Not universal love
But to be loved alone.

These lines need their proper context to be explained, but it may at least be assumed that in the lines just quoted, which are interpolated from the journal Nijinsky kept while under psychiatric care in Switzerland, "to be loved alone" is regarded as the fault of "the normal heart" and as "the error bred in the bone / Of each woman and each man." As the lines' context makes plain, and as Nijinsky's rather mad assertions affirm, the craving "to be loved alone" is selfish, vain, tyrannical—qualities which the poor, demented dancer belatedly attributes to the celebrated impresario, Diaghilev, who had once been his lover.

The other passage consists of the lines "'All our knowledge comes to this, / That existence is enough,'" which recalls,

> Let the winds of dawn that blow
> Softly round your dreaming head
> Such a day of sweetness show
> Eye and knocking heart may bless,
> Find the mortal world enough

from "Lullaby." These lines, as well as the one in the poem under discussion, concern the *contentment* that sexual union provides, and the compensation it affords for our having lost paradise. It will be echoed again in this same volume in a lighter poem eventually to be titled "Heavy Date"; the lines go:

> Crying for the moon is
> Naughtiness and envy,
> We can only love what-
> -ever we possess.

(There is a drawing by Blake of a man yearning for the moon, captioned, "I want! I want!")

*Revenons à nos moutons.* The fourth stanza had adverted to Blake's famous poem called "The Question Answer'd."

> What is it men in women do require?
> The lineaments of Gratified Desire.
> What is it women do in men require?
> The lineaments of Gratified Desire.

This looks very much as if Auden, on the authority of Blake, is speaking of a love that is, first, unashamedly sexual and, second, mutual and reciprocal in the pleasure it bestows, and in this, generous, unselfish,

concerned above all with the satisfaction and gratification of the other—
and therefore, as it would seem, not essentially self-concerned. But the
opening lines of the final stanza explicitly contradict this and point to the
impossibility of such delusional selflessness. For to wish to give pleasure
is to demand that that wish be fulfilled, and to return to all the dangers
and sins of vanity and solipsism. This is a part of the hopeless "Duality"
of man's situation in the fallen world and in this poem, which was later
cunningly titled "The Riddle," perhaps to quibble with Blake's answered
question. For Auden seems to contradict Blake with

> Nowhere else could I have known
> Than, beloved, in your eyes
>   What we have to learn,
> That we love ourselves alone.

That might be thought a curious, if not a chilling, thing to say to a
beloved. And there are a number of ways to annotate it, apart from the
general comment offered above. Freud has one in particular, in his
"Contributions to the Theory of Sex," and particularly in his comments
on sexual inversion, and the narcissism this kind of sexual orientation is
supposed to entail. For the poem's claim that "we love ourselves alone"
may at least be suspected of being descriptive of narcissism. But it is surely
the case that heterosexual love is at least as subject to narcissistic perversion as its homosexual variant—and may in some ways be more pernicious, being less recognized as being so. The fact is that we are beyond
being disinterested in all matters pertaining to love, and this is the
consequence of our fallen state. Even so, we can rejoice in what we are
given, and can find contentment in it; and most amazing of all, we can
see ourselves as being, from the point of view of Eros, at one with all
creatures (from whom, at the poem's beginning, we thought ourselves
divorced), for "Every living creature is / Woman, Man, and Child." It is
important to take note of the "and" in these lines; the poem is not saying
merely that creatures have gender, which matters when they mature,
though not before. It is saying that 1) the creatures are the original forms
of life from which we evolved, and are therefore us in potential form, and
2) in their means of sexual reproduction they are like us (which could
reflect backwards to the homoerotic element that may be latent at the
beginning of the stanza). But finally 3) it seems to me that the creatures,
as is implied by the very term "creatures," are the fundamental qualities
and aspects of Creation; and they therefore represent a universal family

that is archetypally represented (and especially so in traditional paintings of the Nativity) as Woman, Man, and Child.

The second section of this book is called, not without a certain bemused irony, "Lighter Poems." It begins innocently enough, with a poem which, if not a dream poem, is a daydream poem, eventually titled "Heavy Date," an amusing adoption of American teenage heterosexual demotic; but before the section has ended we will have encountered "Epitaph on a Tyrant" and "Refugee Blues," which, whatever else they may be, are "light" only by a perverse extension of the word. Most (though not all) of the poems in this section are explicitly about love in one or another of its protean manifestations. And none addressed the topic with more ease and charm than the first poem, "Heavy Date." It is a putative account of free-associative musings of the poet, who is simply wasting time waiting for the arrival of his beloved. It is filled with the random and the absurd that figure in our unconscious thoughts (but in this case, devoid of anything even remotely threatening).

> Now I hear Saint Francis
> Telling me in breezy
> Tones as we are walking
>   Near a power-house:
> "Loving birds is easy,
> Any fool can do it,
> But I must admit it's
>   Hard to love the louse."

The poem moves from random, surrealist jottings to more coherent meditations on the nature of love.

> Slowly we are learning,
> We at least know this much,
> That we have to unlearn
>   Much that we were taught,
> And are growing chary
> Of emphatic dogmas;
> Love like Matter is much
>   Odder than we thought.

> Love requires an Object,
> But this varies so much,

> Almost, I imagine,
>   Anything will do:
> When I was a child, I
> Loved a pumping-engine,
> Thought it every bit as
>   Beautiful as you.
>
> Love has no position,
> Love's a way of living,
> One kind of relation
>   Possible between
> Any things or persons
> Given one condition,
> The one sine qua non
>   Being mutual need.

We may suppose that the category of "Lighter Poems" will possibly excuse some lapses in logic here, pumping-engines of even the finest manufacture being incapable of expressing "mutual need." And it may be added that "Almost, I imagine, / Anything will do" as an Object to be loved slides smoothly over the feelings of the warped and sadly or dangerously crippled. But the telling detail that as a boy the poet loved a pumping-engine recalls an undiscussed poem in the first part of the book, which may be one of Auden's most personal, and serious, lyrics about love, a poem that begins, "Perhaps I always knew what they were saying." Tucked in as it is among poems either truly impersonal or else in which the poet has deliberately distanced himself from experience, the poem may pass almost unnoticed. But it is an account of how affection of a child for "those beautiful machines that never talked," therefore plainly unreciprocal, enlarged to admit an industrial landscape:

> And all the landscape round them pointed to
> The calm with which they took complete desertion
> As proof that you existed.

This is not easy; the machines and their landscape have been deserted, and the lessons in love that they wordlessly teach is one of stoic endurance, and without promise. Its very bleakness makes the sudden arrival of "you" the more miraculous, and makes all the patient waiting seem not only worthwhile but meritorious.

"Heavy Date" concludes,

When two lovers meet, then
There's an end of writing
Thought and Analytics:
  Lovers, like the dead,
In their loves are equal;
Sophomores and peasants,
Poets and their critics
  Are the same in bed.

The *equality* posited at the end of this cheerful poem will be belied by another of the "lighter" poems, the one called "Victor," in which a man is deranged by the infidelity of his wife, murders her, and, in his frenzy, comes to regard himself as the scourge of the world (not unlike, it may be noted, the speaker of "It's farewell to the drawing-room's civilized cry"). As regards this torment of jealousy and the seething hatred it provokes, Auden (in 1946) said to Alan Ansen, "You know, it's frightening how easy it is to commit murder in America. Just drink too much. I can see myself doing it." And in annotating this comment, the editor of *The Table Talk of W. H. Auden,* Nicholas Jenkins, calls the reader's attention to what he terms "a poem" addressed to Chester, dated Christmas Day, 1941, and recorded in Dorothy Farnan's *Auden in Love,* which reads,

Dearest Chester
  Because it is in you, a Jew, that I, a Gentile, inheriting an O-so-genteel anti-semitism, have found my happiness:
    As this morning I think of Bethlehem, I think of you.

  Because it is you, from Brooklyn, who have taught me, from Oxford, how the most liberal young man can assume that his money and his education ought to be able to buy love;
    As this morning I think of the inn stable, I think of you.

  Because, suffering on your account the torments of sexual jealousy, I have had a glimpse of the infinite vileness of masculine conceit;
    As this morning I think of Joseph I think of you.

  Because mothers have much to do with your queerness and mine, because we both have lost ours, and because Mary is a camp name;
    As this morning I think of Mary I think of you.

  Because the necessarily serious relation of a child to its parents is the symbol, pattern, and warning of any serious love that may later

depend upon its choice, because you are to me emotionally a mother, physically a father, and intellectually a son;
    As this morning I think of the Holy Family, I think of you.

Because, on account of you, I have been, in intention, and almost in act, a murderer;
    As this morning I think of Herod, I think of you.

Because even *les matelots* and *les morceaux de commerces* [the first term meaning "sailors" such as Chester used to pick up, the second meaning pickups in the "rough trade" of tough bars] instinctively pay you homage;
    As this morning I think of the shepherds, I think of you.

Because I believe in your creative gift, and because I rely absolutely on your critical judgement;
    As this morning I think of the magi, I think of you.

Because it is through you that God has chosen to show me my beatitude;
    As this morning I think of the Godhead, I think of you.

Because in the eyes of our bohemian friends our relationship is absurd;
    As this morning I think of the Paradox of the Incarnation I think of you.

Because our love, beginning Hans Andersen, became Grimm, and there are probably even grimmer tests to come, nevertheless I believe that if only we have faith in God and in each other, we shall be permitted to realize all that love is intended to be;
    As this morning I think of the Good Friday and Easter Sunday already implicit in Christmas day, I think of you.

A lot might be made of this very moving declaration. It seems to me, first, not so much a poem as an improvised liturgical chant. And second, it seems like an outline of the central thoughts that will be later embodied in Auden's great work *For the Time Being*. It has a formal and explicitly Christian shape as a meditation, that shape signified in each of its parts by the concluding clauses—as I think of Bethlehem, or the inn stable, or Joseph, or Mary, or Herod, etcetera, I think of you. The clear ingenuity of the text lies in Auden's brilliant capacity to find a point-for-point correspondence between the holy drama and his own personal relationship with Chester. And it may be that the perfection of the correspondence confirmed his faith in the seriousness of the relationship. In any case, when Alan Ansen asked Auden, "What is the connection between 'Victor' and the end of 'The Temptation of St. Joseph'?" Auden replied, "Victor was really somebody by that name. Joseph is me. Victor was at a school where I was; he used to send anonymous letters. He'd told us he'd already done it, evidently hoping no one would suspect him."

As applied to the "light" poem under discussion, however, the claim that "Lovers, like the dead, / In their loves are equal" is belied in other poems within this very book, and seems accordingly like the bemused daydream of a momentarily happy man.

I shall pass over the remaining "lighter" poems, except to say that the ballad about Miss Gee, a sort of Groddeckian case history, has offended some readers by what they take to be its chilling want of sympathy for a poor spinster who clearly suffers from what Auden had called in an earlier poem "the distortions of ingrown virginity." The poem is admittedly shocking, but in this it precisely resembles poems of William Plomer, whose work Auden greatly admired. I am unable to say which poet influenced the other, but it was undoubtedly Plomer who brought the form (a poetic equivalent of the more macabre drawings of Edward Gorey) to the perfection of a very limited kind. Plomer's poems, admired by Dylan Thomas among others, established a purlieu somewhere between the tragic and the vulgar, between mockery and sympathy, and exhibited a "campy" detachment from their not infrequently grisly subject matter. It seems to me that beyond question Auden's "Soldiers' Chorus," which immediately follows Herod's speech in *For the Time Being*, is based unashamedly on Plomer's "Father and Son; 1939," especially as regards the refrains. Plomer, it needs to be said, is a much better poet than has been recognized in this country, and in one of his poems mentions a "habit-forming room" which must be a first cousin to Auden's "habit-forming pain" in "September 1, 1939."

We turn now to the most impressive, as well as the most problematic, section of the book, called "Occasional Poems." These are poems in which Auden takes upon himself a public duty: to think seriously about historical crises of paramount importance, or to celebrate and memorialize certain towering figures whose deaths were symbolic because of the historical roles they played or the dilemmas in which they found themselves. The entire section is filled with the *immediacy* of historical pressures, and among those pressures is the unsolved problem of historical determinism and free will.

When Robert Frost, in his celebrated statement "The Figure a Poem Makes," asserted that the poem "ends in a clarification of life—not a great clarification, such as sects and cults are founded on, but in a momentary stay against confusion," we may recognize in his reference to "sects and cults" a mild dig at established religions, with which, as with the world, he seemed to have had a long-standing lover's quarrel. A great clarification is presumably a way of explaining not only the condition of the soul but that of fate itself, and of history, the relevance and importance of the fall of a sparrow or a great war, and the joys and hardships of a particular human life. It can thus confer huge resonance to any poem, and can lend to any particular person or situation a large and general perspective that saves him or it from eccentricity or solipsism. But from Frost's presumed point of view, the dangers of such "established religions" are those hardening orthodoxies that in various ways become rigidly fundamentalist and cruelly inhuman. Frost's espousal of fugitive insights, of the small rather than the great clarifications of life, bears a curious resemblance to something Turgenev once wrote: "Everything in the world, good and bad, comes to man not through his deserts, but in consequence of some as yet unknown but logical laws which I will not take upon myself to indicate, though I sometimes fancy I have a dim perception of them." Such laws have always lain behind the universe of literary works; but literary works are in general more orderly than the world and its workings. Yet writers have always attempted to hint at, when they do not actually state, those "logical laws" which govern human destiny, and of which art is merely a reflection. Blake sensed the compulsion to devise or discover such laws on his own terms when he declared in his *Jerusalem,* "I must create a system, or be enslaved by another's."

One of Blake's most devoted students, William Butler Yeats, may have been impelled by something like the same motive in creating the strange blend of psychological typology (a taste that Auden, too, exhibited), historical determinism, lunar and solar influence, and a theory of the soul's journey through this world and the next in what he called *A Vision.* For the ingredient of historical determinism, Yeats may have been indebted to Vico or Spengler, but as an account of historical process, determinism performs for him the same function as melioristic Darwinism performed for Tennyson and Hardy.

Mankind has desired virtually from the start to justify God's ways to man, or, in different terms, to discover a means of accepting not only the normal calamities of existence but the extraordinary ones as well by finding them to be part of some inexorable design. That desire, amounting almost to a need, voices itself in the cry of the psalmist—"Lord, how long shall the wicked, how long shall the wicked triumph?"—and in Jeremiah (upon whom Hopkins based a sonnet referred to earlier), who says, "Righteous art thou, O Lord, when I plead with thee; Yet let me talk with thee of thy judgments: Wherefore doth the way of the wicked prosper? Wherefore are all they happy that deal very treacherously?"

The problem of how to reconcile the concept of freedom of the will with a vaguely fatalistic notion of history was to beset Auden when he addressed himself to the task of writing the poem called "Spain 1937." This may be, of all Auden's poems, the most *engagé* or committed. He had, of course, called for "action" almost from the beginning, but what precisely was entailed in the action was rarely spelled out. There was a repudiation of the authority and hegemony of the past; there was a call for renovation, sometimes inward, sometimes Marxist, often a blend of social and personal change, but rarely programmatic. The "rider," the "farer," the "hearer" of the epilogue to *The Orators* leave behind the timid, feeble doubters who are unable to strike out for a new life; and we are meant to applaud this move to innovation. But we enjoy the luxury of leaving undefined the cost and nature of the alteration. There were many rousing poems of this obscure sort scattered about Auden's early work; and it must be added in fairness that in the poem under considera-tion Auden proposes no explicit program. The poem's political and moral stance is based on the simple distinction between fascism, which Auden finds repugnant, and anti-fascism (including communism), which, what-ever may be said against it, is to be preferred to its alternative.

In the great elegy on Yeats, Auden was famously to state that "poetry makes nothing happen," a comment that has been furiously debated and strangely misconstrued. Auden has been charged with, among other things, maintaining that poetry is irrelevant to events in the real world and can have no effect upon them even indirectly. But Auden himself was perfectly aware that this was not the case, for in May 1937 the poem "Spain 1937" was issued as a pamphlet, with all royalties going to Medical Aid for Spain; and quite apart from the question of whether or not the poem changed anyone's mind about the Spanish conflict, or played even the smallest part in anyone's decision to enlist against Franco, the very fact of the contribution of royalties to even so politically neutral a cause as Medical Aid signifies that, for all its irrelevance to the practical world of political action, poetry can make and has made something happen.

The text of this poem is possibly more in dispute than that of any other, and I shall address the poem in the form in which it appears in *Selected Poems* as being the most interesting and controversial that I am acquainted with, though it is worth adding that this version of the poem, dated by Edward Mendelson as April 1937, differs significantly from the version, also dated April 1937, which appears in *Early Auden,* also edited by Mendelson. Both versions, in turn, differ still more significantly from the greatly modified version that appeared, with highly protective and enigmatic emendations, in *Another Time.* Yet even what I hesitantly take to be the earliest version is full of unresolved mysteries.

Certainly the poem, in all its versions, is hortatory, embattled, and a call to action. It is built rhetorically around the historical trinity of past, present, and future, which recur as rhythmic refrains throughout the poem under the names of "Yesterday," "Today," and "Tomorrow," and in rhythmical, repetitive patterns that are little short of ecclesiastical.

> Yesterday all the past. The language of size
> Spreading to China along the trade-routes; the diffusion
>     Of counting-frames and the cromlech;
> Yesterday the shadow-reckoning in the sunny climates.
>
> Yesterday the assessment of insurance by cards,
> The divination of water; yesterday the invention
>     Of cartwheels and clocks, the taming of
> Horses. Yesterday the bustling world of the navigators.
>
> Yesterday the abolition of fairies and giants,
> The fortress like a motionless eagle eyeing the valley,
>     The chapel built in the forest;
> Yesterday the carving of angels and alarming gargoyles;
>
> The trial of heretics among the columns of stone;
> Yesterday the theological feuds in the taverns
>     And the miraculous cure at the fountain;
> Yesterday the Sabbath of witches; but today the struggle.
>
> Yesterday the installation of dynamos and turbines,
> The construction of railways in the colonial desert;

Yesterday the classic lecture
On the origins of Mankind. But today the struggle.

Yesterday the belief in the absolute value of Greek,
The fall of the curtain upon the death of the hero;
    Yesterday the prayer to the sunset
And the adoration of madmen. But today the struggle.

The liturgical quality of these stanzas derives from the fact that they
are syllabically irregular and therefore recall the prosodic freedom of,
for example, the Psalter. They present a catalogue, rich in anachronism,
of the follies and the triumphs of the past; and the past is viewed as fixed,
unchangeable, and, even in its most deplorable aspects, beyond the
range of moral judgment: it simply is there in all its patchwork variety
of fortunate and unfortunate events. The diffusion of learning is jumbled with the practice of witchcraft; the worship of God mixed with
the persecution of heretics; the worship of madmen such as the insane
Roman emperors who deified themselves is part of a history which
also includes the creation of tragic drama. The past is a bewildering
amalgam of ingredients, some of which include the greatest attainments
of what we prize as our "culture": the carving of angels on cathedrals, the
composing of tragedies, the creation of technological innovations and
reclamation of desert places. We, the living, are free to choose from the
riches and detritus of the past. But we must be aware that we ourselves
are the heirs of all the errors and accomplishments of that past, a past
which, if advanced by wisdom, was hindered by folly. In the immediate
instance we are given the occasion for such a choice as it is presented by
the 1937 political crisis in Spain. The past is there to encourage and to
warn.

As the poet whispers, startled among the pines,
Or, where the loose waterfall sings, compact, or upright
    On the crag by the leaning tower:
"O my vision. O send me the luck of the sailor."

And the investigator peers through his instruments
At the inhuman provinces, the virile bacillus
    Or enormous Jupiter finished:
"But the lives of my friends. I inquire. I inquire."

And the poor in their fireless lodgings, dropping the sheets
Of the evening paper: "Our day is our loss. O show us

> History the operator, the
> Organizer, Time the refreshing river."

And the nations combine each cry, invoking the life
That shapes the individual belly and orders
    The private nocturnal terror:
"Did you not found the city state of the sponge,

"Raise the vast military empires of the shark
And the tiger, establish the robin's plucky canton?
    Intervene. O descend as a dove or
A furious papa or a mild engineer, but descend."

Of these stanzas perhaps the first thing to be noticed is that they anticipate, or are the earliest manifestations of, details that will appear much later in Auden's illustrious career. He may indeed have tried to salvage them from a poem he thought he had dispensed with for good and all. The "investigator" who "peers through his instruments / At the inhuman provinces, the virile bacillus / Or enormous Jupiter finished" is an early incarnation of a scientist who will reappear ten years later in "In Praise of Limestone":

>                . . . these gamins,
> Pursuing the scientist down the tiled colonnade
> With such lively offers, rebuke his concern for Nature's
>     Remotest aspects . . .

And the lines of petition—"Intervene. O descend as a dove or / A furious papa or a mild engineer, but descend"—will later be enlarged to a passage of great irony in Herod's speech as he describes the suspicious religious enthusiasm of his time and place.

> Legislation is helpless against the wild prayer of longing that rises, day in, day out, from all these households under my protection: "O God, put away justice and truth for we cannot understand them and do not want them. Eternity would bore us dreadfully. Leave Thy heavens and come down to our earth of water-clocks and hedges. Become our uncle. Look after Baby, amuse Grandfather, escort Madam to the Opera, help Willy with his home-work, introduce Muriel to a handsome naval officer. Be interesting and weak like us, and we will love you as we love ourselves."

The stanzas just quoted concern the poet, placed in a setting both rural (of pines and waterfalls) and civic (the leaning tower—how precarious are the works of man), who depends, rather shakily, on his "vision," which is ironically to be distinguished from the literal vision of the scientist-investigator, who peers through either microscope or telescope at those natural phenomena, minute or enormous, that seem to have no relationship to the lives of his friends, since neither the course nor crisis of history affects the bacillus or Jupiter (which is finished in the sense that it is beyond either historical or evolutionary development). Then follows the prayer of the poor, which, like the prayers of poet and investigator, asks for revelation, though it is left very unclear to whom the prayer is addressed. History is called "the operator," but it is not to History itself that the prayer is spoken, History being, a little obscurely, some intermediary power, like "The Subalterns" of Thomas Hardy. Nor is Time prayed to, though it is characterized as "a refreshing river," presumably because of its cleansing and altering action. These three cries (all of them prayers) combine in an utterance of the nations, which pray for the commonality and address themselves, not without some mysteriousness, to "the life / That shapes the individual belly and orders / The private nocturnal terror." This addressee is the obscure power that governs the somatic and psychic life, which both know, in their different ways, the courses of evolutionary development. The "life" is the mysterious and inexorable power to which the nations turn for an answer to History's puzzle and predicament; and whatever else it may be, it seems absolute and deterministic, not easily to be distinguished from the Darwinian laws that so beleaguered Tennyson. Yet those laws, or that "life," could scarcely "descend as a dove or / A furious papa or a mild engineer" without gravely changing its nature. The power addressed in the prayers is, in any case, hard to identify.

> And the life, if it answers at all, replies from the heart
> And the eyes and the lungs, from the shops and squares of the
>   city
>      "O no, I am not the mover;
> Not to-day; not to you. To you, I'm the
>
> "Yes-man, the bar-companion, the easily duped:
> I am whatever you do. I am your vow to be
>      Good, your humorous story.
> I am your business voice. I am your marriage.

"What's your proposal? To build the just city? I will.
I agree. Or is it the suicide pact, the romantic
        Death? Very well, I accept, for
I am your choice, your decision. I am Spain."

Many have heard it on remote peninsulas,
On sleepy plains, in the aberrant fishermen's islands
        Or the corrupt heart of the city,
Have heard and migrated like gulls or the seeds of a flower.

They clung like burrs to the long expresses that lurch
Through the unjust lands, through the night, through the alpine
        tunnel;
        They floated over the oceans;
They walked the passes. All presented their lives.

The obscure "life" to which poet, scientist, the poor, and the nations
pray, which shapes our physical and mental existence, answers, if it
answers at all, "from the heart / And the eyes and the lungs, from the
shops and squares of the city." There is something peculiarly, not to say
insanely, circular here, and in which it appears at last that mankind is
praying to itself, and declaring, with suitable modesty, "O no, I am not
the mover." The city shops and squares, like the eyes and lungs, are
symbols of human evolution, and these subalterns answer for the "life"
hidden from view. Through their intermediary roles, "life" identifies itself
ambiguously with all mankind's dreams and weaknesses. The catalogue
that follows (the yes-man, the bar-companion, the easily duped, your
business voice, your marriage; the dream of building the just city or of the
suicide pact) resembles the dramatic jumble of progress and folly that
characterized the past of "Yesterday" at the opening of the poem. In this
case, however, it is clear that we cannot leave events to idle chance (if
there is such a thing) or to some extrahuman historical process. That "life"
is our "choice," our "decision." It is as if not history alone but the entire
biological and mental destiny of mankind were in our hands. And indeed
in the very next stanzas metaphors drawn from the realm of nature (the
migration of gulls and the dissemination of the seeds of flowers) make it
seem that the hidden power of "life" has taken a specific political stance.
Those who, in their inmost being, heard the voice, came at great risk, and
through dangers; "They clung like burrs to the long expresses that lurch /
Through the unjust lands . . . They floated over the oceans," behaving

like those natural movements that preserve plant or animal life by seasonal travel, indifferent to the hostility of the environment. The effect of this metaphor, drawn from natural forces, is to suggest that anyone who behaves indifferently, or negatively, in these circumstances, is perverse or unnatural. Those who heard the voice did not hesitate: "All presented their lives," for their lives were nothing more or less than the "life" that spoke to them through the organs of heart, eyes, and lungs.

> On that arid square, that fragment nipped off from hot
> Africa, soldered so crudely to inventive Europe;
> > On that tableland scored by rivers,
> Our thoughts have bodies, the menacing shapes of our fever
>
> Are precise and alive. For the fears which made us respond
> To the medicine ad. and the brochure of winter cruises
> > Have become invading battalions;
> And our faces, the institute-face, the chain-store, the ruin
>
> Are projecting their greed as the firing squad and the bomb.
> Madrid is the heart. Our moments of tenderness blossom
> > As the ambulance and the sandbag;
> Our hours of friendship into a people's army.

The "arid square" separated from Africa, "soldered" to Europe, is, of course, Spain itself. And it is said to be where "our thoughts have bodies; the menacing shapes of our fever / Are precise and alive." Those menacing shapes might be our nightmares, but more probably they are the manifestations of our illnesses, played out upon the Spanish stage. And if our thoughts have bodies, those bodies can be the sudden realization either that what we had before merely thought about had become real, or else that those engaged in the actual fighting are playing out our own inner turmoil. In any case, we are firmly accused in the following lines, which are about our lazy daydreams of escape, now attacking like "invading battalions." The lines which immediately follow are, in my view, the most repellent in the poem, though it must be added that Auden himself found them wanting and entirely eliminated the second and third stanzas just quoted when he produced the second version of the poem in April 1937, which appears in *Early Auden*. By the most facile kind of transformations, our faces (the sign of identity most easily assumed and falsified) project their greed, and smoothly become "the firing squad and the bomb." The cruelty of what happens in Spain is our own fault, and Auden's familiar equation of the ills of the individual with the ills of society is presented in its crudest and most doctrinaire form. "Madrid is the heart," and therefore the center of the contest of health and illness in our own hearts and bodies. But the next two and a half lines are the most deplorable. If our faces turn into firing squads, our moments of tenderness are transformed into benign instruments of safety and security, like the ambulance and the sandbag which stops bullets. And then, the climactic absurdity: "our hours of friendship" are transmogrified "into a people's army." The reason I find these lines so detestable is not unrelated to George Orwell's objections to other lines later in the poem. Generally speaking, this notion of comradely feeling rising up suddenly into a "people's army" has all the daydream laxity I associate with left-wing, dirty-footed bohemians in Greenwich Village lofts, joining in singing the popular loyalist songs to the accompaniment of somebody's semi-skilled guitar music, and passing the Gallo jug; and it also reminds me of the days when I was teaching at a women's college during the Soviet invasion of Hungary, which so outraged my students that they determined to make quilts and comforters for the oppressed victims of this brutal military action. Fighting a war is not joining a brotherhood of like-minded friends, and "hours of friendship" do not make a fighting force. It is the sheer *unreality* of these details of a poem that so fiercely desires to insist upon reality that makes such passages completely unpersuasive.

> To-morrow, perhaps the future. The research on fatigue
> And the movements of packers; the gradual exploration of all the
>      Octaves of radiation;
> To-morrow the enlarging of consciousness by diet and breathing.
>
> To-morrow the rediscovery of romantic love,
> The photographing of ravens; all the fun under
>      Liberty's masterful shadow;
> To-morrow the hour of the pageant-master and the musician,
>
> The beautiful roar of the chorus under the dome,
> To-morrow the exchanging of tips on the breeding of terriers,
>      The eager election of chairmen
> By the sudden forest of hands. But today the struggle.
>
> To-morrow for the young the poets exploding like bombs,
> The walks by the lake, the weeks of perfect communion;
>      To-morrow the bicycle races

Through the suburbs on summer evenings. But to-day the
struggle.

We are presented here with a utopian vision of a future, with all its
leisure for research as well as the most trifling social pleasure, all of them
to be attained once "the struggle of today" has been successfully completed. Later in his life, Auden had some particularly stern things to say
about utopians. In the essay "Dingley Dell and The Fleet" in *The Dyer's
Hand,* Auden declares,

> The psychological difference between the Arcadian dreamer and the
> Utopian dreamer is that the backward-looking Arcadian knows that
> his expulsion from Eden is an irrevocable fact and that his dream,
> therefore, is a wish-dream which cannot become real . . . The
> forward-looking Utopian, on the other hand, necessarily believes that
> his New Jerusalem is a dream that ought to be realized so that the
> actions by which it could be realized [for example, class struggle] are
> a necessary element in his dream; it must include images, that is to
> say, not only of New Jerusalem itself but also images of the Day of
> Judgment.

That "Day of Judgment" will present itself in the concluding stanzas of
this poem. But first it seems worth noting that one of Auden's most devoted
and eloquent admirers, Joseph Brodsky, has either consciously or unconsciously echoed an image from the lines just quoted, but with a significant
difference of intent. When Auden writes here of "The eager election of
chairmen / By the sudden forest of hands," he is envisioning a spontaneous
unanimity of political sympathy, a perfect and harmonious *civitas* built
along party lines. When Brodsky, in his poem called "Lagoon," writes of
"that nation where among / Forests of hands the tyrant of the State / Is
voted in, its only candidate," he is writing of the reflex-action, knee-jerk
response of party bureaucrats rubber-stamping the whims of a dictator.
It is also to be noticed that whereas bombs only a few stanzas earlier were
the projection of "greed," and symbols of our own ill will, in the new
Utopian society poets will explode like bombs for the pleasure and
edification of the young, an event which we may take to symbolize the
innocent effect of sudden and powerful surprise, in keeping with Auden's
earlier statement about poets: "They can amaze us like a thunderstorm."
    Finally we come to the stanzas that represent, in Auden's own phrase,
"the Day of Judgment."

To-day the deliberate increase in the chances of death,
The conscious acceptance of guilt in the necessary murder;
    To-day the expending of powers
On the flat ephemeral pamphlet and the boring meeting.

To-day the makeshift consolations: the shared cigarette,
The cards in the candlelit barn, and the scraping concert,
    The masculine jokes; to-day the
Fumbled and unsatisfactory embrace before hurting.

The stars are dead. The animals will not look.
We are left alone with our day, and the time is short, and
    History to the defeated
May say Alas but cannot help or pardon.

The first thing to be noted is that these stanzas are offered as a deliberate contrast to the utopian vision that preceded them, and are meant to indicate the cost at which that utopian vision is to be purchased. George Orwell read these last lines with celebrated and withering disgust, which he registered in an essay called "Inside the Whale" in *Such, Such Were the Joys*. He called this

> a sort of thumb-nail sketch of a day in the life of a "good party man." In the morning a couple of political murders, a ten minutes' interlude to stifle "bourgeois" remorse, then a hurried luncheon and a busy afternoon and evening chalking walls and distributing pamphlets . . . The Hitlers and Stalins find murder necessary, but they don't advertise their callousness, and they don't speak of it as murder; it is "liquidation," "elimination," or some other soothing phrase. Mr. Auden's brand of amoralism is only possible if you are the kind of person who is always somewhere else when the trigger is pulled.

The contempt here expressed is not altogether uninvited by the breezy tone of that line about "the conscious acceptance of guilt in the necessary murder," a tone which would satisfy the most bloodthirsty of tyrants. Auden was eventually to change that line and finally to scotch the entire poem, but in defense of that line, and against the attack on it by Orwell, he wrote in a letter to Monroe K. Spears,

> I was *not* excusing totalitarian crimes but only trying to say what, surely, every decent person thinks if he finds himself unable to adopt the absolute pacifist position. (1) To kill another human being is

always murder and should never be called anything else. (2) In a war, the members of two rival groups try to murder their opponents. (3) *If* there is such a thing as a just war, then murder can be necessary for the sake of "justice."

This seems to me as honorable and thoughtful a reply as could be made, and one that I have no difficulty accepting. But I would add, and Auden himself eventually must have felt the same, that the tone of these lines was very disturbing and possibly misleading.

There is a second crux or puzzle that presents itself in the final stanza, to which objection was raised by Auden himself. Edward Mendelson comments: "The critical literature on this stanza is divided between two factions. One of them includes Auden and perhaps no one else . . . he wrote of the final two lines: 'To say this is to equate goodness with success.' He added, 'It would have been bad enough if I had ever held this wicked doctrine, but that I should have stated it simply because it sounds to me rhetorically effective is quite inexcusable.'"

I have puzzled for a very long time about this response of Auden's to his own poem's concluding lines, and it has seemed to me almost more bewildering than anything in the poem itself. I have in due course come to a very hesitant and conjectural way of explaining to myself what Auden meant by his fierce condemnation of his own lines. The key to the puzzle, I currently believe, lies in the ambiguity of the meaning of "history." If we are permitted to view history as purely and severely nothing more than the facts and records of the past, it may be seen as a nonjudgmental, amoral, empirical document of the unalterable events of the past, from which all options have been surgically cut away and all choices removed. This is doubtless a narrow but certainly legitimate way of seeing history, and it is a way that makes perfectly plausible the last two lines of the poem. History, by this interpretation, only records what happened, for better or worse, and therefore can say alas, but cannot help or pardon. This view is not wicked, though it is limited.

Another view of history, however, is one that directs our attention not to the past but to the future; and it is the way we think of history when we say, "History will prove him right." This is a way of envisioning history as an uncompleted ordination of events, possibly predetermined, but possibly not. To the degree that this second view of history provides for the possibility of freedom of action and choice, to say of it that it cannot help or pardon the defeated is to deny the value and importance of any individual human action. And *this,* I think, is the implied doctrine that Auden regarded as pernicious. What I am claiming here is, admittedly, rather unlikely: it is nothing less than that Auden came to misunderstand his own poem because he had changed his views about history, and was, moreover, unaware of this. Shaky as my grounds may be, they are the only ones that at present can satisfactorily explain both the end of the poem and Auden's later reaction to it.

In September of 1939 the world was plunged into a catastrophe it had taken inadequate precautions to avoid. The First World War had been advertised as a crusade, and called, with scarcely believable optimism, "the war to end wars." Nearly twenty years later, a war far more widespread and all-consuming began. At the same time Sigmund Freud died. He had been for Auden from very early on an intellectual hero, with whom he may have quarreled from time to time but whom he reverenced and would have included in the prayer to "publish each healer." The problem that the poet faced in composing the commemorative elegy was to explain both to his readers and to himself why one person's death should be singled out when so much suffering, horror, and death was now the common human lot. And the poem opens on precisely this interrogatory note. But while "In Memory of Sigmund Freud" offers no direct answer, it presents a wonderful indirect one.

> For about him at the very end were still
> Those he had studied, the nervous and the nights,
>> And shades that still waited to enter
>> The bright circle of his recognition
>
> Turned elsewhere with their disappointment as he
> Was taken away from his old interest
>> To go back to the earth in London,
>> An important Jew who died in exile.

In these stanzas—the fifth and sixth—Freud is turned, quite brilliantly, and with restrained skill, into a classical hero, an Odysseus or Aeneas, who visits the Underworld in order to find out some arcane but necessary secret. He has visited among the "shades" and, while he lived, returned with valuable knowledge. But not with complete knowledge, for he was "taken away from his old interest" and died in exile, a Moses forbidden to enter the Promised Land. The poem shifts now into allegorical terms.

Only Hate was happy, hoping to augment
His practice now, and his shabby clientele
  Who think they can be cured by killing
  And covering the gardens with ashes.

They are still alive but in a world he changed
Simply by looking back with no false regrets;
  All that he did was to remember
  Like the old and be honest like children.

"Hate" in these lines is a sort of medical quack who will inherit Freud's leftover patients, who, having abandoned self-inquiry with the death of their honest physician, turn to aggression as in 1939 it is to be universally practiced. So by the end of the eighth stanza, in a poem of twenty, Auden has justified the singling out of one man for commemoration, and has gently characterized him as a culture hero, opposed to everything the world is now engaged in. His achievement is further characterized as nothing less than revolutionary.

No wonder the ancient cultures of conceit
In his technique of unsettlement foresaw
  The fall of princes, the collapse of
  Their lucrative patterns of frustration.

If he succeeded, why, the Generalised Life
Would become impossible, the monolith
  Of State be broken and prevented
  The co-operation of avengers.

There is here, quite suitably for a poem honoring one whose concern was always the psychic life of the individual, a deep suspicion of "the State," which deals with crowds, statistics, "the Generalised Life," a suspicion that would voice itself again in "September 1, 1939" as the unambiguous claim that "there is no such thing as the State."

Of course they called on God: but he went his way,
Down among the Lost People like Dante, down
  To the stinking fosse where the injured
  Lead the ugly life of the rejected.

And showed us what evil is: not as we thought
Deeds that must be punished, but our lack of faith,

> Our dishonest mood of denial,
> The concupiscence of the oppressor.

To the earlier suggestions of Odysseus and Aeneas the figure of Dante, another visitor to the Underworld, is added, another student of the buried life in search of instruction. Freud himself, if not quite an amateur archeologist, nevertheless collected specimens and fragments of ancient art, chiefly classical and Egyptian, with which he decorated his study, and which he identified with those retrieved fragments of the buried life of the psyche that are brought to light by the mechanism of psychoanalysis. But what may be most striking in these stanzas is the identification of evil with "our lack of faith." Doubtless this is a serviceable definition in terms of the individual whose neuroses arise from distrust in himself as well as others. But it also seems like a statement about our social ills and our collective malaise, and, as such, an anticipation of the famous claim, to be considered shortly, that "we must love one another or die."

There follows immediately the famous passage in which it is said of Freud that "To us he is no more a person / Now but a whole climate of opinion." Auden continues,

> He quietly surrounds all our habits of growth;
>      He extends, till the tired in even
>      The remotest most miserable duchy
>
> Have felt the change in their bones and are cheered,
> And the child unlucky in his little State,
>      Some hearth where freedom is excluded,
>      A hive whose honey is fear and worry,
>
> Feels calmer now and somehow assured of escape.

This strikes me as among the feebler and more sentimental claims the poem makes. In a world in which child abuse is rampant, there cannot be many "unlucky" children who are for a moment calmed and soothed by the fact that Freud lived, or that, in parts of society that have nothing to do with such children, his ideas are honored and his methods put into practice. The poem concludes,

>      . . . he would unite
> The unequal moieties fractured
> By our own well-meaning sense of justice,

Would restore to the larger the wit and will
The smaller possesses but can only use
> For arid disputes, would give back to
> The son the mother's richness of feeling.

But he would have us remember most of all
To be enthusiastic over the night
> Not only for the sense of wonder
> It alone has to offer, but also

Because it needs our love: for with sad eyes
Its delectable creatures look up and beg
> Us dumbly to ask them to follow;
> They are exiles who long for the future

That lies in our power. They too would rejoice
If allowed to serve enlightenment like him,
> Even to bear our cry of 'Judas,'
> As he did and all must bear who serve it.

Our rational voice is dumb: over a grave
The household of Impulse mourns one dearly loved.
> Sad is Eros, builder of cities,
> And weeping anarchic Aphrodite.

The "unequal moieties," or portions, are body and mind, body being the larger, but mind being the wittier. They were sundered by our own determination to let the mind tyrannize over the body, a tyranny which has led to illness; and Freud has given back to the body some of its lost authority, just as he returns to the son some of his mother's feminine feelings. (We may debate whether something "ambosexual" is being asserted here, or whether this is merely to say that there is always some feminine component in the male psyche.) He calls for our enthusiasm over the night, the realm of dreams, which he found so enormously fruitful—a realm populated by "delectable creatures" not, in the poem, immediately identified, and deliberately left mysterious. They long to be freed, and their liberation is entirely within our power to grant. Mute and dependent on us though they be, they would be branded as traitors if they were allowed to serve "the enlightenment," a brand that all its servants must bear, including, of course, Freud himself, vilified for his "obsession" with everything society had repressed. The poem closes by revealing the

identities of those "delectable creatures," who appear in an allegorical
tableau, for all the world like the sestet of Drayton's sonnet "Since there's
no help . . .":

> Now at the last gasp of Love's latest breath,
> When, his pulse failing, Passion speechless lies,
> When Faith is kneeling by his bed of death,
> And Innocence is closing up his eyes,
>> Now if thou wouldst, when all have given him over,
>> From Death to Life thou mightst him yet recover.

In proposing this parallel I intend nothing frivolous, nor do I wish to
suggest that Drayton's tone of coyness and sexual gambitry is to be found
anywhere in Auden's poem; but the two poems both close with what
amounts to the funerary postures of allegorical grief. Auden's delectable
creatures, Impulse, Eros, and Aphrodite, are also "exiles," as was Freud
himself, and, as it may be argued without too violent abuse of the word,
so was Auden. The poet had a very alert sense of what "exile" meant,
having written "Refugee Blues," "Roman Wall Blues," and "In Memory
of Ernst Toller," this last to commemorate the death by suicide in New
York of the German Expressionist playwright.

The tragic banishment into exile of Impulse, Eros, and Aphrodite
consorts perfectly with the doctrines not only of Freud himself but of Lane,
Layard, and Lawrence, along with others Auden revered, who champi-
oned these forces that society had so long and vigorously suppressed.
Auden's portrayal of these grieving figures in mourning at the death of
their primary champion and defender is perfectly consistent with Auden's
views throughout his poetry up to this time.

On January 28, 1939, William Butler Yeats died in the south of France,
and Auden got into high gear. His famous elegy is dated February 1939
in *Early Auden,* but he also contributed a prose piece called "The Public
v. the late Mr. William Butler Yeats," which appeared in the spring issue
of the *Partisan Review,* and in order to meet the journal's deadline he may
have had to complete the prose piece first. It was, in any case, composed
near enough to the elegy to serve as an interesting gloss upon it, for it
clearly deals with puzzles about the great Irish Nobel laureate that Auden
was trying to hold in balance in his own mind. The prose piece, in fact,
is deliberately and ostentatiously dialectical, composed of two speeches,
the first by a "Public Prosecutor" and the second by "the Counsel for the
Defense." The piece is clearly lighthearted, even wickedly so, though this

in no way diminishes the seriousness of its concern. For the object of its levity is not chiefly Yeats; it is instead the professional, legal sophistries of the two speakers, who obviously have more in mind the swaying of a gullible jury than arrival at anything so sacred as truth. Both lawyers revel in innuendo, the Prosecutor, for example, declaring, "We are here to judge, not a man, but his work. Upon the character of the deceased, therefore, his affectations of dress and manner, his inordinate personal vanity, traits which caused a fellow countryman and former friend to refer to him as 'the greatest literary fop in history,' I do not intend to dwell."

The Prosecutor indicts the dead man for failing to be a "great poet" on three grounds: he did not, according to the charge, exhibit a gift of a very high order for memorable language, or a profound understanding of the age in which he lived, or "a working knowledge of and sympathetic attitude towards the most progressive thought of his time." As to the first of these charges, the prosecutor rejoices in the smug conviction that not a member of the jury will be able to recall very many of Yeats's lines from memory. So much for the first charge. But this is fortified by the claim that a poet, who has a gift for language, would therefore of necessity be able to recognize that gift in others. And in contemptuous evidence against Yeats, the Prosecutor produces the Irish poet's edition of *The Oxford Book of Modern Verse*. Now this anthology was notorious for its eccentricity. It elevated Sturge Moore and Lionel Johnson to representations of prominence while at the same time denigrating, when not entirely eliminating, those modern poets who were challenging Yeats for prominence, and who had discovered voices of a modernity that decidedly jarred with his own.

In this connection, Frank Tuohy, in his biography of Yeats, has some enlightening comments.

> Yeats had a new project in hand: the editing of *The Oxford Book of Modern Verse*. The letters which Jon Stallworthy [author, among other works, of *Vision and Revision in Yeats's Last Poems,* editor of *Yeats: Last Poems, a Selection of Critical Essays,* and for some time poetry editor at Oxford University Press] has published concerning the choice of editor indicate clearly the confused attitude to modern poetry that prevailed in academic circles at the time. Lascelles Abercrombie, a Georgian poet, had done some work on the anthology, but had resigned rather than risk the enmity of his poetic colleagues. Dylan Thomas, just twenty, was the next candidate

proposed, and then Aldous Huxley, already in California. Yeats seemed an unlikely choice. Earlier he had told James Stephens: "I'm not interested in poetry, I'm only interested in what I'm trying to do myself . . . out of any ten poets who are pushed on you by literary ladies, nine are no good, and the tenth isn't much good." If he changed his mind, it was initially for financial reasons, though his interest was soon aroused. To carry out the work, he said, he needed a problem to solve. His problem would be: "How far do I like the Ezra, Eliot, Auden School and if not why not?" and, equally important, "Why do the younger generation like it so much?"

The strongest part of the Prosecutor's indictment concerns Yeats's profoundly conservative, nearly fascist, political allegiances, together with his cult of irrationality: "What are we to say of a man whose earliest writings attempted to revive a belief in fairies and whose favorite themes were legends of barbaric heroes with unpronounceable names, work which has been aptly and wittily described as Chaff about Bran?"

The Defense summarizes the indictment thus: "Take away the frills, and the argument of the prosecution is reduced to this: 'A great poet must give the right answers to the problems that perplex his generation. The deceased gave the wrong answers. Therefore the deceased was not a great poet.' Poetry in such a view is the filling up of a social quiz; to pass with honours the poet must score not less than 75%." Counsel does not lack for occasions to sneer at his opponent, but his task, in representing the Defense, must of necessity require positive and admiring statements about Yeats. He does so by defining poetic talent as the "power to make personal excitement socially available." This should interest us if for no other reason than that it immediately connects the private and public realms in a way Auden had been striving for from the first. He proceeds to observe:

> The later Wordsworth is not inferior to the earlier because the poet had altered his political opinions, but because he had ceased to feel and to think so strongly, a change which happens, alas, to most of us as we grow older. Now, when we turn to the deceased, we are confronted by the amazing spectacle of a man of great poetic talent, whose capacity for excitement not only remained with him to the end, but actually increased. In two hundred years when our children have made a different and, I hope, better social order [this counsel is detectably a socialist, as other passages make clear], and when our science has developed out of all recognition, who but a historian will

care a button whether the deceased was right about the Irish Question or wrong about the transmigration of souls? But because the excitement out of which his poems arose was genuine, they will still, unless I am very much mistaken, be capable of exciting others, different though their circumstances and beliefs may be from his.

There follows a passage distinctly socialist in its perspective, but claiming that Yeats, whatever his politics may have been, was always an enemy of injustice. And then we are directed to return to a consideration of the poems themselves.

From first to last they express a sustained protest against the social atomisation caused by industrialism, and both in their ideas and their language a constant struggle to overcome it. The fairies and heroes of the early work were an attempt to find through folk tradition a binding force for society; and the doctrine of Anima Mundi found in the later poems is the same thing in a more developed form, which has left purely local peculiarities behind, in favour of something that the deceased hoped was universal; in other words, he was looking for a world religion. A purely religious solution may be unworkable, but the search for it is, at least, the result of a true perception of a social evil. Again, the virtues that the deceased praised in the peasantry and aristocracy, and the vices he blamed in the commercial classes, were real virtues and vices. To create a united and just society where the former are fostered and the latter cured is the task of the politician, not the poet.

For art is a product of history, not a cause.

It needs perhaps first to be acknowledged with what skill, charm, deftness, and capacity to amuse Auden takes on the dual impersonations of these antagonists. And the exchange is apt in another way: nothing was so characteristic of Yeats's poetry as its own dialectical balances of antinomies, and Auden, too, is attempting to be, if not anything so exalted as judicial, then still a fair and thoughtful assessor of all the arguments and presuppositions that belong to the case. But if the prose piece is essentially lighthearted, the poem is not so at all. Second, the alacrity with which Auden undertook to commemorate a poet of such enormous stature (in 1940 Eliot, in the first annual Yeats lecture to the Friends of the Irish Academy at the Abbey Theater, was to call Yeats unequivocally "the greatest poet of our time") indicates that he was quite undaunted by the dimensions of his task, and the poem that he produced, though it generated much debate and in some ways displeased its author, proved in my view a richly deserved justification of his confidence. The poem is divided into three sections, which we may consider separately and in turn.

1

He disappeared in the dead of winter:
The brooks were frozen, the air-ports almost deserted,
And snow disfigured the public statues;
The mercury sank in the mouth of the dying day.
O all the instruments agree
The day of his death was a dark cold day.

Far from his illness
The wolves ran on through the evergreen forests,
The peasant river was untempted by the fashionable quays;
By mourning tongues
The death of the poet was kept from his poems.

But for him it was his last afternoon as himself,
An afternoon of nurses and rumours;
The provinces of his body revolted,
The squares of his mind were empty,
Silence invaded the suburbs,
The current of his feeling failed: he became his admirers.

Now he is scattered among a hundred cities
And wholly given over to unfamiliar affections;
To find his happiness in another kind of wood
And be punished under a foreign code of conscience.
The words of a dead man
Are modified in the guts of the living.

But in the importance and noise of to-morrow
When the brokers are roaring like beasts on the floor of the
    Bourse,
And the poor have the sufferings to which they are fairly
    accustomed,
And each in the cell of himself is almost convinced of his
    freedom;

A few thousand will think of this day
As one thinks of a day when one did something slightly unusual.

O all the instruments agree
The day of his death was a dark cold day.

Auden came to dislike the vocative "O" of the refrain, claiming that it was too Latinate; though it should immediately be added that it did not trouble him in any of the following poems: "O love, the interest itself in thoughtless heaven," "O for doors to be open and an invite with gilded edges," "O lurcher-loving collier, black as night," "O the valley in the summer where I and my John," "O what is that sound which so thrills the ear," "'O where are you going?' said reader to rider," "O where would those choleric boys," and "'O who can ever gaze his fill.'" What he substituted, mistakenly in my view, was the line "What instruments we have agree." This has the undesirable effect of suggesting that when at some future time our technological means are more sophisticated, it will perhaps be demonstrable that the day of the poet's death was *not* a dark cold day; but we are handicapped by our primitive and imperfect instruments. The original refrain was much to be preferred.

This is an elegy for a great poet. There are precedents for such compositions; the one that most immediately leaps to the mind is Milton's. But Edward King, though a poet, was not a great poet, so Auden may be said to have tackled a larger task than Milton. He must, however, have had his predecessor in mind, and "Lycidas" is so singular a poem, so celebrated for its manner, its artificiality, its ancient conventions, and above all its use of the pathetic fallacy, that, I suggest, Auden wished to allude to it by ironic variation. Whereas in "Lycidas" all of nature, and all manifestations of pagan divinity (Nature's personifications), mourn the death of the shepherd, this opening of the poem presents a nature both indifferent to Yeats's death and imitative of it. The day itself becomes a dying patient; coldness and illness and deformity pervade a scene which may be English but is certainly not the south of France, where Yeats actually died. The poem begins in remoteness, but a remoteness different from, though analogous to, Milton's. The wolves pursuing their own ends are not unlike the anonymous persons in "Musée des Beaux Arts," who are unconcerned about the deaths and martyrdoms that take place virtually in their midst. "The peasant river" and "the fashionable quays" are a kind of economic landscape, a tiny *paysage moralisé,* with no pathetic fallacy about them but merely the plausible suggestion that certain classes of people congregate in certain locations. The poet's death is then contrasted to the "life" of his poems, and mourning voices are unable to communicate that death to the poems, which are still alive and necessarily ignorant of his death.

He is then likened to a cityscape, much as Matthew Arnold had been, to the disgust of Jarrell. But the analogy of the human body to the body politic, while admirably suiting Auden's purpose in uniting the individual and society, was a very ancient one, and particularly employed in Shakespeare's plays and the poetry of the English Renaissance. When he dies, the metaphor of human body/body politic fails at the same time: he becomes his admirers in that he now exists only as they read and remember his words. But if he is no longer a city, "he is scattered among a hundred cities," in a way that I think is meant to remind us in the most delicate and indirect way of all the cities that laid claim to being the birthplace of Homer, and perhaps, as well, of Orpheus, the archetypal poet, whose body was rent asunder by maenads, his severed head floating down the Hebrus River and across the sea till it reached the island of Lesbos, the home of lyric poetry. "Another kind of wood" may gently remind us of Yeats's poem (and book) "In the Seven Woods," a part of Coole Park, Lady Gregory's estate, where Yeats was protected and happy. To "be punished under a foreign code of conscience" is in fact the potential fate of all artists and writers; they are judged by governments, by censorious boards and illiterate senators, by rabid and narrow moralists who simply assert the superiority of their morality to any other. Against their demagoguery a poet (such as Yeats's friend John Synge) is often powerless, and not least when he is dead. But he will have his way, though it may be slowly. For

> The words of a dead man
> Are modified in the guts of the living.

The first thing that needs to be said about these two lines is that they serve as a necessary gloss upon the later statement that "poetry makes nothing happen." Surely the words of the dead have an effect (often a cherished and benign effect) upon the living, and if this were not so, education itself would be almost impossible. But I would like to add that I never read these lines of Auden's without being reminded of some others by Eliot.

> What is woven in the councils of princes
> Is woven also in our veins, our brains,

Is woven like a pattern of living worms
In the guts of the women of Canterbury.

"To-morrow" will insist upon its importance and will make its noise, not only by the roaring of brokers "like beasts on the floor of the Bourse," but by the absolute significance of the immediate present conferred by newspapers, radio, and "all the instruments" that draw our attention to the present, unstable, ever-changing moment. These devices and our own self-concern divert us from recollections of the past. And "the poor," who, as the gospels remind us, are always with us, continue to suffer, unnoticed and unrelieved, are no more than a standardized background for the brokers and their frenzied concerns for the latest quotations. "And each in the cell of himself is almost convinced of his freedom": this prison imagery will be picked up in the poem's last lines, but it appears here as a sign of our psychological isolation, our distrust of others, our dangerous solipsism. The passage ends with touching and delicate understatement.

The second part of Auden's poem consists of ten lines.

2

You were silly like us: your gift survived it all;
The parish of rich women, physical decay,
Yourself; mad Ireland hurt you into poetry.
Now Ireland has her madness and her weather still,
For poetry makes nothing happen: it survives
In the valley of its saying where executives
Would never want to tamper; it flows south
From ranches of isolation and the busy griefs,
Raw towns that we believe and die in; it survives,
A way of happening, a mouth.

I must fuss a bit about Auden's unconventional punctuation, for its own sake in this passage, but also because in "September 1, 1939" the same eccentricities become crucial. Normal practice would reverse the punctuation marks in the first line. There should be a pause amounting almost to a full stop after "us," and since the second part of the line represents a neat syntactical balance to the first, a semicolon would be appropriate. At the same time, the line ought to end in a colon, for what follows that line is a little catalogue of all those things which the poet's "gift" was able to survive. We are able to make sense of his poem partly by disregarding his pointing.

It is possible to suspect that the opening accusation that Yeats was "silly" is adapted from the Prosecutor's indictment in Auden's *Partisan Review* piece, where, addressing the jury, that attorney declares, "You may say, he was young; youth is always romantic; its silliness is part of its charm." Here in the poem the force of the accusation is judicially modified by the claim that "you were silly like us," an acknowledgment that whoever is free of silliness has a right to cast the first stone. What Yeats's gift was able to survive turns out interestingly to be a catalogue of things both unfortunate ("physical decay") and at least superficially fortunate ("the parish of rich women" who acted as confidantes, patronesses, and supporters), including the faculty of being able to triumph over his own limitations as an individual to produce poems with universal relevance. He was, for instance, able to universalize and mythologize his unrequited passion for Maud Gonne. To be "hurt" into poetry does not suggest anything easy or facile, and it connects personal turmoil with public chaos and instability.

And now comes a little phrase that has raised as many hackles as nearly anything else Auden ever wrote. An awful lot of foolish commentary has been devoted to, mainly attacking, Auden's claim that "poetry makes nothing happen." It has been mocked as meaning nothing more or less than that poetry has no effect whatever on anyone or anything. Auden himself must have become annoyed by these misinterpretations and made a number of statements to indicate as much. In *New Year Letter*, dated January 1, 1940, he appears to repeat the claim made in his elegy when he writes,

> Art is not life and cannot be
> A midwife to society,
> For art is a *fait accompli.*

In a collection of apothegms titled "Squares and Oblongs," he states,

> Two theories of poetry. Poetry as a magical means for inducing desirable emotions and repelling undesirable emotions in oneself and others, or Poetry as a game of knowledge, a bringing to consciousness, by naming them, of emotions and their hidden relationships.
>
> The first view was held by the Greeks, and is now held by MGM, Agit-prop, and the collective public of the world. They are wrong.

In claiming that poetry makes nothing happen, Auden must have had in mind the extravagant claims made in poetry's behalf by some of the Romantics, by Shelley in particular. The extraordinary Shelleyan claim that

"poets are the unacknowledged legislators of the world" may have provoked him, though the ridiculous spectacle of most of the "protest poetry"
composed and read aloud from forum and platform during the Vietnam
era would only have confirmed his suspicions. Indeed, among other
apothegms in the same collection, Auden writes, "How glad I am that the
silliest remark ever made about poets, 'the unacknowledged legislators of
the world,' was made by a poet whose work I detest. Sounds more like
the secret police to me." (Of Shelley's claim Allen Tate once charmingly
remarked that it was one he could wholeheartedly accept, provided
enough emphasis were placed on "unacknowledged.") Auden also wrote,
in his commonplace book, *A Certain World,* "By all means let a poet, if
he wants to, write engagé poems, protesting against this or that political
evil or social injustice. But let him remember this. The only person who
will benefit from them is himself; they will enhance his literary reputation
among those who feel as he does. The evil or injustice, however, will
remain exactly what it would have been if he had kept his mouth shut."

What Auden actually meant, in positive rather than negative terms,
would, I should think, be what Northrop Frye asserts when he states in
*Anatomy of Criticism,* "Poetry is a disinterested use of words." And I
take this to echo what Keats wrote in a letter to Reynolds (February 3,
1818), "We hate poetry that has a palpable design upon us." And since
so much ink has been spilt and idiocy aired on this topic, there seem to
be two other texts that invite citation. One of these is by Yeats himself.
Though he wrote poetry of a very martial character for a very doubtful
cause indeed, he was equivocal, or thoughtful, enough to have had his
doubts about the efficacy of such poetry, and famously wrote, in answer
to a request, conveyed by Henry James from Edith Wharton, during the
First World War, "On Being Asked for a War Poem":

> I think it better that in times like these
> A poet's mouth be silent, for in truth
> We have no gift to set a statesman right;
> He has had enough of meddling who can please
> A young girl in the indolence of her youth,
> Or an old man upon a winter's night.

The second text to which I appeal, and which I am pleased to think of
from time to time as the definitive gloss on the problem stated in Auden's
line, is by Howard Nemerov. Its specific occasion was an advertisement
taken out by one Charles Rubenstein in the November 3, 1966, edition
of the *New York Times.* The ad's title was "An Open Letter to Yevgeny

Yevtushenko, Poet Extraordinary of Humanity," but Nemerov's title, "On Being Asked for a Peace Poem," clearly alludes to Yeats's poem, and Nemerov's poem wonderfully addresses Auden's statement.

> Here is Joe Blow the poet
> Sitting before the console of the giant instrument
> That mediates his spirit to the world.
> He flexes his fingers nervously,
> He ripples off a few scale passages
> (Shall I compare thee to a summer's day?)
> And resolutely readies himself to begin
> His poem about the War in Vietnam.
>
> This poem, he figures, is
> A sacred obligation; all by himself,
> Applying the immense leverage of art,
> He is about to stop a senseless war.
> So Homer stopped that dreadful thing at Troy
> By giving the troops the Iliad to read instead;
> So Wordsworth stopped the Revolution when
> He felt that Robespierre had gone too far;
> So Yevtushenko was invited in the *Times*
> To keep the Arabs out of Israel
> By smiting once again his mighty lyre.
> Joe smiles. He sees the Nobel Prize
> Already, and the reading of his poem
> Before the General Assembly, followed by
> His lecture to the Security Council
> About the Creative Process; probably
> Some bright producer would put it on TV.
> Poetry might suddenly be the in thing.
>
> Only trouble was, he didn't have
> A good first line, though he thought that for so great
> A theme it would be right to start with O,
> Something he would not normally have done,
>
> O
>
> And follow on by making some demands
> Of a strenuous sort upon the Muse

Polyhymnia of Sacred Song, that Lady
With the fierce gaze and implacable small smile.

To return to Auden's elegy, if poetry makes nothing happen, it nevertheless survives "in the valley of its saying," at which point the poet adopts a "submerged" river imagery; the "valley" is low, obscured from easy sight and access, as it has been in earlier Auden poems. In this one it means that poetry is no part of the discourse of the roaring brokers or other public, and largely urban, figures. The poetic language, avoiding the realm (and interest) of executives, "flows south," perhaps in the Lawrentian direction of the feelings and the sexual origins of life, away from "ranches of isolation and the busy griefs, / Raw towns that we believe and die in." For poetry, though it relates to, and deals with, the familiar world we all inhabit, and deals with it by means of an unestablished code of correspondences, nevertheless creates what Auden was later, in his Eliot lectures, to call a "Secondary World." Whereas the Primary World we all live in is contingent, inconclusive, shapeless, and beyond easy solution, Secondary Worlds are shapely, comprehensible, selective, and meaningful. This section of the poem ends with a repetition and an echo. The repetition is "it survives," which also appeared at the end of the fifth line; the echo is "a way of happening." If poetry "makes nothing happen," this is because it is instead "a way of happening," and we should attend to its activities instead of demanding that it precipitate activities in the Primary World. The last words of the section, "a mouth," refers to poetry simultaneously as a mode of human expression that characteristically employs words, and as the delta of the submerged river image that issues into the general sea.

The elegy's third section goes as follows:

3

Earth, receive an honoured guest;
William Yeats is laid to rest:
Let the Irish vessel lie
Emptied of its poetry.

Time that is intolerant
Of the brave and innocent,
And indifferent in a week
To a beautiful physique,

Worships language and forgives
Everyone by whom it lives;

Pardons cowardice, conceit,
Lays its honours at their feet.

Time that with this strange excuse
Pardoned Kipling and his views,
And will pardon Paul Claudel,
Pardons him for writing well.

In the nightmare of the dark
All the dogs of Europe bark,
And the living nations wait,
Each sequestered in its hate;

Intellectual disgrace
Stares from every human face,
And the seas of pity lie
Locked and frozen in each eye.

Follow, poet, follow right
To the bottom of the night,
With your unconstraining voice
Still persuade us to rejoice;

With the farming of a verse
Make a vineyard of the curse,
Sing of human unsuccess
In a rapture of distress;

In the deserts of the heart
Let the healing fountain start,
In the prison of his days
Teach the free man how to praise.

As everyone knows, Auden deleted the second, third, and fourth stanzas of this section, feeling perhaps uncomfortable about the claims he made for Kipling and Claudel, or at least embarrassed about the insoluble issues he had raised in naming them. I think the sacrifice of those lines was mistaken, and not least because they contain a clear allusion to some lines of Yeats's. These trochaic tetrameter quatrains, rhyming *aabb,* are modeled on, and are meant to recall, Blake's "The Tyger," as the seventh stanza makes abundantly clear: "Follow, poet, follow right / To the bottom of the night" is a very clear echo of "Tyger! Tyger! burning bright /

In the forests of the night." Yeats had been a student of Blake and an editor of some of his works, an enthusiasm he shared with Auden himself. The same meter (though with a different rhyme pattern) is used by Yeats in a poem called "In Memory of Eva Gore-Booth and Con Markiewicz." It is a poem concerned with the ravages of both politics (including war) and time, so it must have been either consciously or unconsciously a part of Auden's mind when he wrote his poem. It contains the lines

> The innocent and the beautiful
> Have no enemy but time,

which seem to anticipate Auden's reference to "the brave and innocent" towards whom Time is intolerant.

There are two other late poems by Yeats that, as Daniel Albright has valuably and generously pointed out to me, may have echoed in Auden's mind as he was composing this elegy. Of these the first may be recognized by the explicit rhyme of *voice-rejoice* in Yeats's "The Gyres."

> What matter? Out of cavern comes a voice,
> And all it knows is that one word 'Rejoice!'

The second and more telling one is "The Man and the Echo." The poem directly concerns the existential effect of a poet's words upon the world of politics and the lives of fellow humans. It is a poem filled with anguish and troubled doubts about what the Man's poems may have led others to do. It, too, rhymes *voice* with *rejoice,* and its debate about the value of poetry and the social role of the poet, all framed in rhymed tetrameter couplets, like this final section of Auden's poem, contains all the dialectical contrasts so characteristic of Yeats, and embodied in the paradoxes that conclude Auden's poem. In addition, as Professor Albright shrewdly observes, Auden enjoys a sly joke in conceiving Yeats as the Man and himself (echoing Yeats's form and matter) as the Echo. But in the course of making language the only survivable monument in a world of inevitable decay ("And for short time an endlesse moniment"), Auden deliberately courts controversy by raising the old problems of an author's views, as distinct from his "art." It may be perhaps that the factional differences that kept Guelf and Ghibelline at one another's throats are matters of utter indifference to us, and are not likely to determine our view of the stature of Dante. Nevertheless, we often find it extremely difficult to divorce an author's views—moral, political, social, religious—from the work that is held up for us to honor. When Auden writes of Time as pardoning "cowardice" and "conceit" in writers, we know he is telling a truth, though it may enrage us, and not least because he will seem to be offering an elitist argument that literary geniuses are entitled to behave any way they want, as long as they write nicely. It's clear that Auden thought a good deal about this moral puzzle. Oscar Wilde was one of those who maintained that there was a total divorce between the moral character of the artist and the work of art he produced. As late as 1968, in an essay about Kierkegaard called "A Knight of Doleful Countenance," which appears in *Forewords and Afterwords,* Auden wrote, "The question 'Is X a good or a bad poet?' and the question 'is X a good or bad husband?' have nothing to do with each other." And at one time Auden wrote some lines that he may have intended to introduce into the Yeats elegy, but which he salvaged for his *New Year Letter.*

> Great masters who have shown mankind
> An order it has yet to find,
> What if all pedants say of you
> As personalities be true?
> All the more honor to you then
> If, weaker than some other men,
> You had the courage that survives
> Soiled, shabby, egotistic lives,
> If poverty or ugliness,
> Ill-health or social unsuccess
> Hunted you out of life to play
> At living in another way.

This view of art as imaginative compensation for a damaged life is a not uncommon one. But this is the sort of thing that would turn the stomach of a good Marxist, or even a good socialist; yet strangely enough it is to be encountered in George Bernard Shaw. In his preface to *The Doctor's Dilemma,* Shaw wrote, "No man who is occupied in doing a very difficult thing, and doing it very well, ever loses his self-respect . . . The truth is, hardly any of us have ethical energy enough for more than one really inflexible point of honour . . . An actor, a painter, a composer, an author, may be as selfish as he likes without reproach from the public if only his art is superb; and he cannot fulfil this condition without sufficient effort and sacrifice to make him feel noble and martyred in spite of his selfishness." What may be thought of as the "opposite" point of view is reported by Peter Quennell in *The Sign of the Fish,* in a comment on

Robert Graves: "His view of life at that time was still intensely puritanical; and he even asserted that a 'bad man'—bad in the accepted moral sense—could scarcely hope to be a good artist."

The truth of the matter, for any given writer, may fall anywhere between these extremes. Kipling was often (though not always) a bland apologist for British imperialism, and nowhere more condescendingly than in his poem about "the White Man's Burden." Claudel was an archconservative, an anti-Dreyfusard, a pro-Franco apologist who would later write an ode to Pétain, and for a while a fervent admirer of Charles Maurras, the rabid anti-Semite and founder of *Action Française,* who was so much admired by T. S. Eliot. The "him" in the sixteenth line is, of course, Yeats. The image of intellectual disgrace staring "from every human face" may also have its source in Blake's "marks of weakness, marks of woe." But apart from any derivations, the claim of intellectual disgrace as detectable in "every" human face firmly indicts us all, and makes us as responsible as Kipling or Claudel. If our disgrace is so universal, where are we to turn for help or encouragement? The answer, I believe, is stated in the last three quatrains, addressed to a nameless and generic poet. It is poets who are to help us in our distress, those poets who were instructed by Yeats himself: "Irish poets, learn your trade, / Sing whatever is well made." Such training will permit them to "follow right / To the bottom of the night" of our distress and our misery without flinching. It was what allowed Yeats to journey in the footsteps of Dante himself:

> Such thought—such thought have I that hold it tight
> Till meditation master all its parts,
> Nothing can stay my glance
> Until that glance run in the world's despite
> To where the damned have howled away their hearts,
> And where the blessed dance . . .

All poets are now enjoined in the three final stanzas to take up the task laid down by Yeats, and presumably these poets include Auden. The task is not only difficult, given the historical crisis in the midst of which it must be undertaken, but filled with the paradoxes that fill the last lines. The challenge to "make a vineyard of the curse" is almost Biblical, but it also speaks to that redemptive function that poetry can perform by transmuting into art what in nature was tragically flawed and painful. It is even suggested that, like Moses in the desert, the poet can draw life-sustaining water from a rock; and the last two lines remind us that though we are time-bound and parochial in our knowledge and vision, we are freed by, if nothing else, poetry itself.

I turn now to a poem which means a great deal to me, as it does to many others, and which I admire despite the fact that I think it clearly, and perhaps seriously, flawed, though for different reasons from those of Auden himself. The poem is "September 1, 1939," and Auden famously toyed and fiddled with one line of it, "We must love one another or die," tinkered with it and recast it, and finally eliminated the entire stanza in which it had appeared. There may perhaps be something wrong with that line, but it seems to me of less consequence than some of the other problems the poem presents. Nevertheless, like many poetry readers of my generation, I continue to be enormously grateful for this poem. No one else took it upon him- or herself to address directly and unequivocally the massive crisis that was inevitably to become the Second World War. There were, in the course of time, some other war poets, some of them very good; but either they wrote about personal experience with warfare, or they wrote with a deliberate metaphoric distancing, as Eliot did in the quartets. Auden addressed the crisis at its inception, regarded it with historical perspective that in no way diluted the force and horror of its importance; made the crisis psychological, personal, and universal, and did so in passages that are nothing less than memorable. I feel sure that many others share with me the sense of the timely importance of this poem, and who cherish it as I do for a literary monument. I was just coming to military age when the war began. Like many another, I can remember all the anxiety those headlines generated. And Auden gave them wonderful voice. To say this is not to say that the faults in the poem are negligible. Auden brought to the writing of this poem a welter of concerns that had been obsessing him almost from the beginning of his career, and it must eventually have become clear to him that some of his most cherished notions would no longer be able to serve him. This poem was a critical experiment in which some weaknesses in his repertory of argument made themselves apparent.

> I sit in one of the dives
> On Fifty-Second Street
> Uncertain and afraid
> As the clever hopes expire

Of a low dishonest decade:
Waves of anger and fear
Circulate over the bright
And darkened lands of the earth,
Obsessing our private lives;
The unmentionable odour of death
Offends the September night.

Were it not that Joseph Brodsky, a poet and critic of undeniable skills, has worried the word "dives" in the first line, I would leave it alone. But we have been asked to consider that the word indicates Auden's newly acquired fascination with American, as opposed to British, diction. "He surely likes this word if only because he never used it before," says Brodsky, and goes on to suggest that Auden, in this word choice, is engaged in the business of trying to assimilate the newly adopted culture of America.

There is no question about the fact that throughout his career as a poet Auden toyed with British and American dictions regularly and inter-changeably. As an example of British diction, take, from "Talking to Myself,"

please, please, for His sake and mine, pay no attention
to my piteous *Don't*s, but bugger off quickly.

And, as an instance of American parlance, consider, from "Fleet Visit,"

They are not there because
But only just-in-case.

In addition, Robert Craft, in his Stravinsky memoirs (September 19, 1958), records Auden's announcement of his latest project: "He not only plans to translate one of Goethe's prose works, he says, but promises 'to make him sound like a limey.'" Nevertheless, it seems to me that in the case under consideration we would be better advised to consult *The WPA Guide to New York City*, which, as it happens, was first published in 1939, the very year of Auden's poem, and which has been usefully reissued with an introduction by William H. Whyte. The guide reports that "the long block of Fifty-second Street lying in the shadow of Rockefeller Center between Fifth and Sixth Avenues has won recent renown for its night clubs." It goes on to list the most glamorous, expensive, and exclusive of these: the Little Club, the Famous Door, the Onyx, Leon and Eddie's, the

Twenty-One Club, Tony's, and Hickory House. These places were the resorts of celebrities, reported on by such columnists as Walter Winchell and Leonard Lyons, and many a country bumpkin visited these establishments in the hopes of catching a glimpse of one or another famous personage. Auden's deliberate use of "one of the dives" is simply a way of indicating that he has not situated himself in one of these tourist traps. His bar is a humble one, and eminently suitable to his purposes in this poem. In *Memoirs of a Bastard Angel* Harold Norse reports:

> At the end of August [1939], when Wystan and Chester returned [from a trip to California], Chester and I spent our first night at a notorious gay bar called the Dizzy Club on West Fifty-second Street, three blocks from my room. The dive was the sex-addict's quick fix, packed to the rafters with college boys and working-class youths under twenty-five. From street level you stepped into a writhing mass of tight boys in tighter pants . . . Having decided that he must see it, we told Wystan, who loved sleazy dives, about the Dizzy Club. The next night, September 1, without our knowledge he went alone . . . He didn't go to pick up a boy; however, aware of the age difference and quite shy, he would have selected one of the two unused corner tables at the rear of the bar, which was usually deserted except for those too drunk to stand, from which he could observe boys kissing and groping under the bright lights, packed like sardines pickled in alcohol. There he would begin to write the most famous poem of the decade. Surely he jotted notes, or even the first stanzas, for it begins with the immediacy of composition in situ.

What does a man do, alone in a bar? And why is he there? One kind of answer Auden was himself to provide in the prose prologue to *The Age of Anxiety:* "When the historical process breaks down and armies organize with their embossed debates the ensuing void which they can never consecrate, when necessity is associated with horror and freedom with boredom, then it looks good to the bar business." Good enough; though perhaps we may consider some other factors. A bar is the normal resort of both the gregarious and the lonely, of those who want company and those who wish to be left alone, of those who ambiguously wish to enjoy solitude in the midst of strangers, and as a locus for sexual encounters. To this should be added the fact that Auden was an uncommonly heavy drinker. In his Stravinsky memoirs, Robert Craft, among other equally bibulous entries, reports on January 21, 1964:

New York. Auden for dinner. He drinks a jug of Gibsons before, a bottle of champagne during, a bottle (*sic*) of Cherry Heering (did he think it was Chianti?) after dinner. But the different qualities for delectation in these fluids hardly seem to count compared to their effect as a means of conveyance—supersonic jet, one would suppose—to the alcoholic Eden. Despite this liquid menu, he is not only unblurred, but also performs mental pirouettes for us, as if the alcohol were transformed into an intellectual ichor.

In any or all of these cases, the poet finds himself in a New York dive, "As the clever hopes expire / Of a low dishonest decade." The only "clever hope" must have been Neville Chamberlain's delusion that in sacrificing the Czechoslovakian Sudetenland to Hitler's demands at Munich in September of 1938, "peace in our time" had been secured. As for the chronology that made up the "low dishonest decade," it would include Japan's invasion of, first, Manchuria ('31) and then China ('32), Germany's withdrawal from the League of Nations and Hitler's ascendancy to the German chancellorship ('33), the murder of Engelbert Dollfuss, Austrian chancellor ('34), Italy's invasion of Ethiopia ('35), Germany's violation of the Locarno Pact by occupation of the Rhineland and the beginning of the Spanish Civil War ('36), Germany's repudiation of the Versailles Treaty and of German "war guilt" ('37), the invasion of Austria and Chamberlain's Munich capitulation ('38), and the dissolution of Czechoslovakia, the Hitler-Stalin ten-year nonaggression pact, and the German-Italian political and military alliance. *There*'s something to drink about.

We may assume that the "waves of anger and fear" are both literal airwaves, radio broadcasts, and the emotional vibrations of the world's masses. By the same token, "the bright / And darkened lands of the earth" are simultaneously those engulfed in literal blackouts and those, like America, not exposed to the same immediate dangers, and therefore lit at night; those lands lit by knowledge and freedom, as contrasted with benighted countries; and those which, at the moment the poet is writing, are exposed to daylight, as contrasted with the hemisphere engrossed in night. The waves "circulate" over these lands, "obsessing our private lives," and with these lines begins a strand of the poem that will run throughout its length and entangle Auden in the end. The fact of war forces a collectivity upon us, a collectivity we can neglect or ignore in times of normal peace. This invasion of our private lives by an outside,

irresistible, historical force reminds us of our necessary bond of brotherhood, but it is also potentially a peril to our individuality; and the
uneasiness with which the poet views this emotionally ambiguous situation haunts the whole poem. In fact, the uncertain center of the poem
may lie in a view resembling Trotsky's in "Literature and Revolution":
"the tragedy of our period lies in the conflict between the individual and
the collectivity, or in the conflict between two hostile collectivities in the
same individual." "The unmentionable odour of death" is a deliberately
dainty euphemism, conveying how something outside the bounds of
decent society has intruded vulgarly upon us. A sense of fastidiousness
has been violated, but this is not a prissy attitude. It is instead an
expression of the sort of shock effect presented by the discovery of the
corpse in detective fiction. (Auden has written thoughtfully and intelli-
gently about the structure of murder mysteries in his essay called "The
Guilty Vicarage," whose very title indicates the intrusion of evil into a
realm it is commonly thought not to inhabit.)

> Accurate scholarship can
> Unearth the whole offence
> From Luther until now
> That has driven a culture mad,
> Find what occurred at Linz,
> What huge imago made
> A psychopathic god:
> I and the public know
> What all schoolchildren learn,
> Those to whom evil is done
> Do evil in return.

The diagnostic skill implied in "accurate scholarship" is a twofold
aptitude: both historical and psychological. The investigation will perhaps
begin in the realm of history, but before the one-sentence stanza is
completed we will have followed the argument out of history, into
psychology, and then into the region of folk wisdom and fairy tales of the
Grimm variety. This movement is one from the "general" pattern of
history to the personal and "individual" pattern of psychology, and back
to the "general" one of folk tradition, thus oscillating between collectivity
and privacy.
        "Unearth" is a colloquialism for something as innocent as "reveal," but
it carries the murder-mystery overtones and criminal flavor that were

introduced by "the unmentionable odour of death." As for "the whole offence," it should be noted that "offence" recalls the odor that "offends" in the previous stanza, and as to what the offense consists of, Auden himself has supplied what may be the most concise comment in his introduction to the volume of medieval and Renaissance poets, in the five-volume sequence of *Poets of the English Language* he edited with Norman Holmes Pearson. In that introduction Auden contrasts the popular notion of the Renaissance as something that began promptly in 1450, and whose beginning consisted in the complete eclipse of what was known as medieval man, with a more accurate description, consisting of what he terms "the real revolutionary events":

> the publication of Luther's ninety-five Theses in 1517, of Machiavelli's *Prince* in 1513, and of Descartes' *Discours de la Méthode* in 1637. With these end five centuries of uninterrupted humanism, during which the energies of European civilization were directed towards making the whole of reality universally visible to the physical eye or to the eye of reason, on the assumption that there was no truth, however mysterious, that could not be objectified in an image or a syllogism. This humanistic period begins with Anselm's ontological proof of the existence of God; it receives a temporary check with the condemnation of Abelard through the efforts of St. Bernard; it is seriously challenged by the Cathar Movement with its doctrine that matter was incapable of salvation. But after the crusade against the Albigenses in 1226, the orthodoxy of Christian humanism remains secure until Luther.

Luther, of course, split Christianity irrevocably, but he did more than that. The Thirty Years War was a secular conflict as well as a religious one, and society was divided against itself in ways that were both novel and terrible. That war, and the doctrinal, political, and philosophical disputes from which it began, was the first flowering of the "offence." It is an offense that, the poet claims, "has driven a culture mad." The normal reading of "culture" here has assumed, not incorrectly, that it refers to Western civilization, and certainly the "low dishonest decade" was composed of vicious and criminal acts, as well as negligence and ruthless self-interest, that in retrospect would convict virtually everyone. Nevertheless, the stanza which cites an offense that begins with Luther, and continues to include "what occurred at Linz," seems to present a more localized indictment of a specifically German culture. It was in Germany that the crime began; it is in Germany that it is now recurring in its most virulent form. If this is what is being said, or even part of it, it becomes a painful acknowledgment for Auden, who was always partial to Nordic, including German, culture, and whose heroes included Goethe and, with deliberate allowance for his hateful personality, Wagner. When, after coming down from Oxford, he decided to spend some time on the continent, it was to Berlin he went, in explicit preference to Paris in particular and France in general. Initially he had said that since everyone else went to France, he was not going to do so; it seemed, at least to him, an act of independence. He had not been indifferent to French culture as a young man; his prose was studded with quotations from French poetry, and his own poems testified to an interest in writers as various as Rimbaud, Voltaire, Rousseau, Pascal, and Flaubert. But his strong identification with Nordic culture, fortified by the sagas he read as a boy, strengthened by his Icelandic ancestry, colored by his love for *Tristan* and the *Ring,* never flagged; and when he came, late in life, to purchase the only house he ever owned, it was in Kirchstetten, Austria, not far from the great operatic center of Vienna. With time, also, his impatience with French culture grew into an amusing foible that was not free from contempt. In the journal of his friendship with Stravinsky, Robert Craft reports Auden at a dinner (August 17, 1951) contending that "Italian and English are the languages of Heaven, 'Frog' the language of Hell . . . The 'Frogs' were expelled from heaven in the first place because they annoyed God by calling him *cher maître.*" (This speculation about the language of Heaven is not wholly frivolous; Milton believed it to be Hebrew, which would silence a good number of people.)

With "what occurred at Linz" we move directly into the psychoanalytic segment of the stanza, and to the childhood of Hitler, who, among other things, lost his father at an early age and had to supply one of his own manufacture: the "huge imago." He also was denied the chance to pursue his most cherished ambition—to be an artist and an architect. How much that thwarted desire may have turned him into a mechanism of revenge only "accurate scholarship" could determine. But child psychology, and our earliest experiences of pain and frustration, as well as the folk literature of our childhood, confirm the old rule of reciprocal hurt. It is nothing more or less than the absolute inversion of the Golden Rule: Do unto others as you would be done by. And the law of children, Auden suggests, quickly becomes the law of nations.

It may be worth remarking at this point that, though Auden's punctuation continues to be eccentric, it is clear that this poem consists of nine eleven-line stanzas, each of which is composed entirely of one sentence. On purely technical grounds, this formal precision is worthy of admiration: Auden's thought units correspond perfectly to his grammatical and syntactical forms. The third stanza is about "Exiled Thucydides," who, in his exile, bears comparison with Auden, who is also writing his poem in exile. In addition, Thucydides' great work, the *History of the Peloponnesian War,* is in its own right an example of the "accurate scholarship" mentioned in the second stanza. In this case it reveals all the familiar crimes of politics and warfare, the hypocrisy, the cant, the use of patriotism to mask open greed and crude ambition. The Greek historian is stunningly impartial in his indictments, and neither Athens, Sparta, nor any of their allies or dependents emerges as untainted by the corruptions of expedience and self-aggrandizement. Bernard Knox, in an essay on Thucydides' history, comments,

> The trouble with Athenian democracy was, of course, that it was direct democracy. The modern slogan we used to hear so often from our radical left, "All power to the people," exactly describes it. Policy was decided in an assembly which any citizen could attend; clever orators could play on passions and fears to promote their own interests, as Alcibiades did in his advocacy of the expedition to Sicily . . . When Thucydides puts into the mouth of Alcibiades at Sparta the statement that democracy is a system which is "generally recognized as absurd," one cannot help feeling, with all due allowance made for the slipperiness of Alcibiades and for the fact that he was addressing a Spartan audience, that Thucydides may have been to some extent in agreement.

That war was a long one, and though interrupted by a short interval of peace, it dragged on for twenty years. This poem is being written at the beginning of what is to be a world war, the duration of which no one can possibly foresee.

> Into this neutral air
> Where blind skyscrapers use
> Their full height to proclaim
> The strength of Collective Man,
> Each language pours its vain

> Competitive excuse:
> But who can live for long
> In an euphoric dream;
> Out of the mirror they stare,
> Imperialism's face
> And the international wrong.

This air is "neutral" because the poem is set in New York, outside the realm, for the moment, of conflict. It is also neutral because New York is a melting pot, where "Each language pours its vain / Competitive excuse," and the contentions of warfare to the east are apologies and excuses in this part of the West. It is "Collective Man" who has strength; and, by implication, such collective strength is the only thing that counts in wartime. The "blind" skyscrapers are impartial, neutral as the air, though they betoken the strength of massed men. But in the midst of this image of massive security (engendered not least, perhaps, by the shadow of Rockefeller Center), the truth of our predicament, the fragility of our euphoric dream, becomes apparent. We are back in the bar (having mentally journeyed through a large segment of history into the region of mental pathology and the reflections of Thucydides), where we see, reflected in the bar's mirror, our own faces, which turn out to be "Imperialism's face / And the international wrong." By this time Germany is no longer the only culprit; the collective guilt is epitomized in each individual face, though those faces have generalized themselves into "Imperialism's face."

> Faces along the bar
> Cling to their average day:
> The lights must never go out,
> The music must always play,
> All the conventions conspire
> To make this fort assume
> The furniture of home;
> Lest we should see where we are,
> Lost in a haunted wood,
> Children afraid of the night
> Who have never been happy or good.

The collective, imperial face is fractured by the bar mirror into the individual faces of the barflies who represent general American humanity, concerned to cling to the cherished dream that everything is all right; and the routines, though yesterday a terrible bore, today can seem a symbol of security. The stanza is wonderful in the metamorphoses of its metaphors. We begin in a bar which, in our need for self-protectiveness, becomes a fort against outside dangers; but because a fort is itself a symbol of defense against potential danger, it is immediately transformed into "home." But that "home" is also a disguise to keep us from seeing where we really are. And it turns out that, like Hansel and Gretel, we are still subject to all the irrational childhood terrors we thought we had escaped, and we are about to be sentenced to death by the world of grown-ups, who always have held the power. They are perhaps our superegos; they remind us that we have been naughty children; they confirm our sense of guilt. This amazing metaphoric "journey" takes us from adulthood right back to the Freudian and folkloristic origins of things, confirming the cited adage: "Those to whom evil is done / Do evil in return." The cycle is endless, Oedipal, an unavoidable "curse," like those of the generations both in Greek tragedy and in the Biblical curse of God who will visit "iniquity of the fathers upon the children unto the third and fourth generation." An unavoidable curse, I have just claimed, were it not, both in Greek tragedy and in the Bible, for the one redemptive factor, which is love. In *Oedipus at Colonos* that very word is singled out by the hero, before he is taken to the bosom of the gods, as that which makes all life, including the worst suffering, worthwhile. And the Bible, of course, makes its own celebrated case for love. And this poem is certainly about both the curse and the cure.

> The windiest militant trash
> Important Persons shout
> Is not so crude as our wish:
> What mad Nijinsky wrote
> About Diaghilev
> Is true of the normal heart;
> For the error bred in the bone
> Of each woman and each man
> Craves what it cannot have,
> Not universal love
> But to be loved alone.

For the most part, commentators have behaved as though the two final lines of this stanza were limpidly clear, and have breezily avoided comment on the (admittedly) puzzling and not wholly lucid diary of Nijinsky. But it must be pointed out that while "universal love" could be the sort of adulation offered by the multitudes to rock or movie stars, it could also be the love of God. At the same time, may not the monogamous love of marriage be the same as being "loved alone"? And if so, why can we not "have" it? It will be necessary to consult Nijinsky's difficult text to resolve these problems.

But before we do, we must begin with "The windiest militant trash / Important Persons shout . . ." This is, first of all, facile war propaganda, and secondly it is no less facile wish-fulfillment assertions of certain victory. In both cases, it is an infantile and irrational division of the moral world into the "good guys" and the "bad," a crudeness that lacks all human subtlety and reality, and which contradicts our own quiet and secret acknowledgment that the guilt for what has come to pass is to be seen in the face in the bar-room mirror.

Nijinsky's diary was composed in 1918–19, in St. Moritz, Switzerland, where he and his wife and daughter were awaiting the end of international hostilities, and not long before he was institutionalized. Both Freud and Jung had been consulted about his condition but were unable to help. The notion of keeping a diary was apparently his own. In the confusion of events and his hospitalization, the diary was lost; recovered in 1936, it was, according to his wishes, published shortly thereafter.

It is an excruciating text to read. Nijinsky, now a husband and father, is violently guilt-ridden, especially about his homosexual past. He writes,

> I did not like Diaghilev, but lived with him; I hated Diaghilev from the first days of our acquaintance, because I knew his power. I was poor and 65 rubles [the monthly salary for dancers at the Imperial Theater, after they graduated from the Imperial School] were not enough to keep my mother and myself from starvation. We rented a flat with two rooms for 35 or 37 rubles a month . . . Ivor introduced me to Diaghilev, who asked me to come to the Hotel Europe, where he lived. I disliked him for his too self-assured voice, but went to seek my luck. I found my luck. At once I allowed him to make love to me. I trembled like a leaf. I hated him, but pretended, because I knew that my mother and I would die of hunger otherwise. I understood Diaghilev from the first moment and pretended to agree with him at once. One had to live, and therefore it was all the same to me what sort of sacrifice I had to make. I worked hard at my dancing and was

always tired. But I pretended not to be tired at all in order that Diaghilev should not be bored with me. I know what he felt, he loved boys and therefore could not understand me.

What is, of course, important here is not whether this is an accurate account of Nijinsky's feelings at the time of his initial encounter with Diaghilev, but what he felt about it (now a husband and father) at the time of writing. Clearly he views himself as a powerless martyr, monstrously taken advantage of, and money is made the sole and exclusive cause of what appears to be uncomplicated prostitution. So strongly does this view of himself as martyr figure throughout the diary that Nijinsky has no trouble (and no embarrassment) about identifying himself with Christ. This identification, however, consorts awkwardly with his no less consistent feeling of guilt, and his text oscillates constantly between these opposing attitudes.

In order to understand the brief passage to which Auden's poem alludes, I think it may be useful to cite a few earlier passages that seem to lead up to it.

> People will say that Nijinsky pretends to be mad on account of his bad deeds. Bad deeds are terrible and I hate them, and do not want to commit any. I made mistakes before because I did not understand God.

> I smell out the poor like a dog scenting out game. I smell very well. I will find the poor without their advertisements. I need no advertisements. I will go by scent. I will not be mistaken. I will not give money to the poor, I will give them life. Life is not poverty. Poverty is not life. I want life. I want love.

> I want love and therefore want to throw aside all sordid money—dirt. I will give life to the poor.

> The eagle is a bird of God and one must not kill tsars, emperors, and kings. I like tsars and the aristocrats, but their deeds are not always good deeds. I will give them a good example, by not destroying them.

> Diaghilev is a terrible man. I do not like terrible men, but I will not harm them. I do not want them to be killed. They are eagles.

> The Tsar is a man like the rest of us, and therefore I did not want his death. I am sorry for the Tsar.

> I often state, but am not always understood, that we are all equal.
> By that I mean that one should love everyone.
>
> I know that Clemenceau is honest; he is the policy of France. He is a
> hard-working man, but he was mistaken when he sent France to her
> death. He is a man who seeks goodness, a child with a tremendous
> brain. Some politicians are hypocrites like Diaghilev, who does not
> want universal love, but to be loved alone. I want universal love.

The first thing worth noting is that the last of these passages makes the
same transition from politics to love that Auden makes in the stanza under
discussion. The second thing that needs to be noted is that the assembled
passages tend to define what Nijinsky means by "universal love." It is the
love Biblically enjoined upon all men and women to love their neighbors
as themselves. This love, espoused here by Nijinsky, is, according to him,
rejected by Diaghilev, who, as virtually the entire diary insists, is vain,
selfish, self-aggrandizing, and tyrannical.

But whether or not such accusations against Diaghilev are valid, they
are in any case, Auden asserts, "true of the normal heart." Diaghilev, by
this equation, is simply a symbol for our own habitual self-concern: an
"error bred in the bone / Of each woman and each man." And we are all
indicted by the words of a madman who is also a gifted artist suffering
from the guilt that has erupted in Europe into a world war.

"September 1, 1939" continues:

> From the conservative dark
> Into the ethical life
> The dense commuters come,
> Repeating their morning vow;
> "I *will* be true to the wife,
> I'll concentrate more on my work,"
> And helpless governors wake
> To resume their compulsory game:
> Who can release them now,
> Who can reach the deaf,
> Who can speak for the dumb?

In the *Selected Poems,* Edward Mendelson has emended the punctuation
at the end of the penultimate line; for the period that appears there in the
first American edition of *Another Time* he has supplied the more intelligible comma. I have retained the original punctuation, not because I think

it is right, or even because I think it was what Auden intended, but because
we will shortly come to a serious crux in the poem in which punctuation
plays an important part, and it is useful to notice how promiscuous and
haphazard are Auden's ways with these pointings.

The stanza moves between the poles of sleep and waking, though that
movement is also a birth of sorts. We move from the "conservative dark"
of the womb into the "ethical life," and the realm of sleep is a kind of
infancy. Moreover, we are "commuters" because we return to sleep, as
we shall also return to oblivion after our lives are done. On the literal
level, of course, Auden is writing about those people who live in the
suburbs of New York and have to get up before dawn to commute into
the city for work. They begin the day with the daily resolutions, prisoners
not only of their work but of lives of moral rectitude they must themselves
police. If they are the victims of compulsions, so are those who govern
them, and whom we commonly suppose to be free. All of society (or, as
the very next stanza will state, both "the citizen" and "the police") are
compelled, either by acquired and life-denying habits, or by the strenuous
and undeniable forces of history itself. The stanza, in a way that remains
irritatingly unclear, seems to present a deterministic picture of the human
predicament, though the series of interrogatories with which the stanza
closes suggests that some "release" is possible.

> All I have is a voice
> To undo the folded lie,
> The romantic lie in the brain
> Of the sensual man-in-the-street
> And the lie of Authority
> Whose buildings grope the sky:
> There is no such thing as the State
> And no one exists alone;
> Hunger allows no choice
> To the citizen or the police;
> We must love one another or die.

The first thing that needs to be observed is that while each stanza in this
poem is composed of a complete sentence, and while each of these
sentences has the grammatical independence of a paragraph, so that the
sequence is not a logical one, the stanza now under consideration depends
directly upon the previous stanza. It begins by providing a tentative
answer to the three questions that were just asked: "Who can release them

now, / Who can reach the deaf. / Who can speak for the dumb?" The poet has only his voice with which to hope to cure these handicapped and disabled fellow humans, and that voice must be used to disabuse them of all the habitual tricks and rationalizations they have cherished to get through their tormented lives. There are two such deceptions or rationalizations: "The romantic lie in the brain / Of the sensual man-in-the-street" is the first of these. The second line is an adaptation of the French expression *l'homme moyen sensuel,* your average self-satisfied sensualist, who rejoices in the conviction that if all his daily needs are met, there are no problems. The second lie is "the lie of Authority." We are encountering again the double standard of the previous stanza, the putative division between the "commuters" and the "governors." Here, the sensual man-in-the-street is the unembarrassed solipsist, who thinks only of himself. "Authority," however, is not merely some class of power or wealth but what we encountered earlier as "Collective Man," whose strength was proclaimed by the "blind skyscrapers" of New York. And here again, Authority's "buildings grope the sky." I suggest, other opinions to the contrary notwithstanding, the "groping" here is a groping for answers; and the strength of Authority's buildings will, in search of those answers, be no more effective than the solitary inquiries of the ordinary man.

And now I must be fussy about punctuation, about which Auden himself seems so cavalier. Every stanza in this poem contains, rather oddly, a colon. For the most part, we can read the poem without being disturbed by this, and assume that Auden is using the mark in a vague, unorthodox way, to indicate some kind of major pause. Indeed, it could fairly well be argued that he uses the colon and semicolon virtually interchangeably. We find ourselves, in any case, resisting the temptation to construe the mark as indicating (its normal use) that what follows is precisely an illustration of what had just come before. There is, however, in this stanza, a dangerous temptation to suppose that for once Auden is using the colon in the traditional way, and that what follows after it is an example of the "lies" that were described in the early part of the stanza. But this is not the case. What follows after the colon is the truth that the poet, armed only with his "voice," has taken upon himself to reveal. It is a double secret, enraging both to the individual and to the corporate group of "Collective Man" which constitutes "Authority." "There is no such thing as the State" is not merely an attack upon the likes of Hitler and Stalin, and the superstates over which they tyrannize; it declares that government itself is no more than a useful fiction, one which ought to allow us as much independence and freedom from itself as possible. But there is a balancing corollary which is, at the same time, the inverse of this proposition: it is that "no one exists alone." And this means that we are, of necessity, bound to one another, not wholly independent, and thus part of the fictive State. Both those with authority and those without it are caught in this dilemma, both citizens and police.

We come now to the line Auden troubled himself so much about. The story of his discontent with "We must love one another or die" is well known, but we would do well to consider why he wrote the line in the first place. It is very clearly the bald and unambiguous statement of a doctrine he had maintained and employed in many poems from quite early in his career. It was a doctrine he had learned from some of his intellectual heroes, including Lane and Lawrence, Freud and Groddeck: it was the doctrine of love as a curative force, and Auden had come to enlarge it to include the cure for social ills and society as a whole, as well as the psychopathologies of the individual. In addition to this, it is worth adding that, however unconsciously this may have played a part in Auden's thinking, he knew perfectly well that the cure of love is a familiar and orthodox Christian doctrine as well. So the claim that "we must love one another or die" had behind it a certain history and authority.

Having said that, one must also consider the meaning of the line in the context of the poem, and, situated where it is, it is, alas, nearly ludicrous. It invites us to envision the poet, interposing himself between the advancing Panzer divisions and the retreating Polish troops and bearing in either hand a volume of Freud and a Bible, and urging in flawless German, "You need only read these, and all your little differences will be quickly resolved." To voice such sanguine hopes on the very day of the beginning of a world war, must, on reflection, have appeared naive at best.

His awkward (and temporary) solution was to declare, in 1964, "That's a damn lie! We must die anyway." At first he dropped the entire stanza; then later, under urging by the anthologist Oscar Williams, he allowed it to be reintroduced, but with the offending line now changed to "We must love one another and die." The change is deplorable, particularly since Auden, in making it, had lost all sense of its dramatic context. While it is undeniable that all mortals must die, there is a world of difference between dying at peace and "full of days" in bed, as contrasted with being killed in the mindless carnage of war. And the dying this poem is concerned with—"the unmentionable odour of death," "the international wrong"— these are of the second kind and not the first, and it is foolish to pretend they are the same. If we must all die, of what importance can the doctrine of love be? If it is not a cure, what good will it do, and why *must* we embrace it? Auden provides no answer to these questions, and seems awkwardly to believe he has bypassed them by the simple expedient of changing "or" to "and."

But the original version of the line, while admittedly feeble as practical advice in the context of international conflict, still has about it a kind of sense that the second version lacks. The original proposes the alternatives of "love" or "death" that we are familiar with, and not just from Freud and the Bible. In *Henry V,* just before Agincourt, a common soldier remarks: "I am afeared there are few die well that die in battle; for how can they charitably dispose of anything when blood is their argument?" That soldier's "charitably" is the adverbial form of agape, in which, along with Eros, Auden had so long placed his confidence. And in battle these possibly redemptive forces are banished. So, having first struck out the entire stanza and then altered unsatisfactorily the offending line, the poet eventually struck the entire poem from his corpus, and in doing so suggested that all his dissatisfaction lay in this crux. But I believe that this was another case of disingenuousness on his part; for, while admitting there are clear problems with the offending line, I believe that there are still more serious problems in the final stanza.

> Defenceless under the night
> Our world in stupor lies;
> Yet, dotted everywhere,
> Ironic points of light
> Flash out wherever the Just
> Exchange their messages:
> May I, composed like them
> Of Eros and of dust,
> Beleaguered by the same
> Negation and despair,
> Show an affirming flame.

The night that encompasses the final stanza is the one in which "ignorant armies" clash in Matthew Arnold's poem. It is a world of violence and irrationality, the opposite and enemy of all civility and order. In the thick of this darkness appear what Auden nervously calls "ironic points of light." What is chiefly unnerving about the adjective is that it is left unclear at what or whom the irony is directed—and we are not without permission to believe that it is self-directed. The irony they would exhibit would represent the manifest *impotence* of those who were wise enough to see the folly of warfare and the rising, eager barbarity of the world. These points of light (one shrinks to think that Peggy Noonan borrowed them for campaign speeches of George Bush) are the signals and semaphores of "the Just." Not easy, of course, to know who these are, especially in a world now plunged into brutal conflict. Soldiers at war have no time to be "just," and their political leaders are full of the "windiest militant trash" that has nothing whatever to do with justice. In a time of war, only those so fortunately situated as to be comfortably removed from the issues and strategies can venture to be objective enough to attempt to be "just." These persons are privileged, unexposed, sanitized. And in time of war there are very few such persons. This is one of the reasons their signals are flashed to such little effect: they are talking only to one another; in the encompassing dark, they cast scarcely any light. They are, if powerless, nonetheless an elite. It may be that they are the elite that will salvage or, even better, preserve what is best of civilization when the conflict is over. But for the moment, they are few, powerless, and talk only among themselves. No wonder they should be "beleaguered by . . . negation and despair."

Something curious and unexpected has happened to Auden in this bar, or, in any case, in this poem. He began by feeling the mixed recognition of fellowship with others and the apprehension of having his privacy and individuality invaded by the overpowering forces of history. Throughout the poem there is a dramatic, though unreconciled, oscillation between the corporate, or social, and the individual, or private, life. The confrontation of these attitudes is finally and unequivocally stated in the paradoxical, self-contradictory lines "There is no such thing as the State / And no one exists alone." The poem, therefore, like others before it, employs the ambiguous situation of humans as being at once individuals and part of a social fabric, with advantages and disadvantages to either or both roles. But in the last stanza, a new social entity is introduced: in addition to being either private persons or members of a society, we may be, if fortunately endowed, members of an insulated elite, who view the historical calamity not quite with immunity, but with the dispassion that makes them "the Just." It is with this select group that Auden identifies himself. And it must finally be noted that, as he has done in a number of other poems, this one ends in a prayer: "May I . . . show an affirming flame." The prayer is that the poet may count himself among the hopes and resources of humanity. It is a feeble prayer, and we are not invited to inquire about who is being addressed. But it is, after all, a prayer, and given the "negation and despair," prayer may not be entirely out of place. It would, in fact, come to take a greater place in Auden's poetry after this. For I believe that with this poem, or, at least, with this book, Auden begins to take his leave of his faith in the practical utility of love as a social cure, and as represented by the Eros that is both a sexual emancipator and a social reformer. In any case, *Another Time* concludes with the symbolic triumph of Eros in an epithalamion which unites Giuseppe Borgese and Elisabeth Mann, an Italian and a German, an anti-fascist and an anti-Nazi, whose union is meant specifically to oppose the sinister union of the Axis powers, and whose marriage is envisioned as a reconciliation, through the agency of love, of all the warring chaos of the world.

# IV. A Sort of Practical Holiday: *Letter to Lord Byron*

I have argued that a fairly clear and identifiable set of attitudes and preoccupations runs through and effectively unites *On This Island* and *Another Time*. These complex impulses bind the books together, not so much in a natural sequence but as segments of a single thrust or poetic current. It is all the more surprising, in view of this vigorous, imaginative drive, to notice that in fact it was interrupted, and that squarely between the two volumes, in the months of July through October of 1936, Auden wrote a wholly different kind of poetry. It took the shape of his *Letter to Lord Byron* and was published in the collaborative volume *Letters from Iceland,* which he wrote with Louis MacNeice.

So different is this major long poem from the poetry that immediately preceded and followed it as to astonish almost any reader. And what may be most impressive in the final analysis is Auden's extraordinary capacity to pick up the strain of anxiety, the themes of private and public concern, where he had laid them down before embarking on this holiday interlude.

The Iceland trip was a sort of practical holiday: the chance to visit a wholly different and alien landscape with which Auden identified his Nordic ancestors, and the chance to write a "travel book," which had a chance at a wide popular sale (as distinguished from the audience for serious poetry). Auden's choice of Byron to be the recipient of his "letter" is worth a moment's thought, not least because it concerns the reputation of Byron as it has evolved over the years.

It is difficult for the modern reader to realize with what reverence Byron was once internationally regarded. His works, immediately following publication, were translated into all the major European languages, *The Bride of Abydos* into ten, *Cain* into nine. Goethe declared, "The English may think of Byron as they please, but this is certain: that they show no poet who is to be compared with him." His influence extended far enough to find its place in the works of Victor Hugo, Lamartine, and Alfred de Musset in France; of Börne, Müller, and Heine in Germany; Leopardi and

Giusti in Italy; Pushkin and Lermontov among the Russians; Mickiewicz and Slowacki among the Poles. Moreover, this huge and widespread adulation was based on a segment of Byron's poetry that is almost entirely neglected today: the Oriental tales and *Childe Harold*. When, for example, in 1989 Paul Muldoon came to make his selection of Byron's poetry for the volume called *The Essential Byron*, he included none of the poetry that had so much stirred Byron's contemporaries, and focused instead on what we may call "the modern Byron." Auden himself has defined this "modern Byron" for us. "Take away the poems he wrote in [the mock-heroic ottava-rima] style and meter, *Beppo, The Vision of Judgment, Don Juan*, and what is left of lasting value? A few lyrics, though none of them as good as the best of Moore's, two adequate satires though inferior to Dryden or Pope, 'Darkness,' a fine piece of blank verse marred by some false sentiment, a few charming occasional pieces, half a dozen stanzas from *Childe Harold*, half a dozen lines from *Cain*, and that is all."

What so greatly astonished and attracted the readers of Byron's day involved the kind of heroic, defiant, wicked, and Promethean pride he describes as belonging to the hero of his narrative poem *Lara*.

> Too high for common selfishness, he could
> At times resign his own for others' good,
> But not in pity—not because he ought,
> But in some strange perversity of thought,
> That swayed him onward with a secret pride
> To do what few or none could do beside;
> And this same impulse would, in tempting time,
> Mislead his spirit equally to crime;
> So much he soared beyond, or sank beneath,
> The men with whom he felt condemned to breathe
> And longed by good or ill to separate
> Himself from all who shared his mortal state.

This kind of pride, contemptuous both of the moral conventions of society and of ordinary Christianity, expresses itself as well in Byron's play *Manfred*, of which H. G. Schenk in *The Mind of the European Romantics* writes thus:

> Here, clearly, one can see the repudiation of the traditional idea of Christ sitting in judgment, and its substitution by the judgment of the sinner's own mind and conscience. Christ's redemption of sin,

the power to forgive sinners, and consequently the sacrament of penance, consisting of the tripartite process of confession, contrition and absolution by the priest, have ceased to be the realities of faith, and yet Manfred feels an irrepressible urge for expiation. Unable to repent, his sensitive conscience—elsewhere Byron calls man's conscience "the Oracle of God"—refuses him self-absolution, and it is for this reason that Manfred insists that he has been and will hereafter be "his own destroyer."

Byron's contemporaries had no difficulty identifying him with his own protagonists, a facility which some facts about his life encouraged, and we can see in this association something like the beginnings of the concept of the *poète maudit*. A delicious *frisson* seemed to be engendered by men so solitary, independent, doomed (and not least if they were also exceptionally handsome aristocrats), but Byron's doomed heroes were themselves the heirs to a frame of mind that had already been expressed (and thus their way prepared for) by Rousseau's *Les Rêveries d'un promeneur solitaire* and Goethe's *Die Leiden des jungen Werthers*. This frame of mind is briefly characterized by Schenk in his description of another of Byron's forerunners, Chateaubriand, and his novel *René*.

All the characteristics of unredeemed *Weltschmerz* are present in René: the introspection, the misanthropy and quest for solitude, the unbounded craving of the soul as well as the perpetual dissatisfaction, the *ennui* and resultant melancholy, the disgust with life and the attempted flight—past civilization, to nature, to the New World, or even to suicide.

So whatever it was that prompted Auden's choice of addressee for his verse letter, it was not Goethe's Byron that he had in mind. In a prose letter to his wife, Erika Mann, contained in *Letters from Iceland,* he wrote, "I brought a Byron with me to Iceland, and I suddenly thought I might write him a chatty letter in light verse about anything I could think of, Europe, literature, myself. He's the right person I think, because he was a townee, a European, and disliked Wordsworth and that kind of approach to nature, and I find that very sympathetic."

By the fifth rhyme-royal stanza of the poem itself, Auden acknowledges that his verse letter is the pretext for a sort of gossipy confession and *portmanteau* discourse, freely designed to accommodate anything that comes to hand.

> So if ostensibly I write to you
>   To chat about your poetry or mine,
> There's many other reasons: though it's true
>   That I have, at the age of twenty-nine
>   Just read *Don Juan* and I found it fine.
> I read it on the boat to Reykjavik
> Except when eating or asleep or sick.

Though employing a different (and easier) stanzaic form, Auden's letter resembles *Don Juan* in a number of respects. Travel and gossip are important ingredients of both. Both delight in inventive and unexpected rhymes: in Auden, for example, *easy* with *civilisé*. Both are "light" in being a sort of *vers de société*. Both are remarkably personal, and both governed by the impulses of digression (even when claiming, "It is the strictly relevant I sing"), witty and subversive candor, condemnations at once devastating and charming. All these qualities in both poets would themselves be enough to explain the choice of Byron to be the recipient of Auden's letter.

In an introduction to the *Selected Poetry and Prose of Byron*, Auden made the following astute observation about the relationship between the formal aspect of verse and the subject matter of poetry:

> In the process of composition, as every poet knows, the relation between experience and language is always dialectical, but in the finished product it must always appear to the reader to be a one-way relationship. In serious poetry thought, emotion, event, must always appear to dictate the diction, meter and rhyme in which they are embodied; vice versa, in comic poetry it is the words, meter, rhyme which must appear to create the thoughts, emotions, and events they require.

But we may be entitled to look further still, and to find in Byron a kind of casual aesthetic doctrine Auden would come more and more earnestly to espouse. On October 3, 1810, Byron wrote to Francis Hodgson, "The end of all scribblement is to amuse." And Auden, in the course of his letter, asserts, "Art, if it doesn't start there, at least ends, / Whether aesthetics likes the thought or not, / In an attempt to entertain our friends." These two statements, while not identical, are enough alike to represent a view that is by no means universally entertained. It is, moreover, a view that cannot comfortably be applied to large segments of Auden's own *oeuvre*.

Within the brief space of ten years, this notion had expanded in Auden's mind into something approaching a doctrine, and more specifically, a doctrine with theological underpinnings. Alan Ansen records him as saying, on March 19, 1947,

> I think that poetry is fundamentally frivolity. I do it because I like it. The only serious thing is loving God and your neighbor. Because you can say, "I am not a mathematician," or "I'm not an artist, and that's all right because I have no talent for it." Everything that isn't required of you is fundamentally frivolous. Now you can't say about loving your neighbor that you have no talent for it. It's required of everyone. No, it isn't harder for one than another. It only looks harder to the individual who is confronted with his own problems and can't see someone else's. Of course, the human race as a whole is unlovable. If it weren't, there wouldn't be any problems. Yes, you can see that some people have a special propensity for evil.

I should like to add to this a personal recollection which appeared in an interview I gave to the *Paris Review*. It recalls an acquaintance I had with Auden on the island of Ischia around 1950.

> He was fond of maintaining that art should be amusing, accessible, and without pretensions to *ultimate statements,* to solemn pomposities. All such art he found a bore, and he used to taunt us by saying that anyone who claimed to enjoy Beethoven's late quartets was simply putting on airs. He carried this argument to extremes, I may add, to the point of insisting that art and its subject ought to be nearly frivolous. It was a strong argument for camp taste, but what was interesting about it was its theological foundation. [He proposed a game that] invited participants to imagine that they knew they were to die in a state of grace in six months with complete assurance of a heavenly estate after death. This meant that they were free from all anxieties, and had no need for penitential thoughts or actions, nor spiritual clysters or edification. There was no need to be, as the phrase goes, "uplifted." His argument was that a lot of people foolishly confuse being "uplifted" with aesthetic enjoyment, when in fact they're only hankering after a cheap and artificially induced elation, which they associate with rectitude and purity and upon which they congratulate themselves. So, given these remarkable conditions, we were all asked to say what novel or novels we would read; what lyric

poems; which paintings we would like to look at, and what music we'd like to hear. Remember that the central point is that there was no need to do anything "improving," only to enjoy yourself—which Auden insisted was all art was meant to do. I remember his choices. He wanted to read the novels of Ronald Firbank, the lyrics of Tennyson, look at the paintings of Caravaggio, and listen to, this last pains me, the overtures of Rossini. But I must add that my fondness for Bach pained him.

The problem is, of course, highly complex, and Auden knew perfectly well that it was. He knew, for example, that there is a good deal of superb religious music, much of it of a very solemn and transcendent character, and his argument tends to sidestep this kind of music. He touched upon it only indirectly when talking to Ansen. "When you go to Mass, it makes absolutely no difference whether you're emotionally excited or not. Religious emotion, like any other kind of emotion, is irrelevant to religious duty." The severity of this view is little short of Savonarolan. He might well have gone on to say, "And aesthetic emotion is still more irrelevant." Perhaps this is true, though I am by no means sure; but it is clear that religious ceremonies and buildings have been not only beautifully embellished, but adorned in ways that were thought to *add* to their religious effects. Surely neither Palestrina nor Giotto thought he would play any role in *diverting* congregations from their piety or worship.

There are certain statements of Auden's that appear not so much to condemn art which is serious or solemn, but rather to condemn art which, in its seriousness and solemnity, has no moral or religious motive to it, and which therefore has the effect of making art itself the subject of our whole satisfaction, and perhaps to suggest the old Arnoldian wish that it might come to serve as a substitute for religion. There are times when it almost seems that Auden still regards Arnold as the most dangerous heretic around, and the cause of all the irreverent and self-admiring aestheticism that followed him. In any case, in the essay called "The Virgin and the Dynamo" he concludes by saying,

> The effect of beauty . . . is good to the degree that, through its analogies, the goodness of created existence, the historical fall into unfreedom and disorder, and the possibility of regaining paradise through repentance and forgiveness are recognized. Its effect is evil to the degree that beauty is taken, not as analogous to, but identical with goodness, so that the artist regards himself or is regarded by

others as God, the pleasure of beauty taken for the joy of paradise, and the conclusion drawn that, since all is well in the work of art, all is well in history. But all is not well there.

One cannot fail to note how poorly such a view consorts with Auden's notions, elsewhere stated, about the essential frivolity of poetry, and it might serve as a caution to any who take such frivolity as a seriously adopted and thoroughgoing doctrine. There are a great number of muddles in this short passage, and its first sentence alone could certainly suggest that it is wrong to write beautiful secular poems. And this is not a view that Auden, with his abiding love of the lyrics of Thomas Campion, could ever seriously have entertained. Secondly, the veriest child quickly learns that the paradisiacal pleasures of the imaginary world of his nursery library are daily confuted by what Auden grandly calls "history," which impinges upon childhood relentlessly and invincibly. No one who is reasonably sane is likely to confuse one of these realms with another.

Yet one does not have to be a committed religionist to regard art, and especially High Art, as in danger of pompousness, self-glorification, given to vanities and a foolish reordering of priorities, from which, in Auden's view, the artist as well as the rest of the world has suffered since at least the beginning of the Romantic movement. In this connection, Auden inclines, rather astutely, to identify Byron not with his contemporaries but with Pope, whom both Auden and Byron so much admired. And it is not difficult to imagine so policed a profligate (and self-lacerating a Calvinist) as Byron adopting an aesthetic that sees art as frivolous, and a belief that "the end of all scribblement is to amuse." Yet it is worth remembering at the same time that a doctrine very much like this was enunciated by that severest, most austere, most self-denying of poets, T. S. Eliot. In the preface to the 1928 edition of *The Sacred Wood*, a book to which Auden expressed particular indebtedness, Eliot writes, "Poetry is a superior amusement: I do not mean an amusement for superior people. I call it amusement, an amusement *pour distraire les honnêtes gens,* not because that is a true definition, but because if you call it anything else you are likely to call it something still more false." One cannot too much enjoy the pleasure of debating whether it is to Byron or to Eliot that Auden owes his views.

There may be a still more buried reason for Auden to identify himself so directly with Byron, and I approach it with an avowed tentativeness. I want to propose a cluster of associations that seem to me linked in Auden's mind over a rather long period of time: such a cluster as Caroline Spurgeon proposed about Shakespeare in pointing out his association of dogs with candy, and both with a fawning sycophancy. The cluster I have found involves Byron, Don Juan (that is, Don Giovanni), and Tristan, and finally Tristan with his (that is, Auden's) mother.

The juxtaposition of Don Giovanni and Tristan appears in two consecutive stanzas in Auden's poem "In Sickness and in Health."

> Nature by nature in unnature ends:
> Echoing each other like two waterfalls,
>   Tristan, Isolde, the great friends,
> Make passion out of passion's obstacles,
> Deliciously postponing their delight,
> Prolong frustration till it lasts all night,
> Then perish lest Brangaene's worldly cry
> Should sober their cerebral ecstasy.
>
> But, dying, conjure up their opposite,
> Don Juan, so terrified of death he hears
>   Each moment recommending it
> And knows no argument to counter theirs:
> Trapped in their vile affections, he must find
> Angels to keep him chaste; a helpless, blind,
> Unhappy spook, he haunts the urinals,
> Existing solely by their miracles.

To Alan Ansen he remarked, "Don Giovanni is a certain type of male homosexual. Neither extreme, Tristan or Don Giovanni, is compatible with heterosexual love." Even the essay on Byron's *Don Juan* in *The Dyer's Hand* does not fail to mention Tristan, and the two names are linked again in the essay called "Notes on Music and Opera" in the same volume. In a review of Robert Gutman's *Richard Wagner: The Man, His Mind, and His Music,* reprinted in *Forewords and Afterwords* under the title "The Greatest of the Monsters," Auden writes, "Anyone who pays close attention to the text and the music in [*Tristan*] is aware of the homosexual triangle Mark-Melot-Tristan. In his long monologue after the lovers are surprised, Mark ignores Isolde completely and addresses himself to Tristan alone, causing problems for the stage director." Auden then goes on to quote Gutman on this very point to this effect: "For all practical purposes Isolde might well vanish from the garden with Mark's entry . . . How many Isoldes have desperately rearranged their veils a thousand times while awaiting those few lines near the end of the act!" Auden continues, "(Flagstad solved this problem by sitting down with her back to the audience.) And at the end of the third act, Melot dies with the name of Tristan on his lips."

Ursula Niebuhr, in her essay "Memories of the 1940s," recalls a review Auden wrote in *The Nation* of Denis de Rougemont's *Love in the Western World.* She writes, quoting liberally from the review,

> De Rougemont's book looked at the history of romantic love—or passion—from its "inception in the courtly love of Provence to contemporary personal and political forms." "At the root of the romantic conception of ideal sexual passion lies Manichaeism, a dualistic heresy introduced into Europe from the East, which held matter to be the creation of evil and therefore incapable of salvation." Thus "all human institutions like marriage are corrupt, and perfection can be reached only by death, in which the limitations of matter are finally transcended and the soul is merged into the infinite nothingness of the logos." All this finds expression in the Tristan legend. The love of Tristan and Isolde cannot find fulfilment, for it exists only in the economy of negation. Therefore death, rather than life together "in honour preferring one another" has to be the fate of the lovers.
>
> This legend (Wystan pointed out) in its turn creates a mirror image, the legend that . . . culminates in Mozart's Don Giovanni . . . Tristan sees time as something evil to be aggressively destroyed. The former is a suicide, the latter a murderer . . . The two sides of the myth can combine only in a collective form, in warfare where every individual is at one and the same time the masochistic murderee and the sadistic murderer, or in the political relationship of the impassioned leader and the impassioned masses. Equally opposed to both isotopes of Eros stands the Christian doctrine of Agape (of unselfish love).

It may be that the most protracted and detailed comparison and linkage of Don Juan/Giovanni and Tristan is the one that covers several pages in Auden's essay "Balaam and His Ass." It seems almost as if Auden is unable to think of one without thinking of the other. And both of them seem to represent to him false, dangerous, and deforming versions of love, which are, moreover, homosexually tainted. The taint I refer to

here is not the conventional one of moral blame or heterosexual condescension, but the one to which Auden himself refers when speaking to
Alan Ansen: "The reasons Americans pretend so hard about the subject
[of homosexuality] is that America is really a very queer country. I've
come to the conclusion that it's wrong to be queer, but that's a long story.
Oh, the reasons why are comparatively simple. In the first place, all
homosexual acts are acts of envy. In the second, the more you're involved
with someone, the more trouble arises, and affection shouldn't result
in that." As if in confirmation of this view, Auden wrote, in an essay on
J. R. Ackerley, that "few, if any, homosexuals can honestly boast that
their sex-life has been happy."

Finally, Byron's hero, in contradistinction to Mozart's, is ridiculously
passive, a fact which lends a wonderful comic irony to his entire reputation as seducer. But it does something else as well: it certifies his innocence.
And it may be recalled that Tom Rakewell, too, is characterized by his
absolute passivity, as is Alan Norman in *Dog-Skin*.

The cluster of associations I have outlined might allow Auden to
identify Byron's hero with homosexuality (as Byron was himself so
identified in his coy letters about Ali Pasha, and the young Greek boy with
whom he fell in love near the end of his life) and Juan with Mozart's
irresistible seducer, and both with Tristan, and Tristan with the erotic
duets the child Auden sang with his mother; and finally, all of these with
*innocence*. There can, in any case, be no question that the tone and
atmosphere of the *Letter to Lord Byron* is lighthearted and free of any
burden of anxiety such as haunted the poetry that came immediately
before and after it.

And alongside of it as well. *Letters from Iceland* contains at least one
lyric of the kind that both preceded and followed that book. Later titled
"The Price," and beginning, "O who can ever praise enough / The world
of his belief," it is a painful poem about, among other things, "the
exhaustion of weaning," the cost of being forced to give up the childhood
world of kindly illusion, to end in solitude and fear. It unobtrusively
connects the strains of anxiety that came before with those that would
follow.

The *Letter to Lord Byron,* which is divided into four parts, begins on
a sly erotic note by commenting (as though this were a shared burden or
nuisance) on how authors (presumably both Byron and Auden, as well,
incidentally, as Pope—remember the Epistle to Arbuthnot) are flooded by
mail from total strangers, some of it frankly lewd in character, and

occasionally including "the correspondent's photo in the nude." We are allowed to assume that Auden himself must have received such notes, and it is furthermore suggested (as a compliment) that Byron must be familiar with such overtures, since it is said that to him "a poet's fan-mail will be nothing new." But in addition to this, the intimacy of the discourse throughout suggests that this is itself such a licentious letter, Byron being, because of his youth and good looks, the proper recipient of this sort of mash note in which Auden intends to include some items that will not be part of the poem, and therefore probably not available to the reading public at large.

> Every exciting letter has enclosures,
>     And so shall this—a bunch of photographs,
> Some out of focus, some with wrong exposures,
>     Press cuttings, gossip, maps, statistics, graphs.

The erotic note seems to me to be recalled only a few stanzas later, when, acknowledging that he is in a foreign country where he cannot speak the language, he declares,

> At any language other than my own
> I'm no great shakes, and here I've found no tutor
> Or sleeping lexicon to make me cuter.

It is possible (and has been suggested) that the "sleeping lexicon" is a recording device that one plays as one is about to go to sleep, and which continues to play all night, thereby subliminally educating in whatever subject is desired. If this reading is accepted, then "cuter" is simply an abbreviation of "acuter." But we are also, I think, entitled to suppose that a "sleeping lexicon" is a bed companion who knows Icelandic, and that the cuteness in question is sexual as well as intellectual.

There follows a stanza that seems to be devoted to the requisite documentary details that any travel diary is necessarily based upon.

> The thought of writing came to me today
>     (I like to give these facts of time and space);
> The bus was in the desert on its way
>     From Mothrudalur to some other place:
>     The tears were streaming down my burning face;
> I'd caught a heavy cold in Akureyri,
> And lunch was late and life looked very dreary.

The charm of this lies in its putative concern to record literal facts, no matter how "unpoetic" they may be, together with our recognition that the genre of "light verse"—Byron's especially—permits, and indeed encourages, the constraints of rhyme to govern the materials of discourse, thereby often inviting digressions because some unexpected rhyme has suggested them. As Auden himself will shortly say,

> . . . it's in keeping with the best traditions
> For Travel Books to wander from the point
> (There is no other rhyme except anoint).

The last full stanza quoted above suggests that the "heavy cold," and the streaming tears that accompanied it, were themselves, in some obscure way, the cause of Auden's decision to write to Byron in the first place. This is presently explained as follows:

> Professor Housman was I think the first
> To say in print how very stimulating
> The little ills by which mankind is cursed,
> The colds, the aches, the pains are to creating;
> Indeed one hardly goes too far in stating
> That many a flawless lyric may be due
> Not to a lover's broken heart, but 'flu.

The stanza is, like many a stanza to come, at least superficially anti-Romantic, and the first indication of this is that poor Housman should be identified as "Professor," a reliable dry-as-dust, who will not be given to any Shelleyan posturings or impostures. Secondly, and centrally, there is the claim that love poetry does not necessarily have anything to do with love. What could be more anti-Romantic than that? But Housman's name itself reminds us that the classical and stoic tone of so much of his poetry was nothing more or less than an inversion of the familiar Romantic attitude, based on suppressed feelings and expressed as controlled anguish and cruel irony. It in fact suggests very strongly that art is the product of the suffering artist, and it was Housman who used the analogy of the necessary irritant of the grain of sand that provokes the oyster to secrete its pearl.

Auden goes on to acknowledge that besides having brought a volume of Byron with him on his journey he has brought one other author, and had for a while been uncertain to which of them to address his verse letter. The other author is Jane Austen, who resembles Byron in being deeply concerned with the foibles and conventions of society, and is generally anti-Romantic, as well as the fact that she—again, like Byron—displays a lively taste for gossip. But Auden rejects her as a recipient.

> Then she's a novelist. I don't know whether
>   You will agree, but novel writing is
> A higher art than poetry altogether
>   In my opinion, and success implies
>   Both finer character and faculties.
> Perhaps that's why real novels are as rare
> As winter thunder or a polar bear.
>
> The average poet by comparison
>   Is unobservant, immature and lazy.
> You must admit, when all is said and done,
>   His sense of other people's very hazy,
>   His moral judgements are too often crazy,
> A slick and easy generalization
> Appeal[s] too well to his imagination.

It may be that the best gloss on these stanzas is Auden's sonnet "The Novelist." John Fuller declares that this view of the novelist's art was based on Auden's admiration for the work of Isherwood, and Mendelson declares in a note that the claim for the absolute superiority of the novelist is taken from Henry James's preface to *The Ambassadors,* but I think we may be allowed to suppose that E. M. Forster would also have prompted such a view. And there is, moreover, a plain and obvious truth in the observation, especially if we allow ourselves to think of the poet as the conventional Romantic who seems unaware of anything outside of his own psyche. The novelist's art requires a deep interest in others, in people very different from himself, in the forms and ways of society, in the conventions of daily life, and in the dirty ways of financial transactions, the stuff of daily and ordinary (as distinct from extraordinary—"They can amaze you like a thunderstorm") events.

Having gone on to describe the sort of "enclosures" he plans to include with his letter, Auden now writes frankly about the form it will take.

> I want a form that's large enough to swim in,
>   And talk on any subject that I choose,
> From natural scenery to men and women,
>   Myself, the arts, the European news:

> And since she's on a holiday, my Muse
> Is out to please, find everything delightful
> And only now and then be mildly spiteful.
>
> Ottava rima would, I know, be proper,
>   The proper instrument on which to pay
> My compliments, but I should come a cropper;
>   Rhyme-royal's difficult enough to play.

It is astonishing how many critics of Auden, in the plain face of the last four lines quoted above, declare quite heedlessly that Auden has simply appropriated Byron's *Don Juan* stanza unchanged. The form he has adopted will allow Auden to compose what was in time to become a form characteristically associated with him: the verse essay, an elastic genre that could embrace as much learning and diverse information as he cared to pour into it. The verse essay is obviously related to the kind of poetry Byron himself was writing in *Don Juan*, in which the narrative is little more than a pretext for social commentary and gossip. Auden goes on to acknowledge that the sort of light verse he has elected to write has not in modern times produced the kind of mastery that Byron evidences, and Auden humbly declares himself prepared merely to pasture his "poor silly sheep with Dyer / And picnic on the lower slopes [of Parnassus] with Prior." He also admits that he is not qualified to class himself among the top travel writers, either. He furthermore disqualifies himself as any sort of explorer, declaring at the end of the First Part,

> The shades of Asquith and of Auden Skökull
>   Turn in their coffins a three-quarter circle
> To see their son, upon whose help they reckoned
> Being as frivolous as Charles the Second.
>
> So this, my opening chapter has to stop
>   With humbly begging everybody's pardon.
> From Faber first in case the book should flop,
>   Then from the critics lest they should be hard on
>   The author when he leads them up the garden,
> Last from the general public he must beg
> Permission now and then to pull their leg.

That reference to "Auden Skökull," Carpenter helpfully tells us in his biography, concerns the fact that Auden's father believed "that he himself was of Icelandic descent." He "apparently believed that his family was descended from or related to, a certain Auðun Skökull, who is recorded as one of the first Norse settlers in Iceland in the ninth century." Furthermore, Carpenter supplies a footnote that reads, "The name 'Skökull' means 'carriage-pole,' and seems to have been used as slang for 'penis.'" In this way Auden contrives to insinuate the erotic into the close as well as the opening of the First Part.

This First Part, which is thirty stanzas long (the remaining sections are forty-seven, thirty-eight, and forty-four stanzas long respectively), serves as a general and lighthearted introduction to the whole work, which is an especially informal version of the essay poem that Auden would eventually make his own, and is, in its meandering character, to be related to the dream poems of Auden's earliest composition, which seemed to be governed by free association.

Part II opens "Upon a primitive, unsheltered quay / In the small hours of a Wednesday Morning" with the poet writing his "letter." He goes on to say that, like most Englishmen, he finds it very difficult to sleep at a latitude where the sun never sets, so we are allowed to suppose that he is down on that primitive quay because he has chosen it as an isolated place to compose. Nothing he says in the course of Part II dissuades us from believing this, though the last stanza of the section begins, "We're out at sea now, and I wish we weren't." But at that point in the poem, Auden has outlined so many vexing problems of modern society that we are inclined to read the line about being "at sea" in commonplace metaphoric terms, meaning that we are completely bewildered. And the only thing to prevent us from continuing to adopt this meaning is that the first line of Part III reads, "My last remarks were sent you from a boat." In other words, between the beginning and the end of Part II, Auden has boarded a boat, and continued his verse epistle without mentioning the embarkation. There is, of course, nothing wrong with this, except for the fact that earlier he so very pointedly announced, "(I like to give these facts of time and space)." And so we are reminded that what seems to pass for the verisimilitude of reportage is really no more than the license of the wandering mind.

The letter-writer assumes that the first thing Byron will want to know will be *unserious:* the most frivolous gossip about the most frivolous part of society, "what sort of things *La Jeunesse* do and say," the latest word about those who in the early thirties were known in England as "the Bright Young Things." So Auden prepares to "take a Rover's breath / And skip a century of hope and sin—," the century between the death of Byron (1824) and, roughly, the present. "A Rover's breath" seems like the equivalent of "a deep breath," and "rover" is defined in the *OED* as a rugby player; but it is also defined in the same place as "a male flirt," which has little enough to do with drawing any kind of breath. Still, I think we may be allowed to imagine that Auden may have wanted both meanings.

So the point of departure of his "report" on the modern age, while making a very knowing obeisance to Lewis Mumford's *Technics & Civilization,* concerns the general antiseptic, mechanized, and chilling "decor" of the day: "A world of Aertex underwear for boys, / Huge plate-glass windows, walls absorbing noise, / Where the smoke nuisance is utterly abated / And all the furniture is chromium-plated." Auden does not conceal his nostalgia for an earlier style, which, at this writing, has already become obsolete. It is the industrial north of England, where he spent his childhood, and he describes it in the frankest terms, which are little short of Dickensian.

> Slattern the tenements on sombre hills,
>   And gaunt in valleys the square-windowed mills
> That, since the Georgian house, in my conjecture
> Remain our finest native architecture.
>
> On economic, health, or moral grounds
>   It hasn't got the least excuse to show;
> No more than chamber pots or otter hounds;
>   But let me say before it has to go,
>   It's the most lovely country that I know;
> Clearer than Scafell Pike, my heart has stamped on
> The view from Birmingham to Wolverhampton.
>
> Long, long ago, when I was only four,
>   Going towards my grandmother, the line
> Passed through a coal-field. From the corridor
>   I watched it pass with envy, thought 'How fine!
>   Oh how I wish that situation mine.'
> Tramlines and slagheaps, pieces of machinery,
> That was, and still is, my ideal scenery.

This requires some comment, because initially it may seem so unlikely a taste to admit to. It is worth noting, for example, that one of the photographs in Charles Osborne's biography of Auden, a remarkably forbidding view of a steel-girdered bridge over the cement embankment of a stream with warehouses and other industrial buildings on either side, is captioned: "Oxford gasworks and the river at St. Ebbe's. Walks such as this were thought by Auden to be the most beautiful in Oxford." When Auden was one and a half, his family moved from York to Solihull, near Birmingham. Carpenter reports, "Nothing was more exciting to Wystan than a train ride from Solihull into the city with its smoking chimneys and huge warehouses, and then (if he was lucky) onwards by another train, further north, where the line ran to Wolverhampton—past the canal, and between mile after mile of blackened factories with furnaces flaring up as the train passed."

We should also remember his precocious fascination with machinery and mines. As children Auden and his two brothers, one of whom became a geologist, were taken on visits to the Blue John Caves, and "were guided down long steep passages to caverns hollowed out by underground rivers, whose roofs, hung with stalactites, echoed to the perpetual trickle of water," a description of Carpenter's worth recalling when we come to a consideration of "In Praise of Limestone." The biography continues,

> Wystan was greatly impressed, but what struck him as still more dramatic were the disused lead mines whose remains could be seen here and there on the moors. He began to be fascinated by lead mining, and from now on, in his imagination, "thought myself a mining engineer."
>
> This is how he described his private passion: "I spent a great many of my waking hours in the construction and elaboration of a private sacred world, the basic elements of which were a landscape, northern and limestone, and an industry, lead mining." In his imagination he was, he said, the "sole autocrat" of this dream country—whose features also included narrow-gauge tramways and overshot water-wheels.
>
> He took his landscape seriously, and asked his mother [his father was serving overseas during WWI] and other adults to procure for him textbooks with such titles as *Machinery for Metalliferous Mines* ... and he persuaded them to take him down a real mine if ever there was a chance.

Osborne's book also contains a photograph of the three Auden boys perched on a large "pumping engine," and we are reminded not only of the lines from "Heavy Date,"

When I was a child, I
Loved a pumping-engine,
Thought it every bit as
  Beautiful as you,

but also of that far more serious and important poem from *Another Time* which begins, "Perhaps I always knew what they were saying . . . Those beautiful machines that never talked . . ."

Without question, this interest was instinctive as well as obsessive; yet when Auden came to write poetry later in his life, and had spent a certain amount of time in Germany, he may well have developed a more complex and sophisticated sense of the significance of his interest in mines and the industrial equipment that belongs to them. And this more complex knowledge may well have affected his poetry. What I am thinking of is most succinctly put in a review, by Heinz Kuehn, of a section of *German Romanticism and Its Institutions* by Theodore Ziolkowski.

Mining no longer stimulates the poetic imagination. In the Germany of the time of the romantics, however, mining did not serve the ex-traction of coal, iron production, and industrialization, but the extraction of ore—gold and silver and other precious metals. It was, moreover, a highly dangerous operation whose efficiency depended entirely on the skill, experience, and devotion of the individual miner. For the romantic mind it thus became "the archetypal image of de-scent into mysterious subterraneous caverns under the guide of wise old men in search of lore symbolized by glittering stones and precious metals." Mining became a descent into history, into moral order, into sexuality, in short, an "irresistible image of the human condition." That image in German romantic literature became widespread since every major writer of that period either was a professionally trained mining engineer or was otherwise closely associated with or intensely interested in that institution. The roster includes Novalis, Hölderlin, Goethe, Clemens Brentano, Joseph von Eichendorff, Alexander von Humboldt, and E. T. A. Hoffman. We can still get an inkling of their "obsession with mines" when we think of the continuing popularity of the legends of Tannhäuser and the Mountain of Venus.

Let me add finally that the kind of heroism identified with the mining enterprise figures importantly in Auden's early poem "Who stands, the crux left of the watershed."

Having dealt in a cursory way with architecture and interior decor, the poet now proceeds to other sociological observations.

> To start with, on the whole we're better dressed;
>   For chic the difference to-day is small
>   Of barmaid from my lady in the Hall.
> It's sad to spoil this democratic vision
> With millions suffering from malnutrition.

This is a nice point against the inefficiency and hypocrisy of democratic institutions, and one that would have pleased Byron's ironic sense of the malfunctions of society. But this condescension to "democracy" has its slight taint of snobbery, as if Auden and his predecessor-counterpart, *Lord* Byron, would both look down with Parnassian disdain upon the sins and self-delusions of twentieth-century society. This rather haughty tone is embarrassingly reinforced in the next stanza.

> Again, our age is highly educated;
>   There is no lie our children cannot read,
> And as MacDonald might so well have stated
>   We're growing up and up and up indeed.
>   Advertisements can teach us all we need;
> And death is better, as the millions know,
> Than dandruff, night-starvation, or B.O.

The MacDonald mentioned is Ramsey MacDonald, Socialist prime minister (who submitted to the League of Nations a plan called The Protocol that envisioned the elimination of war and the submission of all disputes to arbitration, after general mutual disarmament). But there is to this stanza an unpleasant whiff of snobbery toward "the millions" and their pathetic inability to free themselves from the delusions of the press and the advertising industry. The first line hints at the ineffectuality of education, as if the several Education Acts passed in England in the mid-nineteenth century had done nothing to advance the condition of ordinary people. This is not far from the view that if you give bathtubs to the poor, they will only fill them with coal. The note of snobbery presently becomes more explicit.

> You lived and moved among the best society
>   And so could introduce your hero to it
> Without the slightest tremor of anxiety;

Because he was your hero and you knew it,
He'd know instinctively what's done, and do it.
He'd find our day more difficult than yours
For industry has mixed the social drawers.

We've grown, you see, a lot more democratic,
    And Fortune's ladder is for all to climb;
Carnegie on this point was most emphatic.
    A humble grandfather is not a crime,
    At least, if father made enough in time!
Today, thank God, we've got no snobbish feeling
Against the more efficient modes of stealing.

An easy equation is implied here between ruthless laissez-faire capitalism and democracy, and both are regarded with a superior and nearly aristocratic contempt. We are a long way from the poem called "A Communist to Others." There follows a *Vogue*-like catalogue on what is "in" and "out" of fashion in the leading social circles. Sibelius is in; Elgar is out.

The vogue for Black Mass and the cult of devils
    Has sunk. The Good, the Beautiful, the True
Still fluctuate about the lower levels.
    Joyces are firm and there there's nothing new.
    Eliots have hardened just a point or two.
Hopkins are brisk, thanks to some recent boosts.
There's been some further weakening in Prousts.

This stock-market parlance follows directly from earlier references to Carnegie and the "industry" that "mixes social drawers." And, alas, it is all too true that not just the general public but book publishers themselves regard their vocation as a straightforward moneymaking proposition, a fact that is crudely reflected in the annual American Book Awards, which for some years now have attempted to imitate the Hollywood Oscars in vulgarity and ballyhoo, but which early decided to give no award in the field of poetry since not enough was involved in the way of money—a policy only recently, and shamefacedly, reversed. Auden is himself perfectly aware that snobbery is the essence of what he's writing about, and he expressly mentions it. And eventually he turns his disdain upon "the average man" of his own day, of whom it is said that in a few superficial ways he resembles his counterpart of Byron's day.

But he's another man in many ways:
  Ask the cartoonist first, for he knows best.
Where is the John Bull of the good old days,
  The swaggering bully with the clumsy jest?
  His meaty neck has long been laid to rest,
His acres of self-confidence for sale;
He passed away at Ypres and Passchendaele.

That last line speaks volumes, and the glosses upon it—or in any case upon the devastating effect of WWI on England, and the disillusionment with military and governmental authority that beset the survivors and the generation just too young to serve—have been many and eloquent. What happened to England's "self-confidence," as represented by the hypothetical "average man," was disastrous; but Auden will almost immediately characterize him simply (and rather unfairly) as cowardly, at least in comparison with the mindless bully, John Bull.

Begot on Hire Purchase by Insurance,
  Forms at his christening worshipped and adored;
A season ticket schooled him in endurance,
  A tax collector and a waterboard
  Admonished him. In boyhood he was awed
By a matric, and complex apparatuses
Keep his heart conscious of Divine Afflatuses.

'I am like you,' he says, 'and you, and you,
  I love my life, I love the home-fires, have
To keep them burning. Heroes never do.
  Heroes are sent by ogres to the grave.
  I may not be courageous, but I save.
I am the one who somehow turns the corner,
I may perhaps be fortunate Jack Horner.

'I am the ogre's private secretary;
  I've felt his stature and his powers, learned
To give his ogreship the raspberry
  Only when his gigantic back is turned.
  One day, who knows, I'll do as I have yearned.
The short man, all his fingers on the door,
With repartee shall send him to the floor.'

What is ridiculed here as the impotent rebuttal to authoritarian power will, in due course, come to be praised (in "Under Which Lyre") in the lines

> By night our student Underground
> At cocktail parties whisper round
>      From ear to ear;
> Fat figures in the public eye
> Collapse next morning, ambushed by
>      Some witty sneer.

The abject spinelessness of this poor man in the face of the ogre, Authority, is almost brutally conveyed.

> He dreads the ogre, but he dreads yet more
>      Those who conceivably might set him free,
> Those the cartoonist has no time to draw.
>      Without his bondage he'd be all at sea;
>      The ogre need but shout 'Security'
> To make this man, so lovable, so mild,
> As madly cruel as a frightened child.

The tone has lapsed a good deal from the jaunty, carefree, and gossipy level at which the poem began, and by this time it has become hostile and little short of cruel. To be sure, the object of scorn here is the abstract "average man," so it can be claimed that no blood wound has been inflicted. Still, we have gotten pretty far from amiable discourse, and even from the genial mode of satire. Auden proceeds to defend Byron against those who fancy he would have sympathized with the ogre of Authority and put himself at the head of a body of storm troopers. This seems to Auden very unlikely, though he concedes, for the sake of argument (and some comic effects), that "Nothing, says science, is impossible," and goes on, in this speculative frame of mind, to suppose that "Someone may think that Empire wines are nice, / There may be people who hear Tauber twice." The reference, very "knowing" and unashamedly snobbish, is to Richard Tauber, the Wagnerian tenor, famous for his performance of Tristan.

In any case, Auden rises in defense of Byron, declaring that while Byron would surely have opposed everything represented by the ogre (Reaction or Authority), the force of the ogre's pernicious influence is still felt throughout modern society.

His many shapes and names all turn us pale,
For he's immortal, and today he still
   Swinges the horror of his scaly tail.
Sometimes he seems to sleep, but will not fail
In every age to rear up to defend
Each dying force of history to the end.

We are about to receive a brief history lesson, but before we do, a couple of things are worth noting in the lines just quoted. The third line is a misquotation from Milton's "On the Morning of Christ's Nativity," and comes from a description of Satan. We may excuse Auden's faulty memory on the grounds that he is traveling, with only a copy of Byron at hand. Anyway, the coming history lesson will begin with Milton, and we may take it that this allusion prompted the citation of his name. Secondly, it could be argued that it is wrong to accuse Auden of snobbery, to align him with Byronic aristocracy, and oppose him to the servile horde of the "average man," since in these lines he expressly uses the inclusive pronoun "us," and thus identifies himself with all the weak and cowardly people he has been finding fault with. Granted, but it should also be pointed out that such inclusiveness is mitigated by the fact that it is Auden who has drawn up so formidable a list of indictments against cowardice and supinity; and secondly, the "us" is more or less forced upon Auden by the homogenized, populist dictates of modern democratic society, in which the vulgar majority prevails. And so we turn to the history lesson, of which the subject is "the ogre, dragon, what you will."

Milton beheld him on the English throne,
   And Bunyan sitting in the Papal chair;
The hermits fought him in their caves alone,
   At the first Empire he was also there,
   Dangling his Pax Romana in the air:
He comes in dreams at puberty to man,
To scare him back to childhood if he can.

Banker or landlord, booking-clerk or Pope,
   Whenever he's lost faith in choice and thought,
When a man sees the future without hope,
   Whenever he endorses Hobbes' report
   'The life of man is nasty, brutish, short,'

The dragon rises from his garden border
And promises to set up law and order.

He that in Athens murdered Socrates,
    And Plato then seduced, prepares to make
A desolation and to call it peace
    Today for dying magnates, for the sake
    Of generals who can scarcely keep awake,
And for that doughy mass in great and small
That doesn't want to stir itself at all.

Forgive me for inflicting all this on you . . .

A number of things need to be said about these lines, and perhaps the first of them is to take notice of their remarkable earnestness, for which, it may be, the last line quoted is a sort of lame apology. Auden is aware of how schoolmasterish he has turned, and how patronizing his tone is in respect to the nominal addressee of his letter. Secondly, it is worth correcting a common misreading of Hobbes that Auden rather injudiciously adopts. Hobbes did not say that man's life was nasty, brutish, and short. What he said was something rather more complicated.

Hereby it is manifest, that during the time men live without a common power to keep them all in awe, they are in a condition that is called war; and such a war, as is of every man, against every man. For WAR, consisteth not in battle only, or the act of fighting; but in a tract of time, wherein the will to contend by battle is sufficiently known: and therefore the notion of *time*, is to be considered in the nature of war; as it is in the nature of weather . . . so the nature of war, consisteth not in actual fighting; but in the known disposition thereto, during all the time there is no assurance to the contrary. All other time is PEACE.

Whatsoever therefore is consequent to a time of war, where every man is enemy to every man; the same is consequent to the time, wherein men live without other security, than what their own strength, and their own invention shall furnish them withal. In such condition, there is no place for industry; because the fruit thereof is uncertain: and consequently no culture of the earth; no navigation, nor use of the commodities that may be imported by sea; no commodious building; no instruments of moving and removing, such things as require much force; no knowledge of the face of the earth; no account of time; no arts; no letters; no society; and which is worst of all, continual fear, and danger of violent death; and the life of man, solitary, poor, nasty, brutish, and short.

In fact, so much are Hobbes's words taken by Auden out of context that it could almost be argued that the two actually are speaking from diametrically opposed points of view—Hobbes from the conviction that the absence of law and order entails the chaos of society at war with itself that results in all the deprivation he so eloquently describes, Auden from the position that authoritarian law and order is itself precisely the enemy. Indeed, it is Hobbes's distinction between what he calls war and peace that probably leads Auden to adapt a phrase from Tacitus' *Agricola.* There, one of the Briton leaders of opposition to Roman occupation characterized the imperial forces thus: "To robbery, slaughter, plunder, they give the lying name of empire; they make a desert and they call it peace." Part II concludes with two stanzas of what may best be described as lighthearted anguish—an attempt to return to the urbane tone without quite repudiating the seriousness of what has just been stated.

Part III, after the acknowledgment that "My last remarks were sent you from a boat," begins on a "let's see; where was I?" note, and resumes the cordial, rather chummy attitude towards Byron with which Part I began, and in which Auden cozily remarks, "I think it's time now for a little shop." This promise of shoptalk presumes a comfortable equality between the two poets; and, more than that, a likelihood of shared views, tastes, and prejudices.

> I like your muse because she's gay and witty,
>    Because she's neither prostitute nor frump,
> The daughter of a European city,
>    And country houses long before the slump;
>    I like her voice that does not make me jump:
> And you I find sympatisch, a good townee,
> Neither a preacher, ninny, bore or Brownie.
> . . . . .
> You've had your packet from the critics, though:
>    They grant you warmth of heart, but at your head
> Their moral and aesthetic brickbats throw.
>    A 'vulgar genius' so George Eliot said,
>    Which doesn't matter as George Eliot's dead,

> But T. S. Eliot, I am sad to find,
> Damns you with: 'an uninteresting mind'.

A number of things might be noted in these lines. To begin with, in his essay on *Don Juan,* Auden makes a rather troubling, obscure, and possibly specious distinction between the adjective "boring" and the noun "bore," and tries to show that they apply to wholly different topics. The distinction is based, at least covertly, on an aesthetic doctrine about solemnity in art, which, in turn, is based upon an unenunciated theology. It allows Auden to pronounce, not without some pompousness, to this effect: the last quartets of Beethoven, Michelangelo's Sistine frescoes, and the novels of Dostoievski are all bores, though not (or seldom) boring. Verdi, Degas, and Shakespeare may sometimes be boring but are never bores. What appears to be his favorite category is made up of Rossini, the drawings of Thurber, and P. G. Wodehouse, which he characterizes as neither boring nor a bore. And he furthermore defines "everything which is to any degree a bore, that is, . . . all forms of passionate attachment, whether to persons, things, actions, or beliefs," the final term of which licenses him to call God the "absolute bore." It is important to be aware that this claim is made not out of disrespect but, paradoxically, with "all due reverence." Like love, God is a "bore" because He cannot be *discussed!*

The line about "country houses long before the slump" certainly brings Wodehouse to mind, and links him with Byron, both in this poem and in the essay mentioned. Finally (and this seems to me important), there is the dissent from the taste and point of view of T. S. Eliot. I think this important because it will figure more prominently later in this account, and because Auden's attitude towards Eliot was interestingly equivocal. Eliot had been his early champion, had published *Paid on Both Sides,* for example, in *The Criterion* in 1930, had been his editor and publisher at Faber, and had advanced his career in important ways of which he was perfectly aware and for which he was genuinely grateful. And Auden's capacity for gratitude was serious and admirable. At the same time, and despite what was to become an allegiance to the same Anglican faith, there was a difference in their regard of most important things, probably including theology, and certainly in regard to aesthetics.

The poem now embarks on its attack upon Wordsworth, under the pretext of sharing a prejudice with Byron.

> I'm also glad to find I've your authority
>   For finding Wordsworth a most bleak old bore,

Though I'm afraid we're in the sad minority
  For every year his followers get more,
  Their numbers must have doubled since the war.

. . . . .

'I hate a pupil-teacher,' Milton said,
  Who also hated bureaucratic fools;
Milton may thank his stars that he is dead,
  Although he's learnt by heart in public schools,
  Along with Wordsworth and the list of rules;
For many a don while looking down his nose
Calls Pope and Dryden classics of our prose.

And new plants flower from that old potato.
  They thrive best in a poor industrial soil,
Are hardier crossed with Rousseaus or a Plato;
  Their cultivation is an easy toil.
  William, to change the metaphor, struck oil;
His well seems inexhaustible, a gusher
That saves old England from the fate of Russia.

The mountain-snob is a Wordsworthian fruit;
  He tears his clothes and doesn't shave his chin,
He wears a very pretty little boot,
  He chooses the least comfortable inn;
  A mountain railway is a deadly sin;
His strength, of course, is as the strength of ten men,
He calls all those who live in cities wen-men.

There is something remarkably disingenuous about this. Even in his letters, where he speaks confidentially and freely, Byron was never so hard on Wordsworth as Auden is here. Byron suspects that Wordsworth never got drunk, a characteristic which he finds blameworthy. He also declares that Wordsworth has sometimes, in his performances after *Lyrical Ballads*, failed to live up to his undeniable talents, and says that "there is undoubtedly much natural talent spilt over 'The Excursion' but it is rain upon rocks where it stands and stagnates." In the context of Auden's poem, however, we are cozened into supposing that Auden is sharing in the strictures against Wordsworth that Byron introduced into the dedicatory stanzas at the opening of *Don Juan,* which effectively dismiss the leading Romantic poets, with particular attention to Southey, Coleridge,

and Wordsworth. But the fact is that Byron castigates his Romantic
contemporaries not on poetic but on ideological grounds.

> Bob Southey! You're a poet—Poet Laureate,
>     And representative of all the race;
> Although 'tis true that you turned out a Tory at
>     Last,—yours has lately been a common case;
> And now, my Epic Renegade! what are ye at?
>     With all the Lakers, in and out of place?
> A nest of tuneful persons, to my eye
> Like "four and twenty Blackbirds in a pye;"
>
> . . . . .
>
> I would not imitate the petty thought,
>     Nor coin my self-love to so base a vice,
> For all the glory your conversion brought,
>     Since gold alone should not have been its price.
> You have your salary; was't for that you wrought?
>     And Wordsworth has his place in the Excise.
> You're shabby fellows—true—but poets still,
> And duly seated on the Immortal Hill.

Between these two stanzas there is the claim that anyone capable of
understanding Wordsworth's "Excursion" would "be able / To add a
story to the Tower of Babel." But it is clear that the chief indictment, both
of Southey and of Wordsworth, is the one Browning seconded in "The
Lost Leader": the capitulation to reactionary politics as the ransom paid
for financial security. In 1813 Wordsworth had accepted a government
sinecure; Byron noted, "the converted Jacobin having long subsided into
the clowning sycophant of the worst prejudices of the aristocracy."
Browning's subsequent condemnation was based upon Wordsworth's
appointment to the Laureateship in 1843, as well as his acceptance of a
Civil List Pension of three hundred pounds in 1842. Byron contrasts both
Southey and Wordsworth to Milton.

> If, fallen in evil days on evil tongues,
>     Milton appealed to the Avenger, Time,
> If Time, the Avenger, execrates his wrongs,
>     And makes the word "Miltonic" mean "*Sublime*,"
> *He* deigned not to belie his soul in songs,
>     Nor turn his very talent to a crime;

*He* did not loathe the Sire to laud the Son,
But closed the tyrant-hater he begun.

So, to return to Auden's verse comments on Wordsworth, there is
something very suspect about the statement that "I'm also glad to find
I've your authority / For finding Wordsworth a most bleak old bore."
Nor does Auden give the least hint of anything concerning turncoat
politics that so affronted Byron. Instead, he makes a mockery, even a
witty political mockery, of Romantic pastoralism, beginning with a
comic botanical metaphor of flowers grown from an old potato.
"They thrive best in a poor industrial soil" works ingeniously in terms of
hardy weeds, and at the same time, in terms of the lower classes of the
industrial midlands who are likely to be seduced by the pastoral myth.
"Their cultivation is an easy toil" because weeds don't need much care,
and because it is easy to cultivate the credulity of simple people. Then, at
least as much for rhyming purposes as anything else, the metaphor
changes to Wordsworth striking oil: "His well seems inexhaustible, a
gusher / That saves old England from the fate of Russia." There is a good
deal of bitter wit and intelligence to these lines. They imply that
Wordsworth's ready embrace of the pastoral tradition was a shrewd way
to keep the lower classes, the proletariat, in their place by allowing them
to congratulate themselves on the moral and spiritual superiority that
belongs to the poor, on the authority both of the Bible and of the classical
pastoral tradition, which represented shepherds and all the innocent
inhabitants of Arcadia as the only people in this world gifted with true
happiness. And the conviction that this is so is, Auden claims, what
prevented the English poor from rising in revolution against their capitalist oppressors. (And perhaps some readers will be grateful to have it
explained that "wen-men" is Auden's coinage, formulated from the
observation of William Cobbett, author of *Rural Rides,* that London is
"the great WEN of all.")
Auden continues his campaign against pastoralism ("This interest in
waterfalls and daisies, / Excessive love for the non-human faces") always
on the pretext that this is a view he shares with Byron, whose Muse he
has already characterized as "the daughter of a European city," by which
characterization he chooses to neglect a good deal of *Childe Harold,* to
say nothing of *The Giaour, The Bride of Abydos, The Corsair,* and *Lara.*
Wittily focusing his anathemas at those who lack all sense of human
fraternity but are overcome with compassion for plants, he writes,

I dread this like the dentist, rather more so:
  To me Art's subject is the human clay,
And landscape but a background to a torso;
  All Cézanne's apples I would give away
  For one small Goya or a Daumier.
I'll never grant a more than minor beauty
To pudge or pilewort, petty-chap or pooty.

Art, if it doesn't start there, at least ends,
  Whether aesthetics like the thought or not,
In an attempt to entertain our friends;
  And our first problem is to realize what
  Peculiar friends the modern artist's got;
It's possible a little dose of history
May help us in unravelling this mystery.

There's a lot crammed into these stanzas, including, as I said, the breezy assumption that they state a view that Byron would share. But this vigorous anti-pastoralism seems to me to have other roots. Of these, one of the first may lie in Auden's well-known myopia. He was functionally disqualified from caring much about landscapes, since at a distance of more than twelve or fifteen feet he had great trouble recognizing people he knew perfectly well. Perhaps at least as much to the point is the fact that one other possible source of this sentiment is not Byron but Sydney Smith, a wit and "townee" much admired by Auden, who hated the country and who wrote once to the newly married wife of Sir Humphrey Davy, when the couple were away on their continental honeymoon, "I am astonished that a woman of your sense should yield to such an imposture as the Augsburg Alps—surely you have found out by this time that God has made nothing so curious as human creatures."

And now Auden provides us with what he mischievously calls "a little dose of history," which is, by his own admission, biased and neither entirely accurate nor coherent. He elects to begin with the eighteenth century, at which time he claims we find (for the first time, it is implied) two arts: one of them courtly and high-brow, the other popular and vulgar. (It is absurd, of course, to suppose that such a division—as that between Spenser and Sidney on the one hand, and the pamphlets of Greene, the broadside ballads, and song lyrics on the other—did not exist in the Elizabethan period. But, as Auden says, never mind.) This division, the poem asserts, continued peacefully, each form of art addressing its own constituency, until suddenly and quite inexplicably artists decided that they didn't like being servile, and each one decided "To get a patch of ground which he can call / His own. He doesn't really care how small, / So long as he can style himself the master: / Unluckily for art, it's a disaster." What we are being given is really far more a sociology than a history of art, and Auden blandly confesses, "I've simplified the facts to be emphatic, / Playing Macaulay's favorite little trick / Of lighting that's contrasted and dramatic."

A rather truer, and almost equally brisk, account of the changing relationship of the poet and artist to his society is given by Alvin Kernan in *The Death of Literature*.

In the Renaissance and the Enlightenment, the courts and the aristocracy fostered the arts, and poetry was defined in ways that suited ruling-class interests and values. Most of the writers were men, rarely women, of taste and means, or, like William Shakespeare, Gent., who bought a coat of arms, they pretended to gentility and made every effort to acquire property. The crown controlled all writing, directly through censorship and patronage, and indirectly through a courtly poetics that eventually developed into the firmness of neo-classicism. Imitation of the ancients, maintenance of decorum, and the observance of such rules as the unities in order to control the sprawl of native writing gave aesthetic form to such aristocratic social values as hierarchy, restraint, and rigidly codified behavior.

Courtly poetry decayed rapidly during the course of the eighteenth century, when historical shifts we collectivize as the French Revolution and the Industrial Revolution were making aristocratic and authoritarian kingdoms into liberal parliamentary societies, agricultural into capitalist economies. Science was at the same time replacing religion as the primary epistemology, and an orientation towards tradition and the past was swinging towards the future and progress ... Print created an open market place for books and ideas, made censorship and patronage uneconomic, transferred literary power to an increasingly literate public of "common readers," as Samuel Johnson styled them, and fostered a new type of professional writers who made their livings and reputations by providing what the market would buy. Samuel Johnson in England, Jean-Jacques Rousseau in France, and Gotthold Lessing in Germany represented in their different ways these new professional writers of the print era, which for the first time included women, Hester Lynch Piozzi, Anna Letitia Barbauld, Hannah More, Frances Burney, Elizabeth Inchbald, and Maria Edgeworth, to name only the most notable in England.

Johnson's famous letter to Lord Chesterfield—asserting that the author, not the aristocratic patron, owned the King's English that Johnson had just made the author's English in a dictionary defining words by the usage of the best writers—formally marks the end of the old courtly order of polite letters. It was also the beginning of what would in the romantic future become literature when authors like Wordsworth, Sainte-Beuve, and Arnold established a different way of thinking about literary things . . .

Appearing in conjunction with an intellectual, political and economic revolution, literature was allied—"Bliss was it in that dawn to be alive"—with forces that overthrew kings and swept away impediments to freedom. A list of names like Shelley, Heine, Hugo, Lorca, Brecht, Sartre, and Mailer testifies that literature never entirely abandoned its early revolutionary zeal, even though individual writers like Goethe, Wordsworth, Yeats, and T. S. Eliot adjusted, compromised, or went into reaction. But as the features of the bourgeois state began to emerge from enlightenment and revolution, and 1789 gave way to 1830 and 1848, literature and the other arts, still identifying with the original idealism of revolution, chose increasingly to be at odds with the new world of money, cities, factories, and machines portrayed most extensively in France by Balzac and in England by Dickens.

This account by Kernan of the emergence of the revolutionary, emancipated (and eventually alienated) artist is a useful one, and not least for its lists of names, which, almost by themselves, can indicate something of Auden's not altogether comfortable or easy posture. Vigorously and mockingly anti-Romantic, a passionate detester of Shelley (to Alan Ansen: "Perhaps my dislike of Brahms is extra-aesthetic. But whenever I hear a peculiarly obnoxious combination of sounds, I spot it as Brahms and I'm right every time. I feel the same way about Shelley. He's the only English poet I really dislike"), Auden would have found it difficult to align himself with the "revolutionary" zealots from Shelley to Mailer, and in the course of his career he came to express a good deal of dislike for Brecht and Sartre. Indeed, he shared with Byron a deep admiration for Pope as well as Dryden, whose art surely represents the old, rather than the new, order. We have seen how equivocal he felt about Yeats, and we shall see that he felt similarly awkward about Eliot. All this means that the blithe tone of this verse epistle conceals a troubled and uncertain mind which does not find itself at ease in either the old or the new dispensation.

The fourth and final section of the *Letter* is a remarkably candid self-portrait and autobiography, the details of which are only glossed, but never, so far as I can determine, contradicted, by so diligent a biographer as Carpenter. The biographical facts, and the narrative of events, correspond in the poem to Carpenter's account, so I will address myself only to those details that seem to invite special notice.

First of all, at several points early in this section, Auden returns to the subject of his precocious interest in mining and mines, declaring that in his fantasy world, "from my sixth until my sixteenth year / I thought myself a mining engineer." But Auden acknowledges that the preoccupation was more than literal. He says, in the very beginning of this account: "I see the map of all my youth unroll, / The mental mountains and the psychic creeks, / The towns of which the master never speaks," and we know that he himself knows what a serious and symbolic role this interest played in his life and was to play in his poetry. Its effect, even here, is pervasive:

> . . . I like a weight upon my bed;
>   I always travel by the Underground;
>   For concentration I have always found
> A small room best, the curtains drawn, the light on;
> Then I can work from nine till tea-time, right on.

His parents are written of with filial respect and reverence, and he observes that "My grandfathers on either side agree / In being clergymen and C. of E." This ecclesiastical note continues, not without a touch of levity:

> My home then was professional and 'high'.
>   No gentler father ever lived, I'll lay
> All Lombard Street against a shepherd's pie.
>   We imitate our loves: well, neighbors say
> I grow more like my mother every day.
> I don't like business men. I know a Prot
> Will never really kneel but only squat.

Lombard Street is a banking area of London, probably so called because the natives of Lombardy were well known as bankers, moneychangers, and pawnbrokers. But the slight, amused snobbery in "'high,'" with its repugnance at kneeling, and the unabashed identification with his mother (and mother church) are worth noting.

From his forebears, his earliest years, and the beginning of the Great War, Auden turns to the first teacher who was ever to have a lasting influence upon him, and whose identity he discreetly veils.

> Surnames I must not write—O Reginald,
>     You at least taught us that which fadeth not,
> Our earliest visions of the great wide world;
>     The beer and biscuits that your favorites got,
>     Your tales revealing you a first-class shot,
> Your riding breeks, your drama called *The Waves*,
> A few of us will carry to our graves.
>
> 'Half a lunatic, half a knave.' No doubt
>     A holy terror to the staff at tea;
> A good headmaster must have soon found out
>     Your moral character was all at sea;
>     I question if you'd got a pass degree:
> But little children bless your kind that knocks
> Away the edifying stumbling blocks.

There is, again, a slightly insolent religious note in the allusion to the First Epistle of Peter (5:4): "A Crown of glory that fadeth not away." Whatever it was that Captain Reginald Oscar Gartside-Bagnall imparted, it must have had little enough to do with what St. Peter wrote about. The other literary reference (to Yeats's "All Souls' Night") is part of a tolerant view of someone distinctly unworthy. What is perhaps most delicate and tactful about these lines concerns the careful juxtaposition of "Your moral character was all at sea" with its rhyming mate, "I question if you'd got a pass degree," which allows the reader to suppose that the Captain's delinquency might be entirely a matter of faking his academic credentials—a surmise that consorts perfectly well with the rest of what is said about him. But Carpenter, who has supplied his full name, describes Auden's later recollection of the man reciting his play "'in a Henry Irving voice to his awed and astonished favourites.'" These favorites, Carpenter continues, "may perhaps have had sexual advances made to them, for

Wystan recorded cryptically that 'Reggy's' moral character was 'all at sea.'" This seems an important consideration because Auden himself was to become a schoolmaster, during which time he did not attempt to disguise his sexual orientation; because some schoolboys accompanied him and MacNeice on the journey to Iceland; and because later (1948), in an essay called "The Greeks and Us," he wrote as follows:

> Even within [the culture of] a single country different Greeces coexist. For instance here are two English caricatures:
>
> Professor X. Reade Chair of Moral Philosophy. 59. Married. Three daughters. Religion: C of E (Broad). Politics: Conservative. Lives in a small suburban house stuffed with Victorian knick-knacks. Does not entertain. Smokes a pipe. Does not notice what he eats. Hobbies: gardening and long solitary walks. Dislikes: foreigners, Roman Catholicism, modern literature, noise. Current worry: his wife's health.
>
> Mr Y. Classical tutor. 41. Unmarried. Religion: none. Politics: none. Lives in college. Has private means and gives wonderful lunch parties for favorite undergraduates. Hobbies: travel and collecting old glass. Dislikes: Christianity, girls, the poor, English cooking. Current worry: his figure.
>
> To X, the word Greece suggests Reason, the Golden Mean, emotional control, freedom from superstition; to Y it suggests Gaiety and Beauty, the life of the senses, freedom from inhibitions.

In the context of the poem, Reginald's moral lapses are referred to with cunning ambiguity, but the man is unambiguously revered in memory. And that reverence leads directly into an anathema-apostrophe addressed, as though she were equivalent to Pope's Goddess of Dulness in *The Dunciad,* to "Goddess of bossy underlings, Normality! / What murders are committed in thy name!" "Normality" indeed comes in for a lot of ridicule and rebuke, and is compared, as later Tristan and Isolde would be, to "the topping figure of the hockey mistress." Auden then turns to his public school, and somewhat coyly announces that he will omit all discussion of intimate matters: "Those who expect them, will get no such thing." We are told instead about his general tastes and interests, and the comment from a fellow student that led him to begin writing poetry.

He then moves on to Oxford, where his taste in poetry develops from Edward Thomas and Thomas Hardy to T. S. Eliot: "For gasworks and dried tubers I forsook / The clock at Grantchester, the English rook." He is "mute" before the verdict of *The Criterion* (which would soon publish his work), and he came, along with others, to embrace the dogma of T. E. Hulme: "'Good poetry is classic and austere.'" And then finally, after having toyed with sexual suggestion for some time, the poet acknowledges that besides Art, "Life had its passions too."

> We were the tail, a sort of poor relation
> To that debauched, eccentric generation
> That grew up with their fathers at the War,
> And made new glosses on the noun Amor.

Even here, of course, the tantalizing particulars are left out; but by this time we are entitled to recognize a trend. There follows now a passage of great interest, not simply because it outlines something about Auden's intellectual development (a topic others have dealt with more carefully and in greater detail) but because of the detached, amused, and distinctly condescending tone he adopts towards enthusiasms he has now outgrown or risen above; and these enthusiasms have played a great part in his early poetry.

> I met a chap called Layard and he fed
> New doctrines into my receptive head.

> Part came from Lane, and part from D. H. Lawrence;
>     Gide, though I didn't know it then, gave part.
> They taught me to express my deep abhorrence
>     If I caught anyone preferring Art
>     To Life and Love and being Pure-in-Heart.
> I lived with crooks but seldom was molested;
> The Pure-in-Heart can never be arrested.

> He's gay; no bludgeonings of chance can spoil it,
>     The Pure-in-Heart loves all men on a par,
> And has no trouble with his private toilet;
>     The Pure-in-Heart is never ill; catarrh
>     Would be the yellow streak, the brush of tar;
> Determined to be loving and forgiving,
> I came back home to try and earn my living.

This return home is from Berlin ("not Carthage," he feels obliged to state), though at the time of Auden's German sojourn not much distinction could have been made. We should interest ourselves not only in the doctrines that affected Auden's early poetry but in his current attitude towards them. And that attitude is somewhat patronizingly expressed by the phrase "Pure-in-Heart." The couplet about living in perfect security with crooks and being exempted from danger because of being Pure-in-Heart may well describe the curious situation in which Auden found himself among the boy bars and brothels of Berlin; but it also bears a striking resemblance to a well-known ode of Horace's that begins *Integer vitae,* and which has been translated by Joseph P. Clancy.

> A clean record and a clear conscience
> can do without Moroccan Javelins
> or bow and quiver stuffed with poisoned arrows,
>     my dear Fuscus,
>
> Whether one's way is through the blazing sand of
> Africa, the unwelcoming heights of Caucasia,
> or through the land of legends where the Indus
>     pours its waters.
>
> For when I met a wolf in the Sabine woods,
> as I was singing the praises of Lalage, walking
> far from my farm, not a care in the world,
>     unarmed: he ran.
>
> Was he a monster! That soldiering country Apulia
> couldn't grow his equal in its broad oak forests,
> barren Numidia, nourisher of lions, breeds
>     not a bigger.
>
> Put me on barren plains, where never a tree
> renews its leaves in breezes of the summer,
> a foggy country where the sky hangs low
>     upon the earth;
>
> put me where the chariot of the sun comes
> swinging so low that no one can live there:
> still will I love my Lalage, her laughter is sweet,
>     her chatter charming.

But there is another matter that seems to call for attention. Whether Auden, like Horace, is saying that his excellent character and purity protected him, as it were, supernaturally from circumambient dangers;

and whether or not he anymore admires the doctrines of Layard, Lane, Lawrence, and Gide that he had embraced at one time, we must puzzle about that exclamation, referring to the Pure-of-Heart, "he's gay." This, of course can mean gay in the sense of carefree. But, given the drift of sections of this poem, we may wonder if something else may not have been part of the meaning. Here, on the homosexual meaning of the word, is part of an essay called "The Political Vocabulary of Homosexuality" by Edmund White.

No one I know has any real information about the origin of the word *gay;* the research all remains to be done. Those who dislike the word assume that it is synonymous with *happy* or *lighthearted* and that its use implies that homosexuals regard heterosexuals, by contrast, as "grim." But *gay* has many meanings, including "loose" and "immoral," especially in reference to a prostitute (a whorehouse was once called a "gay house"). In the past one asked if a woman was "gay," much as today one might ask if she "swings." The identification of *gay* with "immoral" is further strengthened by the fact that *queen* (a male homosexual) is almost certainly derived from *quean* (the Elizabethan word for prostitute).

In American slang at the turn of the century, a "gay cat" was a younger, less experienced man who attached himself to an older, more seasoned vagrant or hobo; implicit in the relationship between gay cat and hobo was a sexual liaison. Yet another slang meaning of *gay* is "fresh," "impertinent," "saucy" (not so very distant from "immoral"). In French *gai* can mean "spicy" or "ribald." My hunch (and it's only a hunch) is that the word may turn out to be very old, to have originated in France, worked its way to England in the eighteenth century and thence to the colonies in America. It has died out in Europe and England and is now being reintroduced as a new word from the United States. But this is only speculation.

If the exact etymology is vague, no wonder; the word served for years as a shibboleth, and the function of a shibboleth is to exclude outsiders. Undoubtedly it has had until recently its greatest vogue among Americans. In England, the standard slang word has been *queer.* In Bloomsbury *bugger* was the preferred term, presumably because it was salty and vulgar enough to send those rarified souls into convulsions of laughter. One pictures Virginia Woolf discussing "buggery" with Lytton Strachey; how they must have relished the word's public school, criminal and eighteenth-century connotations.

Today heterosexuals commonly object to *gay* on the grounds that it has ruined for them the ordinary festive sense of the word; one can no longer say, "How gay I feel!" It seems frivolous, however, to discuss this semantic loss beside the political gain the word represents for American homosexuals.

The *Letter to Lord Byron* is approaching its conclusion, and a few more biographical details are added, including coming back home "to earn my living" by teaching at a public school. The boat brings the poet back to England, and from the port he takes a railroad train (his favorite mode of transportation).

> The line I travel has an English gauge;
>   The engine's shadow vaults the little hedges;
>   And summer's done. I make the usual pledges
> To be a better poet, better man;
> I'll really do it this time if I can.

It remains only to observe that the book called *Letters from Iceland,* in which the poem under discussion first appears, is dedicated to Auden's father, so that the candor of what he has written is the more impressive. Secondly, those "pledges" appearing in the penultimate stanza are not unlike New Year's resolutions; and the entire poem itself is a kind of intellectual and spiritual stock-taking that one is conventionally supposed to undertake before making such resolutions. It is, moreover, not an uncommon thing for Auden to take an inventory of his ideas and beliefs and the ways in which he has changed them. Such an impulse governs another long poem he was to write, the *New Year Letter.*

# V.  A Civitas of Sound:
## *New Year Letter*

A mere four years after the *Letter to Lord Byron* Auden was to compose another verse epistle of a rather different kind, and yet taking up in important ways where the earlier poem left off and advancing some of its themes and concerns. The intellectual stock-taking and spiritual self-assessment that began in the earlier long poem is resumed with great seriousness and in a wholly different verse form. The *New Year Letter* employs as a premise our start-of-the-year convention of self-examination, acknowledgment of our faults, and resolution to change, which is a secular equivalent of the confession that would lead to absolution in religious terms. And the *New Year Letter*, as it progresses, becomes more and more clearly oriented towards religious answers to what were once secular questions.

The American edition of the poem was called *The Double Man*, and it bore a significant epigraph from Montaigne that Auden had found quoted in Charles Williams' book *The Descent of the Dove*, a book Auden acknowledges in his notes as having a profound influence on the poem here discussed. The Montaigne quotation runs: "We are, I know not how, double in ourselves, so that what we believe we disbelieve, and cannot rid ourselves of what we condemn." The doubleness expressed here has a number of analogues in Auden's long poem, and among them are the divisions of public and private life that had concerned him for some time. But there are others as well. In 1938, in a review of Laurence Housman's memoir of his poet brother, Auden began,

> Heaven and Hell. Reason and Instinct. Conscious Mind and Unconscious. Is their hostility a temporary and curable neurosis, due to our particular pattern of culture, or intrinsic to the nature of these faculties? Can man only think when he is frustrated from acting and feeling? Is the intelligent person always the product of some childhood neurosis? Does Life only offer two alternatives: "You shall be

happy, healthy, attractive, a good mixer, a good lover and parent, but on condition that you are not overcurious about life. On the other hand you shall be attentive and sensitive, conscious of what is happening round you, but in that case you must cease to expect to be happy, or successful in love, or at home in any company. There are two worlds and you cannot belong to them both."

The dilemmas and alternatives described here are also part of the doubleness that the poem addresses.

The poem begins with a recollection that exactly four months before this holiday evening, on September 1, 1939, when the war broke out, Auden was visiting the home of the hostess to whom the poem is dedicated. Part III of the poem furthermore recalls that he was also a guest in her house at Christmastime, a week previous to this New Year's Eve. There is, therefore, an ample "compositional span" to account for so long and complex a poem; and yet there are, I think, detectable signs of headlong speed of composition, including lapses of syntax, perilously long sentences that border on the inchoate, and dull passages of compounded abstractions. This is not, in any case, a poem one rejoices at the thought of reading again and again.

If the poem bears some resemblances to the *Letter to Lord Byron,* it differs in being addressed to a living person, Elizabeth Mayer, a German refugee and the wife of Dr. William Mayer, a Jewish psychiatrist who had had to flee the Nazis and had settled in a tiny cottage on the grounds of a clinic in Amityville, Long Island. Elizabeth Mayer was considerably older than Auden, and, according to Carpenter, who cites Auden's brother John as his authority, bore "a striking resemblance to Auden's own mother." She was not herself Jewish, and had distressed her aristocratic and distinctly Christian family ("her own father had been chaplain to the Grand Duke of Mecklenburg") by marrying Dr. Mayer instead of a young man they had thought more suitable. She had pretensions towards being a patroness of the arts, and was particularly kind to Benjamin Britten and Peter Pears, who introduced Auden to her, and she indulged him like a spoiled child, which he must have liked very much. However, not everyone cared for her, and when a friend of Auden's asked him, after observing that she "behaved like a celebrity, a *grande dame,* talked constantly, dropped names," why he was so attracted to her, Auden answered, with a quote from Goethe that appears in the poem under consideration, "Das Ewig-Weibliche!" (the Eternal Feminine).

The poem's rhyming tetrameters also distinguish it from the earlier verse epistle, and recall Swift and Prior, Blake's "The Everlasting Gospel," and Butler's *Hudibras*. But perhaps most distinctly of all, this poem entirely lacks the cheerful frivolity of the *Letter to Lord Byron*. Its earnestness is apparent throughout; and the New Year holiday, with its self-inquisition and in a wartime setting, is vastly different from the Iceland holiday of escape.

In reading this "letter," we cannot fail to become conscious of Auden's explicit debt to Dante. Its triadic structure is evident everywhere. It is divided into three parts (though they are vastly unequal, in contrast to the *Commedia*); in the poem's course he arraigns himself before three judges; but most noticeably of all, the poem is filled with a rhetorical form called the tricolon: an arrangement of words or phrases in groups of three. These are so frequent as to be a significantly formal feature of the poem; and we are reminded that to Dante the numeral three was a central feature of the *Vita Nuova* as well as the *Commedia*. Within the first eleven lines of the poem the pattern figures several times.

> Under the familiar weight
> Of winter, conscience and the State,
> In loose formations of good cheer,
> Love, language, loneliness and fear,
> Towards the habits of next year,
> Along the streets the people flow,
> Singing or sighing as they go:
> Exalté, piano, or in doubt,
> All our reflections turn about
> A common meditative norm,
> Retrenchment, Sacrifice, Reform.

The second, the eighth, and the last of these lines employ the tricolon, and inaugurate a series of them so striking that at least a few need to be cited by way of indicating how consciously they became a formal device of the poet's.

> Terror, concupiscence and pride

> Of fear and faithfulness and hate

> If loud, lugubrious and long

With swimming heads and hands that shake
And stomachs that keep nothing down.

A particle, I must not yield
To particles who claim the field,
Nor trust the demagogue who raves,
A quantum speaking for the waves,
Nor worship blindly the ornate
*Grandezza* of the Sovereign State.

His trade, his corner and his way

Eccentric, wrinkled, and ice-capped

We know no fuss or pain or lying
Can stop the moribund from dying

We see, we suffer, we despair

Entombed, hilarious, and fed

To serve, enlighten and enrich

Unhindered, unrebuked, unwatched,
Self-known, self-praising, self-attached.

The Not, the Never, and the Night
The formless Mass without a Me,
The Midnight Woman and the Sea

Our loves, authorities, and friends

Where Freedom dwells because it must,
Necessity because it can,
And men confederate in Man.

. . . the world we know
Of war and wastefulness and woe

Develop, understand, refine.

Each a unique particular
That is no giant, god, or dwarf

The grinning gap of Hell, the hill
Of Venus and the stairs of Will.

One other feature (or perhaps eccentricity) of the poem deserves notice here: the notes. They were dropped when Auden reissued the poem, and are omitted from the *Collected Poems*. But they are curious and interesting for a number of reasons. The first is their sheer volume. In the Faber edition, the poem proper runs to fifty-eight pages, the notes to eighty-one. And one cannot read any annotated modern poem without being forced to think of *The Waste Land*. It is, accordingly, reasonable to suppose that Auden intends an allusion (and this may be confirmed by an explicit citation from Eliot's poem in Auden's notes). We are still left, however, to determine whether this allusion is meant mockingly or admiringly.

Both Eliot's and Auden's notes employ buried, or private, jokes, meant to be grasped only by the initiate, or perhaps reserved for the solitary pleasure and relish of the poet himself. There are at least two such jokes in the notes to *The Waste Land*. One of these annotates line 68, which closes a description of the crowd of living dead, on their leaden way to work every morning over London Bridge "To where Saint Mary Woolnoth kept the hours / With a dead sound on the final stroke of nine." The note comments, "A phenomenon which I have often noticed." The reason the ninth stroke sounds like a death toll is that office workers who were not at their desks and at work by that final stroke were docked a day's salary, and Eliot himself worked under that danger. The second such joke is the note to line 98 of Part II: A Game of Chess. The line reads, "As though a window gave upon the sylvan scene," and the note identifies the words "sylvan scene" as coming from Book IV, line 140 of *Paradise Lost*. Eliot's contempt of Milton, though published in an essay of 1936, was already a prejudice he obviously entertained. For it is manifestly ludicrous to cast about in an epic poem of 10,566 lines of blank verse for so commonplace and conventional a phrase as "sylvan scene," which might belong to a work of prose criticism as well as to a poem. Auden, too, has a multitude of jokes among his notes; and so does Pope, in his embellishment of *The Dunciad*. But Pope's notes are always relevant, while Auden's are often tangential or seemingly gratuitous. (In the essay of 1941 called "Criticism in a Mass Society," Auden was to cite Dante, Langland—who is quoted in Auden's notes to the *New Year Letter*—and Pope as being "the three greatest influences on my own work.") What allows us to suspect that Auden might be mocking Eliot's notes is the sheer imbalance between the poem and its gloss. We know today that Eliot furnished his notes only to oblige Leonard and Virginia Woolf, who, when they set the poem up for publication at the Hogarth Press, found that the book's signatures provided a lot of wasteful blank pages at the end, which they felt might usefully be filled with something or other. But this was not known in 1941.

The notes, however, do serve a serious and useful function in that they provide a sort of bibliography of authors or of works that were preoccupying Auden at the time he was writing this poem, and the list is delightful and profoundly interesting in its range and diversity. I offer here a mere selection.

F. L. Wells: *Values in Social Psychology*
Tchekov
C. M. Child: *The Beginnings of Unity and Order in Living Things*
Goethe's *Faust* [importantly]
Spinoza
Milton
Wolfgang Kohler: *The Place of Value in a World of Facts*
Pascal [importantly]
Margaret Mead
Kierkegaard [importantly]
*Time Magazine*
Baudelaire
Rilke
Wagner libretti [importantly]
Blake
Collingwood
Flaubert
Jung
Nietzsche
Eliot
Groddeck
R. S. and H. M. Lynd: *Middletown in Transition*
Tillich

Nijinsky's *Diary* [see "September 1, 1939"]
Henry Adams
Kafka
C. S. Lewis
Whitman
Thomas Mann
Charles Williams [very importantly]
Christopher Smart
Donne
St. Augustine
St. Bernard
St. Anthony
St. Polycarp
Jacopone da Todi
Rimbaud
Henry James
Werner Jaeger
Maritain

Some of this is pure levity, as if to relieve the earnestness of the poem it presumes to gloss. One such note, for example, reads,

> Four men were discussing which organ of the body it would be most dreadful to lose. "I am a painter," said the first, "if I lost my hand, life wouldn't be worth living." "I love music," said the second, "I can imagine nothing worse than being deaf." "I would rather be deaf than blind," said the third. "Think of not being able to see the country in summer or a pretty face." "Well, what do you think?" they all asked the fourth, who had so far not taken any part in the argument. "My navel." "Your navel? But why?" "Well, you see, I like to eat celery in bed, and if I had no navel where should I put the salt?"

Other notes are more pertinent but no less amusing, as when, for example, a passage from Hans Spemann's *Embryonic Development and Induction* is juxtaposed with a passage from Henry James's preface to *The Spoils of Poynton,* having to do with the "germ" of a story and how it "develops." Needless to say, a critical commentary that took careful account both of the poem and of its notes would gravely unbalance the overview of Auden's work I mean to present here; so from here on I will concern myself almost entirely with the poem.

Part I begins with the triadic oppression of "winter, conscience and the State," instantly linking the private and interior world to the outward one of weather and politics. It is wartime, and the conventions of the New Year, as well, perhaps, as self-examination, call for the triad of "Retrenchment, Sacrifice, Reform." The poet recalls that exactly a year before, he was in Brussels. While, according to Carpenter, this was a productive (and remarkably carefree) period in Auden's career, it is here painted as rife with all the anxiety and expectation of an approaching catastrophe that would sort with a "low dishonest decade."

> All formulas were tried to still
> The scratching on the window-sill,
> All bolts of custom made secure
> Against the pressure on the door,
> But up the staircase of events
> Carrying his special instruments,
> To every bedside all the same
> The dreadful figure swiftly came.

There is a clear relationship between such lines and the only slightly earlier but much better known lines "All the conventions conspire / To make this fort assume / The furniture of home . . ."

But the poet finds himself fortunately situated (and not without a twinge of "conscience" therefore) in a cottage on Long Island, where Elizabeth Mayer is his hostess, and

> Where Buxtehude as we played
> One of his *passacaglias* made
> Our minds a *civitas* of sound
> Where nothing but assent was found,
> For art had set in order sense
> And feeling and intelligence,
> And from its ideal order grew
> Our local understanding too.

This is a remarkable acknowledgment of the therapeutic, the virtually redemptive, powers of art by a poet who had already claimed, and was later still to claim, that art was no substitute for religion and had no purpose but to entertain. Buxtehude was, of course, a composer of religious music, but that is irrelevant to Auden's dogmatisms about the place of art. In the case of the passage above, the *civitas* of sound created by the music (which we may assume is "played" on a recording, not as live performance) stands as remedy or corrective to the chaos of a world gone mad.

"To set in order" leads the poet to consider those orders that govern, or attempt to govern, Life and Art. And Part I of this poem very seriously continues a theme of the *Letter to Lord Byron* four years earlier: the place of the artist in modern society, and the way that place has changed from earlier centuries. In these opening passages it is taken virtually for granted that artistic order may serve as a paradigm for the human desire to impose order upon life itself. Yet Auden perfectly well recognizes that the great artists who created their great artistic order did not necessarily lead lives that were orderly or admirable. The following lines from the *New Year Letter,* quoted earlier in my discussion of Auden's elegy for Yeats, seem worth repeating here:

> Great masters who have shown mankind
> An order it has yet to find,
> What if all pedants say of you
> As personalities be true?
> All the more honor to you then
> If, weaker than some other men,
> You had the courage that survives
> Soiled, shabby, egotistic lives,
> If poverty or ugliness,
> Ill-health or social unsuccess
> Hunted you out of life to play
> At living in another way.

This notion of art as compensation for an unhappy or troubled life will, later in the poem (with suitable adjustment of Art to Theory), be applied to Karl Marx. But we may observe for the present that art is not only a compensation for personal misery (or even criminality) but a dream-like perfection, an imagined Eden, a faultless dream world that need have no correspondence to the artist's real moral life.

Selfishness is among only the milder vices great artists have been known to possess, and Auden was conscious of the presence of many such vices in an artist he admired all his life and wrote about in the essay called "The Greatest of the Monsters," Richard Wagner. (Among other things Wagner was an outright crook.) Needless to say, this discrepancy between the personal moral disorder of the individual artist, and the artistic order (with its moral implications) that such artists create, is not a matter that is solved or settled here. Auden goes on to claim that poetry is "the greatest of vocations," and, apparently at the urging of both his artistic and moral conscience, he arraigns himself before a "summary tribunal" of great writers who are to sit in judgment upon him.

> Although they delegate to us
> Both prosecution and defence,
> Accept our rules of evidence,
> And pass no sentence but our own,
> Yet, as he faces them alone,
> O who can show convincing proof
> That he is worthy of their love?
> Who ever rose to read aloud
> Before that quiet attentive crowd
> And did not falter as he read,
> Stammer, sit down, and hang his head?

There is evidently something distinctly Dantean in the self-arraignment and self-sentencing described here, and Auden proceeds to confront the three poets who shall judge him. Despite the fact that there are a number of other writers to witness the proceedings—Dryden, Catullus, Tennyson, Baudelaire, Hardy, Rilke—there are only three who sit in judgment: Dante, Blake, and Rimbaud. And these three have in common the fact that they are "experts" on Hell. Dante's credentials are well enough known; Blake wrote "The Marriage of Heaven and Hell," while Rimbaud wrote *Une Saison en enfer*. And a knowledge of Hell (which is to be the obsessive subject of Part II) is particularly required of this poem that is concerned both with the inward consciousness of personal guilt and with the outward manifestations of it in a world at war.

Auden first accuses himself of artistic lapses: "For I relapse into my crimes, / Time and again have slubbered through / With slip and slap-dash what I do, / Adopted what I would disown, / The preacher's loose immodest tone." That evangelical tone was his in those earlier, almost doctrinal poems that saw a cure for England's, and the world's, malaise in the ideas of Lawrence or Lane or other intellectual heroes that inhabit the early poems. But from this self-indictment, the poem turns to the general public shame, which is brilliantly described (in a passage too long to quote) in terms of the crime in detective fiction, and which begins, "The situation of our time / Surrounds us like a baffling crime. / There lies the body half-undressed, / We all had reason to detest, / And all are suspects and involved / Until the mystery is solved." In his essay about detective fiction, "The Guilty Vicarage," Auden would pursue this analogy between police-blotter crime and social evil, and he would do so in terms that are at once those of Greek tragedy and those of Christian theology. So satisfactory did this analogy seem to him that it became the basis of the short poem in syllabics, "To T. S. Eliot on His Sixtieth Birthday," of 1948.

> When things began to happen to our favorite spot,
> A key missing, a library bust defaced,
>> Then on the tennis-court one morning,
>> Outrageous, the bloody corpse and always,
>
> Blank day after day, the unheard-of drought, it was you
> Who, not speechless from shock but finding the right
>> Language for thirst and fear, did much to
>> Prevent panic. It is the crime that
>
> Counts, you will say. We know, but would gratefully add,
> Today as we wait for the Law to take its course,
>> (And which of us shall escape whipping?)
>> That your sixty years have not been wasted.

I think we are entitled to notice how tempered and qualified is the tenor of this praise, but the chief point of the birthday tribute may have to do with a shared admiration for detective fiction (Eliot not only admired Conan Doyle but wrote about police-blotter crime in a number of his poems and in *Sweeney Agonistes*) as well as a shared theology.

The *New Year Letter* continues by turning from the symbolic crime to the actual events that have incriminated the whole world for years. The indictment is terrible, including "The Asiatic cry of pain, / The shots of executing Spain . . . The Abyssinian, blistered, blind, / The dazed uncomprehending stare / Of the Danubian despair, / The Jew wrecked in the German cell, / Flat Poland frozen into hell . . ." In the face of such terrible events, such accusing violence, what is the poet, what is any artist, to do? Auden returns to the claim he made in the elegy for Yeats that "poetry makes nothing happen," a claim for which he was to suffer various kinds of rebuke, particularly from "socially conscious" writers, who felt he had betrayed his early allegiances to social causes, and who treated him much as, in Part II of this very poem, he would treat the elderly Wordsworth. In the immediate context he writes,

Though language may be useless, for
No words men write can stop a war
Or measure up to the relief
Of its immeasurable grief,
Yet truth, like love and sleep, resents
Approaches that are too intense,
And often when the searcher stood
Before the Oracle, it would
Ignore his grown-up earnestness
But not the child of his distress,
For through the Janus of a joke
The candid psychopompos spoke.

There is in these lines a rather cunning equation between art and truth which Keats's Urn would have endorsed and Eliot deplored. But the passage ends with a reference to Hermes, the "psychopompos," and god of dreams, or deep truths, and a claim that the ambiguities ("the Janus of a joke") of the unconscious contain a more enduring answer than immediate calamity can understand or make use of. More important still, Part I now concludes with a prayer, a more than rhetorical form of petition that has appeared in earlier Auden poems. This one goes,

May such heart and intelligence
As huddle now in conference
Whenever an impasse occurs
Use the good offices of verse;
May an Accord be reached, and may
This *aide-mémoire* on what they say,
This private minute for a friend,
Be the dispatch that I intend;
Although addressed to a Whitehall,
Be under Flying Seal to all
Who wish to read it anywhere,
And, if they open it, *En Clair*.

John Fuller remarks of these lines that they are a "public explanation of what to many in wartime England seemed a kind of defection." This seems to me true, and borne out by passages that will appear later in the poem. The "Accord" prayed for here (the term clearly comes from the discourse of international diplomacy) is that between heart and intelligence, in the hope that this *aide-mémoire* will turn out to be such a "*civitas* of sound" as Buxtehude exemplified at the opening of the poem.

Part II is the *Inferno* of this tripartite poem; Part III will be the *Purgatorio,* and there will be no *Paradiso* because we are never allowed to lose sight of the fact that we are now in the midst of the greatest and most costly and terrible war in human history, and because Auden has not achieved the beatific vision, though he feels, by the poem's end, that he is moving in the right direction.

Part II opens with the line "Tonight a scrambling decade ends," and we remember the "low dishonest decade" alluded to in Part I. We immediately encounter a symbolic landscape, one of many that have appeared in Auden's poem and will continue to present themselves. This one may be said roughly to correspond with a Dantean one, and it is in any case a *paysage moralisé.* This one is infernal, and only in part because the temporal context of the war demands something of the sort. We are brought to confront our weaknesses, which are not military but moral, and they include "terror, concupiscence and pride." But they furthermore include the impotence of "language" to set things right. This is a particularly humiliating admission for a poet, who cannot more ruthlessly be shown how marginal to society in a crisis is his "sedentary trade." And among other weaknesses—observe how the self-inquisition of Part I continues here—there is our childish wish (which includes the dream of never growing old) for a *fixed* reality. This wish, however, is authored by the Prince of Lies, who presides in this part of the poem.

> But who, though, is the Prince of Lies
> If not the Spirit-that-denies,
> The shadow just behind the shoulder
> Claiming it's wicked to grow older,
> Though we are damned if we turn round
> Thinking salvation has been found?

(If "fixed reality" is a lie of the Devil, we may be entitled to read these lines as Auden's apologia for changing some of his views about society.)

Now Mephistopheles is addressed directly in the second person, but, suddenly (and inexplicably), the voice of the poem and its grammar shifts to the third person. The Devil is the ruler of the literal world, which is ephemeral and untrue (though this would be a poor consolation to those who are maimed or killed in the war).

Against his paralysing smile
And honest realistic style
Our best protection is that we
In fact live in eternity.

But he is quite prepared to repudiate reason, logic, and what seems literal reality, if this should suit his satanic purposes. He is even given a chance to speak in his own oily voice—a kind of aria that mocks intelligence as the source of all human misery, saying, among other things,

'O when will men show common sense
And throw away intelligence,
That killjoy which discriminates,
Recover what appreciates,
The deep unsnobbish instinct which
Alone can make relation rich,
Upon the *Beischlaf* of the blood
Establish a real neighborhood
Where art and industry and *moeurs*
Are governed by an *ordre du coeur?*'

There is much cunning here. That *"Beischlaf* [sexual life] of the blood" may be both the Lawrentian doctrines that Auden earlier espoused, now being recommended by the Devil, and also some of the racial doctrines of Nazi Germany. This identification of "instinct" with the advice of the Devil is a complete volte-face from the view expressed in the closing, moving lines of the syllabic poem which mourns the death of Sigmund Freud:

One rational voice is dumb: over a grave
The household of Impulse mourns one dearly loved.
        Sad is Eros, builder of cities,
        And weeping anarchic Aphrodite.

Auden is also supremely aware that the infernal powers can corrupt art as well as anything else in the human domain. Sin is defined as a species of rebellion: "To sin is to act consciously / Against what seems necessity . . ." And the Devil's means of seduction are always ingenious.

The False Association is
A favorite strategy of his:
Induce men to associate
Truth with a lie, then demonstrate

The lie and they will, in truth's name,
Treat babe and bath-water the same,
. . . . .
Thus WORDSWORTH fell into temptation
In France during a long vacation,
Saw in the fall of the Bastille
The Parousia of Liberty,
And weaving a platonic dream
Round a provisional régime
That sloganized the Rights of Man,
A liberal fellow-traveller ran
With Sans-culotte and Jacobin,
Nor guessed what circles he was in,
But ended as the Devil knew
An earnest Englishman would do,
Left by Napoleon in the lurch,
Supporting the Established Church,
The Congress of Vienna and
The Squire's paternalistic hand.

One cannot read these lines without thinking of Randall Jarrell's mocking and dismissive review of this poem in the April 12, 1941, issue of *The Nation,* the beginning of which, an imaginary dialogue with the ghost of Alexander Pope, was quoted earlier. And not that review alone, but some of Jarrell's equally disapproving essays recall how, to the younger poet, Auden seemed to have betrayed his liberal beginnings. These lines about Wordsworth clearly show how Auden was aware of, and went in fear of, that particular temptation. And insofar as I am aware, Auden, though he became quite conservative in religious matters, remained truly liberal in political matters (as distinct from a number of well-known writers, including Pound and Eliot and Lawrence).

Indeed, the topic of Wordsworth's ideological shift to reaction immediately calls the person of Marx to Auden's mind; and he is treated in much the same way as were the "great masters" (all of them poets) in Part I. That is to say, he is described as though his personal errors and private unhappiness had been sublimated into a serious and valuable vision of what life ought to be.

[Some] found their humanistic view
In question from the German who,

Obscure in gaslit London, brought
To human consciousness a thought
It thought unthinkable, and made
Another consciousness afraid.
What if his hate distorted? Much
Was hateful that he had to touch.
What if he erred? He flashed a light
On facts where no one had been right.
The father-shadow that he hated
Weighed like an Alp; his love, frustrated,
Negating as it was negated,
Burst out in boils; his animus
Outlawed him from himself; but thus,
And only thus, perhaps, could he
Have come to his discovery.

. . . . .

As he explored the muttering tomb
Of a museum reading room,
The Dagon of the General Will
Fell in convulsions and lay still;
The tempting Contract of the rich,
Revealed as an abnormal witch,
Fled with a shriek, for as he spoke
The justifying magic broke;
The garden of the Three Estates
Turned desert, and the Ivory Gates
Of Pure Idea to gates of horn
Through which the Governments are born.

Not only do these lines identify Marx with the great poets of the past by suggesting that, like them, he has made something fine out of an imperfect life, but that "father-shadow that he hated" sounds familiarly like the "huge imago" that, in "September 1, 1939," made Hitler into a "psychopathic god." And there is another echo of the shorter poem: the last lines quoted above recall the assertion that "there is no such thing as the State," an assertion that Marx is here credited with demonstrating. Furthermore, the poem goes on to describe Capitalistic Man,

Whose love of money only shows
That in his heart of hearts he knows

His love is not determined by
A personal or tribal tie
Or colour, neighborhood, or creed,
But universal, mutual need;
Loosed from its shroud of tempter, his
Determinism comes to this:
None shall receive unless they give:
All must co-operate to live.

And these lines sound remarkably like the one that so much annoyed Auden in "September 1, 1939," which he tampered with before repudiating the entire poem: "We must love one another or die." In any case, the Marxist dream of a stateless and classless society did not come to pass.

We hoped; we waited for the day
The State would wither clean away,
Expecting the Millennium
That theory promised us would come,
It didn't. Specialists must try
To detail all the reasons why;

But we must be on guard against the sin of disillusionment and the accidie that is likely to accompany it.

Here's where the devil goes to town,
Who knows that nothing suits his book
So well as the hang-over look,
That few drunks feel more awful than
The Simon-pure Utopian.
He calls at breakfast in the role
Of blunt but sympathetic soul:
'Well, how's our Socialist this morning?
I could say "Let this be a warning,"
But no, why should I? Students must
Sow their wild oats at times or bust.
Such things have happened in the lives
Of all the best Conservatives.
I'll fix you something for your liver.'
And thus he sells us down the river.
Repenting of our last infraction
We seek atonement in reaction

And cry, nostalgic like a whore,
'I was a virgin still at four.'

Again, the temptations to political (that is, public) corruption are no more real and dangerous than the temptations to personal (that is, private moral and artistic) corruption. For the Devil tempts us not with anything so vulgar and transparent as outright lies, but with "half-truths," and as one of Auden's notes explains, "The Devil indeed is the father of Poetry, for poetry might be defined as the clear expression of mixed feelings." What are we to make of the Shakespearean claim that "the truest poetry is the most feigning"? Can poetry be made "responsible" to society? Part II does not end on a prayer, but instead ends upon a note of hope that we can somehow see through the tricks of the Devil.

Part III is the longest, the most complicated, the most difficult, and the most personal segment of the poem. Its lines are deeply troubled by a complex sense of guilt, only the most superficial part of which is due to the state of exemption from the center of hostilities that Auden is enjoying by virtue of being an expatriate. His absence from England, not regarded with sympathy by many of his countrymen, was attacked in the press of that country and mentioned with rancor on the floor of the House of Commons. And the chances are fairly good that he knew of at least some of these attacks. But the theological tenor of this section of the poem is concerned with many darker and deeper weaknesses and sins than the one bruited about in the British press, a matter which Auden may have had no private reason to be ashamed about, since there was very little he could do, either as a man or as a poet (as this poem has repeatedly shown) to advance or assist the military or political cause of his country.

So at the opening of Part III the poet acknowledges that it is "hard liquor" of the holiday celebration (there is no need to mention geographical distance, or the fact that the United States is not at the moment a belligerent) that "causes everywhere / A general *détente*, and Care / For this state function of Good Will / Is diplomatically ill . . ." This use of the language of diplomacy has its own burden of irony in a world at war; but the irony is reinforced (as it is in the bar-room setting of "September 1, 1939") by the fact that the civility of *détente* is engendered by booze, which serves both to celebrate the holiday in traditional ways and to blunt the mind's knowledge of its and the world's predicament.

As if to confirm both the irony and the guilt, the poem immediately recalls the Christmas Eve of a week before, spent in the same home on Long Island where the poem began with the commencement of the war.

Warm in your house, Elizabeth,
A week ago at the same hour
I felt the unexpected power
That drove our ragged egos in
From the dead-ends of greed and sin
To sit down at the wedding feast,
Put shining garments on the least,
Arranged us so that each and all,
The erotic and the logical,
Each felt the placement to be such
That he was honoured overmuch,
And SCHUBERT sang and MOZART played
And GLUCK and food and friendship made
Our privileged community
That real republic which must be
The State all politicians claim,
Even the worst, to be their aim.

There is much to be noted here, including the unfortunate repetition of "each" in the eighth and tenth lines above. But what is more important is Auden's acknowledgment of the "unexpected power" that invaded him on Christmas Eve. This is far more precise and specific than anything that appears in the poem beginning "Out on the lawn I lie in bed." The language of the first half of these lines is clearly religious, and the note on "the erotic and the logical" comes from Jacques Maritain. Greed and sin are both dead ends, the hang-outs of our "ragged egos"; just possibly a reference to the "Dead-End Kids" of the movies is intended. The wedding feast, as redemptive, may come from "The Ancient Mariner."

In any case, the "privileged community" becomes a richly ambiguous term, since, on its most superficial level, it means exemption from the dangers of war; but it also recalls the "*civitas* of sound" with which the poem began. Here that *civitas* and community is described as "that real republic" which is the ideal of even the worst of politicians—which, presumably, must include Adolf Hitler. What needs emphasis here is the linkage of the aesthetic order of art with the most benign order of politics.

That invasive power, however, is fleeting, and "though it happens every day / To someone," it cannot be *willed* into being, and we have trouble in our search for it. Even so, it reasserts itself "casually" as "an accidental happiness" by which we are briefly removed from the flux of Becoming and dwell, however briefly, in the serene realm of Being. "But perfect Being has ordained / It must be lost to be regained."

These fugitive intuitions or experiences of grace from which we lapse back into our familiar and ordinary world, return us to the topic of Hell, in these lines:

> Hell is the being of the lie
> That we become if we deny
> The laws of consciousness and claim
> Becoming and Being are the same,
> Being in time, and man discrete
> In will, yet free and self-complete.

The notes furnish an interesting and serious gloss on these lines.

> It is possible that the gates of Hell are always standing wide open. The lost are perfectly free to leave whenever they like, but to do so would mean admitting that the gates were open, that is, that there was another life outside. This they cannot admit, not because they have any pleasure in their present existence, but because the life outside would be different and, if they admitted its existence, they would have to lead it. They know this. They know that they are free to leave and they know why they do not. This knowledge is the flame of hell.

What is remarkable about this note is the stunning way it applies to most of our common secular life itself. We are all immersed in mindless and compulsive habits, some of which, like sloth itself, are sins. And with the supinity of addicts we make ourselves content with our lots. Nevertheless, given the momentary glimpses of grace afforded to us, we come to find ourselves most frequently shuffling up the Purgatorial Mount.

> Precisely what our fear suspected,
> We have no cause to look dejected
> When, wakened from a dream of glory,
> We find ourselves in Purgatory,
> Back on the same old mountain side
> With only guessing for a guide.
> To tell the truth, although we stifle
> The feeling, are we not a trifle
> Relieved to wake on its damp earth?
> It's been our residence since birth,

Its inconveniences are known,
And we have made its flaws our own.
Is it not here that we belong,
Where everyone is going wrong,
And normal our freemartin state,
Half angel and half *petite bête?*
. . . . .
O once again let us set out,
Our faith well balanced by our doubt,
Admitting every step we make
Will certainly be a mistake,
But still believing we can climb
A little higher every time,
And keep in order, that we may
Ascend the penitential way.

Something about man's place in the Great Chain of Being is implied by
making him half angel and half beast, a troubled hybrid for which the
animal-husbandry term of "freemartin" carries as well the less well known
meaning of "hermaphrodite." Those who are put off by the religious tenor
of this poem may take little comfort in the line "Our faith well balanced
by our doubt," as though Auden were withdrawing with one hand what
he had offered with the other, for the note on this line directs us to Pascal,
who observes that to deny, to believe, and to doubt are to man what
running is to a horse.

And now, in a brilliant analogy, the fall of Rome (which is presented
as a sort of counterpart of barbarian forces at work in modern Europe)
is likened to the Shakespearean Hell of lust described in sonnet 129, where
"Th' expense of spirit in a waste of shame" is examined. The wrecking of
civilization, represented by cities that are allowed to "fall," is expressed
by the claim that "This lust in action to destroy / Is not the pure instinctive
joy / Of animals, but the refined / Creation of machines and mind." Not
only not angelical, but even without the dignity of being truly bestial, for
lust is the erotic life divorced from love, and war is not the satisfaction of
an animal's hunger. And now, as has been so often and variously
acknowledged in the past poetry, the two realms of private and public are
brought face to face with one another.

There are two atlases: the one
The public space where acts are done,

In theory common to us all,
Where we are needed and feel small,
The *agora* of work and news
Where each one has the right to choose
His trade, his corner and his way,
And can, again in theory, say
For whose protection he will pay,
And loyalty is help we give
The place where we prefer to live;
The other is the inner space
Of private ownership, the place
That each of us is forced to own,
Like his own life from which it's grown,
The landscape of his will and need
Where he is sovereign indeed.

We are approaching here the edgy topic of loyalty to place, a matter to be clarified, or at least interpreted, a few lines further on. There is a fine play on the word "own," which is obviously linked to "ownership" in the previous line, but which very likely is meant to convey the slightly archaic meaning of "acknowledge" as well as the more conventional meaning of "possess." There is a clear paradox in being "forced" to possess something, as if one wished to disburden oneself of one's interior life—and this may point to a knowledge of sin that preoccupies this part of the poem. In any case, when Auden goes on to say, "England to me is my own tongue," he may well be saying that 1) he has not defected, since he still uses it, and 2) he is at home in a land where the language is used, and therefore is at least figuratively where he belongs.

England to me is my own tongue,
And what I did when I was young.
If now, two aliens in New York,
We meet, Elizabeth, and talk
Of friends who suffer in the torn
Old Europe where we both were born,
What this refutes or that confirms,
I can but think our talk in terms
Of images that I have seen,
And England tells me what we mean.
Thus, squalid beery BURTON stands

For shoddy thinking of all brands;
. . . . .
YE OLDE TUDOR TEA-SHOPPE for
The folly of dogmatic law,
While graceless BOURNEMOUTH is the sloth
Of men or bureaucrats or both.

What this *paysage moralisé* means is that he has never left home and
continues to think in terms furnished by a thoroughly English past. This
may be a rebuttal to British reproaches, the rationalization of a guilty
conscience, but it may also be a simple declaration of a primal loyalty.
And indeed, in a passage that follows almost immediately, Auden describes the primal Eden of his childhood (assimilated to a local English
river) and the subsequent Fall from Paradise that is the psychological lot
of all men. As Auden wrote in an essay called "The Prolific and the
Devourer" (terms, incidentally, that will be used in this poem), "The Fall
is repeated in the life history of each individual, so that we have a double
memory of Eden, one from personal experience, and one social-historical.
These two memories are not always identical."

An English area comes to mind,
I see the nature of my kind
As a locality I love,
Those limestone moors that stretch from BROUGH
To HEXHAM and the ROMAN WALL,
There is my symbol of us all.
There, where the EDEN leisures through
Its sandstone valley, is my view
Of green and civil life that dwells
Below a cliff of savage fells
From which original address
Man faulted into consciousness.

That this landscape is truly the symbol of us all is to be reinforced later
in the triumphant poem "In Praise of Limestone." But here the adequacy
of the symbol is made universal in its application to our shared discovery
of the imperfection of life and our recollection of the innocent bliss of
childhood. "Faulted" of course is both a geological term and a moral one,
and "consciousness" is the self-consciousness which is the sign of our
sinfulness. The fall which takes place is also our introduction to terror as
part of the private world.

In ROOKHOPE I was first aware
Of Self and Not-self, Death and Dread:
Adits were entrances which led
Down to the Outlawed, to the Others,
The Terrible, the Merciful, the Mothers;
Alone on a hot day I knelt
Upon the edge of shafts and felt
The deep *Urmutterfurcht* that drives
Us into knowledge all our lives,
The far interior of our fate
To civilize and to create,
*Das Weibliche* that bids us come
To find what we're escaping from.

If the childhood landscape is a symbolic map of Eden, it is also the place where we (and Auden as our representative) are initiated into the domain of terror. The "adits," which are entrances to mines, are also entrances into the nether regions; and suddenly we come upon one of the only two lines in the entire 1,707-line poem that violate the tetrameter pattern: "The Terrible, the Merciful, the Mothers." (The other pentameter line is the final one.) The line under discussion here is glossed by Auden with a quotation from Goethe's *Faust*, Part II, Act I, Scene 5. The notes give four and a half lines of German, spoken by Mephistopheles, which have been translated as follows:

Loth am I higher secrets to unfold.
In solitude where reigns nor space nor time,
Are goddesses enthroned from early prime;
'Tis hard to speak of beings so sublime—
The Mothers are they.

(Faust is reduced to terror at hearing this.) The passage seems to recall the classical Furies, frequently propitiated by being called by nice epithets, but inspiring absolute dread. It is the very dread expressed in the German word *Urmutterfurcht*, a primal terror of the Mother "that drives / Us into knowledge all our lives" ("knowledge of good bought dear by knowing ill," in Milton's words). We may recall how much terror mothers have inspired in Auden's earlier work, and how, in a very late poem, "A Lullaby," he writes,

Now for oblivion: let
the belly-mind take over

> down below the diaphragm
> the domain of the Mothers,
> They who guard the Sacred Gates.

Moreover, *Urmutterfurcht* is also annotated. It comes from the text of Wagner's *Siegfried;* it is spoken by Wotan, ruler of the gods, as he commands the Earth goddess, Erda, to sink back down into the bowels of the earth.

At this point Auden makes a brilliant and characteristic shift from private psychic and spiritual history to the public historical domain. The child's fall from an Edenic condition is likened to what happened to the world at large when the unity of Western culture was rent by the Renaissance and the Reformation. If the *Letter to Lord Byron* offered a potted history that began with the eighteenth century and was concerned chiefly with the role of the poet in society, we are now favored with another, much broader encapsulation involving "LUTHER's faith and MONTAIGNE's doubt." This faith and doubt, which could cohabit in such a mind as Pascal's, are now irrevocably split, and both now lead to the modern discomfort and anarchy represented by "Empiric Economic Man." The note, quoted from *Middletown in Transition,* on this modern phenomenon, reads,

> Middletown believes:
> —That progress is a law of life.
> —That men won't work if they don't have to. "Work is not fun. None of us would do a lick of work if he didn't have to."
> —That too much education and contact with books and big ideas unfits a person for practical life.
> —That schoolteachers are usually people who couldn't make good in business.
> —That leisure is a fine thing, but work comes first.
> —That all of us hope we'll get to the place some time where we can work less and have more time to play.
> —But that it is wrong for a man to retire when he is still able to work. "What will he do with his time?"
> —That "culture and things like that" are more the business of women than of men.
> —That leisure is something you spend with people and a person is "queer" who enjoys solitary leisure.
> —That a person doesn't want to spend his leisure doing "heavy" things or things that remind him of the "unpleasant side of life."

—But that leisure should be spent in wholesomely "worth-while" things and not just be idle or frivolous.

—That it is better to be appreciative than discriminating.

—That anything widely acclaimed is pretty apt to be good.

—That Christianity is the final form of religion and all other religions are inferior to it.

—But that which you believe is not so important as the kind of person you are.

—That preachers are rather impractical people who wouldn't be likely to make really good in business. [This clearly dates the book as having been published before the advent of the television evangelists and Billy Graham.]

—That I wouldn't want my son to go into the ministry.

—That preachers should stick to religion and not try to talk about business, public affairs, and other things "they don't know anything about."

What is being described here is the absolute divorce of the secular and practical domain from the religious one, and the enormous trivialization and enfeeblement of the latter. This is also a world that regards "culture" as effete, if not actually effeminate, and a world that is crudely communal and conformist. Among the other ironies implicit in these notions is that the coercive conformity described above is enforced in the name of freedom and individualism, the great heritage of the Renaissance:

> The individual let loose
> To guard himself, at liberty
> To starve or be forgotten, free
> To feel in splendid isolation
> Or drive himself about creation
> In the closed cab of Occupation.

A further and valuable gloss on these lines, especially the ones about driving about creation in a closed cab, is furnished by the memoir of Auden in the forties by Ursula Niebuhr that appeared in Spender's volume of tributes. Recalling a conversation at Middagh Street in Brooklyn (where this poem was probably written), she writes,

> We talked about all sorts of things and particularly Detroit. George Davis [who would become the fiction editor of *Harper's Bazaar*] had come from there and Reinhold [Niebuhr, Ursula's husband] had lived

and worked there for fifteen years as pastor of a church. It was the Detroit of Henry Ford, and the First World War and the twenties, and Reinhold accordingly had learned the facts of life about industrial production, and at first hand from his parishioners of the toll technological development took in terms of human and social values. Wystan was fascinated by the descriptions his friend George Davis and Reinhold gave of Henry Ford and of his Jekyll-and-Hyde personality. The technical genius who gave the world the Model T and the assembly line was presented by his public relations office as a great humanitarian, and largely was accepted as such, but to his sub-executives and to his workers, he was known as a cruel and exacting employer, who exhibited at times a definite streak of sadism.

There have been articulate denouncers of this economic system and its mechanical, inhuman tyranny, and the poem specifically mentions Blake, Rousseau, Kierkegaard, and Baudelaire; but they were members of a tiny and powerless minority, while mankind willingly or supinely enslaved itself: "Whichever way we turn, we see / Man captured by his liberty," and economic necessity presents us with the grotesque spectacle of

> Boys trained by factories for leading
> Unusual lives as nurses, feeding
> Helpless machines, girls married off
> To typewriters, old men in love
> With prices they can never get,
> Homes blackmailed by a radio set,
> Children inherited by slums
> And idiots with enormous sums.

Though it may be that such a catalogue, chilling as it is, loses some of the power of indictment by its wit and its variety, we are, I think, entitled to recall, apropos of those slum children, Samuel Johnson's observation that "a decent provision for the poor is the true test of civilization," and to reflect that by such elementary standards, the world that Auden is describing and that we inhabit is pretty far from civilized.

And from the collective guilt of Economic Man the two national antagonists now facing one another have inherited the errors of their ways:

> Upon each English conscience lie
> Two decades of hypocrisy,

And not a German can be proud
Of what his apathy allowed.

Auden traces these errors which have led to tyranny and force to their archetypal spokesmen, Plato and Rousseau. Plato's "lie" is the lie of the "intellect," the heresy which accepts only an immaterial Reality, to the disgrace, and in contempt, of the physical world. To Auden it is a species of the Manichaean heresy. Its notional opposite, while equally wrong, is Rousseau's "falsehood of the flesh," which embraces and deifies the "Irrational," to the disgrace, and in contempt, of the powers of the rational mind. These errors appear to be diametrically opposed, yet they descend from "one common cloud," the Ego, the author of all these errors, and of our consequent miseries. The Ego is given a feminine gender, and of her it is said,

All happens as she wishes till
She asks herself why she should will
This more than that, or who would care
If she were dead and gone elsewhere,
And on her own hypothesis
Is powerless to answer this.
Then panic seizes her . . .

Her inability to choose is due to the fact that she acknowledges no criterion or gauge, apart from her own solipsism, by which to evaluate anything. She is characterized as a self-tortured "Witch," who "worships in obscene delight / The Not, the Never, and the Night / The formless Mass without a Me, / The Midnight Woman and the Sea." That "sea," of course, is the primal chaos to which her worship returns us. She is glorified by Wagner, whose "mental hero," Siegfried, becomes a "huge doll" who "roars for death and mother, / Synonymous with one another." In Auden's essay "Mimesis and Allegory," as David Mason, in an unpublished dissertation, has pointed out to me, the poet declares that Siegfried's attraction to Brünnhilde is incestuous: "When in the third act of *Siegfried,* the young hero awakens Brünnhilde, the libretto makes it very clear that he regards her as a mother and that she regards him as a son, even, in a sense, a rejuvenated father."

At this point the discursive impetus of the poem is arrested by the coming of dawn—it is now New Year's Day in the United States, a nation with "secular cathedrals," the huge skyscrapers of "September 1, 1939," a nation new enough to be comparatively unscarred by such a history of

tragedy and calamity as has ruined Europe time and again. But the factions
and heresies that have so bloodily warred in Europe may be reasoned
about in the calm precincts of the United States:

> More even than in Europe, here
> The choice of patterns is made clear,
> Which the machine imposes, what
> Is possible and what is not,
> To what conditions we must bow
> In building the Just City now.

And this consideration is, among other things, a justification and apologia for Auden's being in America rather than England. I may add that I
do not think it an insincere rationalization. The whole poem has been
moving steadily towards a light which is essentially religious, though
it may also be quasi-Marxist in its outrage at the crimes of modern
capitalism.

The choice required of us entails a quest, and in the Faber edition of
the poem, it was followed first by a sequence of poems (most but not all
of them sonnets) and then by an epilogue. The sequence was called "The
Quest." But here, in the body of the long poem, several such quests
are alluded to: the corporate-knight, GAWAINE-QUIXOTE, Melville's
ISHMAEL, and KAFKA's protagonists. Among these questers and the tasks
assigned them, mention is made of "An unrobust lone FISHER-KING," and
a note to that line refers the reader to some familiar lines in Eliot's *The
Waste Land*. There is something dimly amused, or arch, about calling the
Fisher-King "unrobust," a term that does not quite do justice to a figure
who is either impotent or castrated. But Eliot's presence here in this
American or economic version of a waste land is important for two
reasons. Auden supplies a further note in which Eliot figures.

> It is, perhaps, significant that the first American writer to have
> influence on European writers was Edgar Allan Poe. The American
> literary tradition, Poe, Emerson, Hawthorne, Melville, Henry James,
> T. S. Eliot, is much nearer to Dostoievski than to Tolstoi. It is a
> literature of lonely people . . . Even the violence of the characters in
> "tough" American novels seems a reaction of despair against their
> loneliness. Afraid to be alone, they drink or kill.

The final observation about the characters in "tough" American fiction
would perfectly apply to a number of Eliot's Sweeney poems, as well as

to *Sweeney Agonistes*. But Auden's direct allusion to *The Waste Land* reminds us that in the essay called "Criticism in a Mass Society," mentioned earlier, Auden makes the following observation about Eliot's famous poem:

> Dr. [I. A.] Richards once said that *The Waste Land* marked the severance of poetry from all beliefs. This seems to me an inaccurate description. The poem is *about* the absence of belief and its very unpleasant consequences; it implies throughout a passionate belief in damnation: that to be without belief is to be lost. I cannot see how those who do not share this belief, those who think that truth is relative or pragmatic, can regard the poem as anything but an interesting case history of Mr. Eliot's neurotic state of mind.

This essay was published in 1941, very shortly after the poem under discussion. And we may assume it was, in this segment, intended to defend the seriousness and sincerity of Eliot's religious quest, which is taken to be an analogue to the Grail quest on which *The Waste Land* is partly based.

But Eliot himself has put this matter in doubt, having acknowledged that at the time of writing his great poem he had entertained the idea of becoming a Buddhist; as well as by his statement, quoted by Theodore Spencer and recorded by Eliot's brother, Henry, "Various critics have done me the honour to interpret the poem in terms of criticism of the contemporary world, have considered it, indeed, as an important bit of social criticism. To me it was only the relief of a personal and wholly insignificant grouse against life; it is just a piece of rhythmical grumbling."

With all due allowance for Eliot's presumably self-deprecating modesty, it is very difficult to reconcile this statement with Auden's far grander claim. Moreover, recent criticism has tended to bear out the not entirely baseless suspicion that the nervous condition for which Eliot was being treated at Lausanne had a specific and detectable bearing upon the poem itself. These personal matters about Eliot, of course, were not widely known in 1941, and Auden's "protectiveness" of someone who was a fellow poet, his editor, and a co-religionist, may have been a covert self-defense.

In any case, the consideration of the "loneliness" of American writers (which corresponds to the loneliness of the quester, and makes America the ideal place for such a writer-quester) leads directly to the statement:

> And all that we can always say
> Is: true democracy begins
> With free confession of our sins.

This remarkably intimate linkage of politics and religion also links the private and personal concern with public and general welfare; and it prepares us for the end of the poem, which is not only composed of a set of prayers but expressed in a litany of apostrophes and invocations each embellished with a vocative O, that Latinate rhetorical form which had so annoyed Auden that he had removed it from the Yeats elegy. Here it appears in the following sequence:

> O Unicorn among the cedars

> O Dove of science and of light

> O Ichthus playful in the deep

> O sudden Wind that blows unbidden

> O Clock and Keeper of the years, / O Source of equity and rest

All of these are certainly religious in character, and are epithets for some aspect of divinity. To speak only of a few of them, the unicorn was proverbially a beast whose power could be tamed and controlled only by a pure virgin, and it thus became a symbol of Christ. A fifth-century bestiary says, "Sic et dominus noster Iesus Christus, spiritualis unicornis, descendens in uterum virginis" (And thus did our Lord Jesus Christ, who is spiritually a unicorn, descend into the womb of the Virgin). Auden's own notes tell us that he adapted some lines of Chaucer's, which were applied to Apollo, in which that pagan deity was called a "God of science and of light," and he has, as it were, baptized the line by associating it with the Dove of the Holy Spirit. "Ichthus" (Fish) became an early Christian symbol because of the chastity of its mating habits, and because the word was composed of the initial letters of *Iesus Christus Theos*. The Wind is spoken of in St. John's Gospel 3:8, "The wind bloweth where it listeth, and thou hearest the sound thereof, but canst not tell whence it cometh, and whither it goeth: so is everyone that is born of the Spirit." The prayer that immediately follows these invocations goes,

> Instruct us in the civil art
> Of making from the muddled heart
> A desert and a city where

> The thoughts that have to labor there
> May find locality and peace,
> And pent-up feelings their release,
> Send strength sufficient for our day,
> And point our knowledge on its way,
> O *da quod jubes, Domine.*

Of this prayer perhaps two things may be noted. By the desire to make *both* "a desert and a city" of the heart we may presume Auden to mean by "desert" a symbolic place of penitence. And the prayer for the "release" of "pent-up feelings" seems very likely a prayer for erotic fulfillment.

The very last lines are addressed to his hostess and dedicatee, Elizabeth Mayer, and it consists of further prayers: that his end may be more worthy than his beginning, and that he may be blessed in time with her "learned peacefulness." She becomes at the end a modest kind of Beatrice who emanates a radiant warmth, "A calm *solificatio*" that touches all about her. Coming, as this recognition does, at the very end of the poem, it is too late for a conducted tour of the paradisiacal condition. But if Auden brings his poem to a halt at the border of a greater revelation than any he has yet described, we are certainly allowed to suppose that he is at the beginning of one, as well as at the end of another, quest and adventure. He concludes by saying,

> And love illuminates again
> The city and the lion's den,
> The world's great rage, the travel of young men.

Like the desert, the "lion's den" is both a place of spiritual testing and the arena of terror, fully described in the catalogue of the modern world's inhumanity, as well as represented by the world war currently in progress, that has served as part of the setting of the poem. That war is also "the world's great rage," which is contrasted to the quest represented in the final words about "the travel of young men." We may take that quest to be both symbolic and literal: it leads directly to the poem sequence called "The Quest," with all its explicit religious significance, and it also accounts for Auden's expatriate existence in the United States, where he has come to make the discoveries that he could not make elsewhere because it is here that "the choice of patterns is made clear." He has fused private and public issues, religious and secular ones, and the poem is a serious meditation on the need for and hope of redemption.

# VI. God Will Cheat No One: *For the Time Being*

*For the Time Being* is subtitled *A Christmas Oratorio,* and it was, rather surprisingly, submitted to Benjamin Britten for musical setting. Britten, who had relocated in England, was apparently himself surprised upon receiving the text, and his friendship with Auden was greatly strained and tested by his ultimate refusal to undertake the project, a refusal that was nicely couched in terms of their geographical distance from one another. But even to this day one cannot help wondering at the extraordinary naiveté Auden exhibited, a naiveté the more surprising in coming from a poet so professionally concerned with opera, the writing of libretti, and the setting of poetry to music, both his own works and the songs of the Elizabethans. The simple length of *For the Time Being* would make it impossible for even the most parsimonious of composers to set in any way that would take less than an insupportable amount of time to perform. Music as an art demands repetition, parallelism, patterns recalled through variation and return. And this means that any text it embellishes must be suitably lean as well as clear, and therefore either simple or familiar in order to give the music its opportunity to share in the attention and appreciation of the auditor. In preparing a libretto to serve for Verdi's *Otello,* Boito had to condense a play of 3,228 lines to a text of less than 800 for a four-act opera. And one has only to set the text of Auden's oratorio beside the text of that rather lengthy work, Handel's *Messiah,* or even against the text of Bach's *St. Matthew Passion,* to see, by simple word count, how frugal the others are in comparison to Auden's text. (Think of the mileage Handel gets out of "Alleluia" alone.)

The musicless oratorio was composed between 1941 and 1942, and was prompted by the death of Auden's mother, to whom it is dedicated. It is an unambiguously Christian work, as its subject makes plain, though it is based upon the Kierkegaardian dictum that "the quest for faith begins in anxiety." It can be claimed that such anxiety haunts the entire work, beginning, middle, and end, and that it would continue to inform a great deal of Auden's future work, not least, of course, *The Age of Anxiety*. This anxiety takes many forms, including the ordinary, familiar, secular kinds that characterize much of modern life. But they also, and relatedly, involve that kind of *doubt* with which faith has somehow to deal, and which, therefore, is not like the doubt of Montaigne but instead like the doubt of Pascal. It is a doubt expressed in the concluding lines of the second stanza of "Atlantis," a "quest" poem written at about the same time, which envisions a journey to a desired and fabulous Edenic paradise.

> Should storms, as well may happen,
>   Drive you to anchor a week
> In some old harbour-city
>   Of Ionia, then speak
> With her witty scholars, men
> Who have proved there cannot be
>   Such a place as Atlantis:
>   Learn their logic, but notice
> How their subtlety betrays
>   A simply enormous grief;
> Thus they shall teach you the ways
>   To doubt that you may believe.

*For the Time Being* was written at roughly the same time as another major work which in some ways it resembles, *The Sea and the Mirror*. Auden told Alan Ansen, "*A Christmas Oratorio* was written before *The Sea and the Mirror*. It's the only direct treatment of sacred subjects I shall ever attempt. [This prophecy of November 16, 1946, would turn out to be untrue.] My mother had just died, and I wanted to write something for her. I hesitated before deciding in which order the two things should go." It should be explained that the decision concerned the fact that both were published in the same volume by Random House.

These are both major works, and bear an astonishing resemblance to one another. They are both what may be called suites of lyric poems, employing a rich and inventive variety of forms, some traditional but many invented, and both involving large and spacious prose arias of great wit, subtlety, and even parody. (There is, for example, a good deal of fun to be savored in finding that Caliban, who in his unregenerate life had said, "You taught me language; and my profit on't / Is, I know how to curse. The red plague rid you / For learning me your language!" should, in his redeemed condition, speak like the later Henry James.) Both works are tours de force of technical virtuosity, as well as of great psychological understanding. But the differences are just as striking. The work under consideration here is religious, while the other is secular. But far more important, *For the Time Being* enjoys the advantage of its Biblical narrative background, which gives to it a meaningful sequence of events that the other work quite simply lacks. *The Sea and the Mirror* cannot be said to "take up the action" of *The Tempest* where the playwright had set it down, though everything in Auden's work takes place after the curtain falls on the last act of Shakespeare's play; for Auden's work does not involve any *action* whatever; it is a set of meditations, and lacks all narrative impulse. It shares in this a static and undramatic quality that had characterized Auden's plays and would later taint the libretto of *The Rake's Progress,* which is remarkably devoid of dramatic action, and which tends, as does much of Auden's work, to allegory. Auden himself, in *Secondary Worlds,* acknowledges the passivity of Tom Rakewell, and the problems this posed in terms of dramatic action. In addition, there is the central fact that the oratorio is in some ways a more personal work than its companion piece, as what follows will try to show.

The writing of a "Christian" work raises a number of issues, one of them centering on the problem of belief. Auden had come a long way, as *For the Time Being* makes dramatically clear, from the Pisgah view of distant salvation expressed, or at least implied, in the *New Year Letter.* At the same time, he could see perfectly clearly how irrelevant to the operations of the world at large was this change in the quality and nature of his belief—and this lack of correspondence, this open indifference, is a constant theme of the oratorio, as it was in one of his essays on Kierkegaard when he wrote: "Today, in our part of the world, society could not care less what one believes; to be a Christian is regarded by the majority as a rather silly but quite harmless eccentricity, like being a Baconian or a flat-earth man." He knew perfectly well whereof he was writing, and the general secularist view of such Christian faith has been expressed far more contemptuously and dismissively than Auden suggests in the passage just quoted. In his book called *Milton's God,* William Empson says flatly, "I think the traditional God of Christianity very wicked, and have done since I was at school, where nearly all my little playmates thought the same." Even Auden's good friend Isherwood took a rather dim view of the poet's religious propensities, and in describing their collaboration in the writing of plays he commented in 1937:

Auden is a musician and a ritualist. As a child, he enjoyed a high Anglican upbringing, coupled with a sound musical education. The Anglicanism has evaporated, leaving only the height: he is still much preoccupied with ritual, in all its forms. When we collaborate, I have to keep a sharp eye on him—or down flop the characters on their knees (see *F6 passim*): another constant danger is that of choral interruptions by angel voices. If Auden had his way, he would turn every play into a cross between grand opera and high mass.

Ours is a world in which a believer had to contend with the rest of the population of "the moderate Aristotelian city / Of darning and the Eight-Fifteen, where Euclid's geometry / And Newton's mechanics would account for our experience, / And the kitchen table exists because I scrub it," in the closing words of the oratorio's Narrator. But Auden had become a serious and believing Christian who could hope for and imagine the reconciliation of the churches sundered by the Reformation, which he had characterized as "a scandal." In the spirit of this conciliatory hope, Auden wrote, in an essay on Erik Erikson's biography of Martin Luther, "In terms of religious history, Newman's conversion to the Roman Church in 1845 marks the beginning of our era. The Christian doctrine which Protestantism emphasizes is that every human being, irrespective of family, class, or occupation, is unique before God; the complementary and equally Christian doctrine emphasized by Catholicism is that we are all members, one with another, both in the Earthly and the Heavenly City."

I would be prepared to argue that this passage is nothing more nor less than a theological elaboration of the public/private antinomies that had obsessed Auden's poetry and thought from the first. They are to be found in two verse epigraphs in his very first book, *Poems*. The opening dedicatory verse "To Christopher Isherwood" reads,

> Let us honour if we can
> The vertical man
> Though we value none
> But the horizontal one.

A clear and permissible reading of these lines enjoins us to pay suitable respect to the active, living human being, as opposed to the standard and traditional pieties of reverence for the dead. But it is equally possible to read these lines as suggesting that we must respect the "public" aspect of man when he is up, dressed, and about his business, though we value him more when he is recumbent as a sexual partner. Later in the same volume, *The Orators* is dedicated to Stephen Spender with the following lines:

> Private faces in public places
> Are wiser and nicer
> Than public faces in private places.

The last line here bears a not altogether concealed reference to oral sex, along with the suggestion that celebrities would do well to watch themselves. But the pairing of public and private is firmly and clearly made in both cases.

Faith is one matter; the question of "Christian art" is another. And on this topic Auden had some very firm views. In an undated essay in *The Dyer's Hand* called "Postscript: Christianity and Art," Auden has two paragraphs that need quotation here.

> There can no more be a "Christian" art than there can be a Christian science or a Christian diet. There can only be a Christian spirit in which an artist, a scientist, works or does not work. A painting of the Crucifixion is not necessarily more Christian in spirit than a still life, and may very well be less.

> I sometimes wonder if there is not something a bit questionable, from a Christian point of view, about all works of art which make overt Christian references. They seem to assert that there is such a thing as a Christian culture, which there cannot be. Culture is one of Caesar's things. One cannot help noticing that the great period of "religious" painting coincided with the period when the Church was a great temporal power.

These passages raise a multitude of problems, and they express a view that is by no means universally shared. To take only the question of whether there is such a thing as a "Christian culture," Auden's view flatly contradicts the one expressed by T. S. Eliot in his 1948 book, *Notes Towards the Definition of Culture,* in which he writes, "when, as in what follows in this chapter, I discuss Christian matters, that is because I am particularly concerned with Christian culture . . ."

The views expressed in the second of Auden's paragraphs above are a further echo of his general view of art as frivolity in contradistinction to the "seriousness" of religion—a distinction which must necessarily find any mixture of the two debasing and deplorable. But we must remember that Auden's resolve, after finishing *For the Time Being*, never again to attempt "a direct treatment of sacred subjects" was one that he consciously and deliberately violated; so we may conjecture that his categorical assertions here, as in many other places, were in large part the result of forensic and rhetorical habit. (Auden's propensity for making "definitive" statements has been widely noticed, and could be documented at considerable length.)

As to the question of whether or not there can be such a thing as "Christian art," Auden seems to me to be begging the question when he acknowledges that there can be a "Christian spirit" in which the artist paints. Agreed, there can be very bad religious art, and it is everywhere to be seen: dashboard Madonnas, cement saints, holy cards in Hallmark, Easter-egg colors. And there is indisputably much good religious art, too well known to need identification. But can there be good art on religious subjects that may be said to "lack a Christian spirit"? I think there can be; and I think furthermore that this is in fact what so troubles Auden here, though he is not quite candid about it. The truth of the matter is that Caravaggio, who may have been Auden's favorite painter, often painted religious subjects, but the feelings conveyed in many of them are undisguisedly erotic—and, moreover, homoerotic. One need list only a few: the *John the Baptist* at the Capitoline Museum in Rome; the nearly naked executioner, as well as several other nearly nude figures, in the *Martyrdom of St. Matthew,* San Luigi dei Francesi, Rome; *John the Baptist,* in the Öffentliche Kunstsammlung, Basel; *John the Baptist,* Nelson Gallery, Kansas City; and perhaps most suggestively of all, the embracing angels in *The Seven Acts of Mercy* in the Church of Pio Monte della Misericordia.

In any case, we cannot address ourselves to a major modern religious poem without taking into account the presence and influence of T. S. Eliot. "Burnt Norton" had been published in 1938; "East Coker" in 1940; "The Dry Salvages" in 1941; and the final quartet, "Little Gidding," would be published in 1942. It would have been virtually impossible to write a religious poem in English as though this monumental undertaking of Eliot's were not going on. And there are two poetic concerns of Eliot's that Auden was himself to take up.

Of these the first is expressed in "Burnt Norton" in the familiar lines,

> Footfalls echo in the memory
> Down the passage which we did not take

Toward the door that was never opened
Into the rose-garden.

Christian poetry does not always concern itself with gardens, and Eliot's
garden here is primarily the garden of an English country house, and is
recalled in a spirit of renunciation as a wistful acknowledgment of what
might have been. As Daniel Albright has astutely pointed out to me, Eliot
had even earlier, in "Ash Wednesday," made a Christian use of the garden
in his poetry, and, more pertinently, to Auden's purposes, had identified garden and desert: "The desert in the garden the garden in the
desert." In Auden's case, since his subject is the events leading up to,
during, and immediately following the Nativity, we must note that there
is no specific authority in the Gospels themselves for any allusions to
gardens. And yet "the garden" or "the rose garden" is mentioned at least
nine times in the oratorio. Gardens, of course, do figure prominently in
the New Testament narratives and at crucial junctures: the Agony in the
Garden, which marks the beginning of Christ's Passion, is perhaps the
chief of these. And the garden which is the setting for the beginning of
human history is linked with the paradisiacal garden which shall come at
the ending of time by various Biblical gardens, including the one in the
Song of Songs. The gardens mentioned so prominently and frequently at
the beginning of Auden's long poem will be contrasted with the de-
sertscape with which the poem ends in the final section called "The Flight
into Egypt," and which represents both the world of Israelite bondage
from which Christ would deliver mankind, and the aridity of the modern
secular world.

The other matter that figures so obsessively both in Eliot's quartets and
in Auden's poem concerns time. Eliot begins the first of his quartets with
the words, "Time present and time past / Are both perhaps present in time
future, / And time future contained in time past." The final section of his
final quartet begins, "What we call the beginning is often the end / And
to make an end is to make a beginning." Time, and the illusion of Time,
figure as topics in a great deal of religious poetry. They have a bearing on
our very notions of history; and it is a Christian commonplace that the
miracle of Christ's birth, ministry, death, and resurrection, and the
salvation it brought, all took place in historical time—that, according to
Eusebius, "it was the forty-second year of Augustus' reign, and the
twenty-eighth after the subjugation of Egypt and the deaths of Antony
and Cleopatra, the last of the Ptolemaic rulers of Egypt," and "while

Quirinius was governor of Syria," that Jesus was born, and that he suffered death thirty-three years later, under the reign of the Emperor Tiberius. Time, its fusions and confusions, has been incorporated into Christian faith almost as one of its mysteries. For Christ is also born every year at Christmas; and he is born every day at the first of the canonical hours. And these repetitive patterns all operate simultaneously. This mysterious simultaneity not only allowed but encouraged Milton to resurrect the Latin tense of historic present in his "On the Morning of Christ's Nativity," of which the first verse of the hymn proper goes:

> It was the winter wild
> While the Heav'n-born child
>   All meanly wrapped in the rude manger lies;
> Nature in awe to him
> Had doffed her gaudy trim,
>   With her great Master so to sympathize;
> It was no season then for her
> To wanton with the sun, her lusty paramour.

(Anyone inclined to suppose that "lies" is a grammatical lapse into the present tense employed to accommodate the exigencies of rhyme will be disabused by Milton's deliberate continuation of slipping back and forth between the past and the present tense throughout the length of this poem of 244 lines. It may also be added, parenthetically, that this arrogation of "historicity" to the New Testament events is a curious matter in view of the prominent role it plays in many parts of the Old Testament, including the ending of Hebrew Scripture, in which, in the closing verses of Second Chronicles, mention is made of that "good" emperor, Cyrus of Persia.)

There can be no doubt that Auden felt a strong correspondence between the past and the present as represented by the world of Rome, at the time of Christ's birth as well as later, and the world of repression and disorder in which he himself was living. In an essay called "Augustus to Augustine" he wrote, "Our period is not so unlike the age of Augustine: the planned society, caesarism of thugs or bureaucracies, paideia, scientia, religious persecution, are all with us." And in the essay "Heresies" he wrote, "The Roman Empire had evolved legal, military and economic techniques for maintaining internal law and order, defending itself against external enemies, and managing the production and exchange of goods; in the third century these proved inadequate to prevent civil war, invasion by barbarians and depreciation of the currency. In the twentieth century, it is not the failure but the fantastic success of our techniques of production that is creating a society in which it is becoming increasingly difficult to live a human life." It must be stated that to recognize these correspondences is not by any means to subscribe to such cyclical theories of history as are to be found in Vico or Spengler or Yeats. It is merely a way of seeing the degradations of secularism as being "always with us," like the poor.

In the nineteenth and early twentieth centuries there was a characteristic smug and condescending view of Roman culture that saw it as utterly lacking in those ingredients that we associate with "high culture." Such views can well be represented by W. Warde Fowler, who, in his book on Rome, writes with unapologetic self-congratulation, "Imagination in action takes the form of adventurousness, as we may see in our own history; the literary imaginativeness of Elizabethan England had its counterpart in the adventurous voyages of Elizabethan seamen. The Romans were not an adventurous people; they were not imaginative enough to be so." (As if Virgil, Horace, Catullus, Juvenal, Apuleius, Petronius, and Vitruvius had never lived, Plautus and Terence never written, Etruscan votive and funerary sculpture never been created.) Fowler continues in his characterization of the Romans: "It was in another direction that their genius for practical work drew them: to the arts and methods of discipline, law, government . . . It was this power of ruling, which itself implies a habit of discipline, that marked out Rome as the natural successor of Greece in European civilization; and it grew naturally out of the purely practical bent of the early Romans, who were unhampered in their constant activity by fancy, reflection, or culture."

Before coming directly to grips with the poem, one more general consideration needs to be mentioned: numerology. I took notice earlier of Auden's allusiveness or indebtedness in the *New Year Letter* to some of Dante's formal patterns. Such patterns become decidedly more pronounced in *For the Time Being,* and it may be well to review some of these basic matters. *The Divine Comedy* is parted into three great divisions, which may be said to represent the Trinity. Each division is in turn divided into thirty-three cantos, the first one, the *Inferno,* being provided with an extra canto as prologue to the entire work. There are, therefore, exactly one hundred cantos in the work; and one hundred is the square of ten, which, in Dante's time, was regarded as a perfect number. Nine, which is the square of three, figures importantly in each of the three divisions. In the *Inferno,* souls are arranged into three main groups and occupy nine circles. The *Purgatorio* is arranged in a series of seven levels, one for each of the seven deadly sins, which, with the addition of an ante-Purgatory and the Earthly Paradise, make up a total of nine. The *Paradiso* ascends through the circles of the seven planets, then through the circle of the fixed stars and the *primum mobile,* and finally to the Empyrean, or Heaven itself, for a total of nine. There cannot be the slightest doubt that Auden had precisely such numerical patterns in mind in composing his oratorio.

*For the Time Being* is divided into nine parts, and it opens with three choral passages, separated by brief syllabic semi-choruses. The chorales proper are complexly composed in sonnet-length trimeter strophes, rhyming *a b a c d a e c b e f d f a,* with the added provision that the final line is an exact repetition of the first, and that the sixth line, again in each of the three stanzas, is the same as the first and last, except that it begins with an unaccented "As," meaning "at the same time that . . ." And all three choral passages are concerned with time, either as stagnant and repetitious or as ominous and portentous. All three also deal with anxiety generated by oppressive world conditions, as well as quotidian miseries that are at once both ancient and contemporary, so that Auden's fruitful anachronistic juxtapositions of the ancient and the modern world begin right at the start.

This first part, which involves another complexity of time warp, is called "Advent." This is the season celebrated on the four Sundays before Christmas, and in the Roman rite Advent begins with the eyes firmly focused on the Second Coming of Christ, an event which will entail the ultimate Judgment—which means that, at best, Christmas is anticipated with deeply mixed feelings. "Advent" will be followed in Auden's work by the second part, which is "The Annunciation"; and this will accord with the proper sequence of events as described in the Gospel of St. Luke. But in another way of reckoning time, the Annunciation took place nine full months before the Nativity, and is celebrated on March 25, and therefore, by any strict accounting, precedes rather than follows Advent. Here is the first choral passage.

> Darkness and snow descend;
> The clock on the mantlepiece
> Has nothing to recommend,
> Nor does the face in the glass
> Appear nobler than our own
> As darkness and snow descend

> On all personality.
> Huge crowds mumble—'Alas,
> Our angers do not increase,
> Love is not what she used to be;'
> Portly Caesar yawns—'I know;'
> He falls asleep on his throne,
> They shuffle off through the snow:
> Darkness and snow descend.

The mantlepiece clock is confounded with Caesar in ambiguous or indeterminate time; the darkness and snow (that we in the north associate with the Christmas season) eclipse "all personality," just as the clock, with "nothing to recommend," eclipses time, by insisting it is utterly repetitive and routine and beyond the hope of change. We become inured to our own face in the glass, long since having lost any dream of heroism or nobility. And the same snow in the second choral passage "Abolish[es] the watchman's tower / And delete[s] the cedar grove." The second passage begins (and concludes), "Winter completes an age." It does so by bringing an annual cycle to its end, but the words are cunningly proleptic in that they reveal to us almost unaware that on this particular winter an age of error will come to an end. When, in this second choral passage, it is said that "The prophet's lantern is out," a reference is being made to Micah 3:6—"and the sun shall go down over the prophets, and the day shall be dark over them." The third, and final, choral passage goes,

> The evil and armed draw near;
> The weather smells of their hate
> And the houses smell of our fear;
> Death has opened his white eye
> And the black hole calls the thief
> As the evil and armed draw near.
> Ravens alight on the wall,
> Our plans have all gone awry,
> The rains will arrive too late,
> Our resourceful general
> Fell down dead as he drank
> And his horses died of grief,
> Our navy sailed away and sank;
> The evil and armed draw near.

It has been plausibly conjectured that the "resourceful general" here is Alexander the Great, whose terminal illness seems to have been inaugurated by wild carousing, and who was mourned by his whole Macedonian army. And yet "the evil and armed" are not merely the enemies of the civilized Hellenistic world but the modern barbarians who are endangering civilization even as Auden is writing in the early 1940's. Death's "white eye" suggests his blindness, which in turn suggests his bland impartiality and democratic indifference. Collectively the three choral passages are dirge-like, hopeless, and oscillate between feelings of being numbed and being terrified.

They are followed by a protean, chameleon-like Narrator, whose voice and point of view shift continuously throughout the oratorio, and sometimes within the confines of a single speech. At times he presents himself as a crude and unfeeling spokesman for the Powers That Be, employing their obvious euphemisms. Again, he becomes an apologist for the Christian point of view, yet even at the end his dubiety is felt. He is an equivocal spokesman, in any case. In his first speech he begins briskly, and in the manner of a radio (these are pre-television years) commentator. But he is more than a neutral commentator; he is propagandist, an apparatchik, who flimsily veils a grotesque reality—at least at the beginning of his speech.

> If, on account of the political situation,
> There are quite a number of homes without roofs, and men
> Lying about the countryside neither drunk nor asleep,
> If all sailings have been cancelled till further notice,
> If it's unwise to say much in letters . . .
>     . . . . .
> That is not at all unusual for this time of year.

What is being described here is a world devastated by war, with corpses strewn over the landscape. And the comparatively serene tone of the last line quoted reflects the classical view (still much admired and espoused) that war is as necessary and natural a part of existence as peace, and that, according to the view of Empedocles, Love and Strife are always giving way to one another. (Santayana had adopted much the same view in an essay called "Tipperary.") The numbed acceptance of "These after all are our familiar tribulations, / And we have been through them all before, many, many times" cannot fail to recall the opening chorus of *Murder in the Cathedral*, and the words, "What danger can be / For us, the poor, the poor women of Canterbury? What tribulation / With which we are not already familiar?"

The events of Time and Space invoked by the Narrator "occur again and again, but only to pass / Again and again into their formal opposites, / From sword to ploughshare, coffin to cradle, war to work, / So that, taking the bad with the good, the pattern composed / By the ten thousand odd things that can possibly happen / Is permanent in a general sort of way." The complacency of this voice and view, however, is about to be altered in mid-speech. The change is brought about by a dim recognition of the insignificance of human life when viewed *sub specie aeternitatis.* It is brought on by an intuition, which is terrifying, of eternity itself. Such an intuition makes ordinary life seem quite simply *unreal,* and therein lies its terror. And so the speech, which had begun with such breezy confidence, ends,

> We are afraid
> Of pain but more afraid of silence; for no nightmare
> Of hostile objects could be as terrible as this Void.
> This is the Abomination. This is the wrath of God.

The "Void" spoken of here is what Pascal writes of in the *Pensées* thus: "When I consider the short duration of my life, swallowed up in the eternity before and after, the little space which I fill, and even can see, engulfed in the infinite immensity of spaces of which I am ignorant, and which know me not, I am frightened, and am astonished at being here rather than there; for there is no reason why here rather than there, why now rather than then . . . The eternal silence of these infinite spaces frightens me."

There follows an impressive choric lyric in four stanzas, which speak of the dead end of an old and exhausted dispensation. The second stanza—

> Where is the Law for which we broke our own,
> Where now that Justice for which Flesh resigned
> Her hereditary right to passion, Mind
> His will to absolute power? Gone. Gone.
> Where is that Law for which we broke our own?

—seems to be predicated on the "Christian fiction" that the Jews lived only by the Law, which was to bring them unassisted to their salvation; and that the Law was concerned wholly with Justice, as distinguished from Love. This is essentially a Pauline doctrine. The refrain lines, the first and the last, suggest that in the deluded hope of being saved by orthodox religious law, the people of Israel had surrendered either the voice of private conscience or the mores and regulations of secular society. And the invocation of Flesh, contrasted with Mind, should recall a similar opposition of the same faculties, represented by Rousseau and Plato, in the *New Year Letter.* The chorus as a whole describes a despair, frenzy, and enervation, an absolute lack of confidence also described by Gilbert Murray in the penultimate chapter of *Five Stages of Greek Religion,* called "The Failure of Nerve." The refrain of the final stanza, "We who must die demand a miracle," combines the salutation of the Roman gladiators with the demand, reported in Matthew and in Mark, on the part of the Pharisees for "a sign."

In the recitative that follows, the grounds, essentially spiritual, are laid out of the necessary preconditions before a miracle can take place. In the course of defining these requirements, Auden writes,

> For the garden is the only place there is, but you will not find it
> Until you have looked for it everywhere and found nowhere
>     that is not desert;
> The miracle is the only thing that happens, but to you it will not
>     be apparent,
> Until all events have been studied and nothing happens that you
>     cannot explain;
> And life is the destiny you are bound to refuse until you have
>     consented to die.

To be sure, Christian theology abounds in paradox (the Word made Flesh, "the first shall be last"), but these lines, while they are unassailably within the Christian tradition, sound familiarly like the litany of paradoxes in Eliot's "East Coker."

> You say I am repeating
> Something I have said before. I shall say it again.
> Shall I say it again? In order to arrive there,
> To arrive where you are, to get from where you are not,
>     You must go by a way wherein there is no ecstasy.
> In order to arrive at what you do not know
>     You must go by a way which is the way of ignorance.
> In order to possess what you do not possess
>     You must go by the way of dispossession.

In order to arrive at what you are not
  You must go through the way in which you are not.
And what you do not know is the only thing you know
And what you own is what you do not own
And where you are is where you are not.

The concluding chorus of "Advent," in elegiacs, expresses continued bewilderment about the place of man in the universal scheme, and accentuates his divorce from the world of nature, and from the classical world of nature deified, a world in which he is as yet unwedded to anything.

The second part, "The Annunciation," is based loosely on the account in the first chapter of Luke. It begins with the Four Faculties, which, as a number of commentators have observed, are derived from the psychology of Jung, and which here speak both in unison and independently. They are Intuition, Feeling, Sensation, and Thought, which Jung characterized roughly as follows: Intuition tells us of future possibilities and gives us information of the atmosphere which surrounds all experience; Feeling weighs issues and situations and evaluates them; Sensation is perception through our senses; and Thought furnishes meaning and understanding. According to ancient and commonly accepted ideas, these faculties were once perfectly united in the person of Adam before the Fall; but Original Sin separated them and unbalanced their harmony. The faculties stand in relation to one another much as do the four humours or temperaments of medieval anatomical theory, which in turn corresponded with the four elements of earth, air, fire, and water, the basic materials of all creation. These, again, were supposed to have been perfectly mixed and blended within mankind and throughout the universe until the Fall. It should be added, moreover, that the four faculties are represented in Auden's later baroque eclogue, *The Age of Anxiety*, by the four characters in the cast: Quant represents Intuition; Malin represents Thought; Rosetta represents Feeling; and Emble represents Sensation. These nearly allegorical figures proceed to enact some of mankind's familiar, as well as Auden's personal, agonies.

The Four Faculties introduce themselves, and then break out in a tutti of galloping dactyls. Though nothing in the text describes them, it is easy to think of Auden imagining them as high-spirited chorus girls, brazenly playing the roles of temptresses. But after the dactylic song-and-dance they become deeply serious, and each speaks in alarming, nightmarish terms that remind us by turns of the Nazis, some of the more lurid dream sequences in *Crime and Punishment,* and the dreadful torments in the paintings of Breughel and Bosch. This is not a patent contradiction on Auden's part. The lure of the temptresses is the lure to perdition, so that they are simultaneously alluring and horrifying, like the Sirens in the *Odyssey,* and we are always self-damned. In any case, the Faculties reintroduce the theme and frequent mention of "the garden," and serve as prelude to the appearance of Gabriel and Mary. After commanding Mary to wake, Gabriel addresses her in terms that are rather surprising.

> Mary, in a dream of love
> Playing as all children play,
> For unsuspecting children may
> Express in comic make-believe
> The wish that later they will know
> Is tragic and impossible;
> Hear, child, what I am sent to tell:
> Love wills your dream to happen, so
> Love's will on earth may be, through you,
> No longer a pretend but true.

There is, as often enough with Auden, the eccentricity of punctuation, which more conventionally, and certainly more clearly, would have enclosed the third through sixth lines in parentheses. But what troubles yet more is the pseudo-childlike "baby-talk" adopted by overbearing adults towards children in a manner that seems to assume that youngsters are not quite bright, that their intelligence is as limited as their vocabularies. There is something rather off-putting about "a pretend" that carries with it all the grown-up condescension towards children who, it is assumed, need to be instructed about the firm and absolute difference between their own private worlds of fantasy and the real, objective world, with the implied admonition that it is naughty or backward to confuse the two. To be sure, one of the points Auden is trying to make is that habitual reality is irrelevant to *this* situation, but that does not alleviate our discomfort at Gabriel's tone here. Mary is addressed as if she were a little girl who still plays with dolls, and whose "comic make-believe" is that maternity is a changeless, happy, and virtually celibate condition. It is child's play, which adults must give up, as St. Paul so sternly insisted. But an exception is to be made in Mary's case. To be sure, Mary's "youth" may be a further index of her innocence, or Auden's way of representing it. But this premise is somewhat compromised by the language she uses in response to Gabriel, which is that of mature and revelatory rapture. So grown up does Mary seem as to make Gabriel in retrospect look rather foolish; and her ecstatic joy immediately evokes recollection of the traditional Seven Joys of the Virgin, which (as well as the Seven Sorrows) she was supposed to have known at the very moment of her having accepted her role as the vessel of God by her words, "Behold the handmaid of the Lord; be it unto me according to thy word." The Seven Joys are identified as the Annuciation itself, the Visitation, the Nativity, the Epiphany, the Finding in the Temple (when the child Jesus was for a while lost to his parents), the Resurrection, and the Ascension.

Mary, in any case, responds to Gabriel's tetrameter announcement with trimeter lines which are questions. She, in turn, is answered by Gabriel's tetrameters in terms wholly different from his first speech, being full of sophistication and indeed playing upon the philosophical concepts of Love, Flesh, and Knowledge in ways that presuppose a highly cultivated and intellectual auditor, thus:

> When Eve, in love with her own will,
> Denied the will of Love and fell,
> She turned the flesh Love knew so well
> To knowledge of her love until
> Both love and knowledge were of sin:
> What her negation wounded, may
> Your affirmation heal today;
> Love's will requires your own, that in
> The flesh whose love you do not know,
> Love's knowledge into flesh may grow.

There is a good deal of almost "metaphysical wit" in this, of the sort that Dryden said "perplexes the minds of the fair sex with nice speculations of philosophy, when [a poet] should engage their hearts, and entertain them with the softnesses of love." Gabriel is informing Mary that she has it within the power of her will to redeem from its fallen state the Flesh of Mankind, the knowledge of love, and bring about the birth in Flesh of Love itself. Upon Mary's full and unqualified assent, Gabriel continues once more in the high philosophic vein, this time on the topic of freedom and necessity and the problem of choice.

> Since Adam, being free to choose,
> Chose to imagine he was free
> To choose his own necessity,
> Lost in his freedom, Man pursues

The shadow of his images:
Today the Unknown seeks the known;
What I am willed to ask, your own
Will has to answer; child, it lies
Within your power of choosing to
Conceive the Child who chooses you.

This "choice" or assent of Mary's symbolizes St. Augustine's declaration, quoted by Auden in *Secondary Worlds:* "God, who made us without our help will not save us without our consent." The section ends with a voice solo and choral rejoicing. It is perhaps worth noticing that Mary's role is composed entirely of acquiescence, while Gabriel's task is entirely expository, in the course of which he speaks three times.

The third section is called "The Temptation of St. Joseph." Of this matter St. Matthew is the only narrator who comes close to touching upon the subject, even remotely and indirectly.

> Now the birth of Jesus Christ was on this wise: When as his mother Mary was espoused to Joseph, before they came together, she was found with child of the Holy Ghost.
>
> Then Joseph her husband, being a just man, and not willing to make her a public example, was minded to put her away privily.
>
> But while he thought on these things, behold the angel of the Lord appeared unto him in a dream, saying, Joseph, thou son of David, fear not to take unto thee Mary thy wife; for that which is conceived in her is of the Holy Ghost.

So discreet and terse an account as this, though canonical, scarcely hints at the long tradition which extrapolated, either mockingly or sympathetically, the suspicion of Joseph's cuckoldom. And it is precisely this aspect that Auden elects to make much of. As he touchingly confided to a few friends, Chester Kallman's infidelities to a relationship Auden regarded as solemnly as a marriage, and which he had celebrated in a poem whose title, "In Sickness and in Health," was taken from the marriage vows, so unhinged him that he found himself momentarily capable of murder. Carpenter reports, "Auden went completely to pieces. 'I was forced to know,' he afterwards wrote of the days that followed his discovery of Chester's unfaithfulness, 'what it is like to feel oneself the prey of demonic powers, in both the Greek and the Christian sense, stripped of self-control and self-respect, behaving like a ham actor in a Strindberg play.' "

The tradition which makes Joseph the butt of mockery and the suspected victim of cuckoldry goes back to the Apocryphal Books of the New Testament, from which the following account in Protevangelion, 9:23–10:13, is taken.

> But perceiving herself daily to grow big, and being afraid, [Mary] went home, and hid herself from the children of Israel; and was fourteen years old when all these things happened.
>
> And when her sixth month was come, Joseph returned from his building houses abroad, which was his trade, and entering into his house, found the Virgin grown big:
>
> Then smiting upon his face, he said, With what face can I look upon the Lord my God? or, what shall I say concerning this young woman?
>
> For I received her a Virgin out of the temple of the Lord my God, and have not preserved her such!
>
> Who has thus deceived me? Who has committed this evil in my house, and seducing the Virgin from me, hath defiled her?
>
> Is not the history of Adam exactly accomplished in me?
>
> For in the very instant of his glory, the serpent came and found Eve alone, and seduced her.
>
> Just after the same manner it has happened to me.
>
> Then Joseph arising from the ground, called her, and said, O thou who hast been so much favored by God, why hast thou done this?
>
> Why hast thou debased thy soul, who wast educated in the Holy of Holies, and received thy food from the hand of angels?
>
> But she, with a flood of tears, replied, I am innocent, and have known no man.
>
> Then said Joseph, How comes it to pass you are with child?
>
> Mary answered, As the Lord my God liveth, I know not by what means.
>
> Then Joseph was exceedingly afraid, and went away from her, considering what he should do with her.

Auden's adoption of this uncanonical tradition is useful to him in several ways, of which perhaps the most touching is that it affords him the means for expressing deep personal anguish in dramatic and quasi-Biblical disguise. In addition, the tradition allows Auden to take seriously and sympathetically the plight of the cuckold, which the larger part of Western literary tradition, for which Molière may stand as a representative example, regards as ridiculous.

Joseph's lyric reflections, with their refrain line, "My own true Love," are filled with rich and deliberate anachronism. The refrain itself is Elizabethan in character. In the first of three identical stanzas he is getting himself all togged out as for an important date, at which he arrives "too late," since some inexplicable disaster has occurred ("A star had fallen down the street") and the police have surrounded the house. In the second, waiting at an attractive bar which is to be a trysting place and rendezvous, he overhears the knowing voice of a stranger expressing impersonal mockery; and in the third, he is mocked not even by a stranger but by an ass, and is refused sympathy by a desert anchorite, who presumably has foresworn the gratifications of wedlock and of companionship. These three lyrics are interspersed with "off-stage" choruses, brief, snickering, full of hints and innuendo, and after the third of them Joseph speaks in truly moving terms.

> Where are you, Father, where?
> Caught in the jealous trap
> Of an empty house I hear
> As I sit alone in the dark
> Everything, everything,
> The drip of the bathroom tap,
> The creak of the sofa spring,
> The wind in the air-shaft, all
> Making the same remark
> Stupidly, stupidly,
> Over and over again.
> Father, what have I done?
> Answer me, Father, how
> Can I answer the tactless wall
> Or the pompous furniture now?
> Answer them . . .

> GABRIEL
> No, you must.

> JOSEPH
> How then am I to know,
> Father, that you are just?
> Give me one reason.

> GABRIEL
> No.

JOSEPH
All I ask is one
Important and elegant proof
That what my Love has done
Was really at your will
And that your will is Love.

GABRIEL
No, you must believe;
Be silent, and sit still.

There is a great deal here to admire. Joseph's misery seems real and unfunny, his repetitions of "everything, everything" and "stupidly, stupidly" are eloquent in their insistence on the unevadability of this seeming betrayal of love, while the walls, the furniture, all the inanimate appurtenances of daily life, rise up as accusers and mockers. Joseph's request for "one reason" and "one / Important and elegant proof" recalls those other Biblical occasions (the testing of Abraham and Isaac, the tribulations of Job) when inexplicable demands or impositions required superhuman and heroic resolve. The expression "elegant proof" comes from the discourse of mathematics, and denotes parsimony of means to an inviolable conclusion. It is a desire precisely opposed to Tertullian's *credo quia absurdum*, and to the ideas of Kierkegaard, as expressed by Justin Replogle in his valuable book on Auden's poetry: "Kierkegaard's philosophy is the Marx-Engels epistemology plus God. Put simply, it is an empirical philosophy insisting, contrary to empirical evidence, that God exists. That such a belief is logically contradictory and absurd is precisely Kierkegaard's point. Life *is* absurd, precisely because though God exists men, confined to their empirical knowledge, cannot know him, or even demonstrate his existence." And Gabriel's injunction, "Be silent, and sit still," will recall the lines from T. S. Eliot's "Ash Wednesday" that go, "Teach us to care and not to care / Teach us to sit still." And these lines in turn probably owe something to Pascal's comment in the *Pensées:* "I have discovered that all the unhappiness of men arises from one single fact, that they cannot stay quietly in their own chamber."

There follows a lyric speech of the Narrator, didactic in character and addressed to Joseph. It is brilliantly complex in form, exhibiting intricately elaborate ten-line stanzas of the kind favored by the seventeenth-century metaphysical poets, and of which the fourth stanza demands special notice for the deftness and sinuosity of its syntax. The speech is in

large part a catalogue of the historical and habitual faults of male arro-
gance and chauvinism, beginning with the (Biblically accredited) claim of
Adam that the temptation and fall in the Garden were entirely due to the
weakness of Eve. The list of indictments is partly comic but essentially
serious, and at the end of each stanza Joseph is told that it is now his task
to do penance for the entire human male gender. In the supernatural
context of the oratorio, Mary's role is not merely more prominent, it is
more heroic than Joseph's; and he must take upon himself the burdens of
passivity and meekness commonly assigned to women. The lyric is not
without its Eliotic paradoxes: "The Exceptional is always usual / And the
Usual exceptional."

This section of the oratorio concludes with a series of semi-choruses
and a final chorus, all of them addressed jointly to Mary and Joseph as
tutelary saints of the nuclear family, and as ones who have endured its
most terrible stresses. The first of these begins,

> Joseph, Mary, pray for those
> Misled by moonlight and the rose,
> For all in our perplexity.
> Lovers who hear a distant bell
> That tolls from somewhere in their head
> Across the valley of their dream—
> 'All those who love excessively
> Foot or thigh or arm or face
> Pursue a louche and fatuous fire
> And stumble into Hell'—

and it concludes,

> Pray for us, enchanted with
> The green Bohemia of that myth
> Where knowledge of the flesh can take
> The guilt of being born away,
> Simultaneous passions make
> One eternal chastity:
> Pray for us romantics, pray.

It is important to notice that the word "romantics" is in lower-case, and
does not refer to either poets or lovers of the nineteenth century. Indeed,
the heresy described in the concluding lines is the one made most familiar
by some of John Donne's love and seduction poems, including "The

Ecstasy" and "The Canonization" but also such lines from "The Relique" as these:

> First, we loved well and faithfully,
> Yet knew not what we loved, nor why,
> Difference of sex no more we knew,
> Than our guardian angels do;
> Coming and going, we
> Perchance might kiss, but not between those meals;
> Our hands ne'er touched the seals,
> Which nature, injured by late law, sets free:
> These miracles we did; but now alas,
> All measure, and all language, I should pass,
> Should I tell what a miracle she was.

The second of these passages is a prayer in behalf of "us / Independent embryos," sung by a "boys' semi-chorus," and descriptive of the inherited Original Sin, traceable not merely historically to the disobedience in the Garden but genetically to "the germ-cell's primary division" at which point "Innocence is lost and sin . . . Once more issues as an act." A third semi-chorus implores blessing in behalf of the conventionally married, who take their domestic lives indolently and for granted, being so unaware of unconscious rebellions that their "will / To civil anarchy / Uses disease to disobey / And makes [their] private bodies ill." The familiar territories of Freud and Groddeck are invoked, and the crime of incest, as specifically distinguished from adultery, is characterized as the besetting hazard of "the bourgeoisie." The fourth of these passages of prayer, following plainly from the invocation of Freud, concerns infantile sexuality, "whence each derives / A vague but massive feel / Of being individual." This is the beginning of solipsism and of selfishness, and the whole section of the oratorio ends with the formerly separated semi-choruses joined at last in a final chorus of prayer.

> Blessed Woman,
> Excellent Man,
> Redeem for the dull the
> Average Way,
> That common ungifted
> Natures may
> Believe that their normal

Vision can
Walk to perfection.

This prayer in behalf of the ordinary and the humble, those so distinctly different from the Holy Family, is also a prayer for those who differ from the worldly learnedness and wisdom of the Magi, who will be the principal figures in the following section, called "The Summons."

This fourth section is a curious mixture and not altogether comfortable blending of religious and secular, miraculous and mundane. Doubtless Auden's deliberate intention was to show the intrusion upon the secular-political world of the inexplicable workings of divinity. But his way of doing it in this part of the poem seems no more than a crude juxtaposition of, first, the journey of the Magi, and second, a ludicrous paean to Caesar. The first half, which constitutes the summons of the Magi by the appearance of the "Star of the Nativity," gives that star a voice, which speaks in an adapted Spenserian nine-line stanza. The star introduces itself as the opponent of orderly, rational thought, of "orthodox sophrosyne" (which the *OED,* citing these lines, defines as "prudence, moderation, soundness of mind"), as well as of all that is conventional, convenient, and taken for granted. The Star furthermore acknowledges that to follow its summons is to undertake a dangerous and unpleasant quest through one of Auden's familiar symbolic landscapes and *paysages moralisés* in the course of which the pilgrim will encounter "that Glassy Mountain where are no / Footholds for logic," and a "Bridge of Dread" that Auden slyly appropriated from the anonymous lyric "A Lyke-Wake Dirge," in which the pilgrim soul must pass through purgatorial tests. In the Star's version, the tests turn out to include "confusion, cripples, tigers, thunder, pain."

After the stately and ominous pronouncements of the Star, the three Magi present themselves in rollicking stanzas and headlong rhythms, and Auden ingeniously turns them into his own version of the Three B's: not Bach, Beethoven, and Brahms, but instead Bacon, Bergson, and Bentham. Bacon, the First Wise Man, declares that "With rack and screw I put Nature through / A thorough inquisition," and represents the unadulterated positivistic empiricist. But having found that Nature will not reveal her secrets as easily as he had counted upon, and having found her a deceiver, he now, in his perplexity, determines to follow the Star which will repudiate all his science. The Second Wise Man is Bergson, the philosopher of Time, whose concern with "the immediate data of consciousness" made him an opponent of nineteenth-century positivism, which he countered with a dependence upon intuition, defined as a way of "thinking in duration." As distinct from the so-called "objectivity" of the empiricist, Bergson is the spokesman for the highly subjective. But his theory has led him to the discovery that "We anticipate or remember but never are," so he too must make himself a pilgrim. The third of these comic wise men is Bentham, who devised a "calculus of social happiness" as a means of arriving at an optimum condition of well-being for society. But so cold-blooded and calculating a world view, he discovered, "left no time for affection, / Laughter, kisses, squeezing, smiles." And so, like a reformed beadle in a Dickens novel, a regenerated Mr. Gradgrind, he joins his colleagues, acknowledging that he failed in his system to take account of "love," and he too takes on the burdens of pilgrimage.

Given the subject matter itself, one cannot fail to notice the pains that Auden has taken *not* to draw any parallels or possibilities of comparison with Eliot's "Journey of the Magi." Auden's figures are comics, allegorical, clownish, and keep up their spirits during the difficult trek with what they themselves characterize as "a silly song." The difference could not be more pronounced. Joining together in a trio, they sing, "At least we know for certain that we are three old sinners, / That this journey is much too long, and that we want our dinners." This is not merely different from Eliot; it seems a repudiation of his speaker's solemnity and lack of good humor. Auden's Magi make light of their discomforts and exhibit a cheerful (or perhaps mindless) stoicism Eliot's speaker never entertains. After the trio sing in unison, the Star speaks once again, and for the last time, in commanding utterance.

> Descend into the fosse of Tribulation,
> Take the cold hand of Terror for a guide;
> Below you in its swirling desolation
> Hear tortured Horror roaring for a bride:
> O do not falter at the last request
> But, as the huge deformed head rears to kill,
> Answer its craving with a clear I Will;
> Then wake, a child in the rose-garden, pressed
> Happy and sobbing to your lover's breast.

I must confess to finding this passage the most unsatisfactory one in the whole poem. I am not persuaded by any of the Terror or the Horror, possibly because they seem too allegorical—whereas other poets (Hopkins, for one) have made them very real indeed. What Auden is trying to describe, of course, is the "fear and trembling" upon which Kierkegaardian doctrine is premised, and the "leap of faith" that it demands. But what we seem to get instead resembles the nursery story of the "Frog-Prince," who must be kissed in his unmetamorphosed condition before he turns into a matinée idol. The fairy-tale aura is greatly emphasized by the concluding lines.

Still, we can take seriously the notion of heavenly demands. Such demands are immediately contrasted with the secular demands of tribute and obeisance to Caesar, who is said to have established "our Just society." All citizens are commanded to "stand motionless and hear / In a concourse of body and concord of soul / His proclamation." Caesar is virtually deified, as many caesars were, by the virtues and beneficent powers he is said to exhibit. His voice, which turns out to be the proxy voice of a herald, is made to contrast ironically with the voice of divinity whose proxy is the Star. After the herald's announcement (which turns out to be the decree from Caesar Augustus mentioned in the second chapter of Luke and which has about it all the totalitarian compulsion of the Nazi dictatorship), the vast and silenced citizenry is commanded to disperse in order to carry out Caesar's commands, but not before first giving thanks and praise to him "Who overcame implacable Necessity / By his endurance and by His skill has subdued the / Welter of Fortune."

What follows is a witty "Fugal-Chorus" of praise, which is tantamount to a pledge of allegiance. It is also praise that is predicated on a naive conception of progress. Each of the seven stanzas begins, "Great is Caesar: He has conquered the Seven Kingdoms." These kingdoms turn out to be Philosophy, Physics, Mathematics, Economics, Technology, Medicine, and Psychology. Since it can be claimed that progress has been made (at least anachronistically) in each of these domains, or that previous errors have been discovered and repudiated, the multitude join in this paean even as they acknowledge, in the final stanza, that they are the passive victims of political brainwashing. The kingdoms Caesar has conquered are intellectual kingdoms, all of them conceived in defiantly secular terms, as well as in terms that would have perfectly agreed with W. Warde Fowler's view of Roman civilization as not merely derivative but as lacking in what he called "fancy, reflection, or culture." This is not to say Auden's view of Rome is the same as Fowler's; on the contrary, the society Auden presents would border on parody were it not being enacted by the dictatorships of Europe and apparently embraced by their citizenry.

At this point the Narrator reappears with one of those puzzling speeches that vary in tone from the blandly optimistic confidence of a Chamber of Commerce booster to that of penitential sinner. The speech begins with unqualified cheerfulness.

> These are stirring times for the editors of newspapers:
> History is in the making; Mankind is on the march.
> The longest aqueduct in the world is already
> Under construction: the Committees on Fen-Drainage
> And Soil-Conservation will issue very shortly
> Their Joint Report; . . .

The fatuous satisfaction of these opening lines could find its echo in political spokesmen for virtually all public works projects. But into the midst of this euphoric description of community enterprise, Auden cunningly insinuates a very odd note indeed.

>                     even the problem of Trade Cycles
> And Spiralling Prices are regarded by experts
> As practically solved; and the recent restrictions
> Upon aliens and free-thinking Jews are beginning
> To have a salutary effect upon the public.

The phrase "free-thinking Jews" sticks in the mind (as in the craw), and we recall at once that it is Eliot's phrase, notoriously used in an anti-Semitic context of which he was sufficiently ashamed to suppress it, forbidding republication. The phrase occurs in Eliot's collection of lectures at the University of Virginia, published under the title *After Strange Gods*, itself a condemnation. In these lectures Eliot tries to envision an ideal community, and he says,

> The population should be homogeneous; where two or more cultures exist in the same place they are likely either to be fiercely self-conscious or both to become adulterate. What is still more important is unity of religious background; and reasons of race and religion combine to make any large number of free-thinking Jews undesirable. There must be a proper balance between urban and rural, industrial and agricultural development. And a spirit of excessive tolerance is to be deprecated.

Eliot published the book in which these words appear in 1934. It is worth remembering that in the previous year the Nazis had set fire to the Reichstag building and blamed it on poor Van der Lubbe in particular and the Communists in general. Dachau had not merely been established but enlarged. On March 9, the *Manchester Guardian* had reported that many Jews were beaten in Berlin "until the blood streamed down their heads and faces, and their backs and shoulders were bruised. Many fainted and were left lying on the streets." The account of atrocities committed against the Jews of Germany in the single year of 1933, including the random execution of individuals in their homes by shooting and by hanging, cases of torture and mutilation, the suicide of many, the flight into exile of others, all this was attested to in the public press. Einstein was among those forced to flee. Under the circumstances, Eliot's remark about "free-thinking Jews" and the error of "excessive tolerance" seems, at the very best, in shockingly bad taste, if not actually grotesque.

There can be little doubt that Auden himself must have been appalled by Eliot's phrase, since he puts it into the mouth of someone who, in the first half of this speech, presents himself as a shameless jingoistic spokesman for imperial policy and totalitarian power—and not alone of Roman power. We are made absolutely conscious that the political and practical virtues being extolled here are precisely those envisioned by the Nazis in their dream of the "thousand-year Reich," since the Narrator concludes this first half of his discourse with "Our great empire shall be secure for a thousand years."

The second half of this speech, however, is another matter altogether, and not easy, at least, psychologically, to reconcile with the first. It deserves full quotation.

> If we are never alone or always too busy,
> Perhaps we might even believe what we know is not true:
> But no one is taken in, at least not all of the time;
> In our bath, or the subway, or the middle of the night,
> We know very well we are not unlucky but evil,
> That the dream of the Perfect State or No State at all,
> To which we fly for refuge, is part of our punishment.
> Let us therefore be contrite but without anxiety,
> For Powers and Times are not gods but mortal gifts from God;
> Let us acknowledge our defeats but without despair,
> For all societies and epochs are transient details,
> Transmitting an everlasting opportunity
> That the Kingdom of Heaven may come, not in our present
> And not in our future, but in the Fullness of time.
> Let us pray.

The Narrator has transformed himself, quite suddenly and inexplicably, from extrovert to introvert; from chauvinistic encomiast and xenophobic bigot to meditative penitent, whose sight reaches beyond the limits of ordinary human time, and specifically beyond a "thousand years." Moreover, while the first half of the speech is highly *public* in its nature, concerned with large and corporate projects, the second half speaks to us when we are specifically "alone." It is then that we are obliged to acknowledge certain truths that our public life, in its officious busyness, can usually eclipse. The Platonic dream of the "Perfect State" is equated with the Marxist utopian dream of the complete withering away of the State, and both are seen now as naive delusions. More precisely, they are symbolic forms of twin Christian heresies. The Platonic is the absolute repudiation of the material by the spiritual, and is therefore a species of the Manichaean heresy; Marxism is rank materialism, which repudiates the spirit; both, by their exaggerations, are in error. Auden is shyly, parenthetically, incidentally, repudiating a political dream of his own past, as the second half of the speech repudiates the first, so that we may read the reproach to Eliot as balanced by another reproach of Auden to himself. That the Narrator says we must wait in a spirit of contrition "without anxiety" may seem to run contrary to the Kierkegaardian Christianity that is so clearly espoused in this work; but we must remember that this speech is historically *pre-Christian,* that the Narrator is either a Jew or a Gentile (very probably a Jew) who awaits the coming of the Messiah as prophetically promised, as widely expected, and as immediately recognized (as shall shortly come to pass in this work) by the shepherds, by the Wise Men, and by Simeon.

This part of the oratorio ends with a chorale, the only fragment of Auden's text as it now stands that was actually set to music by Britten, though I have learned from David Mason that an abridged version of the oratorio was set by Marvin David Levy and performed at Carnegie Hall on December 7, 1959. The final chorale employs a traditional hymnal stanza, and is unexceptionable except for one striking detail in the second of the three stanzas, specifically in its two final lines:

> And for thy Goodness even sin
> Is valid as a sign.

Admittedly, everything lies within the power and grace of God, including the totally unexpected. But the paradox in these lines is familiar, and it was made familiar by Eliot in his 1930 essay on Baudelaire, in which he wrote,

It was once the mode to take Baudelaire's Satanism seriously, as it is now the tendency to present Baudelaire as a serious and Catholic Christian . . . I think that the latter view—that Baudelaire is essentially Christian—is nearer the truth than the former, but it needs considerable reservation. When Baudelaire's Satanism is dissociated from its less creditable paraphernalia, it amounts to a dim intuition of a part, but a very important part, of Christianity. Satanism itself, so far as not merely an affectation, was an attempt to get into Christianity by the back door. Genuine blasphemy, genuine in spirit and not merely verbal, is the product of partial belief, and is as impossible to the complete atheist as to the perfect Christian. It is a way of affirming belief.

It is of interest to notice how Eliot, embarking from a specific and focused interest in Baudelaire, his Christianity and his Satanism, proceeds to what seem general and universal conclusions. He goes on to say,

The possibility of damnation is so immense a relief in a world of electoral reform, plebiscites, sex reform, and dress reform, that damnation itself is an immediate form of salvation—of salvation from the ennui of modern life, because it at last gives some significance to living.

As we read on it seems more and more as though Baudelaire were merely a pretext for a very peculiar kind of religious homily on Eliot's part:

What distinguishes the relations of man and woman from the copulation of beasts is the knowledge of Good and Evil (of *moral* Good and Evil which are not natural Good and Bad or puritan Right and Wrong) . . . So far as we are human, what we do must be either evil or good; so far as we do evil or good, we are human; and it is better, in a paradoxical way, to do evil than to do nothing: at least we exist.

This very puzzling doctrine seems to owe something to the theology and poetry of Dante, a fact of which Eliot seems glancingly aware, since at the very opening of his essay he writes, "Baudelaire has, I believe, been called a fragmentary Dante, for what that description is worth." In the third canto of the *Inferno*, in the vestibule or antechamber of Hell, Dante, the pilgrim, encounters a host of tormented spirits blown about like sand in a windstorm. "Ed egli a me: 'Questo misero modo / tengon l'anime triste di colore, / che visser senza infamia e senza lodo.'" In Charles Singleton's

English this is rendered, "And he [Virgil] to me: 'Such is the miserable condition of the sorry souls of those who lived without infamy and without praise.'" Virgil, Dante's spokesman, proceeds to compare these spirits with "that base band of angels who were neither rebellious nor faithful to God, but stood apart." As regards this "moral neutrality," Singleton furnished some valuable notes. He writes:

> Although no mention of neutral angels is made in the Bible, the notion of moral neutrality stretches back into very early legends. The long tradition is represented in the many versions of Brendan's voyage, in Wolfram von Eschenbach's *Parzival*, Walter Map's *De nugis curialium*, and the epic poem, *L'image du monde*, as well as, among patristic writings, in Clement of Alexandria's *Stromata* . . . The theological problem of the angels' neutrality has been studied by J. Freccero (1960) who says (pp. 13–14): "[The neutral angels] simply did not act [as did those who rebelled with Satan], but remained frozen in a state of aversion from God. It is pointless to ask whether they were better or worse than the lowest of sinners, for they do not fit into any category, after the initial division of heavenly light from infernal dark. With the aversion from God, the bond of charity was smashed; with the abstention from action, they deprived themselves of the one positive element which could win them a place in the cosmos. They are as close to nothing as creatures can be and still exist, for by their double negation, they have all but totally removed themselves from the picture. To be deprived of action is to be deprived of love, and love is the law of Dante's cosmos, determining all classifications. There remains nothing for them but the vaguely defined vestibule of hell, and they merit no more than a glance from the pilgrim before he passes on to the realm of love perverted."

It is to be noted that all this commentary is addressed to the problem of the "moral neutrality" of angels, while nothing is said of this matter as regards mortals; it is simply assumed that the moral predicament involved is comparable or analogous in some way. But I am by no means persuaded that it is, and I find Eliot's somewhat confused statements quoted above a confirmation of my views. For I find it always requires active moral energy simply to keep from doing harm to others even inadvertently, and that, in view of the ever-present inequities in human life, we can never be unaware of the unmerited suffering around us which we cannot hope ever fully to repair. Even passive consent to the pain of others is sinful, or certainly anything but neutral, so that the realms of moral experience available to us on the most elementary level are three: active benevolence, active or passive harm. Rarely, however, is the choice that simple, since we are rarely, if ever, able to foresee the consequences of our actions, which, even when undeniably well-intentioned, may have deplorable results—as Eliot himself seems to have perfectly acknowledged when, in "Gerontion," he wrote, "Unnatural vices / Are fathered by our heroism. Virtues / Are forced upon us by our impudent crimes." This is to say, there is no intermediate, neutral ground. And in this very essay Eliot seems to hold that view himself when he declares, "So far as we are human, what we do must be either evil or good," which leaves no room for the "neutrality" of "doing nothing." Failure to do good is not "doing nothing"; it is doing harm. And when Eliot proceeds to embrace the paradox that "it is better to do evil . . . than to do nothing," it seems to me he is entering upon grounds where I cannot follow him, and suspect him of being in grave danger. I should not myself care to defend the position that the mass murders of Stalin and Hitler were in any way morally superior to some form of human behavior, if there be such, that could be described as "morally neutral." To do nothing may be wicked, but to classify active crime as "morally superior" to it seems to me a sophistical exercise in perversity. And there was that in Eliot that was always attracted to the perverse. Apart from the evidence of certain of his poems and of *Sweeney Agonistes,* there is his considered endorsement of the scene of bestiality that takes place in a chapel and before an altar at the end of Djuna Barnes's *Nightwood.*

The fifth section is called "The Vision of the Shepherds," and it bears a not unexpected kinship to *The Second Shepherds' Play* by the so-called Wakefield Master. The shepherds, three innocent ones, as in the play (but without the play's "villain," Mak) exchange comments on the familiar pastoral complaints, and on the skewed and unequal relationship between themselves and their social and economic betters. It must be acknowledged that these matters of social injustice are dealt with far more realistically and dramatically in the old play than in the new oratorio, though some of the same topics are mentioned. Auden's shepherds are very civilized in their reprobation of those inclined to patronize them, who, as usual, turn out to be the pastoral poets, the *laissez-faire* capitalists, and the evangelical Marxists.

THE FIRST SHEPHERD

We observe that those who assure us their education
And money would do us much harm,

How real we are just as we are, and how they envy us,
    For it is the centreless tree
And the uncivilized robin who are the truly happy,
    Have done pretty well for themselves:

THE SECOND SHEPHERD
Nor can we help noticing how those who insist that
    We ought to stand up for our rights,
And how important we are, keep insisting also
    That it doesn't matter a bit
If one of us gets arrested or injured, for
    It is only our numbers that count.

There could be no more apt gloss upon the First Shepherd's observations than Gray's "Elegy Written in a Country Churchyard," in which the deprivations of the poor, being customary, are made to seem slight, and almost benign, in comparison with the mental torments and near insanity of the Regius Professor of Modern History at Cambridge. Virgil's shepherds did not enjoy any comforting acquaintance with the Emperor Augustus, and had to make do for themselves in a world in which the most serious fault the poet allowed to intrude was a broken love affair. Auden's Second Shepherd takes aim at the Marxists, and their clarion call for the workers of the world to unite. The dream of the dictatorship of the proletariat is based purely on numerical force, is itself coercive, and is unconcerned with the "spiritual" welfare of any individual in and for himself—which is, presumably, the one concern of God. Instead of trying to improve their lot by revolutionary or other political means, the shepherds are, as they explain, "waiting." They do not say for what, and possibly don't know, though we who are familiar with the story know perfectly well. But the fact that they are "waiting" bears directly on the meaning of Time as it figures in this work, and on "the Fullness of Time," as it is meant in its Christian sense. Such "waiting" requires patience.

THE SECOND SHEPHERD
That is why you should not take our conversation
    Too seriously, nor read too much
Into our songs;

THE THIRD SHEPHERD
    Their purpose is mainly to keep us
From watching the clock all the time.

This is another instance of Auden's half-seriously entertained doctrine about the essential frivolity of art, only religion being worthy of serious and solemn meditation. As I have indicated earlier, this was a doctrine that Auden himself could not have completely believed. And there is, moreover, a very perdurable quality to the "pastoral myth," as there is to the value of what we conventionally call "primitive art." Nor can such art, or poetry, be easily dismissed by any such slighting word as "frivolous." Clearly the problem is a complex one, since a distinction needs to be made between truly "untutored" art and the art attributed to untutored artists, that is to say, the art composed for them by such sophisticated artists as Virgil or Theocritus and presented as the work of uncouth and natively inspired poets. So persuasive is this myth of the instinctive artist, "warbling his woodnotes wild," that every now and then society discovers one—James Hogg the Ettrick Shepherd, John Taylor the Water Poet—and our faith in his reality is part of our faith in the inspiration of shepherds, including the Shepherd-King, David, in the Old Testament, and in the inspiration that made so mysteriously articulate the humble fishermen who were the Apostles (though Luke and Paul enjoyed the benefit of sound education). This tradition, which would also include the poet Caedmon, in any case, associates art, and poetry in particular, with very serious matters, and on that ground alone commands more respect than Auden's doctrine of the frivolity of art would allow.

The three shepherds join in singing a song whose burden is shockingly suicidal—which is to say, anything but frivolous. Their language is that of modern factory workers, with their sense of mechanical and mindless repetition and heartless routine. (One is reminded of Reinhold Niebuhr's years of ministry in Detroit.) In any case, the angels make their appearance, and, addressing the three shepherds in three choral passages, direct them to "run to Bethlehem" because forgiveness and good will to all men—"all, all, all of them" (that is, not just some of a certain religious persuasion or of a certain "cultural background")—is at hand. The word "all" is thrice repeated; the granting of this clemency is stated three times.

The sixth part, called "At the Manger," begins with a lullaby sung by Mary to the Child, and composed of three stanzas. It is worth observing that a lullaby is what may be an archetypal version of pastoral poetry. It is sung by a knowing, experienced adult to an inexperienced and innocent child. Its drama and emotion are predicated on the sophisticated knowledge of the former, which includes a foreknowledge that an infant's innocence and heedless bliss is doomed in the very nature of things to be lost. It soothes and comforts any tendency to childish tears, while withholding the bitter knowledge that there will be much more serious and terrible griefs to come. It encourages the child to sleep and to dream as an avenue of escape from the worldly miseries that crowd upon the consciousness of the adult. It presents, in other words, a benign relationship between the stronger and the weaker, between the figuratively rich and the figuratively poor, between the shepherd and his sheep, between those with power and those without. It moves us by its deliberate omission of bitter truths that, as adults, we know to be inevitable, and that we know are left unmentioned out of love for the infant and respect for its innocence. The lullaby partakes, in other words, of the "pious fraud" that is part of the now completely secularized tradition of Santa Claus. A lullaby involves loving deception.

But in the context of the Nativity scene, it becomes far more complex and dramatic. Tradition maintains that Mary could not have been duped into taking upon herself the supreme maternal role; so that before she acquiesced to her destiny, which was made manifest by Gabriel, she was granted absolute foreknowledge of what that destiny entailed, for herself, for her child, and for mankind. Such foreknowledge included the Seven Joys of the Virgin; but it also included the Seven Sorrows of the Virgin. In this role of *Mater Dolorosa,* Mary is often depicted with seven swords piercing her breast or framing her head, representing, among other things, the Seven Deadly Sins by which men vitiate the sacrifice of her son's life. But they represent more particularly the prophecy of Simeon in the temple: "This child is destined to be a sign which men reject; and you too shall be pierced to the heart" (Luke 2:34–35). This is merely the first of the sorrows, the other six being the Flight into Egypt, Christ lost to his parents when, as a child, he disputes among the doctors in the Temple, the Bearing of the Cross, the Crucifixion, the Descent from the Cross, and the Ascension (which is the final worldly parting of the son from his mother).

In Auden's lullaby there are sufficient hints of these coming sorrows, known to the mother but not the child. The second stanza goes,

> Sleep. What have you learned from the womb that bore you
> But an anxiety your Father cannot feel?
> Sleep. What will the flesh that I gave do for you,
> Or my mother love, but tempt you from His will?
> Why was I chosen to teach His Son to weep?
> Little One, sleep.

And the final stanza concludes: "How soon will you start on the Sorrowful Way? / Dream while you may." Mary's anguish is made the more poignant by the fact that, as though by malicious genetic division, her son will inherit what is painful only from her, what is blessed and perfect only from his heavenly Father. So, in the tradition of lullabies, this one speaks of grief while engaged in concealing or assuaging grief.

At the conclusion of the lullaby the Wise Men present themselves, and after they have made their comments, which chiefly concern the discomforts and inconveniences they have endured in the course of their journey, the shepherds come forward and describe the habitual miseries of their lives. Nobody brings any gifts, save for the explicit acknowledgment of the miraculousness of the event. The Wise Men have been travelers; they are filled with worldly experience, earned in the course of their passages over the face of the earth, so they conclude the account of this latest journey by saying, in unison, "O here and now our endless journey stops." The shepherds, by way of dialectical contrast, are representatives of those poor who are stuck forever in the place and station of their birth, and for whom nothing has ever changed, so that after describing the quotidian routines which have imprisoned them, they join in union to declare: "O here and now our endless journey starts."

The scene of the Adoration concludes with the Three Wise Men and the Three Shepherds speaking in alternating stanzas, each group assigned its own stanzaic form and rhyme pattern as well as its own theme. The Wise Men, who had earlier been so specifically identified with the positivistic heresies, speak continuously and exclusively of Love, while the shepherds, with characteristic humility, speak of the errors of their ways, and all of their speeches are prayers. In the midst of this antiphonal exchange (it cannot be called a colloquy, since neither group takes notice of what the other says), the Wise Men declare,

> The singular is not Love's enemy;
> Love's possibilities of realization
> Require an Otherness that can say *I*.

This is the first instance of a note that will reappear shortly, and which is derived from the I/Thou theology of Martin Buber, in which Auden had taken a serious interest. The final tutti pronounces the reconciliation of Space and Time personified and assimilated by Love.

The seventh section is called "The Meditation of Simeon," and once again we are reminded that this is a subject Eliot addressed. And we note furthermore that, once again, Auden seems to have taken deliberate pains to avoid any suggestion of similarity. Eliot's "Ariel" poem, "A Song for Simeon," gives voice to an elderly and deeply exhausted man, who speaks, symbolically, at the dead end of an exhausted tradition. In a seasonal juxtaposition that Eliot cherished ("April is the cruellest month," "What is the late November doing / With the disturbance of the spring"), Simeon, in his failing days, observes that "the Roman hyacinths are blooming in bowls and / The winter sun creeps by the snow hill . . ." There is in his voice no deep gratitude or sense of revelation. He speaks instead of deprivation: "Not for me the ultimate vision." Instead of viewing Simeon traditionally as the First Convert, Eliot sees him as the last of the heretics in his final feebleness, and his *Nunc Dimittis,* with which the poem ends, is the expression of a man who wants, like the Cumaean Sibyl in the epigraph to *The Waste Land,* to die. (There is certainly a way of reading Eliot's poem as a spiritual statement about his own willingness to "die to this world," but that does not alter the unambiguous tone of resignation and fatigue that characterizes the poem.)

A few words about the traditional Simeon seem in order. He is described as "righteous and devout," or conscientious in regard to God and His law. He is identified as full of expectation for the coming of the Messiah, and as moved by the Holy Spirit (that is, not merely the spirit of prophecy) to believe he would not die before he had seen the Messiah. Guided by the Spirit to the courts of the Temple, he no sooner saw Jesus there than the words of the *Nunc Dimittis* rose to his lips. While Mary was wondering at the meaning of these words, he turned to her and foretold the diverse results of the ministry of Jesus, which would entail the Seven Joys and Seven Sorrows that Mary had foreknown. He then disappears from all record, in a state of rapture and gratitude.

Auden's Simeon is a man of great intelligence and understanding, who speaks in a series of prose passages or prose poems, most of them confined to the length of a single paragraph and separated from one another by an "off-stage" chorus, whose terse, italicized comments are pointedly alliterative. Moreover, Simeon's passages are, for the most part, joined in groupings of three that parallel and fortify one another. The entire "Meditation," which envisions the fate and history of mankind from the Fall to the Incarnation, is nothing less than a series of brilliant aperçus, of carefully deployed and systematized argument; and it is easy to feel that Simeon himself is the one personage in the entire oratorio with whom Auden most willingly identifies himself.

The first three passages of Simeon's meditation are carefully structured in both parallel and mutually exclusive ways. In summary outline, they run as follows:

(1) As long as the apple had not been entirely digested . . . there was still hope that . . . the Fall had not occurred in fact.
(2) As long as there were any roads to amnesia . . . there was still hope that . . . the Fall had occurred by necessity.
(3) As long as there were any experiments to be undertaken . . . there was still hope that . . . the Fall had occurred by accident.

The purport of these three hypothetical situations involves the evasion of our abiding sense of guilt associated with Original Sin. If the Fall had not in fact occurred, we would not be guilty. If it had occurred by necessity, it was not our fault. And neither was it our fault if it had occurred by accident. These are the only three possibilities, and they exhaust our rational attempts to exculpate ourselves, since we are forced to acknowledge, when the full bill of particulars is presented to us, that each hypothesis is false. The third one, for example, is based upon the dream of the secular reform of society, and is sustained only by the hope that we have simply failed to arrive at the right "formula" to solve all our social problems. The second assumes that mankind has always been bestial, and any dream of an earlier prelapsarian, paradisiacal condition is no more than childish self-delusion, based upon the ignorance of youth; so that the "necessity" of the Fall is proven by our unhappy acknowledgment that we have grown up to the truth of our real natures, "necessity" in this case being the inevitable course of human maturity.

The next three passages begin, each in turn, as follows:

(1) Before the Positive could manifest Itself . . .
(2) Before the Infinite could manifest Itself . . .
(3) Before the Unconditional could manifest Itself . . .

The capitalized nouns are, of course, faceless personifications of the Godhead, and the three "conditions" being articulated are the preconditions for the Incarnation and require the defeat of three forms of mental life. The first is utter Subjectivity, with its attendant narcissism and indifference to reality. The second involves wandering in the wilderness of philosophical dilemmas, especially those insoluble ones of "Illusion and Reality," "the One and the Many," which can be resolved only by supernatural solution. The third is the realm of the Unconscious, a depth unfathomable, but which cannot explain Original Sin. And from this Simeon proceeds to affirm that the Old Testament prophecy of the coming of the Messiah "could only be fulfilled when it was no longer possible to receive, because it was clearly understood as absurd." The point is not simply the sudden introduction of a Kierkegaardian concept, but the fact that the nonrational, or suprarational, is being affirmed in a highly organized and meticulously rational argument. And now Simeon adverts to the precepts of another theologian altogether, and it is worth quoting the relevant passage in its entirety.

> But here and now the Word which is implicit in the Beginning and in the end is become immediately explicit, and that which hitherto we could only passively fear as the incomprehensible I AM, henceforth we may actively love with comprehension that THOU ART. Wherefore, having seen Him, not in some prophetic vision of what might be, but with the eyes of our own weakness as to what actually is, we are bold to say that we have seen our salvation.

The glossing of this passage could be quite extensive, but I will confine myself to a few comments. The "incomprehensible I AM" refers to God's identification of Himself to Moses in Exodus 3:14. Moreover, in Exodus 33:18–23, God refuses to show His face to Moses (and this may be an act of kindness, since to behold His face is to perish) and instead allows Moses to view His "back parts." The prohibition against seeing God face to face is most explicit in Exodus 33:20, where it is written of the Lord, "And he said [to Moses] Thou canst not see my face: for there shall no man see me, and live." The Old Testament God is, accordingly, invisible, and, as the books of Job and Jonah both indicate, inscrutable as well. The "mystery" of this God is, according to orthodox Christian theology, made comprehensible to the intellect and accessible to the senses of mankind by means of the Incarnation, by which God takes on human features that may be looked upon and a human nature that may be understood. But the matching of the phrases I AM with THOU ART seems very likely to have been derived from the theology of Martin Buber, who in a work titled *I and Thou* wrote, "Love is a responsibility of an *I* for a *thou*."

There follow very shortly three parallel passages of assurance and hope:

> (1) Because in Him the Flesh is united to the Word without magical transformation, Imagination is redeemed from promiscuous fornication with her own images.

(2) Because in Him the Word is united to the Flesh without loss of perfection, Reason is redeemed from incestuous fixation on her own Logic, for the One and the Many are simultaneously revealed as real.

(3) And because of His visitation, we may no longer desire God as if He were lacking: our redemption is no longer a question of pursuit but of surrender to Him who is always and everywhere present. Therefore at every moment we pray that, following Him, we may depart from our anxiety into His peace.

This synoptic account ends with Simeon's last words, and by the very use of the word "therefore" they enlist the means of logical discourse and forensic argument in the service of that truth which defies rational analysis. They also recall that faith begins in anxiety.

The entire meditation of Simeon offers Auden an opportunity to display his most dazzling capacities of extrapolation and embroidered invention as the techniques for theological persuasion and philosophic demonstration. Many commentators have admired in his prose essays a pervasively categorizing mind in which all possibilities are numbered and itemized. This has the superficial effect of inordinate tidiness, but it has also the compelling force of an argument that leaves nothing out of account. Auden's Simeon is the triumphant Christian apologist.

And now we come, in the penultimate division of the oratorio, "The Massacre of the Innocents," to what may be the most admired, and surely is one of the wittiest, of its parts. It is a prose monologue, putatively "thought" or "spoken" by Herod as he weighs the reasons for his decision to order the massacre. I say "putatively" because in this speech Herod is no more than the spokesman for Roman imperial policy, and moreover, a spokesman for that policy at its most benign, which has widely been thought to be the time of Marcus Aurelius. It was Edward Gibbon who elevated Marcus Aurelius to this most exalted pagan position, and from whose death he dated the beginning of the decline of the Roman Empire, regarding with an impartial dismay the Christians and the barbarians as being equally to blame for the corruption and weakness into which the empire fell. Gibbon wrote: "If a man were called to fix the period in the history of the world, during which the condition of the human race was most happy and prosperous, he would without hesitation, name that which elapsed from the death of Domitian to the accession of Commodus." This period has become known as the Age of the Antonines, and it covered the reigns of Nerva, Trajan, Hadrian, Antoninus Pius, and

Marcus Aurelius. It is a period celebrated by a poem of Melville's, and in
a letter of Flaubert's, in which he writes,

> The melancholy of the antique world seems to me more profound
> than that of the moderns, all of whom more or less imply that beyond
> the dark void lies immortality. But for the ancients that "black hole"
> was infinity itself; their dreams loom and vanish against a back-
> ground of immutable ebony. No crying out, no convulsions—noth-
> ing but the fixity of a pensive gaze. With the gods gone, and Christ
> not yet come, there was a unique moment, from Cicero to Marcus
> Aurelius, when man stood alone. Nowhere else do I find that
> particular grandeur.

While acknowledging that Marcus Aurelius was a persecutor of the
Christians, Russell Kirk virtually exonerated him on the grounds that
"this was undertaken out of pure motives, and from a misunderstanding
of Christian doctrines, caused by the excesses of the fanatics on the fringe
of the then-inchoate Christian church," and furthermore by the Emperor's
generous belief "that wickedness was the consequence of ignorance." Kirk
has formulated some convenient summary remarks about the Stoicism
that served as the basis for the Emperor's famous *Meditations*. He writes,

> The Stoic philosophy . . . commences in a thoroughgoing material-
> ism: this world is the only world, and everything in it, even the usual
> attributes of spirit, has a material character . . . The duty of man is
> to ascertain the way of nature, the manner in which divine Providence
> intends that men should live. An inner voice informs the wise man
> of what is good and what is evil. (Most things, including the fleshly
> enjoyments of life, are neither good nor evil, but simply indifferent.)
> The Stoic, conforming to nature, looks upon all men, even the vicious
> and imbecile, as his brothers, and seeks their welfare. He lives, in
> Marcus Aurelius' words, "as if upon a mountain," superior to
> vanities, and expecting very little of his fellow-men, but helping and
> sympathizing with them, for all that. We are made for cooperation,
> like the hands, like the feet. The Stoic does not rail at misfortune, for
> that would be to criticize impudently God's handiwork; and he does
> not seek gratification of ambition, but rather performance of duty;
> and his end is not happiness, but virtuous tranquility.

What is seen by Kirk as a virtue is seen by Charles Williams as a defect,
when, in *The Descent of the Dove*, he writes,

The "good" Emperors had come to regard Christianity as an evil, as all tolerant and noble non-Christian minds tend to do. Partly, no doubt, the best Emperors had the highest idea of their duty to the safety of the State. But they also had the highest sense of moral balance and the least sense of the necessity of Redemption. The worst Emperors—Commodus, Heliogabalus—had a more superstitious impulse which was certainly more in accord with the asserted dogmas of the Gospel. Gods, and the nature of the Gods, are likely to be better understood by sinful than by stoical minds. [This last sentence might recall Eliot on Baudelaire.]

In any case, Herod's speech begins, in deliberate mimicry of Marcus Aurelius' *Meditations,* with expressions of homage to those who were his teachers and benefactors. Auden has him say,

To Fortune—that I have become Tetrarch, that I have escaped
   assassination, that at sixty my head is clear and my digestion sound.
To my Father—for the means to gratify my love of travel and study.
To my Mother—for a straight nose.
To Eva, my coloured nurse—for regular habits.
To my brother, Sandy, who married a trapeze-artist and died of
   drink—for so refuting the position of the Hedonists.
To Mr. Stewart, nicknamed The Carp, who instructed me in the
   elements of geometry through which I came to perceive the errors
   of the tragic poets.
To Professor Lighthouse—for his lectures on The Peloponnesian
   War.
To the stranger on the boat to Sicily—for recommending to me
   Brown on Resolution.
To my secretary, Miss Button—for admitting that my speeches were
   inaudible.

From the *Meditations,* I present a comparable, though highly selective and abbreviated, list. The Emperor catalogues those from whom he has received benefits of one kind or another.

From my mother, piety and beneficence, and abstinence, not only
   from evil deeds, but even from evil thoughts . . .
From Diognetus, not to busy myself about trifling things, and not to
   give credit to what was said by miracle-workers and jugglers about
   incantations and the driving away of daemons and such things.

From Rusticus I received the impression that my character required
improvement and discipline . . . and to abstain from rhetoric, and
poetry, and fine writing . . .

From Sextus, a benevolent disposition, and the example of a family
governed in a fatherly manner, and the idea of living conformably
to nature; and gravity without affectation, and to look carefully
after the interests of friends, and to tolerate ignorant persons . . .

From Alexander the grammarian, to refrain from fault-finding . . .

Thus Marcus Aurelius, represented by Herod, a surrogate administrator,
is perfectly suited to Auden's purposes, and the technique of anachronism
allows him to borrow the Tetrarch's philosophy from a reign one hundred
and sixty years after the birth of Christ. The Stoic Emperor serves Auden's
purposes precisely because he was so widely regarded as "good." This is
more than simply to demonstrate that so-called good men can commit
crimes, with Herod's Massacre of the Innocents standing for Marcus
Aurelius' persecution of Christians. It is to show that human rules of
morality are irrelevant to the miracle of the Incarnation and the Salvation
it proclaims, since that Salvation precisely involves the forgiveness of sins.

The Herod/Marcus Aurelius figure is the absolute rationalistic empiricist and pragmatic bureaucrat. He sees himself as laboring against an
opposition, even within his own ranks, of ignorance, philistinism, and
stupidity, against which, with inordinate patience and forbearance, he
strives in behalf of an ideal that very few are bright enough to admire or
approve, but which, in his own view, is greater, more magnanimous and
disinterested, than even the well-being of the empire itself. He is dedicated
to nothing less than human enlightenment, as he conceives it. And so in
appraising his opponents, he recognizes the most threatening of them as
those who espouse *irrationality* of any kind whatever, since any appeal
to the irrational, the subjective, and the solipsistic can only undermine the
shared premises and mutually agreed-upon laws of logical inference (to
say nothing of other laws) that it has taken interminable years and
innumerable errors to overcome. To him, it is clear that the imperilment
or destruction of the laws of discourse and reason, which are openly
available to all, is nothing less than a threat to civilization, of which he
regards himself an unacknowledged and self-effacing hero. His distrust of
anything that deviates from generally accepted "reason" makes it impossible for him to distinguish between one apocalyptic or evangelical cult
and another—and at the time of Christ's coming there were many such

cults, some of them very bizarre indeed. To recall Russell Kirk's words, Marcus Aurelius became a persecutor of Christians "from a misunderstanding of Christian doctrines, caused by excesses of the fanatics on the fringe of the then-inchoate Christian church." But a more scholarly mind, that of Gilbert Murray, saw the dilemma even more impartially, and in what may be purely sociological terms.

> To compare [late] Paganism in detail with its great rival [Christianity] would be, even if I possessed the necessary learning, a laborious and unsatisfactory task. But if a student with very imperfect knowledge may venture a personal opinion on this subject, it seems to me that we often look at such problems from the wrong angle. Harnack somewhere, in discussing the comparative success or failure of various early Christian sects, makes the illuminating remark that the main determining cause in each case was not their comparative reasonableness of doctrine or skill in controversy—for they practically never converted one another—but simply the comparative increase or decrease of the birthrate in the respective populations. On somewhat similar lines it always appears to me that, historically speaking, the character of Christianity in these early centuries is to be sought not so much in the doctrines which it professed, nearly all of which had their roots and their close parallels in older Hellenistic or Hebrew thought, but in the organization on which it rested. For my own part, when I try to understand Christianity as a mass of doctrines, Gnostic, Trinitarian, Monophysite, Arian and the rest, I get no further. When I try to realize it was a sort of semi-secret society for mutual help with a mystical religious basis, resting first on the proletariat of Antioch and the great commercial and manufacturing towns of the Levant, then spreading by instinctive sympathy to similar classes in Rome and the West, and rising in influence, like certain other mystical cults, by the special appeal it made to women, the various historical puzzles begin to fall into place.

To believe, with Auden, that the birth of Christ was nothing less than the miraculous and real Incarnation of God on earth, and His deliberate intervention and participation in human affairs, is to repudiate any view such as Gilbert Murray's, as well as those expressed by that champion of "reasonableness," Herod, the Tetrarch. But Auden is wittily aware that in embracing the Miraculous Birth, he will be confounded with all the crackpot cultists that Marcus Aurelius so sensibly distrusted, and some of

the most brilliant parts of Herod's long speech are devoted precisely to
conflating all irrational doctrines and barbaric rituals into a grotesque
composite which can appeal to those unwilling to undergo the fatigue of
thinking for themselves, or not bright enough to do so. Herod makes, in
other words, a pretty strong case for distrusting this newest threat to
reason and order. What is so astonishing and dramatic is that his
very process of reasoning leads him directly to the necessity for mass
murder.

Given his premises, his inferences and conclusions are unimpeachable,
and Auden is triumphant in exhibiting the inhuman consequence of an
absolute reliance on reason. But his very demonstration leads him, in my
view, to the only flaw in this otherwise masterly monologue. For as Herod
begins to realize the homicidal direction in which his thoughts are leading
him, he becomes petulant and quite suddenly drops all the dispassionate
virtues of Stoicism he was initially intended to represent. His last sentences
of whining complaint reduce him to a ridiculous butt who should never
have been taken seriously in the first place—instead of the unfeeling
rationalist he began by being. The ending of the speech seems to me feeble
in itself, with a feebleness that retrospectively weakens the brilliance of
what has gone before.

Herod's speech is followed by Auden's parody of the "Soldiers' Chorus," like that in Gounod's *Faust* or Verdi's *Il Trovatore*. The chorus sings
of "one of their own," a nearly anonymous representative named only
"George" (misspelled "Gearge" in the *Collected Longer Poems*), a mer-
cenary and a coward, whose picaresque career is outlined as a sort of
high-spirited demonstration that, like patriotism in Johnson's definition,
the military is the last refuge of the scoundrel. Moreover, a number of
clear homosexual notes are struck; and we are allowed to infer that an
exclusively male community, as the army has traditionally been, is a
plausible sanctuary for such a "refugee" from ordinary society. The highly
suspect and artificial "heartiness" of the chorus is the more striking in its
welcome of the peregrine George back into the fold "Just in tidy time to
massacre the Innocents."

The chorus is followed by a brief, solemn, and deeply moving speech
of lamentation in free verse, and the speaker, surprisingly, is Rachel. There
is, of course, no Rachel in the New Testament, and she appears principally
in the Old Testament as the wife of Jacob. But she also appears in
Jeremiah, weeping for the loss of her sons, which, in context, means the
children of Israel, and is alluded to in Matthew 2:17-18. She is, therefore,
a prefiguration, or type, of Mary herself, and her grief here is a universal

grief in behalf of "the Innocents." The Innocents are not, however, simply those spoken of in Jeremiah, nor those massacred by Herod, nor even both together, for they surely must include, in view of what was going on in the world at the time Auden was writing, the Jewish victims of genocide throughout the Nazi realm. And it is, moreover, impossible not to recall that Eliot, too, has his Rachel, mockingly designated as "Rachel *née* Rabinovitch," who was involved in murderous and sexual intrigue. There is something opaque about Eliot's phrase, since *née* is conventionally used to indicate the maiden name of a married woman, or of a woman who, for one reason or another, has legally changed her name. But it is never used without its being taken for granted that we know what her changed name actually is, a piece of information that Eliot withholds. Auden's invocation of her name and her eternal sorrow are so striking that it is worth noting that not very long after writing this oratorio, in March 1947, Auden said to Alan Ansen, "I've been increasingly interested in the Jews. Here's a book I've been reading about the Jewish mystics, the Chassidim. There's one man who was the Jewish St. Francis. These were all eighteenth century . . . I wonder what would happen if I converted to Judaism." Auden did not, of course, make such a conversion, nor was Chester Kallman in any way a factor that led him even to entertain the notion as a possibility. But it is worth observing that the two women to whom he proposed marriage, Rhoda Jaffe and Hannah Arendt, were both Jewish, and that from the earliest period of his veneration of Freud he had been a vigorous philo-Semite. By 1941 the Nazi policy regarding the Jews was so thoroughly established and so notoriously effective that the introduction of a mourning Rachel into a "Christmas oratorio" was certainly meant as a clear reference to what lay right before the eyes of a watching and horrified world.

The ninth and final division of the oratorio, "The Flight into Egypt," does not allow us to forget the cause of Rachel's grief. The Holy Family are themselves refugees, or, as they had come to be called in those days, DP's, "displaced persons." They are lucky, of course—providentially lucky to be among the survivors, since the Innocents will all have perished.

The land they enter is a kind of no man's land of aridity that is meant, among other things, to contrast with all the promise implied by the imagery of the garden at the beginning of the oratorio. It is the wasteland of modern society, and is given actual voices, which are, suitably enough, the commercial voices of the travel brochure and of cruise-ship advertising. They are voices we have heard in another form before: the voices of temptation, the siren voices of seduction, which made their first grotesque

appearance and appeal in the second part of the poem, "The Annunciation," where, in the guise of the emancipated Four Faculties, they identified themselves as the "Ambiguous causes / Of all temptation." The
"ambiguity" is made perfectly clear in this final section, where Egypt is
both a desolation and a place of refuge.

The voices are allowed to speak in a rather complicated nine-line stanza
which is actually an amalgam of two parts, and for purposes of discussion
it will be useful to divide the parts from one another, and examine them
as parallel forms. The second half of each stanza is a kind of minimalist
limerick, sardonic in tone, ostensibly a lure to the barren and grief-filled
prospects of the desert. There are four such choral invitations, all printed
in italics, as follows:

> *Come to our bracing desert*
> *Where eternity is eventful,*
>   *For the weather-glass*
>   *Is set at Alas,*
> *The thermometer at Resentful.*

> *Come to our old-world desert*
> *Where everyone goes to pieces;*
>   *You can pick up tears*
>   *For souvenirs*
> *Or genuine diseases.*

> *Come to our well-run desert,*
> *Where anguish arrives by cable,*
>   *And the deadly sins*
>   *May be bought in tins*
> *With instructions on the label.*

> *Come to our jolly desert*
> *Where even the dolls go whoring;*
>   *Where cigarette-ends*
>   *Become intimate friends,*
> *And it's always three in the morning.*

Of the last line it should be mentioned that it alludes to an observation in
F. Scott Fitzgerald's *The Crack-up* (1936), where Fitzgerald wrote, "In

the real dark night of the soul it is always three o'clock in the morning."
And the Egyptian sojourn is symbolically "the dark night of the soul" for
the Holy Family, prefiguring the anguish and sacrifice that is to come, and
which will echo the "despised and rejected" condition that in the land of
bondage the Israelites were made to endure. These little appeals and
invitations are amusing in the bleak candor of their tone, with its
suggestion not only that there is no escape from the vicissitudes of life,
but that in fact these very vicissitudes supply the diversions that our utter
boredom so desperately craves.

The first part of each stanza is wholly different in character, and is
composed of unrhymed tetrameter quatrains with a liberal sprinkling of
anapestic feet. They appear seriatim as follows.

> It was visitors' day at the vinegar works
> In Tenderloin Town when I tore my time;
> A sorrowful snapshot was my sinful wage:
> Was that why you left me, elusive bones?
>
> How should he figure my fear of the dark?
> The moment he can he'll remember me,
> The silly, he locked the cellar for fun,
> And his dear little doggie shall die in his arms.
>
> All Father's nightingales knew their place,
> The gardens were loyal: look at them now.
> The roads are so careless, the rivers so rude,
> My studs have been stolen; I must speak to the sea.
>
> In the land of lilies I lost my wits,
> Nude as a number all night I ran
> With a ghost for a guest along green canals;
> By the waters of waking I wept for the weeds.

It seems to me inarguable that in these lines Auden has consciously
borrowed the manner and idiom of Theodore Roethke. There is the
quasi-surrealism, the elementary diction, the sense of the familiar nightmare, and the easy colloquialisms that had become the hallmark of
Roethke's poems. In his biography of Roethke, Allan Seager testified to
the admiration the two poets had for one another.

After he arrived [at Penn State] from Harvard in 1939, Phillip Shelley
became a good friend of Ted's and he took a flat in the Glennland
Apartments where Ted lived . . .  In a joint effort, he and Ted
arranged to have W. H. Auden come and give a reading. Ted had
been reading Auden's work for some time and he was very excited
about meeting him. The year was 1941 and Auden came and stayed
for ten days. He says he and Ted hit it off at once and they remained
friends. Although boxing was not at all in either Auden's or Shelley's
line, Ted took them to see some College boxing matches.

Early in March of the same year Roethke's *Open House* was published,
and reviewed with unreserved admiration and understanding by Auden
in the *Saturday Review of Literature*.

Mr. Roethke is instantly recognizeable as a good poet . . .  Many
people have the experience of feeling physically soiled and humiliated
by life; some quickly put it out of their minds, others gloat narcissis-
tically on its unimportant details; but both to remember and to
transform the humiliation into something beautiful, as Mr. Roethke
does, is rare. Every one of the lyrics in this book, whether serious or
light, shares the same kind of ordered sensibility: *Open House* is
completely successful.

What Auden was seeking to represent by the voices of the desert was the
"soiled and humiliated" language of the buried psyche that Roethke had
so brilliantly formulated, a language which consorted perfectly with the
despised and rejected condition of which Isaiah spoke and which is native
to the wastes of the desert. Mary and Joseph recognize that they have
come to a region of testing, of deprivation, and of pain, and we know that
region to be our own familiar camping ground, which is a grim substitute
for the dangers of death from which they have escaped. In a recitative in
three stanzas of syllabics we are given the most trenchant commentary on
the antiphon of the Holy Parents and the desert.

Fly, Holy Family, from our immediate rage,
That our future may be freed from our past; retrace
 The footsteps of law-giving
 Moses, back through the sterile waste,

Down to the rotten kingdom of Egypt, the damp
Tired delta where in her season of glory our

> Forefathers sighed in bondage;
>   Abscond with the Child to the place
>
> That their children dare not revisit, to the time
> They do not care to remember; hide from our pride
>   In our humiliation;
>     Fly from our death with our new life.

A number of points need to be raised about this brief lyric. For one thing, the prayer "that our future may be freed from our past" can be understood in at least two ways. The first is the petition of the individual penitent or convert, who envisions the escape of the Holy Family as a sign of the ultimate fulfillment of a promised salvation, and the assurance that past errors are eradicated by present renovation. As such, it is unexceptionable, and may possibly reflect the private prayer of Auden himself, though it is spoken in behalf of us all. But the prayer may also be meant to express the severe Pauline doctrine of the severance of the Old Dispensation from the New, and the consequent necessary repudiation of Judaism, which, given Auden's kindly feelings and respect for that faith, seems to me unlikely. Secondly, there is the description of Egypt not only as the locus where "our forefathers," the children of Israel, "sighed in bondage," but also as "the place / That their children dare not revisit . . . the time / They do not care to remember." To say this is to emphasize the heroism entailed by this journey of the Holy Family into Egypt; but to claim that this is a time the Jews "do not care to remember" is surprisingly to fail to take into account the annual and ritual remembrance of the years of Egyptian bondage in the ceremony of the Passover.

And now we come to the final speech of the Narrator. It is, in my view, a superb achievement, the brilliant culmination of the entire work, exempt from the oscillating shifts of tone that beset the Narrator in his earlier appearances, and triumphant precisely in the muted and uneasy timbre of its triumph. It speaks with the voice of that beleaguered believer Auden had characterized as one who is thought to be an eccentric and a freak by the vast body of secular society in which, whether he likes it or not, he is obliged to live. The world everyone inhabits is a scientific, technological world of expedience and practicality, in which the believer is mocked not only by the doubts of others but by the doubts he himself cannot fail to entertain. This kind of isolation, which does not allow him even the luxury of the company of like-thinking fellows (since each person's private reservations and doubts must always be his own), makes the believer, at least by delicate implication, the sort of martyr-hero who was a prey to the beasts in the Colosseum. And Auden maintained that the tradition of the epic hero gave way to that of the Romantic hero, but that neither was available to modern man, and that the only contemporary hero possible to our imagination was the self-denying saint or martyr.

The Narrator wrenches us suddenly from the context of the predicament of the Holy Family into our own predicament just after the Christmas holidays, when all the agreeable, child-oriented illusions of the vacation must be put away, like the tree ornaments, and we are returned to a world the doubters always insisted was the real and only one, the world of "darning and the Eight-Fifteen." What makes the survival of faith difficult is not merely the hostile and indifferent environment in which it must survive, but the fact that the season of jubilation just past is only the beginning of a faith which leads, very shortly, to the austerities of Lent and the anguish of Good Friday.

But in the subtle course of this most unambiguously Christian speech in the oratorio—unambiguous though expressing the unease of an honest believer—Auden interpolates two distinctly Jewish notes. In the first of these, the Narrator speaks of remembering, after the Christmas holidays are over, "the stable where for once in our lives / Everything became You and nothing was an It." This is an explicit echo of the theological language of Martin Buber. The other concerns the Narrator's closing words, which are wonderfully eloquent.

> The happy morning is over,
> The night of agony still to come; the time is noon:
> When the Spirit must practice his scales of rejoicing
> Without even a hostile audience, and the Soul endure
> A silence that is neither for nor against her faith
> That God's Will will be done, that, in spite of her prayers,
> God will cheat no one, not even the world of its triumph.

Auden has appropriated his last line from the Aphorisms (#51) of Franz Kafka in "The Great Wall of China." One need only observe that very few Christian apologists rely so heavily and so admiringly on Jewish thought.

The work concludes with a brief chorus in three strophes of three lines each. They are tricolons, in which the lines in each stanza exactly reflect the syntax and thrust of the corresponding lines in the other stanzas. The parallelisms can be made explicit by realignment, so that the first lines, in sequence, read,

He is the Way.
He is the Truth.
He is the Life.

The second lines go,

Follow Him through the Land of Unlikeness;
Seek Him in the Kingdom of Anxiety;
Love Him in the World of the Flesh;

And the concluding lines,

You will see rare beasts, and have unique adventures.
You will come to a great city that has expected your return for
years.
And at your marriage all its occasions shall dance for joy.

The phrase about the "Land of Unlikeness," which was the title of Robert Lowell's first and privately published book, appears to come from St. Bernard's *regio dissimilitudinis,* about which Étienne Gilson wrote, in *The Mystical Theology of St. Bernard* (as I have learned from Philip Hobsbaum's excellent book on Lowell), "Man lost his likeness to God in losing his virtues . . . the soul suffers, because she no longer knows how to accomplish in joy what before the first transgression she would have done without effort. Such is the condition of those who live in the Land of Unlikeness. They are not happy there. Wandering, hopelessly revolving, in the 'circuit of the impious' those who tread this weary round suffer not only the loss of God but also the loss of themselves . . . For when the soul has lost its likeness to God it is no longer like itself."

# VII. Amor Loci: *Nones*

*For the Time Being,* including *The Sea and the Mirror,* was published in 1944. In the following year Auden published his celebrated attempt at historical obfuscation, the *Collected Poetry* of 1945, with the poems arranged alphabetically by first line. In 1947 he published *The Age of Anxiety,* a complex and highly mannered, long and alliterative work that owes something to Langland. In 1950 he published *The Enchafèd Flood,* his essays on "the Romantic Spirit," which were delivered as lectures at the University of Virginia. In 1951 he published *Nones,* which, along with *The Shield of Achilles* of 1955, contains what I consider to be some of Auden's best poetry. *Nones* also initiated a new phase in his work, and perhaps more indirectly in his life. The Christmas oratorio, like the poetry that had immediately preceded it, was characterized by a comparative straightforwardness and simplicity of diction and syntax, a policied accessibility and openness: a very public voice. (*The Age of Anxiety* does not fit easily into what preceded or what followed it, with which it seems stylistically at odds—a kind of daring, and not wholly successful, experiment.) With *Nones* Auden inaugurated a style that was consciously different from what he had written before, and which offered difficulties of a different order from those that had characterized his earlier work.

There was, first of all, the employment of an increasingly exotic and recondite vocabulary, only parts of which belonged to a homosexual initiate or camp lingo. We encounter now such words as "fronde," "catadoup," "faffling," "cerebrotonic," "dedolant," "baltering," "soodling," "sossing," "eagre," "qualming," "jussive," "mornes and motted mammelons," and "prosopon," to offer some random examples. Whatever else may be said about this vocabulary, it must be acknowledged that it is quite distinct from common parlance, and from that "language really used by men" which Wordsworth had so deliberately sought in the *Lyrical Ballads.* (It is not to be assumed, by the way, from Auden's gibes at Wordsworth in the *Letter to Lord Byron* that he had no respect for his great predecessor. To Alan Ansen he confided, "I don't dislike Wordsworth at all. He is especially good in his long pieces. *The Prelude* is a marvelous work. I like the same country as Wordsworth but not the same places. My landscapes aren't really the same as Wordsworth's. Mine, and that's a point I haven't written about yet, come from books first.")

There is, in any case, to this new lexicon of Auden's a certain unrepentant elitism, which, I think, will eventually express itself in other ways as well. And almost as conspicuous as the exotic words, there appears a very emphatic use of internal rhymes. We encounter "a seeing being," a "share of care," "Limbs became hymns; embraces expressed in jest," and a stanza such as the following in which the internal rhymes and assonances (which, for the sake of clarity, I shall italicize) seem nearly compulsive, and make for what seems to me a very uncomfortable feeling.

> Somewhere are *places* where we have really been, dear *spaces*
> Of our *deeds* and *faces,* scenes we remember
> As *unchanging* because there we *changed,* where shops have
> names,
> Dogs *bark* in the *dark* at a stranger's footfall
> And crops grow ripe and *cattle fatten* under the *kind*
> Protection of a *godling* or *goddessling*
> Whose affection has been *assigned* them, to *heed* their *needs* and
> *Plead* in heaven the special *case* of their *place.*

At its most maddeningly obsessive, this mannerism can almost completely divert the reader or listener from what has been written or said. In a commissioned text called "The Twelve," an anthem "for the Feast of any Apostle," with a musical setting by William Walton, there is what may be Auden's supreme achievement in this deplorable idiom in a chorus that goes:

> When they heard the Word, some demurred, some were shocked, some mocked. But many were stirred, and the Word spread. Dead souls were quickened to life; the sick were healed by the Truth revealed; released into peace from the gin of old sin, men forgot themselves in the glory of the story told by the Twelve.

> The Dark Lord, adored by this world, perceived the threat of the Light to his might. From his throne he spoke to his own. The loud crowd, the sedate engines of State, were moved by his will to kill. It was done. One by one they were caught, tortured and slain.

This kind of writing can become tiresome very quickly, and it must be said that Auden does not allow himself to indulge this habit at the same annoying density very often. But it is a recognizable component in his new work.

Finally, most personally and most touchingly of all, there appears to be a growing distance in the new poetry between a dream of reciprocated love and of sexual happiness on the one hand, and a presentation of desire or of sexual intercourse that is increasingly coarse and brutal (though some would simply call it frank) and almost despairing. There are still a good number of poems about love, but in them love is attenuated or profoundly threatened. And as his faith in the possibility of a reciprocated love began to fail ("If equal affection cannot be, / Let the more loving one be me"), he found himself writing about the subject in terms that were cold, self-protectively remote, fearful of self-pity, and generally distrustful. For example, "Minnelied," dated ?1967 in the *Collected Poems:*

> When one is lonely (and You,
> My Dearest, know why,
> as I know why it must be),
> steps can be taken, even
> a call-boy can help.
> To-night, for instance, now that
> Bert has been here, I
> listen to the piercing screams
> of palliardising cats
> without self-pity.

He would come to write a covertly acknowledged pornographic poem, "The Platonic Blow," still circulated in *samizdat* fashion, as well as the openly acknowledged "dirty" limericks and the lines in a poem addressed to "a young Viennese named Hugerl, whom Auden had met in a bar," as Carpenter explains.

> Glad, though, we began that way,
> That our life-paths crossed,
> Like characters in Hardy,
> At a moment when
> You were in need of money
> And I wanted sex.

Carpenter also reports of the earlier, Ischian phase of Auden's life that he wrote to Rhoda Jaffe, "The sex situation in Forio is from my point of view exactly what it ought to be. Very few of the men and boys are queer . . . but all of them like a 'divertimento' now and then, for which it is considered polite to give 35 cents or a package of cigarettes as a friendly gesture. It is so nice to be with people who are never shocked or psychologically insecure, though half of them don't get enough to eat." That final clause demonstrates Auden's real honesty, just as the phrase about the "politeness" of bartering a pack of cigarettes or a small tip for sex is a sad evasion of the truth. (I myself lived in Ischia, comparatively newly married, during this period, and a father of many children begged me to take away one of his sons, a particularly good-looking young boy, to America for fear, both financial and sexual, of what might become of the boy if he remained in Forio.) It is in any case sad to think of these lines to Hugerl coming from the same poet who, in the general summation scene of *Dog-Skin,* would have his protagonist say to someone who has had to suppress her sexual longings in order to care for a sick mother, "What you really hate is a social system in which love is controlled by money. Won't you help us destroy it?"

The real poignance of this substitution of prostitution for love is clearest and most dramatic if we contrast those lines to Hugerl, as well as others that will come under consideration, with some representative poems by two of Auden's greatest contemporaries, Yeats and Frost. The notion of such a comparison is not unfair, and might have been consciously invited by Auden. In a poem called "The Willow-Wren and the Stare," the final stanza goes,

> Waking in her arms he cried,
>   Utterly content;
> "I have heard the high good noises,
>   Promoted for an instant,
> Stood upon the shining outskirts
>   Of that Joy I thank
> For you, my dog and every goody."
>   There on the grass bank
> She laughed, he laughed, they laughed together,
>   Then they ate and drank:
> *Did he know what he meant?* said the willow-wren
>   *God only knows,* said the stare.

Certainly that "dog and every goody" undermine the romantic extravagance of the lover, and Auden was handy at such mockery from the first. In "As I Walked Out One Evening," an early ballad, he has his lover go

through the whole conventional repertoire of boasts about the duration
and fidelity of his love, only to have him interrupted by "all the clocks in
the city," which speak for Time itself, and will "prove the child ephemeral" and false. But in the later poem, when Auden has his lover speak,
in a romantic context, of hearing "the high good noises," we are surely
reminded of Yeats's "Solomon and the Witch," and particularly of the
opening lines.

> And thus declared that Arab lady:
> 'Last night, where under the wild moon
> On grassy mattress I had laid me,
> Within my arms great Solomon,
> I suddenly cried out in a strange tongue
> Not his, not mine'.
>                          Who understood
> Whatever had been said, sighed, sung,
> Howled, miau-d, barked, brayed, belled, yelled, cried, crowed,
> Thereon replied: . . .

What Yeats is writing about is nothing less than a revelation brought
about through sexual climax—a kind of superior knowledge also suggested as possibly occurring at the moment of orgasm in "Leda and the
Swan," and which Yeats thought of as comparable to the chaste knowledge granted to the Virgin Mary at the moment of the Annunciation,
which was also the moment of Conception. In Yeats's poems this is an
ecstatic and truthful moment, and in "Solomon and the Witch" the two
lovers come so near to eternal truth that the Queen of Sheba pleads
pantingly at the end: "O! Solomon! let us try again." And we are not, as
readers, inclined to take that line lubriciously. But Auden calls "the high
good noises" into question, not alone by the "dog and every goody" but
by the choral commentary of the two birds.

    As for Frost, he is also slyly invoked by phrases of Auden's. And it must
be acknowledged that he is not given to the extravagant romantic gestures
of Yeats. He wrote with brutal honesty of domestic friction and misunderstanding, for example, in such poems as "Home Burial," "The Hill
Wife," and "The Lovely Shall Be Choosers." He was not a poet who
permitted himself any upholstered illusions about domestic happiness. In
"The Subverted Flower," Frost wrote even more terrifyingly about "the
distortions of ingrown virginity" than Auden had ever done, either in the
sonnet in which these words appear or in the ballad called "Miss Gee."

But for all that, Frost did write "The Silken Tent" and "The Death of the Hired Man" and "West-Running Brook," which exhibit a deeply convincing tenderness in the relations of couples such as had appeared in Auden's early work, particularly in "Lay your sleeping head, my love," but would henceforth be increasingly avoided, denied, and mocked. Some of the cold objectivity which would enter Auden's later poems about love is expressed very clearly in his essay (in *Forewords and Afterwords*) on J. R. Ackerley, called, rather cutely, "Papa Was a Wise Old Sly-Boots."

Few, if any, homosexuals can honestly boast that their sex-life has been happy, but Mr. Ackerley seems to have been exceptionally unfortunate. All sexual desire presupposes that the loved one is in some way "other" than the lover: the eternal and, probably, insoluble problem for the homosexual is finding a substitute for the natural differences, anatomical and psychic, between a man and a woman. The luckiest, perhaps, are those who, dissatisfied with their own bodies, look for someone with an Ideal physique; the ectomorph, for example, who goes for mesomorphs. Such a difference is a real physical fact and, at least until middle age, permanent: those for whom it is enough are less likely to make emotional demands which their partner cannot meet. Then, so long as they don't get into trouble with the police, those who like "chicken" have relatively few problems: among thirteen- and fourteen-year-old boys there are a great many more Lolitas than the public suspects. It is when the desired difference is psychological or cultural that the real trouble begins.

Mr. Ackerley, like many other homosexuals, wanted his partner to be "normal." That in itself is no problem, for very few males are so "normal" that they cannot achieve orgasm with another male. But this is exactly what a homosexual with such tastes is unwilling to admit. His daydream is that a special exception has been made in his case out of love; his partner would never dream of going to bed with another man. His daydream may go even further; he may secretly hope that his friend will love him so much as to be willing to renounce his normal tastes and have no girl friend. Lastly, a homosexual who is, like Mr. Ackerley, an intellectual and reasonably well-off is very apt to become romantically enchanted by the working class, whose lives, experiences, and interests are so different from his own, and to whom, because they are poorer, the money and comforts he is able to provide can be a cause for affectionate gratitude. Again, there is nothing wrong with this in itself. A great deal of nonsense has been spoken and written about the sinfulness of giving or receiving money for sexual favors.

It needs first of all to be said that some of the nonsense Auden deplores here was written by himself. But the cool, Shavian or Olympian tone here is filled, nevertheless, with uncommon sadness, and a sadness of which Auden himself may have been at least partly unconscious. For one thing—and it is no small thing—he calls "the luckiest" of homosexuals those who are "dissatisfied with their own bodies," and for whom love, therefore, begins in self-loathing, has about it no possibility of equality, and is predicated on the supplication of someone who feels himself unworthy. It is a crippled and heart-rending posture. Secondly, Auden makes a chilling mockery of the cherished romantic daydream of Acker-ley's type of homosexual, and contrasts the fallacy of that daydream with the plain and sad "reality" of straightforward commercial sex. In my view, the "affectionate gratitude" Auden speaks of on the part of the poor who receive "money and comforts" from sexual patrons is as much a senti-mental daydream as anything poor Ackerley was said to have entertained. And it is also decidedly elitist. This essay has about it the same disillu-sioned cast that will be found in some of the poems in these two books we are about to explore.

*Nones* opens with a dedicatory poem addressed to Reinhold Niebuhr and his wife, Ursula. Niebuhr was certainly one of the most distinguished of American Protestant theologians and a prolific writer of theological texts, but it is reasonable to assume that his attraction for Auden lay in his dramatic sense of how theological matters presented themselves in the context of actual, practical life. There were all the years of his ministry to the very poor of Detroit; there were books of his with such titles as *Christian Realism and Political Problems* as well as *Moral Man and Immoral Society;* and there was his great service as a teacher at Union Theological Seminary in New York, where one of his students had been Dietrich Bonhoeffer, the German Protestant theologian who resisted Nazism, was consequently imprisoned and then brutally executed, and for whom Auden would write a memorial poem.

The dedicatory poem begins on a deceptively blithe note.

> We, too, had known golden hours
> When body and soul were in tune,
> Had danced with our true loves

By the light of a full moon
And sat with the wise and good
As tongues grew witty and gay
Over some noble dish
Out of Escoffier;
Had felt the intrusive glory
Which tears reserve apart
And would in the grand old manner
Have sung from a resonant heart.

We are alerted to the suspicion that all is not well by the use of the pluperfect, "had known," in the very first line. And the opening words, "We, too," align "us" with unknown others who are said to have enjoyed similar celebratory and revelatory occasions. For what is being described here, allusively but certainly, is a "love feast," which was originally a theological term. It is the equivalent of the Greek agape, and among early Christians referred to a meal partaken, in token of brotherly love, by members of the church, and in connection with the eucharist. Its Greek associations connect it, at the same time, directly with Plato's *Symposium,* which is a banquet of food, wine, and discourse devoted to the topic of love in both the secular and the religious sense (and in which double sense "body and soul were in tune"). The "wise and good," along with the beautiful in the person of Alcibiades, were the *dramatis personae* of Plato's dialogue, and the "intrusive glory / Which tears reserve apart" bears a wonderful resemblance to the event which took place in the summer of 1933 at the Downs School, and which Auden wrote of in the 1964 essay "The Protestant Mystics," discussed earlier. Nevertheless, the joy, benevolence, and freedom of the occasion is ominously hedged about and muted by the subjunctive mood of "would . . . have sung."

And we are not wrong to hold our delight in reserve, for the next lines begin with a telling "but."

But, pawed-at and gossiped-over
By the promiscuous crowd,
Concocted by editors
Into spells to befuddle the crowd,
All words like peace and love,
All sane affirmative speech,
Had been soiled, profaned, debased
To a horrid mechanical screech:

No civil style survived
That pandemonium
But the wry, the sotto-voce,
Ironic and monochrome:
And where should we find shelter
For joy or mere content
When little was left standing
But the suburb of dissent.

It may be noted that the mandatory question mark with which the poem
ought to close was absent from the poem as published in *Nones* but
supplied in the posthumous *Collected Poems*. We may also note a number
of other things. The first is the awkward and conspicuous repetition of
the word "crowd" as a rhyme word. This is a genuine blemish, uncommon
in Auden's work. Secondly, we cannot fail to detect the note of elitism
and condescension in the claim that serious words have been "pawed-at
and gossiped-over / By the promiscuous crowd." This high disdain is not
unlike Yeats's in his poem "The Fisherman," in which, using the same
meter and irregular rhyme scheme, he had deplored

The witty man and his joke
Aimed at the commonest ear,
The clever man who cries
The catch-cries of the clown,
The beating down of the wise
And great Art beaten down.

Auden's refuge from the general debasement is one to which he had
resorted once before. Here it appears as "the wry, the sotto-voce, / Ironic
and monochrome." There is about this the cunning and anonymity of the
subversive, a role Auden had long enjoyed playing. But we may recall the
dedicatory poem (to Erika Mann) of the 1937 volume, *On This Island*,
which also ends in a question.

Since the external disorder, and extravagant lies,
The baroque frontiers, the surrealist police;
What can truth treasure, or heart bless,
But a narrow strictness?

At the time Auden wrote these lines Europe was gravely threatened by
imminent chaos; by the time he wrote the poem for the Niebuhrs that

chaos, "that pandemonium," had come to pass. The word "pandemonium" is Milton's own coinage, and it refers to the dominion of Hell, raised up in envious imitation of Heaven by the Fallen Angels. Its place is perfectly apt in a poem for a theologian and his wife. But it reminds us of the terrific battle in Heaven that Milton takes such pains to describe, and when, at the end of Auden's poem, he declares that "little was left standing / But the suburb of dissent," we are necessarily reminded of the almost total devastation of the European continent. And "dissent" is a "suburb" because it is not densely enough populated to merit bombing.

As a volume of poems, *Nones* is carefully arranged. It begins with "Prime," a poem about awakening, about the world freshly and newly apprehended. It closes with "A Walk After Dark," which envisions retiring for the night, and with a good deal of apprehension in behalf of "My person, all my friends, / And these United States." This suggested cycle running from dawn to dark also suggests a lifespan; and there are many signs in the book that Auden has become increasingly conscious of his age. Roughly three quarters of the way through the book, the title poem, "Nones," appears carefully situated at that three-o'clock-in-the-afternoon position which is its proper place among the canonical hours, and filled with anxiety, desolation, and remorse.

"Prime" begins, in a floodtide of alliteration, with the almost independent awakening of the body (whose "gates," the eyes, "fly open / To its world beyond") and the mind (which also has its classical and traditional gates of ivory and horn, and which open and shut to the realm of dreams). During sleep the body is innocent and at peace, while the mind traffics with "its rebellious fronde," a reference to a party of political opposition during the reign of Louis XIV. That rebelliousness, of course, represents the subversive life of the unconscious; and the brilliantly sinuous syntax of the extended, sixteen-line stanza, which is a single sentence long, requires its full length for the speaker to return to the world, still clothed in innocence, and now divorced from the havoc and dissension of the dream world, as well as from the willed and deliberate activity of the waking one.

The second of the three stanzas is once again a single sentence (although in the first edition of the book it mistakenly had a period at the end of the tenth line). The moment of awakening is recognized as "Holy," and the absolute *otherness* and alterity of the physical world is acknowledged not merely with gratitude but as a welcome release from, and alternative to, the claustral egotism of the self. Having as yet not exercised either his will or his physical body in behalf of anything, the speaker is "Adam sinless in our beginning, / Adam still previous to any act."

But as the third and final stanza (again in a single sentence) makes clear, even the involuntary action of drawing breath (which, of course, has gone on throughout the dormant and innocent night) is now, in the world of consciousness, an act of the will, a wish, an exercise in personal selfishness; and as such it mimics and recapitulates the Fall from grace in the Garden of Eden. And the flesh that earlier in the poem was innocent is no longer an "honest equal but my accomplice now / My assassin to be," and the speaker is left "Afraid of our living task, the dying / Which the coming day will ask." That dying is the conscious acknowledgment of sinfulness and its consequent penalty of mortality. It is also a forecast of the night which will engulf the poet at the end of the book. Finally, it may be worth noting what seems like a family resemblance between the dramatic structure of this poem, in which gradual awakening is likened to a recognition of the Fall from grace, and Richard Wilbur's poem, "Love Calls Us to the Things of This World." Both poems attempt to come to terms not only with our fallen condition but with the daily, yet nonetheless astonishing, miracle of waking into a world that seems newly made, original, faultless, and blessed.

I want now to address what by this time seems to be, by almost universal consent, one of Auden's finest and most successful poems, "In Praise of Limestone," about which I have written an extended essay in an earlier volume, *Obbligati: Essays in Criticism*. I shall try here to summarize those observations, and will begin by saying that I still prefer the early, and un-self-censored, version of the poem as it appeared in its original book publication.

Auden was born and brought up among the Pennines, a limestone region in central England, and from very early in his poetic career he identified landscapes with the female, and more especially the maternal, anatomy ("By landscape reminded once of this mother's figure"). Something both reverent and irreverent is made of that association in this poem. The entire poem is a large-scale *paysage moralisé*, containing three smaller, cameo *paysages* within it, all of them, including the great embracing landscape that dominates the poem, symbolic. The landscape here is not the childhood English one (except by the inference of nostalgia). It is instead the south Italian landscape of Ischia, where Auden summered for many years, a region known to this day by cartographers as Parthenopeia, which includes Naples and its neighboring islands, Capri and

Ischia among them. This area was settled by Greeks, and the name that today is Naples is an adaptation of Neapolis, "the new city," its older, Greek name having been derived from Parthenope, one of Homer's Sirens, whose body was reputedly found washed ashore along the coast of the mainland. The islands were therefore traditionally thought to be the celebrated islands of temptation in the *Odyssey*, which are both seductive and dangerous. And as the poem in its course elegantly makes clear, "this land is not the sweet home that it looks," since it "looks" like both Eden and Mother.

The poem begins in a spirit of delight and affection.

> If it form the one landscape that we the inconstant ones
>   Are consistently homesick for, this is chiefly
> Because it dissolves in water.

Homesickness would be understandable enough on the part of someone brought up in limestone country, but here the connection is far more complex and interesting. The landscape "dissolves in water," and in this way resembles us, because even as it dissolves we become dissolute. It reminds us of our mortality as much as it does of Eden, and is therefore at once alarming and seductive. The lines which immediately follow, and which elaborate on the interaction of water and stone (a twining of elements that resurfaces at various points in this extended poem of free elegiacs), also remind us that the limestone landscape is human in other ways as well. With its "secret system of caves and conduits," it resembles both the human body, with its hidden arterial life, and the human mind, with its buried, nocturnal and subconscious life. In addition to all these affinities, the poet claims that it is a landscape particularly hospitable to humankind—and he will in due course summon up a number of other landscapes which by their bleakness and infertility will contrast dramatically with this lovely rural and small-town Italian one.

We are entitled (and, indeed, invited) to ask just who are "we the inconstant ones," and there seem to be three reasonable answers. The first is homosexuals, who are often thought compulsively promiscuous, as Auden noted in essays on Wilde and Ackerley, and as Isherwood took no pains to conceal about his own sexual life in his numerous autobiographical writings. The second possibility is tourists, northerners, come south to bask in this temperate, gentle climate—Gothic invaders brought south by all the Nordic longings of Goethe (in "Kennst du das Land, wo die Zitronen blühn," and in the *Römische Elegien*, to which this poem bears

a marked resemblance) as well as of the early heroes in the fiction of
Thomas Mann, who delighted in presenting a polarization of north and
south (linked in such a name as Tonio Kröger, opposed in such characters
as Naphta and Settembrini) and more or less explicitly characterized by
Mann's Germanic narrator in the story "Mario and the Magician," who
has come south to Italy with his family for an ill-fated holiday. He speaks
thus of the atmosphere of an Italian summer resort:

> classic weather, the sun of Homer, the climate wherein human culture
> came to flower—and all the rest of it. But after a while it is too much
> for me, I reach a point where I begin to find it dull. The burning void
> of the sky, day after day, weighs one down; the high coloration, the
> enormous naiveté of the unrefracted light—they do, I dare say, induce
> lightheartedness, a carefree mood born of immunity from downpours
> and other meteorological caprices. But slowly, slowly, there makes
> itself felt a lack: the deeper, more complex needs of the northern soul
> remain unsatisfied.

(Clearly Mann, through the mouth of his narrator, is doing some landscape moralizing of his own here.) Finally, there is a third gloss on "we
the inconstant ones": the phrase refers to all mortals, exiled since Adam's
Fall from the ideal Eden but yearning for its likeness if that likeness is at
all to be found on earth. The landscape is inconstant, its very erosion a
sign of our inconstancy, as Auden had intimated in "Lay your sleeping
head, my love, / Human on my faithless arm," and as Catullus had
intimated before him.

But if limestone alarmingly reminds us of our mortality, it also, and
seductively, reminds us of the best and most civilized signs of human
achievement—it is, after all, marble, and thus capable of being turned into
palaces and monuments—into things especially noble and handsome in
worldly terms. We are exhorted to

> examine this region
> Of short distances and definite places:
> What could be more like Mother or a fitter background
> For her son, for the nude young male who lounges
> Against a rock displaying his dildo, never doubting
> That for all his faults he is loved, whose works are but
> Extensions of his power to charm? From weathered outcrop
> To hill-top temple, from appearing waters to
> Conspicuous fountains, from a wild to a formal vineyard,

Are ingenious but short steps that a child's wish
To receive more attention than his brothers, whether
By pleasing or teasing, can easily take.

Well now, "short distances and definite places." This is more than simple topographical description, having as it does both aesthetic and theological meanings. This landscape distinguishes itself from the *indistinct* northern mists, and the disembodied Germanic (which is to say, Lutheran) theology that refuses to acknowledge any priestly intercessor between man and the invisible God to whom the worshiper prays; and the aesthetic component may be described in terms of the wonderfully baroque architecture characteristic of the Italian south, and chiefly the product of the Counter-Reformation, which in its art as well as its theology meant to repudiate the long vistas of Infinity and discarnate Spirituality that the Reformers so puritanically embraced.

Then we have a particularly secular Madonna and child, both of whom are "like" the landscape, beautiful, with the woman's softness and depth, and with the male's external sexuality. If the "nude young male" seems to be an exhibitionist, we will shortly be told that "The blessed will not care what angle they are regarded from, / Having nothing to hide." And in the lines that immediately follow, it turns out that sibling rivalry, the instinct for competition at its most elementary, is the cause and source of all the best of human endeavor. It is this desire to excel that will turn the "weathered outcrop" into a "hill-top temple," will transform "appearing waters to / Conspicuous fountains," will engender much of what we prize in culture, including viniculture and agriculture. Certainly, this desire to excel might be either a good or a bad trait: bad as a symptom of pride, but good as a symptom of the love of excellence, including that special excellence which is divine and beyond us. The people in this poem, and the limestone landscape itself, are constantly exhibiting this doubleness; and both the landscape and its resident humans are frankly pagan—the god who can be "pacified by a clever line / Or a good lay" might easily be Zeus or Apollo, but is certainly not the God either of Milton or of Moses. Yet their pagan carnality itself links them to the baroque spirit of Christian art, with its insistence on the material clothing of the spirit, the curvilinear and fleshly incarnation of the divine, emphasizing at once its familiarity, comfortableness, its playfulness and its mystery. The Christianized pagans who live here are not by the simple fact of their creed prevented from going "to the bad," but when they do, it happens in a comparatively harmless way:

> to become a pimp
> Or deal in fake jewelry or ruin a fine tenor voice
> For effects that bring down the house could happen to all
> But the best and the worst of us . . .

Whatever else they may be, the best and the worst of us are the exception to the normal human rule, and are precisely for that reason attracted by the lure of other symbolic landscapes rather than this so distinctly humanized one. These best and worst now hear as audible voices the Siren songs of enchantment, speaking to some profound need of their natures. The austerity of the "granite wastes," with its reminders of the marmoreal inevitability of death, its *memento mori* bleakness, calls out to the "saints-to-be" and seduces them with its cold appeal. The malleability of the "clays and gravels" makes its appeal not merely to the tyrannical and dictatorial Caesars who rejoice in worldly power, but even to those secular reformers who wish to believe that all mankind's ills can be cured by legislative program and social engineering. The third Siren voice of temptation declares that the only gratuitous act, which is truly free, is suicide, a demonstration that one is emancipated from all the bonds, demands, and needs of the world. The ultimate existential freedom is to have no ties. Fittingly, the voice that whispers this invitation, "an older colder voice," is "the oceanic whisper," the voice of unbridled chaos: "And the earth was without form, and void; and darkness was upon the face of the deep. And the Spirit of God moved upon the face of the waters."

These three Siren songs are temptations to spiritual sins, luring Odysseus, the wanderer, the "inconstant one," to various delusions of *soi-disant* constancy; but they also correspond to the three temptations of Christ in the fourth chapter of Luke. And they correspond as well to the temptations paraded before Tom Rakewell by Nick Shadow, Auden's Mephistopheles, in *The Rake's Progress.*

The speaker now acknowledges, after having described the setting and its inhabitants in the most attractive and endearing terms, that "this land is not the sweet home that it looks," which is to say that, though the Sirens delude and would lure us into the dangers of pride and death, this limestone landscape is neither the Eden we like to imagine it is nor what we think we remember from the Bible or from childhood. It is the fallen world, full of its imperfections, "A backward / And dilapidated province," yet it performs its necessary moral and spiritual function. First, by its flux and changeableness, its capacity to dissolve in water, it "calls into question /

All the Great Powers assume," which is that things can somehow be made stable. It makes the poet, who would interpose no deity between the outward universe and his mind that re-creates it, uneasy, suggesting that there are depths and realities beyond the poet's designs and discoveries. It also rebukes the scientist for his concern with "Nature's / Remotest aspects." These aspects are either astronomical or microscopic, realms not only nonhuman but, without technological assistance, invisible. In the *Letter to Lord Byron,* Auden had already had fun at the expense of those who cherish an interest and "Excessive love for the non-human faces, / That lives in hearts from Golders Green to Teddington; / It's all bound up with Einstein, Jeans, and Eddington."

Nevertheless, though Auden is a poet, he has no difficulty identifying with scientists, and some of those he most revered and honored were physicians and engineers. He made great use of scientific metaphors in his early poetry, drawing heavily from biology. And there is what seems a curious paraphrase of these lines about the scientist in a recollection of Robert Craft's, who visited Auden in Ischia and described him as "outstandingly non-aboriginal . . . His hair is sun-hennaed, and his skin raw with sunburn. Nor is his once-white Panama suit any help as a disguise. A gang of gamins single him out and pursue him as we walk, but though he shouts '*Basta*' at them, the foreign ring of the word only increases his plight."

Like many poems, this one opened with general observations, not in any way seeming to be directed to anyone in particular. But suddenly, with the appearance of its sixtieth line, "They were right, my dear, all those voices were right," a single addressee enters the poem, rather belatedly and, therefore, in a way reminiscent of Wordsworth's "Tintern Abbey." And the final lines of the poem are by this very presence made more personal and intimate and, one may suppose, sincere. They include a confession ("I, too, am reproached, for what / And how much you know") which is able to be understood only by the addressee, and from the full meaning of which all other readers are explicitly excluded. This extreme intimacy of address to a solitary reader has about it some of the mystery and secret significance of a number of the more obscure sonnets of Shakespeare, poems that Auden had loved, taught, and written about. The "innocent athletes and gesticulating fountains, / Made solely for pleasure" are reappearances of the stone and water that have run through the poem (the athletes are public statues). That they are made "solely for pleasure" means that they invite our admiration, and the invitation has its unashamed erotic component. A reader who finds this unsuitable (or worse) in a poem that bears so conspicuous a religious burden would do well to recall Michelangelo's famous tondo (or circular painting) of the Holy Family, with young male nude athletes lounging around in the background. Lest this be thought no more than a sign of Michelangelo's personal sexual predilections, it should be pointed out that a similar group of male nudes (or very scantily clad young men) are to be seen in the tondo of the *Adoration of the Magi* in the National Gallery in Washington, attributed jointly to Fra Angelico and Fra Filippo Lippi, whose sexual tastes have never raised comment before. The fact is that this was an established way of representing the pagan traditions which were outmoded, repudiated and surpassed by the New Dispensation signalized by the birth of Christ, and which Milton, in the poem "On the Morning of Christ's Nativity," represents as the hasty exodus of all varieties of pagan deities.

For Auden, in any case, this mixture of a serious religious concern, expressed by references to "the blessed" and "the life to come," with a particularly worldly sensuality links his poem to a good deal of Italian baroque and mannerist art. Both that art and this poem envision an anti-puritanical ideal, and both are clear repudiations of Manichaean dualism. The poem ends with a line that combines the stone and water with which it began.

"Limestone" is undeniably a personal and in some ways intimate poem, overtly bearing upon a private relationship with a beloved. This relationship, as Carpenter, among others, has revealed, was not, for the most part, a happy one, and one of the tasks Auden seems to have set himself was to write about it with enough "distancing" and objective impersonality to avoid self-pity, or even any clear indication that he was writing about himself. He had already done so in that part of *For the Time Being* called "The Temptation of St. Joseph," as well as elsewhere. And now he was to do so in a number of short lyrics that appear to have no relationship to one another, nor any clear relationship to him. I want to consider, as one particular instance of this, a poem called—with evident appeal to the comparative anonymity of many Elizabethan songs—simply "Song," and beginning,

> Deftly, admiral, cast your fly
>   Into the slow deep hover,
> Till the wise old trout mistake and die;

> Salt are the deeps that cover
>   The glittering fleets you led,
>     White is your head.

What could be more admirably remote from the poet and his own personality? The stanza is about declension and mutability; the admiral is no longer young; the fleets he led are "buried" under water as he himself will shortly be buried under ground. He is loyal to his element of water by turning fisherman, a tame and enfeebled pastime for a naval hero, associated as it is with the meditative and pastoral existence glorified by Izaak Walton, where it is presented as the indolent occupation of leisure and retirement. (It may be worth pointing out that one meaning of "hover" as a noun is an overhanging stone or bank under which a fish can hide.)

The second stanza is a careful and witty parallel of the first.

> Read on, ambassador, engrossed
>   In your favorite Stendhal;
> The Outer Provinces are lost,
>   Unshaven horsemen swill
>   The great wines of the Châteaux
>     Where you danced long ago.

Like the admiral, the ambassador is growing old. He who once literally shaped nations is reduced to the passive pleasure of reading, an even more sedentary occupation than the dancing he used to do. Stendhal alone can resurrect for him an active participation in the affairs of society, and convey the lost glory of old wine and grand Châteaux. The regime served by the ambassador has diminished, its outer provinces lost, either in battle or through diplomatic negotiation and contrivance. The elderly diminishment of personal powers in these two men is set against the alteration and destruction of great political and naval powers.

After these two stanzas, each with its own protagonist, the third stanza links them in their unwittingness or indifference to two other persons.

> Do not turn, do not lift your eyes
>   Toward the still pair standing
> On the bridge between your properties,
>   Indifferent to your minding:
>   In its glory, in its power,
>     This is their hour.

The first adjuration ("do not turn") is addressed to the admiral, who is busy fishing; the second ("do not lift") to the ambassador, who is busy reading. Their eyes are properly focused on what now, in age and retirement, most concerns them, for they have had what is publicly regarded as illustrious careers, and they are now entitled to the peace that is the privilege of the long expenditure of strength and skill, and belongs properly to the age of retirement. We may assume that their "properties" are grand and stately ones, such as have been bestowed upon heroes and diplomats by grateful nations. So the "still pair" standing on the bridge between their properties are interlopers. They are lovers who have found a momentarily secure trysting place, as long as the two old men do not turn or lift their eyes. For the lovers, this "hour," which is brief enough in its duration, confers its glory and power, which must seem pitiful in both its brevity and its inconsequence when compared with the great historical attainments of the two old men. Even so, the whole poem has been steadily making a point about the evanescence of human glory and accomplishment, so the admiral and the statesman may be thought of as having accomplished things only marginally more durable than the love which now is being enacted between their grounds. And so to the final stanza.

> Nothing your strength, your skill, could do
>   Can alter their embrace
> Or dispersuade the Furies who
>   At the appointed place
>   With claw and dreadful brow
>     Wait for them now.

The terrible "retributive justice" that exacts punishment of these lovers for the brief hour of love's power and glory seems at first strangely disproportionate to the secluded and unimportant lives they play in this poem and in the world at large. After all, both the admiral and the ambassador have been responsible for greater and more costly losses. But those Furies are classical and immortal, and they, or something like them, figure throughout tragic literature, which, especially in its form of Greek drama, is invariably focused on some terrible deviation within the intimacies of love and the family. All the great tragedies are domestic: Oedipus, Agamemnon, Medea, Hippolytus, Lear, Hamlet, Macbeth, Othello. The penalty for love is unforeseen and unavoidable, and is often a matter of terrible violence. Auden had once described himself as one possessed by the Furies, able to feel himself "the prey of demonic powers, in both the Greek and the Christian sense, stripped of self-control and self-respect," as he wrote later in recollection of his first discovery of Chester Kallman's infidelities. Such infidelities would, in the course of time, become little short of ostentatious, and manifestly calculated to wound. As Carpenter wrote,

> In [Auden's] eyes Chester's behaviour was not simply a betrayal of a love-affair but a breaking of what Auden regarded as marriage-vows. He had used the term "marriage" to describe his bond with Chester ever since the relationship began, and possibly the two of them had sworn actual vows. Auden's poem "In Sickness and in Health," arising from his love for Chester, implies this when it talks of "This round O of faithfulness we swear."

Carpenter makes these remarks in the context of a description of a summer holiday at Jamestown, Rhode Island, that Auden and Kallman had been invited to spend at the home of Caroline Newton. It was here in this summer retreat that Auden found himself trying to come to terms with his estrangement from Chester, which, Carpenter says, he wrote of only a few months later in the "Temptation of St. Joseph" section of the Christmas oratorio. But infidelity was only a part of the cruelty exhibited by Kallman. Carpenter continues,

> . . . About three weeks after he had arrived at Jamestown, Auden heard from England that his mother, aged seventy-two, had died in her sleep. The news came in a telegram which was read over the telephone to Caroline Newton. That evening, she, Chester Kallman and Auden were due to dine with an Admiral King at Newport, Rhode Island. Caroline Newton gave the news to Chester, asking him to break it to Auden. Chester came into the room, and said: "We're not going to King's." Auden remarked: "Goody, goody." Chester continued: "The reason is your mother has died." Auden sat in silence for a long while. Then he said: "How like her that her last act on earth should be to get me out of a social engagement that I didn't want." Then he burst into tears.

It is not difficult to believe those tears had a number of powerful sources, including the brutality with which the news of his mother's death was imparted to him. The "claw and dreadful brow" of the Furies that lie in wait for lovers was something Auden could write about with some authority.

There is a related poem called "Nocturne II" in *The Shield of Achilles*, which again touches in the most circumspect and guardedly impersonal way on the Nemesis that may lie in wait for lovers—as though sexual happiness exacted a compensatory and terrible forfeit.

> Make this night lovable,
> Moon, and with eye single
> Looking down from up there,
> Bless me, One especial
> And friends everywhere.
>
> With a cloudless brightness
> Surround our absences;
> Innocent be our sleeps,
> Watched by great still spaces,
> White hills, glittering deeps.
>
> Parted by circumstance,
> Grant each your indulgence
> That we may meet in dreams
> For talk, for dalliance,
> By warm hearths, by cool streams.
>
> Shine lest tonight any,
> In the dark suddenly,
> Wake alone in a bed
> To hear his own fury
> Wishing his love were dead.

The poem is framed in the form of a prayer, a familiar enough mode of address from the very beginning of Auden's career as a poet; and in this case the addressee is the Moon. (In his 1948 "historical grammar of poetic myth," *The White Goddess*, Robert Graves, who rather peevishly attacked Auden in his Clark Lectures, though Auden always wrote and spoke well of him, firmly identified the Moon with the Muse of Poetry, and the inspiration of all "true" poets, which could not, according to Graves, include homosexuals. He declares that Ben Jonson "knew the risk run by Apollonians who try to be wholly independent of women: they fall into sentimental homosexuality. Once poetic fashions begin to be set by the homosexual, and 'Platonic love'—homosexual idealism—is introduced, the Goddess takes revenge.")

Auden's Moon in this poem is the regnant deity of *A Midsummer Night's Dream*, the goddess of the dream world, which is also the realm of lovers because, like dreams, love is richly engrossed with illusion, and the connection between love and dream is one that Freud recognized as surely as did Shakespeare. She is a night goddess, and she is besought to "make this night lovable," in which "lovable" can mean "worthy to be loved in and of itself" or "making possible an exchange of love among humans." The first stanza has about it the charm and serene neutrality of Ben Jonson's "Queen and Huntress, chaste and fair," which is one of the most beautiful lyrics in the English language.

But the second stanza introduces a small note to disturb this tranquility: "Surround our absences" is a curiously ambiguous petition, but whatever else it may mean, it signifies that on this particular night not everyone has found his appropriate or desired mate. Still more unsettling is the prayer "Innocent be our sleep," since it reminds us of all the "nocturnal rummage," the dark oubliettes of resentment, envy, and rage buried in the unconscious. Sleep is traditionally identified with innocence, since we are at least inactive when we are in its possession; and a sleeping person usually *looks* innocent simply because he looks vulnerable. Moreover, it is also traditional to identify guilt with sleeplessness, as Shakespeare does both in *Macbeth* and *The Tempest*.

The third stanza makes still more explicit the isolation of some or all for whom the prayer is offered—and it is no small matter that only in the first stanza did the speaker (in "Bless me") pray expressly in his own behalf. The "innocence" of the second stanza is emphasized and made touching by the genuine modesty of the request "that we may meet in dreams," which seems chaste and minimal. The line "For talk, for dalliance," for all its clear suggestion of sexual dalliance, is doubly chaste in that it will take place, if at all, only in the realm of dream (nothing more is being asked for), and also in that the primary meaning of "dalliance" (that is, dawdling or delaying) recalls Ben Jonson's song once again, with its concluding prayer,

> Lay thy bow of pearle apart,
>   And thy cristall-shining quiver;
> Give unto the flying hart
>   Space to breathe, how short soever;
> Thou that mak'st a day of night,
> Goddesse, excellently bright.

Jonson's poem closes with a moving reminder of evanescence and mortality, and this note, while probably not chief among Auden's meanings, is among them nevertheless.

But the real bitterness, carefully couched, distanced, and impersonalized, is reserved for the final stanza. The Moon is besought to "Shine lest . . . any . . . Wake alone in a bed . . ." Since, in the first stanza, it is made clear that the entire prayer is being made in behalf of "me, One especial / And friends everywhere," it concerns an indeterminately but presumably large crowd. And the final prayer is not merely that none of these should be allowed to wake alone, but that none should wake alone "To hear his own fury / Wishing his love were dead." That "fury" we may recognize as "the Furies" who wait for the lovers of the song "Deftly, admiral, cast your fly." The exhortation to the Moon to shine implies that its light can dispel the darkness of the soul as well as of the earth; and it is a way of supplicating the Moon to exhibit the visible evidence of its supernatural and divine authority. In the end, for all the poem's putative impersonality and its request in behalf of any one of a large group, there can be no question of its moving relationship to the speaker of the poem, and of that speaker to the poet himself.

These two poems in turn bear a relationship to another comparatively "impersonal" poem which, whatever else it may be, is, I feel certain, meant to be recognized as an homage to Robert Frost. Its title is "Their Lonely Betters," a title which smacks ever so slightly of the elitism we identify with class distinction, nicely mitigated by the pathos of "lonely," and conveying the ruefully mixed feelings that Shakespeare inspires about monarchs with lines like "Uneasy lies the head that wears a crown," and the long prose speech by the soldier, Michael Williams, in *Henry V,* about the responsibility of a king for the souls of all who die fighting for him in battle.

Auden admired Frost, and published an essay about him in *The Dyer's Hand,* in which he specifically deals with the personal/impersonal qualities in poems. The poem under consideration is written in the iambic couplets and quatrains that Frost favored, and when Auden declares that he listened "To all the noises that my garden made," he has caught Frost's idiom with admiring exactness. More important still, the two poets, different enough in so many ways, were both at different times deeply preoccupied with loneliness. This is a topic Frost addressed in many forms, some of them virtually metaphysical, as in "The Lovely Shall Be Choosers," but often dramatically, as in "The Hill Wife," "An Old Man's

Winter Night," "The Most of It," "Tree at My Window," "Stopping by Woods on a Snowy Evening," "The Tuft of Flowers," and "Acquainted with the Night," to make a by no means exhaustive list. Moreover, Auden's poem closes with words that echo Frost's celebrated conclusion of "Stopping by Woods on a Snowy Evening," "promises to keep." But these very words, both in Frost and in this poem of Auden's, imply a serious commitment to fidelity, and for Auden this had become a very painful subject.

It must be acknowledged, finally, that despite adopting some of Frost's manners, idiom, and theme, Auden was probably unwise to invite a comparison. Though this poem returns to the topic Auden had early and often employed regarding the absolute divorce between mankind and the rest of the natural world (in, for example, "Fish in the unruffled lakes" and "Our Hunting Fathers"), it unhappily and inadvertently betrays the fact that Auden lacks the naturalist's faculties and knowledge that Frost had at his easy command. Concerned as it is with the human, avian, and vegetable kingdoms, the poem is based on the presupposition that plants are incapable of communication (including sexual union) except by the intercession of "some third party" (that is, bees) to assist in the process of pollination; and that birds communicate at best imperfectly, and are blessedly and innocently free from a capacity or a base motive to deceive. But Frost would never have written "No one of them was capable of lying" because he knew perfectly well that certain birds (the catbird, the mockingbird) were brilliantly capable of mimicry and the imitation of the song of other birds; that the cuckoo, whose name is derived from its characteristic note and mating song, gave its name to the cuckold, because of its "infidelitous" practice of laying its eggs in the nests of other birds. Finally, Frost would have known that spousal fidelity is so rare among birds that the exceptions (turtledoves, cardinals, love-birds) are always commented upon. He would therefore not have written a poem in which birds are made at once more ignorant and innocent than humans.

"The Love Feast" is a poem whose title is meant as a grotesque travesty of the Greek word *agape,* a meal celebrating the exchange of brotherly love that was seriously described in the dedicatory poem for the Niebuhrs. If the poem is full of open acknowledgments of the profanation of things at least potentially sacred ("Of love according to the gospel / Of the radio-phonograph"), the indictment is not spoken by some shocked puritan who revels in his own self-righteousness; and indeed the delinquency described in the poem is familiar enough, in terms of the morality not only of the love ballads of popular culture, but of such films as *La Dolce Vita*. There is even, in the brief two lines "Jack likes Jill who worships George / Who has the hots for Jack," a situation remarkably like the one dramatized by Sartre in *No Exit*, a four-character play set in a hotel room that represents Hell. The poem, not despite but because of its profane and libidinous concerns, is filled with religious allusions. "The Love that rules the sun and stars" of the fourth stanza is an adaptation of the last line of Dante's *Divine Comedy*. "The Love that made her out of nothing" comes from St. Augustine, and is quoted again by Auden in *Secondary Worlds*. The last line in Auden's poem, "Make me chaste, Lord, but not yet," comes from Book VIII, chapter vii, paragraph 17 of St. Augustine's *Confessions*, which goes, in part,

> For many of my years (perhaps twelve) had passed away since my nineteenth, when, on the reading of Cicero's *Hortentius*, I was roused to a desire for wisdom; and still I was delaying to reject mere worldly happiness, and to devote myself to search out that whereof not the finding alone, but the bare search, ought to have been preferred before the treasures and kingdoms of this world, though already found, and before the pleasures of the body, though encompassing me at my will. But I, miserable young man, supremely miserable even in the very outset of my youth, had entreated chastity of Thee, and said, "Grant me chastity and continency, but not yet."

The poem's deeply mordant power and authority come chiefly from this searing juxtaposition of religious texts, voices, echoes, with a depiction of ordinary debauchery, part of whose sordidness lies in the very fact of its being commonplace. And I may add that I have never been able to read the line "Catechumens make their entrance" without recalling

> The sable presbyters approach
> The avenue of penitence;
> The young are red and pustular
> Clutching piaculative pence.

Eliot's poem, which closes with Sweeney shifting "from ham to ham" as he stirs the waters of his bath, involves the very same uncomfortable confrontation of the truly religious, the pseudo-religious, and the frankly profane that Auden presents in a far more accessible poem. Auden's poem is, moreover, almost a catalogue; it is an extended list of gossip, hypocrisy, and what Dante asserted all sin was based upon: misdirected love. So when we read that "Willy cannot bear his father, / Lilian is afraid of kids," we are being presented with some among many deviations from that "Love that rules the sun and stars," which permits the very sins which, in His divine ordinance, He forbids. So habituated do we become to this more or less familiar catalogue that we may at first fail to notice the personal presence of the speaker at the end of the poem. To be sure, he has been there from the first—but we had taken him as an observer, even though he says, "See us gathered on behalf / Of love according to the gospel / Of the radio-phonograph." Thereafter, he seems to disappear from view, except in his capacity as reporter. But towards the end his presence as a moral being is made noticeable, since, after the long listing of details he says, apropos of some woman who is telling lies on the telephone, "The Love that made her out of nothing / Tells me to go home." The speaker has taken a moral resolve and is on the point of leaving when the final stanza presents one more, and this one apparently a defeating, temptation:

> But that Miss Number in the corner
> Playing hard to get . . .
> I am sorry I'm not sorry . . .
> Make me chaste, Lord, but not yet.

Just as he is about to leave he spots a "Miss Number" made the more alluring by the highly complex invitation-cum-repulsion behavior of "playing hard to get," which seems to involve a challenge. The term "miss" is widely used as a cant homosexual term to denote a clearly homosexual male, and here it is joined with "number," which the OED defines as "a person, usually a woman," so that a "Miss Number" might be a singularly "pretty" young man. In any case, it is a glimpse of this last, highly elusive person that cancels the speaker's resolve to leave the party, and the poem concludes, very tauntingly, with the suggestion of another complex and possibly sordid story about to begin.

Hitherto Auden had dedicated only a few poems—apart from elegies or epithalamia—to specific people, at least with open and public acknowledgment. A number of poems—for example, "1929," which begins, "It was Easter as I walked in the public gardens"—have unidentified dedicatees, and a number of such poems are among his most intimate, and often exhibit that occult exclusiveness that allows it fully to be understood by the initiate, and perhaps only by the dedicatee himself; and this is also the case with a number of Shakespeare's sonnets. But with the publication of *Nones,* and thenceforward, Auden would increasingly dedicate individual poems (as distinct from the dedication of entire volumes) to individual friends; and as time went on such dedications became a roster of his friendships, old and new. Friends had come to play an increasingly important part in his life, and this was the consequence of his feeling more and more lonely, or at least bereft of real or enduring intimacy. In *The Shield of Achilles,* each of the *Bucolics,* the poem "'The Truest Poetry Is the Most Feigning,'" and, in *About the House,* every room described, has its dedicatee. It is touching to notice this change, and to recognize it as sponsored by a need to be reassured that he was not altogether rejected and abandoned.

"Ischia" is dedicated to Brian Howard, who was at Oxford at the same time as Auden. Evelyn Waugh, who would one day ridicule him in *Brideshead Revisited* under a fictive name, was initially greatly impressed with him, and, of his undergraduate days, wrote, "Brian made himself more than the entertainer, the arbiter, almost the animator, of the easy-going aristocrats whom he set out to reform in his romantic model, like the youthful d'Israeli inspiring 'Young England.'" Howard was ostentatiously, histrionically homosexual; and he was also—what endeared him to some and recommended him to the active interest of many—"amusing." This was a faculty in which Chester Kallman excelled. Like one of his heroes, the Reverend Sydney Smith, Auden especially prized the gift in others of being amusing. To one friend Smith wrote, "You say I have many comic ideas rising in my mind; . . . this may be true, but the champagne bottle is no better for holding the champagne . . . I don't mean to say I am prone to melancholy; but I acknowledge my weakness enough to confess that I want the aid of society and dislike a solitary life." Hesketh Pearson, Smith's biographer, adds, "He candidly admitted that he was not one of those mortals who have infinite resources in themselves, but was fitted up with the commonest materials and had to be amused." And there is for Auden, with the advance of years, an increasing necessity to resist a growing propensity to melancholy in ways that make him resemble not only Smith but Dr. Johnson.

In his largely gossipy book *Children of the Sun,* Martin Green offers some characteristic details of Howard's military service during WWII: "Transferred to another post, Brian formed the habit of referring to his commander as 'Colonel Cutie' (something Basil Seal does in *Put Out More Flags*) and so aroused his hostility. Finally he was given a medical discharge in December 1944." But before that discharge, Brian's flamboy-

ant behavior while in uniform created, not for the first time, a little morsel
of scandal of the kind that would have delighted his friends. Green's
account of it goes, "On another occasion Brian was asked for his name
and service number in the Ritz Bar, where he had again been talking very
loudly and critically about national policy. He was then an aircraftsman,
of the lowest rank, and it was an officer who spoke to him; but Brian
replied over his shoulder, 'Mrs. Smith to you, darling,' still defying
authority."

Given Brian Howard's remarkable and widely known reputation, it is
striking how singularly free from camp affectation of any kind is this poem
dedicated to him, which is actually an ode in syllabics, addressed not to
its dedicatee but to the island of Ischia and the surrounding Parthenopeian
region. Moreover, its opening stanzas are nearly psalm-like in character.

> There is a time to admit how much the sword decides,
> With flourishing horns to salute the conqueror,
>     Impassive, cloaked and great on
>     Horseback under his faffling flag.
>
> Changes of heart should also occasion song, like his
> Who turning back from the crusaders' harbor, broke
>     With our aggressive habit
>     Once and for all and was the first
>
> To see all penniless creatures as his siblings: then
> At all times it is good to praise the shining earth,
>     Dear to us whether we choose our
>     Duty or do something horrible.

To be sure, "the shining earth" is Homeric, but these stanzas bear a
striking kinship to the following verses of the ninety-second Psalm.

> It is a good thing to give thanks unto the Lord, and to sing praises
> unto thy name, O Most High:
>     To shew forth thy loving kindness in the morning, and thy faith-
> fulness every night.
>     Upon an instrument of ten strings, and upon the psaltry; upon the
> harp and with a solemn sound.

There is also, perhaps, an echo of the third chapter of Ecclesiastes:
"To everything there is a season, and a time to every purpose under the
heaven." In any case, there is a note of piety and gratitude that runs

through this poem with a moving persistence, and manages to sound, rather surprisingly, even Wordsworthian.

> Dearest to each his birthplace; but to recall a green
> Valley where mushrooms fatten in the summer nights
>       And silvered willows copy
> The circumflexions of the stream
>
> Is not my gladness today: I am presently moved
> By sun-drenched Parthenopeia, my thanks are to you,
>       Ischia, to whom a fair wind has
> Brought me rejoicing with dear friends
>
> From soiled productive cities.

That sense of liberation "from soiled productive cities," while it resembles Keats's sonnet that begins, "To one who has been long in city pent," seems to me nearer to the opening of *The Prelude,* with its Miltonic, and hence Biblical, grandeur. The religious note is maintained by the early reference to the saint (is it St. Francis?) who saw "all penniless creatures as his siblings." Moreover, the claim that "the shining earth" is "Dear to us whether we choose our / Duty or do something horrible" is a witty and moving assertion of the incontestable value of life itself, and thus the ground for our gratitude and our impulse to give thanks.

Furthermore, the opening of the poem contrasts two dramatically opposed occasions that invite celebration in poetry with a third alternative, unlike either of the others. First there is "the conqueror," who traditionally is honored ceremonially with "flourishing horns" as well as in those poems like Lucan's *Pharsalia* with long passages of tribute intended to butter up the emperor—in that case, Nero. So first there is the public man of power. Secondly, there is a private world of religious conversion exhibited by the saint. But both of these, though different from, and indeed opposed to, one another, are active. Contrasted to both of these is "the shining earth," the landscape we inhabit, which is inactive but the source and sustenance of our lives, and, of course, our Mother.

After the opening stanzas, the poem offers a discursive tour (not without some punctuation and, consequently, syntactical puzzles) of the sights of the island, as delivered by a knowing and appreciative cicerone. Two alternative landscapes may be viewed from the Ischian one under discussion, just as "In Praise of Limestone" presented alternative landscapes with their appropriate modes of life. Here we may view

Vesuvius,

Looming across the bright bland bay
Like a massive family pudding, or, around
    A southern point, sheer-sided Capri, who by herself
Defends the cult of Pleasure,

A jealous, sometimes a cruel, god.

The comparison of Vesuvius to a family pudding has the effect of
reminding us, by its very cuteness and absurdity, of the cataclysmic power
of that volcano, of Pompeii, and of incalculable destruction. Opposed to
it is Capri, "sheer-sided," virtually fortified, and certainly difficult of
access. It may be sacred to the jealous or cruel god of Pleasure, but we are
likely to forget just how jealous and cruel that god can be until we recall
that Capri is the island where the obscenely cruel and pathological
emperor Tiberius built a palace, the ruins of which can still be visited, and
where he had particularly hideous executions performed for his personal
amusement, as Suetonius relates in grotesque detail. The two alternate
places, therefore, are carefully distinguished from the Ischian setting,
which is, by contrast, modest in its attractiveness, and boasting only a
minimal volcano in Epomeo, whose last recorded eruption, Baedeker
asserts, took place in 1302. The unassuming virtues of the place suggest
that it is a kind of microcosm. In fact, there are sufficient signs to remind
"the happy / Stranger that all is never well," and these signs (the bray of
a donkey, the sigh of his master) serve to chasten the happy stranger who,
like any tourist, is in danger of wishing to see only the enjoyable aspects
of an unfamiliar place. Tourists, temporary visitors, "the inconstant
ones," are supremely capable of averting their eyes from the quotidian
concerns of a foreign place, and take upon themselves the passer-by's
immunity from feeling any obligation to love their temporary "neighbor,"
unless it be confined to the disbursement of a few *soldi* to some persistent,
or pathetic, or unavoidable, beggar. But Auden refuses to avert his gaze,
and acknowledges that even in this lovely setting where he enjoys the
privileged life of an outsider, "all is never well." Mention in fact is made
of Santa Restituta, the island's patron saint, about whom a local (and
probably, in origin, pagan) superstition persists, to the effect that there is
destined to be one unnatural death on the island every year, a forfeit
demanded by the saint as a "blood sacrifice." One can understand the
persistence of this superstition as a kind of psychic insurance: once such

a fatality takes place, everyone else is secure for the rest of the year. The poem ends, in fact, with a propitiatory gesture both anxious and grateful, declaring to the saint that "since / Nothing is free, whatever you charge shall be paid," a forfeit that we as readers cannot believe either Auden or we ourselves are exempt from.

The piety, the modesty, the straightforward and open gratitude of this "island poem" is wonderfully contrasted with the poem that immediately follows it in *Nones,* "Pleasure Island," which, while being a discursive description of Fire Island, off the coast of Long Island, bears a distinct kinship with "The Love Feast." It is, as it were, "The Love Feast" in slow motion. It is ingeniously composed of dialectical oppositions. The "surround" or frame of human life and activity has been purified to the infinitudes of the sky and the sea, which in their vastness contrive to trivialize anything of merely human proportions.

> . . . the ocean
>    Stares right past us as though
> No one here was worth drowning, and the eye, true
>    Blue all summer, of the sky
> Could not miss a huddle of huts . . .

The situation is described from the point of view of the huge, impersonal elements of sky and sea. In the lines that immediately follow, the same situation is viewed from the perspective of human impotence: to protest or cry (to the heavens) for help, to address "those dazzling miles" of the sky, "would be rather silly," just as adding "one's occasional tear" to the salt solution of the ocean would in no way ease the grief of or add to the compassion for the human dilemma. The landscape has specifically been pruned of the conventional symbols of hope (a hill to climb) and remorse or dejection (a tree to sit beneath, in the manner of dejected lovers). The coast mentioned is Long Island, the conventional land of churches and routines, which have been prevented, as by a tariff barrier and vigorous customs inspections, from crossing the water into this haven "where nothing is wicked / But to be sorry or sick, / But one thing unneighborly, work." If the landscape initially sounds spare, and to some unappealing, the moral climate must be what many think of as a guiltless and erotic paradise. And it is precisely this suggestion of freedom from blame that is meant to seduce the reader as well as those who have settled into a summer of sand and indolence. Work is not merely discouraged by others, it becomes increasingly difficult to perform where "The plain sun has no use / For the printing press, the wheel, the electric / Light," and where even the most resolute visitor

> ... gives in, stops stopping
>   To think, lets his book drop
> And lies, like us, on his stomach watching
>   As bosom, backside, crotch
> Or other sacred trophy is borne in triumph
>   Past his adoring by
> Souls he does not try to like ...

The itemization of "sacred trophies" will recall the "steep" (which, in connection with eyes, is defined as "prominent, staring or glaring with passion") "enthusiastic eyes," which, in "The Love Feast," "flicker after tits and baskets," the last of those terms being a homosexual cant word for the protuberance of male genitals. What is being described in both poems is an aimless, depersonalized, unfocused eroticism, wholly divorced from any human feelings normally associated with love. And this very absence constitutes the beginning of a series of omens.

> The tide rises
>   And falls, our household ice
> Drips to death in the dark and our friendships
>   Prepare for a weekend
> They will probably not survive ...

And now, in what seems like a tiny "recognition scene," we come to realize where in fact we are, and it is not paradise.

> ... for our
>   Lenient amusing shore
> Knows in fact all about the dyings, is in
>   Fact our place, namely this
> Place of the skull, a place where the rose of
>   Self-punishment will grow.

Turning a wildly permissive summer resort into Golgotha, the aridity of its sand and salt sea made into an equivalent of a place of execution, has, of course, the effect of preparing the reader of *Nones* for the appearance, in due course, of the title poem itself. Moreover, it affirms that the place initially chosen as a refuge from the afflictions of guilt turns out to be, as Dante asserts of the Inferno, the place to which we consign ourselves for punishment, and the punishment which is demanded by our sins. Dante and his realm of torment are firmly called to mind by "some decaying / Spirit" who wanders alone towards the poem's end, "excusing itself / To itself with evangelical gestures / For having failed the test." It does not matter whether we take the test to be the ability to resist the temptations of this abandoned community, or the ability to indulge in them without remorse; in either case the "Spirit" has failed. He is one of two failures with which the poem ends; he is dialectically mated with "Miss Lovely," who need not be female. She awakens from sleep, after having been "the life and soul of the party," to hear a voice

> Ask as one might ask the time or a trifle
> Extra, her money and her life.

"Nothing is free, whatever you charge shall be paid," Auden wrote in "Ischia," and the forfeit here could not be more complete. To have been "the life and soul" of a party is to move towards the relinquishment of life and soul, and the final demand of money *and* life cancels all the oppositions and alternatives with which the poem seemed to begin.

"The Fall of Rome" is dedicated to Cyril Connolly, critic and editor of the British literary journal *Horizon,* who continued to publish Auden's poems in England during WWII, a time when large segments of the British public had written him off as no longer of any consequence. It is a poem in which Auden uses deliberate anachronism with telling effect. There is a certain irony immediately present in the very notion of giving a short lyric the title "The Fall of Rome." Gibbon's monumental work, which in my modest Modern Library Edition runs to 2,759 pages, covers a period that runs from A.D. 180 to 1453, so that it may safely be said that if Rome wasn't built in a day, neither did it fall in one.

The poem is written in tetrameter quatrains rhyming *a b b a,* which is to say in the funereal stanza form of Tennyson's "In Memoriam." The quatrains are grammatically and syntactically discrete, each one ending with a full stop and each one composed of a single complete sentence. The formal qualities of the poem, its reiterative stanzaic structure, is reinforced by its composition as a catalogue of the symptoms of decay—symptoms which, of course, we readily recognize as those of our own contemporary world. Auden begins, as he shall end, as impersonally and objectively as possible, with a landscape totally void of human presence.

> The piers are pummelled by the waves;
> In a lonely field the rain

Lashes an abandoned train;
Outlaws fill the mountain caves.

The "active" verbs here all denote the behavior of the natural elements; such humans as there are have concealed themselves. The opening is cinematic in its desolation, and full of portent. Why is the train, a complex technological vehicle for human locomotion, abandoned? Has there been an accident? Is a war going on? Where, in any case, are the passengers? Have they been robbed, or kidnapped, or killed by the outlaws? We are simply allowed to guess, and the guessing is like the deduction Auden delighted to make in appraising a forsaken industrialized landscape. This instinct figures in his early poems, and will reappear in the volume under consideration in the poem called "Not in Baedeker."

The mention of outlaws leads directly to the next stanza.

Fantastic grow the evening gowns;
Agents of the Fisc pursue
Absconding tax-defaulters through
The sewers of provincial towns.

The evening gowns are presumably worn by persons at the opposite social pole to the outlaws. The diagnostic view that the poem presents will range over the whole gamut of society. The gowns grow fantastic as a symptom themselves of extravagance, and of the depravity of a society in which the rich have long ceased to feel any responsibility for the poor. Social revolutions often express themselves in severe reformations of clothing, as, for example, the sans-culottes and Phrygian caps of the French revolutionaries. It was their aim to distinguish themselves from the hated pomps of the aristocracy. The Fisc (or Fiscus) was the tax-gathering arm of imperial Rome. The word originally meant basket or money bag. By the time of Cicero it had come to mean the state treasury, and under the empire it was nothing less than the emperor's private purse.

Private rites of magic send
The temple prostitutes to sleep;
All the literati keep
An imaginary friend.

Sacred prostitution, usually connected with fertility cults, was commonly practiced in various parts of the pagan world, especially at a shrine devoted to Aphrodite at Corinth, the libertine city whose inhabitants were addressed by letters from St. Paul. It was, of course, the purpose of such prostitutes to serve the gods and goddesses in whose shrines and temples they performed their services. So even the heretical faith is here being undermined. As for the imaginary friends being "kept" by the literati, Auden may be playing upon the complex and deceptive practice of the classical poets of addressing their amatory poems to persons represented under fictive names, like Celia, Delia, Lesbia, etc., a practice continued by such neoclassic poets as Jonson and Herrick, as well as others. The device is a tribute to the practice of earlier poets, who in this way were able to secure the anonymity of the married women with whom they were having affairs. The device also made it possible to pretend to be having an affair even if one wasn't, and to endow the beloved, whether real or not, with exceptional charms which needn't have borne any relation to reality. This touches upon not merely the capacity of poets to tell lies, but the theme Auden would come increasingly to play with: that love poetry has the greatest difficulty being honest, and perhaps ought not to try.

> Cerebrotonic Cato may
> Extoll the Ancient Disciplines,
> But the muscle-bound Marines
> Mutiny for food and pay.

The *OED* defines "cerebrotonic" as "designating or characteristic of a type of personality which is introverted, intellectual, and emotionally restrained, classified by [Dr. W. H.] Sheldon as being associated with an ectomorphic [that is, a lean body-build, distinguished by Sheldon from endomorphic and mesomorphic] physique." The Cato in question is one of an illustrious family. He is Marcus Cato, surnamed Uticensis from his death at Utica, who was the great-grandson of the censor of the same name. He was precocious in his virtue, and at the age of fourteen asked his preceptor for a sword to kill the tyrant Sulla. He was austere in morals and a strict follower of the tenets of the Stoics. He was careless of his dress, often walking barefoot in public, and never traveled but on foot. So much was he a lover of discipline that in whatever office he was employed he always reformed its abuses and restored ancient regulations. The very fact that he was obliged to do so suggests something about the decline in public and governmental morals. When he was set over the troops in the capacity of commander, his removal was universally lamented, and deemed almost a public loss by his affectionate soldiers. His fondness for candor was so great that the veracity of Cato became almost proverbial. But his championship of the Ancient Disciplines will clearly not carry much weight against the mesomorphic Marines, who have strength, numbers, a happy absence of morals, and contempt for tradition on their side.

> Caesar's double-bed is warm
> As an unimportant clerk
> Writes *I DO NOT LIKE MY WORK*
> On a pink official form.

The loves of the Caesars, as reported by the likes of Suetonius, Tacitus, Cassius Dio, the *Historia Augusta,* Aelius Lampridius, and others, were pretty nearly a chronicle of outrageous scandal, involving matters, including incest, that were sometimes known but never spoken or written of. It was at one time widely supposed that Ovid was exiled because he knew more than it was healthy to know about the imperial family. As for the feeble protest of the unimportant clerk, and the plight of such people who, whether they like it or not, are locked into a regime of bureaucracy or business, Auden, in his commonplace book, *A Certain World,* has written very pertinently as follows:

So far as I know, Miss Hannah Arendt was the first person to define the essential difference between work and labor. To be happy, a man must feel, firstly, free and, secondly, important. He cannot be really happy if he is compelled by society to do what he does not enjoy doing, or if what he enjoys doing is ignored by society as of no value or importance. In a society where slavery in the strict sense has been abolished, the sign that what a man does is of social value is that he is paid money to do it, but a laborer today can rightly be called a wage slave. A man is a laborer if the job society offers him is of no interest to himself but he is compelled to take it by the necessity of earning a living and supporting his family.

The antithesis to labor is play. When we play a game, we enjoy what we are doing, otherwise we would not play it, but it is a purely private activity; society could not care less whether we play it or not.

Between labor and play stands work. A man is a worker if he is personally interested in the job which society pays him to do; what from the point of view of society is necessary labor is from his own point of view voluntary play. Whether a job is classified as labor or work depends, not on the job itself, but on the tastes of the individual

who undertakes it. The difference does not, for example, coincide
with the difference between a manual and a mental job; a gardener
or a cobbler may be a worker, a bank clerk a laborer. Which a man
is can be seen from his attitude towards leisure. To a worker, leisure
means simply the hours he needs to relax and rest in order to work
efficiently. He is therefore more likely to take too little leisure than
too much; workers die of coronaries and forget their wives' birth-
days. To the laborer, on the other hand, leisure means freedom from
compulsion, so that it is natural for him to imagine that the fewer
hours he has to spend laboring, and the more hours he is free to play,
the better.

What percentage of the population in a modern technological
society are, like myself, in the fortunate position of being workers?
At a guess I would say sixteen percent, and I do not think that figure
is likely to get bigger in the future.

Those who would object that Caesar did not live in a "modern technological society" will have failed to remember this poem's deliberate use of
anachronism, and its mention of evening gowns, which did not exist in
Roman times, either.

It may be best to speak of the last two stanzas together. The poem began
with a remote, panoramic view of a landscape devoid, for the most part,
of humanity; and it will end in something like the same way.

> Unendowed with wealth or pity,
> Little birds with scarlet legs,
> Sitting on their speckled eggs,
> Eye each flu-infected city.

> Altogether elsewhere, vast
> Herds of reindeer move across
> Miles and miles of golden moss,
> Silently and very fast.

After the intermediate stanzas with their human actors and their deft
ironies, our view is severed from the human perspective, and we are
granted, quite literally, a bird's-eye view of the human predicament. The
birds are among the creatures from which humans are set apart; we are
denied their innocence, and though we enjoy many worldly advantages
over them, we can make no claim upon their sympathy, which is a purely
human feeling. They are therefore a permanent reminder of how alienated

we are from that pastoral union with the natural world that comprises our idea of Eden. Caring for their own unborn, they look out upon a city (a specifically human community) ravaged by a specifically human illness. The illness, a common one in the general index of pathology, stands for the entire range of weaknesses that served slowly, invisibly, and inexorably to undermine the Roman Empire.

The last stanza is a triumph, and this is due in large part to the skill with which its syntactical construction is disposed upon the framework of the rhymed quatrain. In all the previous stanzas the line unit, while not always self-contained, exhibited a kind of unity: the enjambments, when they occurred, were smooth, easy, and normally linked no more than two consecutive lines. Here, for the first time, the syntax is as free as the movement it means to describe. In the first line, the adjective "vast" is firmly severed, by its terminal position, from the noun it modifies, a separation without precedent in the poem. And indeed the first three lines of the final stanza require a seamless continuity, since the preposition "across" demands fulfillment in its object in the third line. This movement of three lines is itself descriptive of a unity of movement on the part of the vast "herds of reindeer," which exhibit a community of instinctual behavior even more removed from the human domain than was the nearby inspection of the birds. The reindeer move in annual migration, presumably in search of feeding grounds, in obedience to the seasons and to elementary instincts of self-preservation, which the citizens of Rome have lost. It remains to be added how powerful is the adverbial phrase of the last line, added (because syntactically quite independent, and unnecessary for the grammatical sense of the stanza) almost as an afterthought. It is the silence and speed of the herd's movement that is wonderfully arresting—the silence perhaps because of the moss, but also perhaps because the creatures are being viewed as very remote. The silence and speed probably both are due to the instinctual wisdom of the creatures and to motivations more primitive and more persistent than those exhibited by any of the humans in the poem. The last stanza presents us not merely with an alternative landscape, but with an alternative sense of the order of time itself as a biological and evolutionary record that makes trivial and brief the imperial ambitions of men.

The poem called "Music Ho" is an amusing little bit of what seems like light verse, but it is connected with some of Auden's central preoccupations. First of all, it is about the power of music to redeem from the region of helpless disbelief even the most outrageous and tiresome plot. It is about

Auden's favorite art form, opera, in which we cease to care that the lovers
both could pass for sumo wrestlers, the dialogue borders on the imbecile,
and the plot creaks with obvious contrivances. This in turn bears upon
the literary (and musical) device of dénouement and closure: the technique
by which a work persuades the reader or listener that, for the duration of
the work of art, a complete and coherent world has been presented, in
which all parts play a perfectly designed role. And this in turn bears upon
the degree to which a literary work is obliged to tell a "lie," since the
world we inhabit is by no means neat in its designs, if indeed it has any
at all. These puzzles are presented at their most extreme in *farce*, where
the wildest improbabilities are not merely permitted, but relished because
the dénouement then becomes a miraculous and gratuitous salvation. The
"rather scruffy-looking god" of this poem, the *deus ex machina*, is simply
a symbol of this compositional contrivance; but he is also a symbol of our
hope that some providential order may also obtain in the world we so
desperately live in.

"Memorial for the City" is a large, complex, and important poem to
which I fear I cannot do justice, since its second, and chief, part is afflicted
with a congestion of internal rhymes to a degree I find insupportable. The
poem has been given careful consideration by Monroe Spears, and I have
little to add to what he has thoughtfully written. The first part of the poem
presents that "removed" and impersonal view of earth which opened and
closed "The Fall of Rome," and which, in its striving for a kind of
impersonal objectivity, can be traced back as far as to the poem of 1930
called "Consider," which begins, "Consider this and in our time / As the
hawk sees it or the helmeted airman . . ." In the later poem we have,
instead of the hawk and the airman, "the eyes of the crow and the eye of
the camera." These viewers are not merely impersonal; they can see no
cause-and-effect relationships. They are without a sense of history. And
a large part of the rest of the poem presents history (from the early Middle
Ages to post-Romantic, psychoanalytic self-consciousness) in what had
become the potted formulae that we saw in Auden's *Letter to Lord Byron*,
as well as in his prose. The third section is a description of our fallen
condition, rendered in terms of a recurrent nightmare, and the final section
is an account of that human weakness which is the weakness not of
deliberate sinfulness but of the essential human condition—for which,
therefore, hope of salvation may still be held out; and the final part of the
poem is the voice of that weakness, the weakness of Man who has built
"Metropolis, that too great city," which has become the symbol of his

defeat. Implicit in Auden's symbol of the city is the double one of a civilized human community on the one hand, and on the other the opposition that St. Augustine makes between the City of God and the "earthly city" that are contrasted at the beginning of Book II of *The City of God.*

The title "Under Sirius" refers to the Dog Star, whose appearance, according to the ancients, always caused great heat on earth, with the accompanying aridity that belongs to the hottest part of summer. Virgil writes of it in the third book of the *Aeneid* thus: "the Dog Star burned / Our green plantations barren, and our grassland / Withered; sickly stalks denied us food." This season of spiritual desolation is the setting of a lovely, minatory, and essentially homiletic poem ostensibly addressed to an early medieval (c. 530–609) bishop of Poitiers and poet, Fortunatus, though I am at one with those critics who feel that, with characteristic modesty and desire for personal concealment, Auden is in fact addressing the poem chiefly to himself, and chiding himself for an insufficient commitment to a faith he has formally embraced. The actual Fortunatus was a native of northern Italy, chaplain to a community of nuns founded at Poitiers by St. Radegunda, who had formerly been the wife of the Frankish king Clotaire I. Fortunatus wrote a number of light epistles in verse to the saint and to her friend, Agnes, who was the superior of the community, as well as some hymns (at least one of them famous) and a long poem (a small epic?) in four books in honor of St. Martin. The famous hymn, *Vexilla Regis,* has been translated into English, and its first, fairly familiar quatrain goes,

> The royal banners forward go,
> The cross shines forth in mystic glow
> Where He, as man, who gave man breath,
> Now bows beneath the yoke of death.

If those of us who think Auden is speaking to himself in "Under Sirius" are right, he has assigned to himself a particularly barren period in the history of Latin poetry, and may in consequence be not merely denigrating the importance of his own work but echoing a witty conceit of Frost's, who, in his poem "The Lesson for Today," which itself is a homiletic title, was poking some not altogether sly fun at T. S. Eliot. In his essay on Dante, Eliot had written that Dante's greatness was not "due to greater genius, but to the fact that he wrote when Europe was still more or less one." (Eliot would elaborate on this idea in "What is a classic?" with reference to Virgil, to this effect: "It did happen that the history of Rome was such, the character of the Latin language was such, that at a certain moment a uniquely classical poet was possible . . . A classic can only occur when a civilization is mature; when a language and a literature are mature; it must be the work of a mature mind.") Frost's poem, written for the June 1941 Phi Beta Kappa ceremonies at Harvard, could not have taken this second essay (1944) into account, but it was in some ways nothing but an extension of what Eliot had stated in 1929. What Frost found most risible was the virtual historical determinism of Eliot, and his claim that poets were doomed to be minor or major by dint of the period into which they were born. He begins his poem with scarcely concealed glee:

> If this uncertain age in which we dwell
> Were really as dark as I hear sages tell,
> And I convinced that they were really sages,
> I should not curse myself with it to hell,
> But leaving not the chair I long have sat in,
> I should betake me back ten thousand pages
> To the world's undebatable dark ages,
> And getting up my medieval Latin,
> Seek converse common cause and brotherhood
> (By all that's liberal—I should, I should)
> With poets who could calmly take the fate
> Of being born at once too early and late,
> And for these reasons kept from being great.

I am not trying to claim that Auden is taking part in this debate on either side; he admired both Eliot and Frost. But surely there is something wry, modest, self-critical, and slightly mocking in his identification of himself with a comparatively minor Latin poet most of whose works, and especially his most ambitious ones, are now forgotten. The poet is self-chiding in another way as well, and in this second way it is more specifically personal. It takes the form of a homily meant to allay the spiritual presumption of a convert, whose eagerness for the total renovation of everything, as a sort of confirmation of his own conversion, has not yet, to his slightly petulant annoyance, been satisfied. It speaks the counsel of patience; and, more than that, it warns that everything is not as smooth and easy as the convert had rather casually supposed. There will be, as the Scripture demands, some serious testing yet to be endured, and some serious questions yet to be answered.

The poem is composed in nine-line stanzas of Auden's own invention. The line lengths in each stanza follow a pattern of 5,3,4,3,5,3,4,3 feet, though Auden is expansively free with his rhythms and allows himself some Hopkinsesque liberties with unaccented syllables. There is also some selective rhyming: the second and fourth lines rhyme, as do the fifth and sixth, and the seventh and ninth. This leaves three lines in each stanza conspicuously unrhymed. The effect is one of pleasant unconstraint, which sorts well with a voice that is meant to sound like the insinuating, casual voice of the conscience.

The "dog-days" with which the poem opens are mere signs of a general malaise. Just as the landscape is arid, so does a general torpor possess everyone from the legions and their commander to the scholar and the Sibyl. The closing lines of the stanza, "Drug as she may the Sibyl utters / A gush of table-chat," remind us that at the principal shrines, including Delphi, the priestess's seat, usually a tripod, was situated above a fissure in a floor of rock out of which fumes and intoxicating gases rose to enhance her visionary faculties. The general sterility described in the stanza presumably has its contemporary analogies, though it may be of little use to point to specific parallels. And the point, in any case, is that from the serious point of view of the soul—which is the view of Eternity— almost any period of history is likely to seem vacant and without promise.

The second stanza draws a parallel between the barren landscape, the emptiness of vocation of soldier, scholar, Sibyl in the first stanza, and the enfeebled condition of the poet himself. As in the first stanza, the feebleness is of two kinds, physical and spiritual. The poet, suffering from "a head-cold and upset stomach," also feels that he has been born into an unpropitious period, such as those Eliot wrote and Frost joked about. Fortunatus daydreams of some apocalyptic event, wishing "some earth-quake would astonish / Or the wind of the comforter's wing / Unlock the prisons and translate / The slipshod gathering"(Acts 16:26). "Comforter" is a title of the Holy Spirit, and is so identified in John 14:16–17, in which Christ says to his disciples, "I will pray the Father, and he shall give you another Comforter, that he may abide with you for ever; Even the Spirit of truth, whom the world cannot receive, because it seeth him not, neither knoweth him; for he dwelleth with you, and shall be in you." Fortunatus' wish is misdirected because it is wholly concerned with externals and with others, as though his own spiritual condition were not open to question. Earthquakes were commonly taken as acts of God, and consequently as judgments against wicked people.

As distinguished from daydream (wishing) there are the deeper dreams of night. These envision a redemptive bliss, the restoration of the fertility of the land, and the arrival of "the three wise Maries." They disembark from their "ivory vessels" in a manner that recalls a Christmas carol in which "three ships come sailing in on Christmas Day in the morning." The three Maries are in all likelihood the three women mentioned in the last chapter of Mark, and who came to the tomb of Jesus after his burial to anoint his body: "And when the sabbath was past, Mary Magdalene, and Mary the mother of James, and Salome, had brought sweet spices, that they might come and anoint him." In the medieval Mystery play called *The Three Maries*, the woman identified in Mark as "Salome" (which, by the way, means "shalom," or peace) is called "Mary Salome." These three women are the first to discover that the tomb is empty and that Jesus has risen from the dead. They are thus the first bearers of the revelation of the Gospel fulfilled. They arrive in Auden's poem in the manner of stately pagan deities, "piloted in / By sea-horse and fluent dolphin," as cannons roar in celebration: "How jocular the bells as They / Indulge the peccant shore." "Indulge" carries the theological meaning of the capacity to "grant an indulgence," and the "peccant," or sinful, shore is to be redeemed from its waywardness by that indulgence. The dream, in other words, is of an easy, gratuitous absolution.

The fourth stanza opens with a complex set of echoes.

> It is natural to hope and pious, of course, to believe
> That all in the end shall be well . . .

The most immediate source of this is probably Eliot's "Little Gidding":

> Sin is Behovely, but
> All shall be well, and
> All manner of thing shall be well.

And the exegetes have told us that Eliot in his turn is quoting from *The Revelation of Divine Love* by the fourteenth-century mystic Julian of Norwich. In the context of Eliot's poem, however, the lines take on a quality that comes rather near to complacency, and thereby touches upon an unavoidable Christian quandary. To abandon all hope in salvation is to deny the mercy and loving-kindness, as well as the power, of God; to count upon that salvation with a careless confidence is to sin and to risk perdition. The assurances given to the visionary Julian (from whose work Auden selected an epigraph to "Memorial for the

City") were vouchsafed in a context that Eliot's appropriation fails to make entirely clear. The anchoress, who gave religious instruction to Margery Kempe, was concerned about the fact that Church teachings declared that "the wicked angels and those that die out of charity will be damned eternally," in the words of James Walsh, from his introduction to his translation of Julian's work. In response to this concern Julian received in a vision this reassurance: "At one time our good Lord said: 'All things shall be well'; and at another he said: 'Thou shalt see thyself all manner thing shall be well.' "

But Auden, in the lines that immediately follow, is quick to recall another part of doctrinal orthodoxy:

> But first of all, remember,
>      So the Sacred Books foretell,
> The rotten fruit shall be shaken.

That warning refers to the Eschatological Sermon in which Jesus speaks (in Matthew 23, Mark 13, Luke 21—the "Sacred Books") of the coming destruction of Jerusalem, and of the Parousia, the Second Coming of Christ as supreme judge of the living and dead at the end of the world. The phrase "Sacred Books" recalls the Sibylline books, largely destroyed, the remnants sold to Tarquin, which were supposed to contain an account of all future time. And the continuation of the stanza is as much a chiding to the complacency of Eliot as it is to Fortunatus, to Auden himself, or to any serious believer. (An "eagre" is a tidal wave of unusual height, and an "insurrected" one is raised or mounted high.)

The threats of the third stanza continue to fill the fourth, couched though it is in the diction of a light and taunting banter. Such a tone is all the more alarming in that we cannot tell just how seriously we are to take this supernatural extravagance, the dangers and the queries it anticipates.

The final stanza envisions a future time that is actually beyond time, in which, in something like Elizabethan diction, "the reborn featly dance" to the music of a "carol" under the boughs of "apple-trees" in what is a lovely and deliberately archaic image of paradise. That "future time" is both in the future and the present, since heaven is constantly present, and the blessed are forever enjoying its bliss. That "future time" looks suspiciously like the eternity that follows any death, when, according to the ominous voice that speaks this poem (the voice of a poet's conscience) "there will also . . . Be those who refused their chance," those who did not do what was required of them, those who complained (in the very

complaints of the first stanza) that they lived in the "dull dog-days /
Between event," which is to say, when nothing of consequence was going
on. Yet complain as they might, at the same time they rejoiced that theirs
was an era of peace, upon which they congratulated themselves, taking
upon themselves the credit for this tranquility, and filled with vanity in
their administrative skills and arts. There is in this, I suspect, a sly joke
about the Pax Romana which Augustan Rome attributed entirely to the
wisdom of the emperor and his administrators, but which Christians
believe was a divinely established peace contrived as the necessary setting
for the birth of the Prince of Peace.

Auden returns to a lasting interest (one might almost say obsession)
with mines in "Not in Baedeker." A number of early poems, for example,
"The Watershed," dealt with mines, and others with mining equipment,
a matter that I have touched upon earlier. The theme is full of symbolic
weight for Auden, suggesting both historical and psychological depths;
and abandoned mines are, to him, very much the equivalent of an
archeological site, requiring both laborious and instinctive interpretive
skill in the reconstruction of an earlier way of life, of industry, of human
undertaking. Such "reconstruction" of a rich past from an impoverished
present goes on throughout the poem, which is filled with parentheses
indicating qualifications, second thoughts, recollections, and insights. The
parentheses are themselves a kind of foraging of the past in the way of
mental life. The poem closes with a mild act of irreverence and profanation, when two English cyclists "stopped here for a *fine*," after which, in
the Shot Tower, the younger of the two

>                     using a rotting
> Rickety gallery for a lectern,
> To amuse his friend gave an imitation
> Of a clergyman with a cleft palate.

The joke is deliberately awkward, and in vaguely bad taste. We are meant
of course to realize immediately how ill-suited to his profession such a
clergyman would be, and how ignorant of his own limitations he was to
have attempted such a vocation. But such folly could potentially belong
to the choice of any vocation, and we can see by this how chancy and
filled with potential disaster have been all our fates. The impudence of the
mimic, in this poem, may carry an autobiographical reproof, for Carpenter tells us that "Auden was no mimic, but he liked acting roles, a favorite
one being that of a lunatic clergyman preaching to his flock."

"Cattivo Tempo" (bad weather) begins by invoking the Sirocco, a hot wind that, in southern Italy, is said to induce petulance, ill humor, negligence, and a vague but powerful sense of discontent—what Auden in this poem calls "the minor devils." He mentions two: "Nibbar, demon / Of ga-ga and bêtise, / Tubervillus, demon / Of gossip and spite." There is a certain amount of commendable courage in Auden's having singled out these two for mention, since he genuinely relished gossip and did not mind passing it along, sometimes fastidiously omitting proper names, though without discouraging some obvious guesses. As for "ga-ga and bêtise," these are particularly the dangers that beset the poet, as the second stanza makes clear. These demons have "Grown insolent and fat / On cheesy literature / And corny dramas," a diet both literally and figuratively repellent. The cheesy literature can infect the work of the poet, the corny drama debase the insinuating inventions of the gossip. The poet's business is always to refuse "The nearly fine / The almost true," the work that is just short of the very best and most accurate of which he is capable. There is a highly moral principle being suggested here, and one which Auden stated in the preface to the 1945 *Collected Poetry*.

> In the eyes of every author, I fancy, his own past work falls into four classes. First, the pure rubbish which he regrets ever having conceived; second—for him the most painful—the good ideas which his incompetence or impatience prevented from coming to much (*The Orators* seems to me such a case of the fair notion fatally injured); third, the pieces he has nothing against except their lack of importance; these must inevitably form the bulk of any collection since, were he to limit it to the fourth class alone, to those poems for which he is honestly grateful, his volume would be too depressingly slim.

There is a rare candor and severe artistic conscience exhibited here, and Auden had from the first declared himself an enemy of the second-rate, even more in his own work than in the work of others.

As for Tubervillus, his kind of evil may be even more serious, since he is demon of venom and malice, and concerned with giving hurt to others rather than merely to himself. In any case, the two of them, inspired by that malevolent wind, attack their victim when he is alone and unprepared to resist them. And how is such resistance to be effected? How do we defy the devils? Luther is supposed to have thrown an inkwell, and St. Dominic a heavy stone that may be viewed in the Dominican Church of Santa Sabina on the Aventine Hill in Rome. But inkwells and stones are not always to hand, and Auden has hit upon a more moral way, which is also, of course, a way of defeating the enervating effect of bad weather.

> The proper riposte is to bore them;
> To scurry the dull pen
> Through dull correspondence,
> To wag the sharp tongue
> In pigeon Italian,
> Asking the socialist
> Barber to guess
> Or the monarchist fisherman to tell
> When the wind will change,
> Outwitting hell
> With human obviousness.

There is something genuinely touching in this. The socialist barber and monarchist fisherman are merely humble citizens who are subject to the same afflictions of bad weather (as well as the bad temper that it brings) as the poet-speaker. Political differences are made slight by the disturbing power of the wind and by universal susceptibility to the corruption of "the minor devils." Moreover, with time Auden had come more and more to feel the overriding *moral* importance of doing small, tedious, and disagreeable jobs promptly and thoroughly. The curious point about this is that as time went on he ceased to make a distinction between this *moral* necessity and the demands of what must finally be called *etiquette*. There is in this very poem at least the hint of such a conflation when Auden speaks of the "proper riposte." And as we proceed we will find that he inclines more and more to rely on what seem like the rules laid down for young gentlemen by nannies, school proctors, and headmasters. To say this is not in any way meant to diminish the seriousness of what he recommends, or to doubt that these irritating tasks should be well and carefully performed, and that the omission of them is truly a moral lapse. But I can't help feeling puzzled about this confusion of virtue with deportment, and we shall see it again in other poems.

"Secrets" may be thought of as an addendum to "In Praise of Limestone," touching as it does upon some of the same topics, the divorce of mankind from the other creatures, our openness to the view of God, our place midway between the divine and mundane, and our susceptibility to various kinds of corruption. It begins with a witty deceptiveness.

That we are always glad
When the Ugly Princess parting the bushes
To find out why the woodcutter's children are happy
Disturbs a hornet's nest, that we feel no pity
When the informer is trapped by the gang in a steam-room,
That we howl with joy
When the short-sighted Professor of Icelandic
Pronounces the Greek inscription
A Runic riddle which he then translates,

Denouncing by proxy our commonest fault as our worst;

This sentence will continue for another seven lines, but by the time of this major stop with a semicolon we have been led to consider what "our commonest fault" is, and, from the evidence so far provided by the poem, it would be reasonable to accuse ourselves of a malicious longing for a comeuppance, a sort of retributive justice that would, by some mysterious but inexorable law, exact a suitable penalty upon those who (even professors with their pretenses to omniscience) regularly humiliate or in some way offend us. This at least, I would claim, is our first impression, if we read no further. But the remainder of the sentence serves wonderfully to modify the first part of it, showing that "our commonest fault" is not what we had supposed but that each instance mentioned is of a secret being violated. The additional instances make perfectly clear our inability to keep secrets; more than that, our positive delight in revealing them: "that, dear me, how often / We kiss in order to tell . . ." The "dear me" seems slightly affected: the voice, one would guess, of a nanny or an aunt. To kiss and tell is as much a heterosexual as a homosexual vice; Byron complained that Lady Caroline Lamb had raised it to the power of "fuck and publish." But whatever it is, it has something to do with social politics, with vanity, with the power to hurt others, with the perishable commodity of reputations, and so it is slightly shocking to find the poet saying that it "defines precisely what we mean by love." That Auden should make such an assertion is perhaps one more small index of how little faith he had come to entertain in durable human relations of any intimacy.

"Nones," the title poem of this volume, and, with "Prime," the only one of the poems on the canonical hours to appear in it, seems to me a brilliantly successful work of very great and yet mysterious power. It is the name of the divine office recited at three o'clock in the afternoon, the symbolic hour of the Crucifixion. Auden had very decided personal views about this time of day. Let me once again have recourse to a recollection of mine that appeared in the *Paris Review* interview. "[Auden] kept to an inflexible schedule of work and play. He rose early, wrote and read before breakfast, which was likely to be no more than coffee. (I was told all this.) Continued work until about three P.M., pausing for a light lunch. The rest of the day was for relaxation and amusement. He used to say that he was never able to work beyond mid-afternoon, but only came to understand the reason for this when he had become a convinced Christian, because he then realized that three P.M. is the canonical hour of the Crucifixion." This fact is worth recording as a serious statement the poet actually made, but it is not entirely clear what he meant by it. How, for example, would he have responded to the suggestion that his loss of power to work that struck about mid-afternoon had something to do with his personal metabolism? That if he rose later he might not be fatigued till later? Such questions were not asked, and perhaps they are impertinent.

There have been many remarkable and powerful poems about the Crucifixion. There is, for example, an anonymous medieval lyric of which the first stanza goes,

> His body is wrappèd all in wo,
> Hand and fote he may not go.
> Thy son, lady, that thou lovest so
> Naked is nailed upon a tree.

There is also Skelton's poem "Wofully arrayed," at least two sonnets of John Donne's, "Crucifying" and "Spit in my face," as well as George Herbert's "The Sacrifice." All of these poems require that the reader regard unflinchingly the torment of physical suffering and hideous death. In not allowing the reader to, as it were, avert his eyes, these poets are in effect following the precepts of St. Paul, who, in writing to the Philippians (3:10), said that he would give everything "that I may win Christ . . . That I may know him, and the power of his resurrection, and the fellowship of his suffering, being made conformable unto his death."

Auden, however, is doing something no less powerful but somehow more subtle. He is writing about the complete sense of desolation engendered by the Crucifixion, the almost inconsolable grief and sense of loneliness that it occasions. He is writing, that is to say, not about the Crucifixion itself, but about its effect upon us—an effect that makes itself felt daily, at three in the afternoon. This is the time of day not only when Auden is overcome with lethargy and unhappiness, but when, throughout most of Italy but especially in the south, and in Ischia in particular, all shops, banks, and other places of commerce close and everyone takes a siesta. Whether this widespread social practice is merely a convention of convenience in a hot climate, or whether it springs from a deep metaphysical impulse, we are not told, though the very notion of writing such a poem as "Nones" presupposes an active sense on the part of the poet that divinity in its workings has a detectable effect upon our lives. The poem, in fact, is not so much about the sacred event itself as it is about *us*, the reluctant witnesses, the unconscious culprits, the unworthy beneficiaries. It is we who, by our guilt, have required the sacrifice that is made to repair our sinful natures; and that guilt is strangely increased by responsibility for the murder itself. (To be sure, both guilts, we are assured, will be assuaged by the sacrifice, but at the hour of the death we are not in the frame of mind to rejoice in this.) In any case, since the poem is so emphatically about *us*, it has the dramatic effect of being, not about a singular and terrible event, but about something universal and inescapable.

What we know to be not possible
  Though time after time foretold
By wild hermits, by shaman and sybil
  Gibbering in their trances,
Or revealed to a child in some chance rhyme
  Like *will* and *kill,* comes to pass
Before we realize it: we are surprised
  At the ease and speed of our deed
And uneasy: it is barely three,
  Mid afternoon, yet the blood
Of our sacrifice is already
  Dry on the grass; we are not prepared
For silence so sudden and so soon;
  The day is too hot, too bright, too still,
Too ever, the dead remains too nothing.
  What shall we do till nightfall?

This is the first of seven stanzas of a poem that in its course will be tainted from time to time with the sort of internal rhymes that trouble my ear and seem to lend a note of unwanted frivolity. In this first stanza one of these appears as just and persuasive: that our sinful nature should be revealed "to a child in some chance rhyme / Like *will* and *kill.*" But almost immediately following this we encounter "the speed of our deed," which, in the words of Edmund, bastard son of Gloucester in *King Lear,* comes in pat, "like the catastrophe of the old comedy." The phrase, of course, is meant to convey something serious: the very rapidity of the flow of events in which we are involved is an index of how little thought we give to our ordinary behavior, and how little time there is for such thought. The terrible sight, which we try to avoid seeing, is emblematically represented by "the blood . . . already / Dry on the grass." The stanza conveys an air of police-blotter crime that is soon to be followed by a coroner's inquest. The normal habits of life have been violently interrupted, and the period between *now* and "nightfall," when the body's clock will demand a restorative meal, and perhaps a conscience-soothing or -obliterating drink, lies before us as a great vacancy and solemn emptiness, as though a death in our own family had bereft us not merely of a person but of the normal habits of life. The shock and the surprise are the more powerful in that the event itself was "time after time foretold." And we realize now that our error was nothing less than a failure of belief.

> The wind has dropped and we have lost our public.
>     The faceless many who always
> Collect when any world is to be wrecked,
>     Blown up, burnt down, cracked upon,
> Felled, sawn in two, hacked through, torn apart,
>     Have melted away: not one
> Of these who in the shade of walls and trees
>     Lie sprawled now, calmly sleeping,
> Harmless as sheep, can remember why
>     He shouted or what about
> So loudly in the sunlight this morning;
>     All, if challenged, would reply
> —"It was a monster with one red eye,
>     A crowd that saw him die, not I—."
> The hangman has gone to wash, the soldiers to eat:
>     We are left alone with our feat.

The first line of this second stanza carries a witty incrimination. To say of us all that "we have lost our public" is to remind us that we usually regard ourselves as actors, that we play roles in order to be regarded in ways that please us, that we are usually hypocrites, and that our sense of identity depends so heavily on the view of others that without them we are scarcely real to ourselves. By this time the damage is done; the world has been wrecked as surely and as brutally as the catalogue of destruction the poem provides—a catalogue that begins with the familiar modes of warfare ("blown up, burnt down") and smoothly proceeds to forms of human mutilation ("sawn in two, hacked through, torn apart," all of which can find their duplicates among the accounts of the martyrs). Our "public" has left us alone: those who came to witness the Crucifixion, who are always attracted by sadistic spectacles of suffering, have gone off to their customary siestas, "harmless as sheep" in sleep, and each convinced of his own complete innocence, prepared to deny even having witnessed the event. Self-exculpation is greatly eased by the oblivion of a mid-afternoon snooze, and makes possible even a kind of spiritual amnesia which blocks out any recollection of having been present at the scene of the crime. But we who have not resorted to such deliberate forgetfulness are now left with what we acknowledge as "our feat." The word has all the justice and irony of "accomplishment."

In the third stanza the "three wise Maries" divert their gaze from us, the authors of this crime, and from our uncompleted projects of construction, our pitiful attempts to repair the world, fixing their view instead upon "our completed work," the crime itself, which the reader of the poem again is not allowed to see. The body hangs on the cross, but what we are aware of is our own obsolescence:

> Outliving our act we stand where we are
>   As disregarded as some
> Discarded artifact of our own,
>   Like torn gloves, rusted kettles,
> Abandoned branchlines, worn lop-sided
>   Grindstones buried in nettles.

Readers of Auden's early poetry will immediately be struck by this catalogue. It recalls "Equipment rusting in unweeded lanes" from the 1929 poem that begins "Since you are going to begin to-day," which would later be titled "Venus Will Now Say a Few Words"; it also recalls "By silted harbours, derelict works" from "Consider this and in our time" (1930), as well as other ruined industrial and mining landscapes that, from the first, were what Auden himself called in retrospect "sacred places." They had for him always a numinous quality which now, in this poem, takes on a significance it never had before. And indeed, the following stanza is a sudden and astonished revelation of the real meaning of idle games and pastimes, many of them from childhood. Everything most familiar, domestic, habitual, diverting now means something different from what we heedlessly thought it meant. Even, or perhaps especially, our exaltations, our "wonder" and our "rapture," will henceforth inevitably recall "the deed to which they lead," and our most supposedly "innocent" behavior or moments of transport are now contaminated. There will be no diversion for us that will not be tainted.

There remain three sixteen-line stanzas to this poem, and like all the preceding stanzas, each one ends with a full stop. No alterations, performed in the name of clarity, have been attempted in any editorial supervision. But I believe that the last three stanzas compose a grammatical and syntactical unit, that they cannot be read independently, and that all but the last should be followed not by a period but by a dash, as a way of indicating a logical and grammatical bond between stanzas.

The first of these stanzas begins with a breath of fresh air, the "cool tramontana," the north wind, stirring the leaves, not only refreshing us but making more plain than ever how everything came to a sudden halt when our paralysis set in. "The shops will re-open at four, / The empty blue bus in the empty pink square / Fill up and drive off . . ." The Ischian bus was in fact blue, and its stop in Forio d'Ischia was indeed a small square of stucco-faced houses painted the identical shade of pink, at least in those years (1949–50) when both Auden and I lived in that town. Doubtless such documentary matters are of small consequence to the reader; but they seem to have had a sufficient importance to Auden to demand accurate report, and in all likelihood this accuracy bears on his sense of the absolute reality of the spiritual condition of which he is writing. At four o'clock, the crisis having passed, the bus having driven off, "we have time / To misrepresent, excuse, deny, / Mythify, use this event . . ." These are all devices of exculpation, of which one, "mythify," is a way of equating the Crucifixion with the death of Adonis or Attis or any of Frazer's sacrificial gods, or the "hanged god" of the tarot pack. But we are destined not to succeed in any of these devices, for soon "the great quell" will begin. That "quell" is a witty and tricky word, suggesting some kind of tranquility but actually meaning a slaughter, and we are being warned about Armageddon. The "triple gallows" of Abaddon (who is the angel of the bottomless pit) surely recalls the three crosses at Golgotha; they are set up "at our seven gates," reminding us of the inherited curse of the children of Oedipus in the *Seven Against Thebes*, where the city itself is vulnerable at its seven gates, but also at the seven portals of the body: two eyes, two ears, two nostrils, and the mouth. It is with these senses or avenues that our life of sin begins. Belial, a name of the Devil or one of the fiends, will "make / Our wives waltz naked" in a frenzied display of debauchery.

> . . . meanwhile
> It would be best to go home, if we have a home,
> In any case good to rest—
>
> That our dreaming wills may seem to escape

I have just quoted the splice between the fifth and sixth stanzas, inserting a dash where Auden and his editors put a period. The word "that" with which the sixth stanza begins means "so that" or "in order that," and refers back to the verb "to rest" in the previous stanza. The body of the sixth stanza is given over to an initially eager dream of escaping "this dead calm," the transfixion of the hour of nones itself, to wander instead in any region of the mind's excitement. "Knife edges" suggests both daring exploratory mountaineering as well as something homicidal. "Black and white squares" suggests the marble floors of grand mansions as well as the challenging ground-plan of a crossword puzzle. In their flight to escape "this dead calm," our wills traverse "moss, baize, velvet, boards," various textures and surfaces that conjure up lost fragments of our lives—the baize, for example, recalling perhaps some fling at a gambling casino where, again, the excitement of risk is diverting. Mention of being "pursued by Moors" may refer to the villainous Monostatos and his henchmen in *The Magic Flute*. As the stanza proceeds, however, it takes on the somewhat vulgar contrivances of an unconscious with the taste and standards of grade-B movies. Something of the crude thriller takes hold of us until, having willingly suspended our disbelief in the cheap fictions of cinema but not in the reality from which we flee, we imagine ourselves about to encounter at last our sinister host, the arch-villain, the person who has contrived with aristocratic decorum to remain absent for almost the entire length of the film. Finally we come upon him, in Poe-like seclusion in "a room / Lit by one weak bulb where our double sits / Writing and does not look up."

The final stanza also begins with "that," and it has the same antecedent—"good to rest"—as the one that began the sixth stanza; so the sixth stanza, too, should end with a dash. The final stanza claims "That while we are thus away" ("thus" meaning while we are resting, our wills having gone off on their hazardous expeditions), "our wronged flesh / May work undisturbed . . ." Our flesh is wronged because our sin has been of the spirit, and because Auden was everywhere the vigorous enemy of any form of Manichaeism and of any other stringent puritanical heresy such as that of the Albigensians, who believed in the depravity of the material world and of the body in particular. The body, in obedience to laws of its own, works on undisturbed, "restoring / The order we try to destroy, the rhythm / We spoil out of spite . . ." Our spitefulness consists of our heretical impulse to blame the body for all our sins, and, more specifically, to blame it for the momentary death we have just experienced when everything came to a sudden halt at three in the afternoon. Nevertheless, "glands secrete, / Vessels contract and expand / At the right moment," as though our continued life was desired by some power or authority apart from ourselves, yet these vital organs are themselves astonished by the shock of the momentary death we have just experienced. They have no spoken language, they do not "know" what happened, but like the inarticulate creatures with which we share our life on earth, they have been "awed / By death," suggesting that our very bodies will never be quite the same. The creatures who live with us are now "watching this spot,"

> the hawk looking down
> Without blinking, the smug hens
> Passing close by in their pecking order,
> The bug whose view is baulked by grass,
> Or the deer who shyly from afar
> Peer through chinks in the forest.

These creatures, from their different perspectives, above, below, and beyond us, remind us that it is we who are the fallen ones, and they do so by "watching this spot," which is ambiguously wherever we happen to be, who are regarded by the creatures instinctively as their natural enemies; and also the spot where "the blood / Of our sacrifice is already / Dry on the grass," where human sinfulness is most clearly manifest. The poem seems to me deeply moving and eloquent, privately personal without any egotistical self-assertion, and written always from the view of the third-person plural except when one of a sleeping crowd is allowed to speak in his own person. It is a modest poem, almost completely untheatrical, even to the movie sequences in the penultimate stanza. And it moves forward with a measured tempo that is stately, quiet, and compelling, especially when the grammatical linkage between the final three stanzas is recognized.

The satiric poem "A Household" is placed dramatically right after "Nones" and could not be more different. It in fact recalls thematically the early poem beginning "Watch any day his nonchalant pauses," and later titled "A Free One." It also resembles some satirical portrait-poems by William Plomer. Like these, it contrasts the admired outward impression that a man creates with the realities behind his facade. In this, it resembles as well some of the poems by Thomas Hardy, especially the group called "Satires of Circumstance." But the poem evades the dismissiveness of simple satire because we are given a glimpse (before the grotesque details of the family life of the central character are revealed) of a genuine tragedy—the early death of his wife, of whom he never speaks. Whether the poisoned relationships of his son and his mother are the result of this death we are permitted only to surmise. In any case, the hypocrisy described in the poem has grown into a compulsive habit, and is not unlike the same social vice as it is portrayed not only in the poems but in the novels of Hardy.

Auden's satiric gifts were in evidence from the first, and now, in his later work, they were, I think, sometimes deftly and covertly directed against himself. I want to propose, with suitable tentativeness, that at least two poems in this book are of that character—poems in which faintly ridiculous women, their longings, their self-dramatizations, their size or their age, disqualify them for the hopelessly romantic image of themselves they would like to entertain. The poems concern lonely women, given to ludicrous fantasies or posturings; and they constitute a sort of self-criticism on the part of a poet who has had some difficulty sustaining any vision of love or fidelity. The longer, wittier, and more histrionic of these poems is called "The Duet." There seem to be overtones of Leoncavallo's *Pagliacci* in the poem, including Canio's famous aria, "Vesti la giubba," in which he complains of the ironic fate that compels him to make an appearance as an actor in a comic play when his heart is breaking. The opera also features an ugly and deformed clown named Tonio, who loves his manager's wife though she is repelled by him.

"The Duet" contains two characters, a "huge sad lady" and a "scrunty beggar," who never meet or interact in any way. Both, however, are singing songs (hence the title) quite independently of one another, and only the audience or reader can hear them both. But the wit of the composer or poet can blend them into a single and harmonious work.

Each sings according to his character: the woman, full of exotic language and surrounded by luxurious comfort, is filled with mawkish self-pity, a sentiment with which, even at his most anguished, Auden had no patience whatever; while the beggar, without privilege and equally alone, is full of cheer and optimistic expectation. The woman sings "of the heart betrayed." She in her warm house complains, "Love lies delirious and a-dying, / The purlieus are shaken by his sharp cry." The personification of Love, perhaps in this case not Eros but Adonis, who actually was killed by a wild boar, is highly literary, as is the archaism "a-dying." Not only are the two characters temperamentally contrasted with one another, but their settings, betokening their class, are similarly contrasted—"dividing / His wilderness from her floral side."

If she is a hopeless, overblown romantic, he is no beauty either, "with one glass eye and one hickory leg." But the poet tells us that he "refused her tragic hurt" and sang to his barrel-organ, *"Lanterloo, my lovely, my First-of-May."* John Fuller explains that "first-of-May" is a cant word meaning a young tramp. The definition, not supplied by the *OED,* is one that makes both characters in the poem, the lady and the beggar, yearn for men. This line is addressed to no one present; indeed, it very much resembles the refrain line of a conventional love ballad. If he has a barrel-organ, she has "her grand black piano" to which "She sang the disappointment and the fear / For all her lawns and orchards," which is to say that she has no more audience than he. The song fragment of hers that follows is again filled with affected language, all the more striking in that it is used to express painfully trite sentiments about time and mutability, those enemies of love. No sooner does she finish bewailing the fact that "The cute little botts [that is, bottoms] of the sailors / Are snapped up by the sea," than "to her gale of sorrow from the moonstruck darkness / That ragged runagate opposed his spark, / For still his scrannel music-making / In tipsy joy across the gliddered lake . . . Cried Nonsense to her large repining." The *OED* defines "scrannel" as now chiefly used in reminiscence of its use by Milton in "Lycidas." As for "gliddered," it means glazed or iced over, and again reminds us of the beggar's cheerful indifference to the harsh elements to which he is exposed, as contrasted with the "warm house" of the lady. For all his misshapen disqualifications, he is able, at the close of the poem, to have the last word as he sings (in implicit criticism of her woeful meditations on decay and death),

> *The windows have opened, a royal wine*
> *Is poured out for the subtle pudding,*
> *Light Industry is humming in the wood*
> *And blue birds bless us from the fences,*
> *We know the time and where to find our friends.*

The other poem in *Nones* that carries something of the same satiric thrust is called "In Schrafft's." The title refers to a small chain of restaurant–coffee shops favored by dowdy upper-middle class ladies of the sort that figured in the *New Yorker* cartoons of Helen Hokinson. And the poem presents itself as an account of just such a woman ("A somewhat shapeless figure / Of indeterminate age / In an undistinguished hat") being carefully observed. The second stanza is the one most like *New Yorker* cartoons in which ladies seem mindlessly unaware of the catastrophes of the world at large but are apprehensive about their begonias or bridge club meetings. It is, however, the third stanza that marks the poem as more serious than a cartoon. The second stanza told us only, as a sort of negative definition, that "When she lifted her eyes it was plain / That our globular furore . . . Was not being bothered about," but the final stanza explains those eyes more specifically and positively: they are smiling. What remains of the poem may be interpreted in two ways. When it is claimed that the smile "attested / That, whoever it was, a god / Worth kneeling-to for a while / Had tabernacled and rested," we may suppose either that the woman in raising her eyes has actually seen some very attractive man who is unnoticed by the speaker—whose attention has been focused exclusively upon her and her demeanor—or that her smile is one of happy recollection. The word "tabernacle" as a verb is not common, but it was used in translating a famous passage in the first chapter of John: what we familiarly know as "And the Word was made flesh and dwelt among us" has also been rendered "and tabernacled among us." The Biblical context is certainly not irrelevant, since "a god" is being spoken of. The infidelitous, conditional nature of the devotion described ("worth kneeling-to for a while") is a mockery not merely of religion but also of those casual attachments that are crowded in under the general rubric of "love." And "tabernacle," which means booth, would have a comic application to Schrafft's, where booths were a standard part of the seating arrangement. It is the casualness and imper-manence of the sexual dream entertained by a curiously unsuitable and nearly featureless lady that is at once touching and ludicrous in the poem, and that achieves a genuine pathos if we allow ourselves to imagine that this was an ingeniously artful way for Auden to write about himself without seeming to.

*Nones* contains two Phi Beta Kappa poems, one for Columbia and the other for Harvard. They are strikingly different, though both deal with the puzzles attending the function of art. Of the two, "Music Is International" (Columbia) is the more frankly difficult of access, the more densely baroque, convoluted, and crammed with exotic and unfamiliar diction. So markedly is this the case that, since it is the practice for Phi Beta Kappa poems to be read in ceremonial circumstances and academic regalia during a special PBK segment of commencement, and only published in some university journal later on, one wonders just how intelligible this poem would have been to uninstructed ears. This tradition (in which a new poem is read aloud to an audience which has neither seen nor heard it before) has afforded opportunity for complicated literary jokes. At an earlier Columbia commencement, the PBK laureate Rolfe Humphries read a poem which to the ear seemed irreproachable, if rather lifeless and of not much moment. Only, however, when the poem finally appeared in the Columbia alumni magazine, long after the ceremonies, did someone notice that the poem was an acrostic, the initial letters of its lines spelling out "Nicholas Murray Butler is a horse's ass."

Auden is not here engaged in playing that sort of trick, but his poem is unashamedly elitist nevertheless, and not only in its vocabulary but in its syntax. He takes pleasure in the Jamesian joke of following an extended rhetorical question with a terse, colloquial reply. Consider, for example, this excerpt from Caliban's Jamesian speech in *The Sea and the Mirror,* which appears to be addressed to Shakespeare himself.

> Can you wonder then, when, as was bound to happen sooner or later, your charms, because they no longer amuse you, have cracked and your spirits, because you are tired of giving orders, have ceased to obey, and you are left alone with me, the dark thing you could never abide to be with, if I do not yield you kind answer or admire your achievements I was never allowed to profit from, if I resent hearing you speak of your neglect of me as your "exile," of the pains you never took with me as "all lost"?
>
> But why continue?

And compare this to the following excerpt from the poem under consideration.

> Do they sponsor
> In us the mornes and motted memelons,
>   The sharp streams and sottering springs of
> A commuter's wish, where each frescade rings
>   With melodious booing and hooing
> As some elegant lovejoy deigns to woo
>   And nothing dreadful ever happened?
> Probably yes.

As Monroe Spears has carefully noted, Henry James may well have been on Auden's mind as he wrote this poem, and not alone with regard to his elaborate syntax. For the poem concerns the uses and abuses of art, and these are questions Auden considered in an essay called "Henry James and the Artist in America," in which, as Spears observes, Auden "notes that the subtlest temptation, the desire to do good by art is powerful in our age of disintegration, in which authorities turn to the artist and promise rewards 'if he will forsake the artistic life and become an official magician, who uses his talents to arouse in the inert masses the passions which the authorities consider socially desirable.'" It may be added that it makes very little difference whether this expressly political use of art is made in behalf of the powers-that-be and takes on the air of "official art," or against them, in insurrectionist rebellion, as with the reams of unreadable poems written to protest American involvement in Vietnam.

In "Music Is International" it may be said that Auden has, in at least one sense, made things easy for himself, since music may be considered a nonreferential, if not in fact a noncognitive, language. Admittedly, this did not prevent Plato from putting it to political uses in his *Republic*, and it is often used to stir emotions for reasons that are specifically nonmusical. A good deal of this skewed and essentially political purpose is expressed in the observation that "military justice is to Justice as military music is to Music," attributed to Georges Clemençeau. Indeed, the first "use" of music in Auden's poem (which is dated 1947) is the sort of music that might be heard by an "unamerican survivor" of the calamities of WWII, who hears the triumphant sounds of military brass bands as proclaiming the absolute conquest (in the next world as here) of American values.

The unamerican survivor
Hears angels drinking fruit-juice with their wives
Or making money in an open
Unpolicied air.

This is followed by a set of rhetorical questions. What do we want music
for? What should it do or be? Should it, for example (to paraphrase a
passage quoted above), conjure before us a kind of universally acceptable
pastoral landscape, "a commuter's wish," in which "nothing dreadful
ever happened"? One may be permitted to doubt whether in fact this is
precisely what happens when we listen to, say, a Bach unaccompanied
violin partita or even a Chopin ballade. Still, Auden is right when he claims
that

We are easy to trap,
Being Adam's children, as thirsty
For mere illusion still as when the first
Comfortable heresy crooned to
The proud flesh founded on the self-made wound,
And what we find rousing or touching
Tells us little and confuses us much.

There follows a passage about the subornation, by the "progressive"
kind of tyrant, of composers who could "melt the legal mind / With a
visceral A-ha," make a dwarf believe he was a giant, bamboozle "the most
oppressed," and so forth, "So that today one recognizes / The Machiavel
by the hair in his eyes, / His conductor's hands." The powers here
attributed to music are extraordinary, and may not be meant to be taken
quite literally. But they point to the serious error of taking art for magic,
and using magic for nonartistic purposes. In the midst of this magic,
however, the poem reminds us, "the jussive / Elohim are here too." There
are a number of meanings to the Hebrew word, and one of them is a name
of God. But the one clearly intended here, as indicated by its use in the
plural, would be roughly equivalent to the potentates and masters of the
earth, who in certain passages of the Bible (Psalms 82:1, for example) are
referred to ironically. So the "jussive Elohim" are the "progressive
tyrants" who are not going to be bamboozled, but instead will commis-
sion the art intended to bamboozle others. Their presence here (they are
"here too") might excite our anger, since they are so clearly the enemies

of art except when it serves a particular end they have in mind. (All considerations of music quite apart, there was much on the public record in the course of Auden's lifetime to justify his deep fear and distrust of "progressive tyrants." To give a single Chinese instance, the Great Leap Forward, 1958–60—an ill-conceived utopian experiment intended, in the words of Tu Wei-Ming, professor of Chinese history and philosophy at Harvard, "to enable China to surpass the West in industrial productivity within fifteen years"—in combination with natural disasters led to massive starvation, killing an estimated forty million people.) But at just this point, Auden's serious religious considerations present themselves, as he recalls that "To forgive is not so / Simple as it is made to sound," yet we are under obligation to forgive even those who would, by the subversion of art, deceive or enslave us. The solution, which is nearly mystical as Auden presents it, is to

> listen
> To the song which seems to absorb all this,
> For these halcyon structures are useful
> As structures go—though not to be confused
> With anything really important
> Like feeding strays or looking pleased when caught
> By a bore or a hideola.

The capacity to "absorb all this" suggests that music can reconcile even its most unworthy enemies with a kind of superior overview that takes everything into account. The structures of music are "halcyon" in their capacity to calm, and, presumably, to reconcile. But their value is *morally* inferior to the ordinary decencies and kindnesses that are enjoined upon us all. Auden has cunningly introduced some moral considerations that do not always play a part in aesthetic discourse, and from which some commentators have explicitly excluded it. Such moral-free discourse conscientiously avoids terms like "use" as being either explicitly or implicitly utilitarian, and thus subject to abuse for nonaesthetic purposes. Its "use" in this poem (after all, Eliot wrote about "The Use of Poetry") turns out to be that, for the undeserving and unexpecting soul, it provides the occasion to rejoice "at the sudden mansion" of joy. And joy itself is a precious commodity, since "We may some day need very much to / Remember when we were happy." At this point the poem imagines two bleak scenarios, the kind in which lonely persons would need to recall an earlier mansion of joy.

One such
Future would be the exile's ending
With no graves to visit, no socks to mend.
Another to be short of breath yet
Staying on to oblige, postponing death.

These are purely imaginary, conjectural endings, but it is impressive that
Auden is able to envision them in all their bleakness, and to feel the
pressing need to express gratitude for any former happiness that he or we
may have encountered in the past. And it may be worth saying that
gratitude is the attractive ingredient of a good number of his poems,
especially the later ones. But the later ones also acknowledge loneliness
and anxiety, and with a witty and slightly operatic bravado, he was able,
in April 1971 (that is, not long before his death in 1973), to write a poem
called "Talking to Myself," in which he addresses his body, concluding
this way:

Time, we both know, will decay You, and already
I'm scared of our divorce: I've seen some horrid ones.
Remember: when *Le Bon Dieu* says to You *Leave him!*,
please, please, for His sake and mine, pay no attention
to my piteous *Don'ts,* but bugger off quickly.

This is clearly a very mixed attitude about one's own death, with presumably equal weight given to both sides. In any case, Auden could envision
wishing to die, and, while he would never have committed suicide, there
is that in Carpenter's account of the position in which his body was found
after death that suggests he had deliberately lain on his left side, the side
which he knew to be most dangerous to the heart which had given him
medical trouble in the past. As for the solitary life of the exile, Auden was
not only himself largely an exile, and often lonely, but he knew and
celebrated a good number of others (like Freud, Toller, Hannah Arendt,
Isaiah Berlin, Elizabeth Drew, Igor Stravinsky, Neil Little, Teckla Clark,
Joseph Brodsky) who also were displaced persons.

The poem closes with a statement about what music actually does; the
claim is a wonderful mixture of modesty and grandeur.

Listen! Even the dinner waltz in
Its formal way is a voice that assaults
International wrong, so quickly,

Completely delivering to the sick,
    Sad, soiled prosopon of our ageing
Present the perdition of all her rage.

Of this a number of things need to be remarked. There is, to begin with, the unassuming modesty of the dinner waltz, the formality of which is of a comparatively elementary kind, yet its voice is said to assault "international wrong," a phrase we will remember from an earlier context, "September 1, 1939," now stricken from the canon:

Out of the mirror they stare,
Imperialism's face
And the international wrong.

It is difficult to say quite how the voice of the waltz assaults this international wrong, but we may assume that there are two ways. First, its very formality speaks of a convention voluntarily accepted and participated in, and therefore representing a mutual accord. Secondly, by presenting the soul with a "sudden mansion . . . of joy," the music repudiates the disorder of states, their hostilities and suspicions. The word "prosopon" is a theological term, and is usually applied to a conception or presentation of one of the three persons of the Trinity, and is one of the meanings of "hypostasis." But it has a secondary meaning, which is the one Auden intends here: outward appearance or aspect. And the poem is asserting that music can deliver "to the sick, / Sad, soiled [appearance] of our ageing / Present the perdition of all her rage." What is described here is nothing less than an Aristotelian catharsis by which all our rage is purged by an art with quasi-religious powers.

The other Phi Beta Kappa poem, "Under Which Lyre: A Reactionary Tract for the Times," is a companion poem to the one just discussed in more than the formal sense of the occasions for which they were both composed. This one, written the previous year for ceremonies at Harvard, also deals with the danger to the artist (and to the soundness and health of the social fabric as well) of attempts on the part of authorities of any stripe to suborn artistic works and force them into the fixed idiom of "official art." This poem is, understandably and deservedly, one of Auden's most popular and admired poems; one reason is that while its theme and the views it expresses are very much those of the Columbia ode, "Under Which Lyre" is much more easily accessible, and is moreover written in a brisk stanzaic pattern that exhibits all the ingenuity of light verse. If "Music Is International" may be called elitist, as I have ventured to do, then "Under Which Lyre" may perhaps be called subversive—though it may also be worth pointing out that often enough the subversive impulse is merely another guise of the elitist, both of them speaking or acting in behalf of an exclusive or excluded minority.

The only time I can remember Auden saying anything about any of his own poems concerned this one. He acknowledged that at least a part of its purpose was to embarrass the "pompous stuffed shirt" who had invited him to write and read a Phi Beta Kappa poem for Harvard. He was much too discreet to say who this was, and the small group of us to whom he was speaking were allowed to conjecture to our hearts' content, Harvard having then as now its full quota of such persons. It was therefore with a sense of having an intuition confirmed that I read the following in Alan Ansen's *Table Talk,* where Auden is quoted as saying,

When I was delivering my Phi Beta Kappa poem in Cambridge, I met Conant for about five minutes. "This is the real enemy," I thought to myself. And I'm sure he had the same impression about me. He is the real Prince Hal and gives the notion of sheer naked power. I took the line of chiming in with him, of being terribly cynical about politics. Of course, I didn't feel that way at all, and I'm sure I didn't take him in for a second.

You know, I should like to ask him whether he was the one that made the final decision to drop the atomic bomb. The scientists got a pledge from Roosevelt that the bomb would not be used until an announcement had been made. But then, of course, Roosevelt died, and after that . . . One shrewdly suspects that Conant gave the deciding word.

My suspicions about who the "stuffed shirt" was that Auden was trying to embarrass may be no sounder than Auden's about who decided to drop the atomic bomb. But the fourth stanza of the poem—

Professors back from secret missions
Resume their proper eruditions,
    Though some regret it;
They like their uniforms a lot,
They met some big wheels, and do not
    Let you forget it.

—would politely camouflage a more specific reference to Conant, who took great pride in having been appointed the United States high commissioner for Germany from 1953 to '55 and the United States ambassador to the Federal Republic of Germany from 1955 to '57. Still more to the point, he had served as chairman of the National Defense Research Committee from 1941 to '46 and did a lot of confidential advising of the administration on scientific matters throughout the war. Within the context of the poem it is clear that in the "dialectic strife" between the followers of "precocious Hermes" and "pompous Apollo," the Apollonians, with Auden as with Nietzsche, stand for a life-threatening order and are associated with all "big wheels," whether in academia or not.

The poem wittily opposes Hermes to Apollo, for both of them are associated with the lyre—hence the title. By noon of the day on which he was born, Hermes had left his cradle and invented the lyre, "killing a tortoise . . . and making the instrument from its shell," as one authority reports. On the very same day, he drove off fifty cows belonging to Apollo, making them walk backwards so that they should not be traced by their hoofprints, and then returning to his cradle. This made him on the day of his birth a rival of Apollo and a patron of thieves (and thus of subversives). The story is told in the Fourth Homeric Hymn.

It's difficult to know what remains to be said about this frequently anthologized and quoted poem. It is written with a cheerful élan and gusto, and it deliberately omits any of the serious, possibly tragic, notes that are sounded in "Music Is International." To the degree that this poem is in any way about Auden himself, it can only be asserted that he decidedly aligns himself on the side of Hermes and those who "do their best when they / Are told they oughtn't." He furthermore identifies himself with Falstaff, in contradistinction to "the prig Prince Hal," with whom, to Ansen, he had identified Conant. The smack at the existentialists, who appear "in fake Hermetic uniforms / Behind our battle-line," is probably directed at Sartre, since it is said of them that, though they are in complete despair, they go on writing, and Sartre was given to an ungovernable prolixity. Of his very long biography of Flaubert, Richard Ellmann commented, "His eloquence about the unknown is staggering. The flimsier the documentation, the more he has to say."

What finally seems to enchant us all is that the poem, while filled with incidental felicities of a witty and charming kind, never flags in its energy or capacity to entertain, and finally culminates in a crowning set of four stanzas that, in an amusing parody of a sacred text, present "the Hermetic

Decalogue," which, being sacred only to Hermes, patron god of subversion, lies, and thievery, has no obligation to be pious in any conventional sense. The laws that are laid down are unfailingly amusing, and most of them, as in their Biblical counterpart, are expressed in terms of prohibitions. But this Decalogue ends with three positive commands.

> Read *The New Yorker,* trust in God;
> And take short views.

*The New Yorker* is presumably enjoined to be read because of its lack of pomposity, and its ability to present serious as well as amusing matters in an engaging way. To "trust in God" is precisely to flout the prudential considerations of the managerial executives who are the butt of this poem, as well as of an earlier one in the same book, called "The Managers." Finally, the brief command to "take short views" is indebted to the Reverend Sydney Smith, the Whig and Anglican clergyman Auden greatly admired. This small detail, shorn of its serious context, may be the nearest Auden comes in this poem to saying anything deeply personal about himself. In 1820 Smith wrote to one Lady Morpeth a letter which contains twenty specific instructions, the very enumeration of which may well have suggested to Auden his own decalogue.

> Dear Lady Georgiana, — Nobody has suffered more from low spirits than I have done — so I feel for you. 1st. Live as well as you dare. 2nd. Go into the shower-bath with a small quantity of water at a temperature low enough to give you a slight sensation of cold, 75 degrees or 80 degrees. 3rd. Amusing books. 4th. Short views of human life — not further than dinner or tea. 5th. Be as busy as you can. 6th. See as much as you can of those friends who respect and like you. 7th. And of those acquaintances who amuse you. 8th. Make no secret of low spirits to your friends, but talk of them freely — they are always worse for dignified concealment. 9th. Attend to the effects tea and coffee produce upon you. 10th. Compare your lot with that of other people. 11th. Don't expect too much from human life — a sorry business at the best. 12th. Avoid poetry, dramatic representations (except comedy), music, serious novels, melancholy, sentimental people, and everything likely to excite feelings of emotion, not ending in active benevolence. 13th. *Do good,* and endeavour to please everybody of every degree. 14th. Be as much as you can in the open air without fatigue. 15th. Make the room where you commonly

sit gay and pleasant. 16th. Struggle by little and little against idleness. 17th. Don't be too severe upon yourself, or underrate yourself, but do yourself justice. 18th. Keep good blazing fires. 19th. Be firm and constant in the exercise of rational religion. 20th. Believe me, dear Lady Georgiana, Very truly yours ,— Sydney Smith.

*Nones* closes with two poems that are prayers of one kind or another. The first, "Precious Five," addresses the five senses in turn and, in the final stanza, all at once. In each case, the individual sense is enjoined to be obedient (the nose to be patient, the ears to be modest, the hands to be civil, the eyes to look straight, the tongue to praise) in pursuance of what seems very much like the ascetic discipline of the Catholic Church known as "the custody of the senses." One of Hopkins' biographers tells us that "during lent 1869 [Father Christopher] Fitzsimon would not allow [Hopkins] to fast, but did give him leave for a custody-of-the-eyes penance which lasted from January to July and entailed looking downwards for most of the time, rather than gazing out on to the garden and the park, or looking at other people when he spoke to them." On analogy to this severe and orthodox practice, Auden undertakes to regulate the sensuous life along honorable and indeed religious lines.

The nose is besought to be patient, as it needs must be, since it has no capacity to anticipate. It therefore must humbly serve "the present moment well," and though by the end of the stanza it may be enjoined to point "from memory to hope," that is a way it cannot take by dint of its very nature. The poem first locates it in "That calm enchanted wood, / That grave world where you stood / So gravely at its middle, / Its oracle and riddle." I am by no means confident that I understand these lines, but I think they mean to represent a child with his nose buried in a book of fairy tales, and where, by the poetic process of synecdoche, it-and-he are in the middle of that world. But by mid-stanza that world has altered, and the nose is now simply a bridge from mouth to brow, a projection "Whose oddness may provoke / To a mind-saving joke / A mind that would it were / An apathetic sphere." The "mind-saving joke" of a mind that would like to regard itself as featureless may merely mean that the mind is given to discarnate vanities and other heretical views. But it may also express the partly concealed unhappiness of one who is embarrassed by his nose, as, for example, Edward Lear was, as Auden's poem about him makes clear; and Lear's pathetic loneliness was something Auden was able strongly to identify with.

Like the nose, the ears too are warned that the mind, now called "paranoic," is their enemy, since it craves to be diverted by any caper upon the stage of life, and being literal-minded, is discontent with fiction (that is, art) and prefers "rumors partly true," which is to say, the normal scandal that passes for the news of the day. The ears are enjoined to submit their quickness and levity to rule, in the manner of the oriental monkey who must "hear no evil." Such discipline will make all sounds grateful to the ear, all shall "seem natural, not one / Fantastic or banal." And just as the nose cannot anticipate, so the ears cannot "place" (that is, identify) their luck, which is the power that created them. (In each of the stanzas, the last line is a statement of the limitations of the sense being addressed.)

The hands (the sense of touch, "these pickers and stealers") are directed to be "civil," and told that though they themselves cannot read, others can read them, which means that they are telltale in the common sense of giving some indication of the kind of work and class to which their owner belongs (as Sherlock Holmes can deduce the precise profession of a man by a glance at his hands), or that they are subject to interpretation by palmists. In either case, they give themselves away, including the outbursts of wrath or greed in which they figured, and will be decoded, whether sympathetically or otherwise, by eyes unknown. The hands are told to honor the labor of their predecessors, those earlier hands who fought, engraved the Decalogue in stone, and served in a world Homeric but immoral and obsolete; those old hands are buried, and are no longer to be imitated. These present hands must make and give to a future they cannot see.

The "naked" eyes, naked because exposed by the peeled-back eyelid and also betokening a special candor and truthfulness, are commanded to look, but not to look at themselves in a mirror, to avoid the sort of narcissism that might be engendered by self-contemplation, "Lest in a tête-à-tête / Of glances double-crossed, / Both knowing and both known, / Your nakedness be lost." The doublecross is not only betrayal but growing cross-eyed from self-approval. The knowingness and being known of this kind of self-consciousness will make the eyes lose their primal innocence. The eyes are further instructed to notice that, looking outward rather than inward (thus being objective and empirical rather than subjective and romantic), they will observe a characteristic asymmetry in the paired eyes of certain kinds of people. These eyes ("one shameless, one ashamed") indicate that their possessor longs for a sexual encounter but fears it at the same time, and so would make a very doubtful sexual partner.

Possessors of such eyes are to be contrasted with the "eyes met now and then / Looking from living men, / Which in petrarchan fashion / Play opposite the heart, / Their humor to her passion." This becomes complicated only because of the numbers of pairs involved. There are first the pair of eyes of the beholder; then the pairs of eyes upon which he gazes, some of them stricken with sexual anxiety, others not. Those that are not set themselves in opposition to the heart "in petrarchan fashion," composing, with the heart, another pairing. The heart, here represented in traditional Petrarchan convention as feminine and the seat of passion, will be courted by the eyes, exhibiting "masculine" humor. And they will further make a contrast of "Her nature to their art / For mutual undeceiving." What we have here is a conventional Petrarchan or courtly courtship of the kind described in Castiglione. The man, represented by the eyes, is witty, charming, deft, and artful; the woman, represented by the heart, is natural and passionate. Each gender exhibits its own special virtues in a conventionally approved style of courtship which involves, in spite of the playing of roles, no deception on either side. Sight can never "prove" belief, though, paradoxically, "seeing is believing." In any case, the eyes can never be the eyes of the beloved, but only of the lover.

The tongue (the sense of taste, but here chiefly the instrument of articulation) is told to praise the Earthly Muse, quite appropriately, since these bodily faculties are the means whereby we apprehend and delight in the world in which we live. The Earthly Muse is to be praised "by number and by name," "number" meaning in verse ("Then feed on thoughts that voluntary move / Harmonious numbers, as the wakeful bird / Sings darkling, and in shadiest covert hid / Tunes her nocturnal note."— *Paradise Lost*, iii, 37–40). As for her name, in a poem in his next book Auden would address her under the name of Gaea. Among her many attributes is the knowledge of everything that is done on earth. The tongue is told to feel no embarrassment in composing verses of praise, since both nimble and lame tongues have found favor in the past. Being earthy, her "port" (meaning "deportment") and sudden ways should not surprise, nor the fact that she is now reasonable, now unreasonable, "now fish-wife and now queen." Being earthly, she is also the figure of mutability, and is thus furnished with Fortune's wheel "of appetite and season." This realm of Temporality which is hers will remind the tongue of its own aging, recalling what the speaker was as a child, and still becomes again "at any drink or meal": an appetitive creature, "Unlettered, savage, dumb, / Down there below the waist." This creature of appetites (includ-

ing, of course, the sexual one) will in its savage state make no discrimina-
tions but simply satisfy as expediently as possible its immediate craving,
forgetting that it has developed in the course of time into an "animal of
taste" that can exercise critical judgment. The two creatures (who, of
course, are simply two aspects of the same person) are described as
"twins." The tongue is finally urged once again to attempt a tribute in
verse to that Muse to whom, because of her infinite variety, "all styles
belong," and to tell "the truth she cannot make," because, Muse though
she be, she is not a poet.

The final stanza addresses all five senses together; and they are told to
be happy. The final stanza is the only one that does not conclude on a
note of disqualification. The senses are instructed to rejoice purely for
their own existence; they are not rational faculties, and should not demand
reasons for rejoicing, though if they care to they may take satisfaction of
immediate appetites ("love or alcohol or gold," the final one appropriate
for those "pickers and stealers") as sufficient cause. There is a slightly
schoolmarmish tone that will continue to resurface now and then in the
later poems, which here is audible in the phrase "do as you are told." The
"I" of the poem, which is rational, could find plenty of reasons to find
fault with "what is going on," which we may take to be the normal and
abnormal calamities of existence. The sky to which those complaints,
groans, and petitions would be addressed "would only wait

> Till all my breath was gone
> And then reiterate
> As if I wasn't there
> That singular command
> I do not understand,
> *Bless what there is for being,*
> Which has to be obeyed, for
> What else am I made for,
> Agreeing or disagreeing.

A number of things might be noted here. To begin with a small one,
Auden's deliberate avoidance of the subjunctive here ("As if I wasn't
there" in a place where "weren't" would have fit the meter just as well)
is an index of how much he had adopted a local American idiom, even
when it was bad grammar. Something of the same abandonment of his
English speech occurs in "The Fall of Rome," where he rhymes "clerk"
with "work." Such a rhyme is decisively American, and clearly distin-

guished from the standard British pronunciation as employed, for example, by William Empson in "Just a Smack at Auden":

> What was said by Marx, boys, what did he perpend?
> No good being sparks, boys, waiting for the end.
> Treason of the clerks, boys, curtains that descend,
> Lights becoming darks, boys, waiting for the end.

More important is the perfect assent to the command to be happy, and, still more, to *Bless what there is for being*. This assent is plainly a religious act of faith, since it is made in obedience to a "singular command," and is made without regard to his capacity to understand, "agreeing or disagreeing." There is to this statement a piety, a patience, a humility, and, in a manner I think characteristic of some of Auden's most engaging poetry, a determination to find grounds for gratitude. Without presumption to any claims of grandeur, it may fairly be pointed out that the command for assent and for praise *without understanding* bears a striking resemblance to the voice which, in chapter 38 of Job, speaks out of a whirlwind and demands, "Where wast thou when I laid the foundations of the earth? declare, if thou hast understanding." And it consorts with Auden's unwillingness to indulge in self-pity.

The concluding poem in *Nones* is "A Walk After Dark." Had he cared to, Auden could have embellished it with an epigraph (a practice in which he seldom indulged) from Kant's celebrated conclusion to the *Critique of Pure Reason:* "Two things fill the mind with ever-increasing wonder and awe, the more often and the more intensely the mind of thought is drawn to them: the starry heavens above me and the moral law within me." The poem is virtually undeviating in its attention to these twinned topics, and they are ingeniously linked to a third, which was always important to the poet—his age. This poem, written in August 1948, when Auden was forty-one, makes a firm point of declaring himself "middle-aged," a condition he had also acknowledged in the 1946 poem "Under Which Lyre," in the lines about "those who like myself turn pale / As we approach with ragged sail / The fattening forties." Auden took a ritual pleasure in celebrating his own birthday, though not, I would imagine, for the usual reasons of wishing to be the center of attention. Indeed, he had been known to leave some of these parties quite early in order to keep to his schedule of rising early and maintaining regular working hours. But he remarked somewhere that it was especially hazardous for a writer to forget his own age, and the celebration of one's birthday is a handy way of being reminded of the passage of time. Auden may have felt this way because, as he wrote, he was the youngest of three sibling boys, in consequence of which he had grown into the habit of feeling the youngest of any company he was in; and such a feeling can lead to all kinds of self-deception. The requirement, therefore, of knowing your own age is a way of facing an important and elementary kind of truth that a lot of people go out of their way to avoid. On this topic, William Plomer wrote a poem that is withering in more than one sense of the word; it is called "The Playboy of the Demi-World: 1938," of which I give the opening and closing lines.

> Aloft in Heavenly Mansions, Doubleyou One —
> Just Mayfair flats, but certainly sublime —
> You'll find the abode of D'Arcy Honeybunn,
> A rose-red sissy half as old as time.
>
> . . . . .
>
> "The kindest man alive," so people say,
> "Perpetual youth!" But have you seen his eyes?
> The eyes of some old saurian in decay
> That asks no questions and is told no lies.
>
> Under the fribble lurks a worn-out sage
> Heavy with disillusion, and alone;
> So never say to D'Arcy, "Be your age!" —
> He'd shrivel up at once or turn to stone.

Auden's "A Walk After Dark" begins in a spirit of cheerfulness and innocence.

> A cloudless night like this
> Can set the spirit soaring;
> After a tiring day
> The clockwork spectacle is
> Impressive in a slightly boring
> Eighteenth-century way.

There is an amiableness here, and an untroubled lightheartedness that can treat as a joke what Basil Willey in *The Eighteenth Century Background* speaks of as "that more subtle modern atheism, that Cartesian teaching which, by reducing the Deity to an abstract first cause, leaves us with a dead universe of matter and motion, virtually untenanting Creation of its God." I am not, of course, accusing Auden of atheism; the charm of the stanza is largely based on its spirit of frivolity, and a lively sense of a "clockwork" universe as being a distinctly passé and outmoded idea that should be classed with perukes, minuets, and sedan chairs. Indeed, it is the very outdatedness of the image that leads directly to a consideration of the poet's past in the next stanza.

> It soothed adolescence a lot
> To meet so shameless a stare;
> The things I did could not
> Be as shocking as they said
> If that would still be there
> After the shocked were dead.

There is something winning and precocious in this view of the witness and antiquity of the firmament. It speaks with all the self-justifying wit and assumed objectivity of the young. Auden is playing with scales of huge difference in size and time, yet in a manner common enough in moral, philosophical, and theological discourse. The diversion of attention to his own youth reminds him that it, too, is démodé.

> Now, unready to die
> But already at the stage
> When one starts to dislike the young,
> I am glad those points in the sky
> May also be counted among
> The creatures of middle-age.

Again we are aware of the good-spiritedness that can liken the middle age of a human to that of a star, continuing to play with the discrepancies of time systems. Astronomers are now bold enough to hazard serious guesses about the age of the solar system, as well as the galaxies beyond it, and even to formulate estimates of the lifespan of stars. But a new note of slight malaise has crept in with the admission of having attained to an age "when one starts to dislike the young." The reason for the dislike is complex; it may well involve envy on the part of one who admits to being no longer young himself; but it probably also involves the easy callowness with which youth justifies itself, as the second stanza indicated. In this second way, the third stanza is the poet's middle-aged criticism of his adolescent self. And the next stanza is composed in the spirit of good-natured acceptance of the poet's present condition—not that he has much choice about it, but as a state in some ways preferable to the earlier one.

> It's cosier thinking of night
> As more an Old People's Home
> Than a shed for a faultless machine,
> That the red pre-Cambrian light
> Is gone like Imperial Rome
> Or myself at seventeen.

"Cosy" is the sort of word that has jarred some of Auden's readers, and its use here suggests that Auden had only the most fugitive sense of what an "Old People's Home" is actually like. Late in his life he did visit such a place, and wrote of it in a 1970 poem called "Old People's Home," which concludes, "Am I cold to wish for a speedy / painless dormition, pray, as I know she prays, / that God or Nature will abrupt her earthly function?" But there is no indication in "A Walk After Dark" that anything is wrong except age itself. I have no doubt that he would have been appalled by the scandals of neglect, cruelty, and avarice that have recently attached to those institutions in the United States. The "shed for a faultless machine," to which the Old People's Home is to be preferred, harks back to the clockwork universe of the first stanza. "Pre-Cambrian" is a geologic term, scarcely surprising in the work of a poet so devoted to geology from his earliest years. It denotes a time in excess of six hundred million years ago, preceding the Paleozoic era. John Fuller explains that "the red light emitted by the furthest stars that are going away from us at great speeds can be used as an indication of their age, and . . . they are often so far away and so old that they may not even exist any longer." There is probably very little regret expressed in the stanza for the passing either of imperial Rome or of the poet as he was at seventeen.

> Yet however much we may like
> The stoic manner in which
> The classical authors wrote,
> Only the young and the rich
> Have the nerve or the figure to strike
> The lacrimae rerum note.

That "lacrimae rerum note" is a matter of some complexity. The phrase is Virgil's, and comes from a speech of Aeneas' in the first book of the *Aeneid*. Having arrived at Carthage, Aeneas, to his great surprise, sees stonework representations, sculpture or bas relief, representing scenes of the Trojan War, and depicting both the Greeks and the Trojans. He sees Agamemnon, Priam, Menelaus, and Achilles, and, in the Rolfe Humphries translation,

> He is moved to tears.
> "What place in all the world," he asks Achates,
> "Is empty of our sorrow? There is Priam!
> Look! even here there are rewards for praise,
> There are tears for things, and what men suffer touches
> The human heart."

This speech is a deliberate imitation of a passage in the eighth book of the *Odyssey,* where, in the court of Nausicaa's parents, Odysseus, having received generous entertainment, asks a blind bard, who has been singing about the adulterous affairs of Ares and Aphrodite, to sing instead about the Trojan War. In Robert Fitzgerald's translation,

> The splendid minstrel sang it.
> And Odysseus
> let the bright molten tears run down his cheeks,
> weeping the way a wife mourns for her lord
> on the lost field where he had gone down fighting
> the day of wrath that came upon his children.

Both Homer and Virgil are concerned with the feeling of grief at the vanishing of past glories. Both protagonists, recalling the same war from the vantage point of a later and comparative safety, weep in gratitude that the past is not wholly obliterated since it is preserved in works of art; but also in grief at irreparable loss. The grief is general, diffused, manly, and stoic, and exhibited by men who, though on opposed sides of the conflict, are both military commanders. When Auden declares that today "Only the young and the rich / Have the nerve or the figure to strike / The lacrimae rerum note," he means that both the rich (who have the nerve) and the young (who have the figure) can feel themselves exempt from the ravages of time, and enjoy a special protection that allows them to adopt heroic posturings. There is here a suggestion that the classical authors themselves are somehow démodé, since the heroic stance is not one that the modern world finds completely plausible. Auden will make this point more seriously, and at greater length, when he comes to write "The Shield of Achilles."

"A Walk After Dark" continues:

> For the present stalks abroad
> Like the past and its wronged again
> Whimper and are ignored,
> And the truth cannot be hid;
> Somebody chose their pain,
> What needn't have happened did.

It is difficult to read these lines without hearing behind them, and in the same metrical pattern, "But who can live for long / In an euphoric dream; / Out of the mirror they stare, / Imperialism's face / And the international wrong." By this point the poem has abandoned the spirit of levity with which it began, and a deeply serious moral tone, reminiscent of much earlier poetry, has supervened. No major international crisis such as the one that occasioned "September 1, 1939" initiated this poem; but "the wronged," like "the poor," are still with us; they still "whimper and are ignored." And "somebody," whose identity is carefully cloaked, is to blame. The concealing of who is responsible does not exempt us from the possibility of accusing ourselves, as the lines of the earlier poem accuse us when seeing the international wrong staring "out of the mirror."

And now, in the penultimate stanza, the most unsettling and ambiguous note in the whole poem is sounded.

> Occurring this very night
> By no established rule,
> Some event may already have hurled
> Its first little No at the right
> Of the laws we accept to school
> Our post-diluvian world:

The unresolvable puzzle here concerns those laws. Certainly our world is in need of regulation, as the Flood itself suggests; but we cannot be sure that the laws we have effected are the right ones, and that they may not, in some grotesque way, be responsible for the miseries of "the wronged." These "wronged" of the present are just like the "wronged" of the past, though we enjoy the delusion that we are much superior to earlier ages. If our laws are just, then the "little No" to them is uttered by ignorant, self-serving malcontents; but if they are unjust, that "little No" is the first sign of what may become insurrection, as, for example, in the first Luddite destruction of textile looms. The stanza allows us the equivocal sense that either side is potentially right or wrong, and that this is itself part of the human dilemma. And the poem has been approaching this state of uneasiness by careful calculation from the first. It closes the collection of poems with these lines.

> But the stars burn on overhead,
> Unconscious of final ends,
> As I walk home to bed,
> Asking what judgment waits
> My person, all my friends,
> And these United States.

The poem is dated August 1948. Some important laws that we accept to "school / Our post-diluvian world" had recently been instituted. WWII had come to an end in 1945. The first General Assembly of the United Nations opened in London on January 10. Twenty-two Nazi leaders were convicted of war crimes at Nuremberg on September 30, eleven of them sentenced to death by hanging on October 1. In the same year, American miners struck for a guaranteed $100-a-month pension for retired mine workers, and they were opposed by the federal government. The laws enacted to regulate our world did not prove to be wiser, or more effective, or more humane than any earlier laws, such as, for example, those of "Imperial Rome." The laws, in their inadequacy, are clearly contrasted to the "judgment" of the final stanza, which has about it a tone that is little short of penitent. The poem's brilliance and "drama" reside in its tonal curve from levity to seriousness, from complacency to something close to anguish. The inquiry about "judgment" is nothing short of prayerful; and the prayer is made in behalf of those, beginning with the poet himself, and enlarging to contain his entire adopted nation, who must find themselves responsible for "the wronged," for what has happened, for the laws that are meant to school us.

# VIII. In Solitude, for Company:
## *The Shield of Achilles*

*The Shield of Achilles* was first published in February 1955. It is one of the most clearly and formally composed volumes Auden ever produced. It begins with one sequence, *Bucolics,* and closes with another, *Horae Canonicae,* and between them appears an intermediary section of assorted lyrics under the general heading *In Sunshine and in Shade.* The very title of this intermediary section indicates its transitional role, participating as it does in the largely cheerful, playful, and secular pleasures of the landscape poems that precede it, as well as in the serious, darkened, tragic tone of blood-sacrifice that haunts all about the religious poems with which the volume ends. There are, moreover, important suggestions that the playful and serious, the mundane and the religious, are not wholly separable but instead intimately linked.

It is my view, which I share with others, that the first sequence, *Bucolics,* is, generally speaking, less successful than the religious sequence, and I shall accord it less careful notice. Every one of its seven constituent poems bears an individual dedication, though Auden, in what seems to me an unprecedented manner, was to change his mind about one of these. The first poem in the sequence, "Winds," is dedicated to Alexis Léger, whom we know more familiarly as St. John Perse, author of a poem called *"Vents,"* published in 1946. The poem, beginning with some of Auden's characteristic randomness of the essay poem, takes up, midway, an Horatian mode of address to the "Goddess of winds and wisdom," who is to preserve mankind (by virtue of the very devious-ness of the winds themselves) from calcified rigidities or doctrinaire inflexibilities.

The second poem, dedicated to the composer Nicholas Nabokov, cousin of the novelist Vladimir, is called "Woods," and concludes with a line that might rejoice the heart of any dedicated environmentalist, "A culture is no better than its woods." On the way to this conclusion, Auden remarks presciently, "This great society is going smash." The poem is written in particularly regular six-line pentameter stanzas, rhyming *a b a b c c,* a form sometimes called "the stave of six." So established and so familiar is this form that we cannot fail to be struck by a serious lapse from it in Auden's second stanza. As it appeared in the first edition of the book, the first two lines of the second stanza read,

> Reduced to patches owned by hunting squires
> Of villages with ovens and stocks,

which was clearly a misprint that Auden failed to catch; but when he came to re-edit, and in some cases revise, his poems for the 1957 *Collected Shorter Poems,* he no less carelessly changed the second of the lines above to read, "Of villages with ovens and a stocks," a reading which, to my considerable surprise, has been maintained in all editions of the *Collected Poems,* including the First International Edition dated February 1991. It seems indisputable from the meticulous observation of formal considerations throughout the rest of the fifty-four-line poem that what Auden intended must have been "Of villages with ovens and with stocks."

"Lakes" is dedicated to Isaiah Berlin, and while formally fastidious in one regard it is less so in another. The first stanza goes,

> A lake allows an average father, walking slowly,
>    To circumvent it in an afternoon,
> And any healthy mother to halloo the children
>    Back to her bedtime from their games across:
> (Anything bigger than that, like Michigan or Baikal,
>    Though potable, is an 'estranging sea').

The stanza alternates hexameter and pentameter lines, unrhymed but formally poised. The quoted phrase is, of course, from Matthew Arnold, and I think it may be worth providing a little of Arnold's context, since the small phrase may have carried a private, and even a painful, burden of meaning for Auden. Arnold's poem, "To Marguerite — Continued," begins and ends this way:

> Yes! in the sea of life enisled,
> With echoing straits between us thrown,
> Dotting the shoreless watery wild,
> We mortal millions live *alone.*
> The islands feel the enclasping flow,
> And then their endless bounds they know.

Who ordered that their longing's fire
Should be, as soon as kindled, cooled?
Who renders vain their deep desire? —
A God, a God their severance ruled!
And bade betwixt their shores to be
The umplumbed, salt, estranging sea.

Right in the first of Auden's stanzas, which embarks on a tone of resolute domesticity with its mention of father, mother, and children, there is the submerged theme of loneliness and isolation of Arnold's poem. The "domestic" note turns out to be Auden's bulwark against the pain of larger, more "estranging" bodies of water; and this defensive posture resembles another, with which the poem ends. Auden employs it elsewhere as well. It is the posture of safety that allows one to examine alternate situations from the dangers of which one is exempted either by choice or by circumstance. We shall encounter this again when we come to consider the poem called "A Permanent Way." And this safety Auden came more and more to feel was imposed upon him by his advancing age, although he associated it more and more with the security of childhood. The final stanza of "Lakes" runs,

It is unlikely I shall ever keep a swan
    Or build a tower on any small tombolo,
But that's not going to stop me wondering what sort
    Of lake I would decide on if I should.
Moraine, pot, oxbow, glint, crater, piedmont, dimple . . . ?
    Just reeling off their names is ever so comfy.

Not a few readers have been made precisely *uncomfortable* by the nursery diction of the last three words. The stanza's little cascade of geological terms, such as were dear to Auden from his childhood, in context bespeak a world of imagination, a safe haven. Carpenter reports Auden as one who, even as a child, carefully formulated and envisioned a unique Eden of his own. "This is how he described his private passion: 'I spent a great many of my waking hours in the construction and elaboration of a private sacred world, the basic elements of which were a landscape, northern and limestone, and an industry, lead mining.' In his imagination he was, he said, the 'sole autocrat' of this dream country—whose features also included narrow-gauge tramways and overshot waterwheels." So I think it can be argued that the "domestic" details of the first stanza are what may be regarded as a proleptic anticipation for a very childlike conclusion, made the more secure and invulnerable because it is purely imagined or, in part, recollected.

This opening and closing gives the poem an initial appearance of shape. (That Auden believed poetry should exhibit such shapeliness is evident from his essay "Making, Knowing and Judging," in which he writes: "A poem is a rite . . . the form of a rite must be beautiful, exhibiting, for example, balance, closure and aptness to that which it is the form of.") The poem in its totality is an essay-poem—one that moves discursively through a lot of interesting, imaginative, unexpected byways in what seems a kind of baroque meander that returns us to something like the childhood setting from which we set out. But I would claim that this is largely illusory, and that the linkages, whether associative or syllogistic, that bound the discourse into coherence in earlier essay-poems are absent here, and that the order of the sequence of the stanzas is entirely adventitious. There are nine stanzas altogether. The first and last are designed as termini. Of the remaining seven, the fifth and sixth are linked by grammatical interdependence, but the rest are completely discrete, isolated, independent, and, I would argue, susceptible of being reordered according to any permutation or sequence the reader might care to invent. If they may be said to lend themselves to anything so ordered as an "argument," it can be only by incremental addition. And this is, when compared to such early essay-poems as the elegy for Freud or the admirable "In Praise of Limestone," a flaccidity and shapelessness that disappoints.

When it first appeared in book form, "Islands" was dedicated to Giocondo Sacchetti; but two years later, when included in the *Collected Shorter Poems,* the dedication was conferred instead on Giovanni Maresca. This is a curious and inexplicable business. Maresca was Auden's Italian translator; Sacchetti was an inoffensive young man who worked as a domestic in Auden's Ischian household. The poem, in neat stanzas of alternating tetrameter and trimeter lines, with only the second and fourth rhyming, is in consequence really made of "fourteeners." The poem is about the temptations, and the dangers, of solipsism and narcissism, the logical end of the isolation that islands symbolize. And the temptation and danger is there, even, or especially, when islands are presumed to be escapes from temptation or danger. The tone throughout is of sly amusement, and the opening stanzas are representative.

Old saints on millstones float with cats
    To islands out at sea,
Whereon no female pelvis can
    Threaten their agape.

Beyond the long arm of the Law,
    Close to a shipping road,
Pirates in their island lairs
    Observe the pirate code.

We can tell something of the tone of this by the rhyming of "sea" with
"agape"; and still more by the deliberate dialectical juxtaposition of saints
and pirates. This juxtaposition is made all the more amusing by the fact
that the saints isolate themselves to avoid erotic temptations, while the
pirates "observe the pirate code," which is buggery. (See *Sodomy and
Pirate Tradition: English Sea Rovers in the Seventeenth-Century Carib-
bean*, by B. R. Burg.)

The best of the entire sequence is "Streams," dedicated to Elizabeth
Drew, an expatriate English scholar who was Auden's colleague during
the time he taught at Smith College in Massachusetts. She was an Oxford
graduate and the author of a number of works, including *Discovering
Poetry, Direction in Modern Poetry, Poetry: A Modern Guide to Its
Understanding and Enjoyment*, as well as a Jungian study of T. S. Eliot.
"Streams" begins in Horatian address to the element of water itself, and,
in its opening, alludes gently and indirectly to Campion, long one of
Auden's favorite poets. Here are the first two stanzas.

Dear water, clear water, playful in all your streams,
As you dash or loiter through life who does not love
    To sit beside you, to hear you and see you,
Pure being, perfect in music and movement?

Air is boastful at times, earth slovenly, fire rude,
But you in your bearing are always immaculate,
    The most well-spoken of all the older
Servants in the household of Mrs. Nature.

The lovely collocation of music and water in the first of these stanzas
cannot fail to remind us of Campion's

These dull notes we sing
Discords need for helps to grace them;

Only beauty purely loving
  Knows no discord,

But still moves delight,
Like clear springs renewed by flowing,
Ever perfect, ever in them-
    selves eternal.

And in the second stanza we encounter some of the cozy domestic diction that opened and closed "Lakes." It is not just the use of the coy "Mrs. Nature," though "Mother Nature" would not have interrupted the metrical pattern at all, while "Mrs." suggests something out of *Peter Rabbit*. It is the presentation of an entire household staff of domestics that might maintain a plush Victorian or Edwardian mansion, with a marked variety in their backgrounds and education. Again, the note of old-fashioned security is sounded.

But in pronounced contrast to "Lakes," this poem, though it meanders hither and yon in the very manner of a stream, moves along its chosen path in continuous and fluently sequential order, touching, in the manner of the essay-poem, upon many diverse and not necessarily related topics, but marshaling them into a plausible and coherent discourse. So fluent and adaptable an element is the water of "Streams" that it allowed Auden to drag in a reference to his favorite *Tristan und Isolde*.

And *Homo Ludens*, surely, is your child, who make
Fun of our feuds by opposing identical banks,
    Transferring the loam from Huppim
  To Muppim and back each time you crankle.

To "crankle" is to zigzag, and the reference to *Homo Ludens* (playful man) is both to a Latinate nomenclature descriptive of general human behavior, and to the book of that title by Johan Huizinga, who, in his chapter called "Play and Contest as Civilizing Functions," writes,

Like all other forms of play, the contest is largely devoid of purpose. That is to say, the action begins and ends in itself, and the outcome does not contribute to the necessary life-processes of the group . . . On a visit to England the Shah of Persia is supposed to have declined the pleasure of attending a race meeting, saying that he knew very well that one horse runs faster than another . . . The outcome of a game or contest—except, of course, one played for pecuniary profit—is only interesting to those who enter into it as players or spectators, either personally or locally, or else as listeners by radio or viewers by television, etc., and accept the rules. For them it is immaterial whether Oxford wins, or Cambridge.

There is, today, a sad irony in Auden's claim about the water of streams, "And not even man can spoil you," especially when, for example, more than half the Rhine has been declared biologically dead. The irony is double in that the statement itself points to man's capacity for despoliation. Despite this capacity, the poem goes on to say, water in its journeying "Tells of a sort of world, quite other, / Altogether different from this one / With its envies and passports, a polis . . ." This polis will remind us of the "Metropolis" and "our Authentic City" of "Winds," and of the many images of the city as emblematic of civilization that run through Auden's poetry almost from the first, and that made the very word "cities" a resonant terminal word in the early sestina "Hearing of harvests rotting in the valleys," which ends,

It is the sorrow; shall it melt? Ah, water
Would gush, flush, green these mountains and these valleys
And we rebuild our cities, not dream of islands.

It will also recall the "*civitas* of sound" created by the music of Buxtehude in the *New Year Letter*. In the present case, however, the polis is "like that / To which, in the name of scholars everywhere, / Gaston Paris pledged his allegiance / As Bismarck's siege-guns came within earshot." Gaston Paris (1839–1903), a professor of medieval French literature, "endeared himself to a wide circle of scholars outside his own country by his unfailing urbanity and generosity," in the praising terms of the *Britannica*. He maintained that French versification was a natural development of popular Latin methods which depended on accent rather than quantity. His polis, therefore, is a supranational one of humane learning such as would be represented by the exiled literary scholar Elizabeth Drew. This very polis, freed from the bonds of strife and politics, recalls the poet to "the loveliest" of all the dales of Yorkshire, in which, "Sprawled out on the grass, I dozed for a second . . ." And this dozing leads directly into a dream, the beginning of which involves "a croquet tournament" such as Huizinga would have found a place for in *Homo Ludens*.

Auden had employed dream sequences in poems often before, and from early in his career—see the suppressed poem that begins "The month was

April . . ." For him dreams were associated with quests as well as with the "nocturnal rummage" of repression and the unconscious, or with psychoanalytic doctrine. Here, in this poem, the dream, good in itself, is also, upon waking, a token or omen of a further goodness. The dream's croquet match might have some connection with *Alice's Adventures in Wonderland,* a world in which, despite the Queen of Hearts' bloodthirsty commands of "Off with their heads," no one gets hurt. In Auden's match, "of all the players in that cool valley / The best with the mallet was my darling." Not everyone, however, is involved with the game, either as player or spectator. There are others in the immediate vicinity, "wild old men" who seem to be archeologists or geologists, as well as bird-watchers. These men not only represent Auden's earliest enthusiasm for excavating the hidden recesses of the earth, but symbolize as well that probing of the buried life that Freud treasured in the form of the ancient artifacts that decorated the consulting room in his Vienna apartment. Then, suddenly, and with all the pomp and majesty of a Stuart masque, "the god of mortal doting" appears. He is not named, though presumably recognized as Eros. The word "doting" carries a pointedly ambiguous burden, since it can mean excessive love or fondness (and such excesses of love were not infrequently the origins of action in Greek tragedy), and can also mean to be foolish or feeble-minded as well as to be senile and in one's "dotage." Something of the potency and danger of the god is conveyed by the demeanor of his henchmen "who laugh at thunderstorms and weep at a blue sky," which is to say that the way of Love is *Sturm und Drang,* and opposed to serenity. Dispensing his largesse and favors to his devotees, he "promised X and Y a passion undying." Our reaction to this bequest is bound to be complex, reminding us as it does of Tristan and Isolde. But we are no less reminded that salvation does not lie in a prudish repudiation of the awful power of Love, as the fate of Hippolytus demonstrated. So the "undying passion" of X and Y might be either fortunate or unfortunate, but whatever it is, it is human, and something commonly yearned for. X and Y are kept tauntingly anonymous, and are presumably to be distinguished from the poet and his "darling," though not necessarily. But in the light of Auden's jaundiced views of sexual fidelity that have presented themselves in the poetry of these years, we may be entitled to doubt that he is speaking of himself unless it is a way of saying that he can enjoy the "promise" of such fidelity only in dreams. By the same token, if X and Y are two other people, then the god has pointedly denied his boon to the poet. In either case, there follows a wild dance of celebration, in which the poet and his beloved take part without any evidence of regret or suspicion. The dance is commanded by the god, and in accordance with the conventions of the masque.

> With a wave of his torch he commanded a dance;
> So round in a ring we flew, my dear on my right,
>    When I awoke. But fortunate seemed that
>    Day because of my dream and enlightened . . .

There is a possible ambiguity in the placing of the clause "my dear on my right," which can refer either to the relative positions of the two as "round in a ring we flew," or to their positions "when I awoke." That the beloved had appeared so far only in the dream sequence would not prevent the dream from "coming true." Certainly, "because of my dream," that day seemed "fortunate" as well as "enlightened," which may mean "enlightening." If the day seemed both fortunate and enlightened, water itself seemed dearer than ever, as the final stanza affirms.

> And dearer, water, than ever your voice, as if
> Glad—though goodness knows why—to run with the human
>    race,
>    Wishing, I thought, the least of men their
>    Figures of splendor, their holy places.

The water is praised here as perhaps the inspirer of the dream of sustained and "undying" erotic happiness. In Campion's words, "Like clear springs renewed by flowing, / Ever perfect, ever in them- / selves eternal." But perhaps the best gloss on this final stanza may be taken from the opening chapter of Huizinga's *Homo Ludens.*

Inside the play-ground an absolute and peculiar order reigns. Here we come across another, very positive feature of play: it creates order, *is* order. Into an imperfect world and into the confusion of life it brings a temporary, a limited perfection. Play demands order absolute and supreme. The least deviation from it "spoils the game," robs it of its character and makes it worthless. The profound affinity between play and order is perhaps the reason why play, as we noted in passing, seems to lie to such a large extent in the field of aesthetics. Play has a tendency to be beautiful. It may be that this aesthetic factor is identical with the impulse to create orderly form, which animates play in all its aspects. The words we use to denote the element of play belong for the most part to aesthetics, terms with which we try to describe the effects of beauty: tension, poise, balance, contrast, variation, solution, resolution, etc. Play casts a spell over us; it is "enchanting," "captivating." It is invested with the noblest qualities we are capable of perceiving in things: rhythm and harmony . . .

We found that one of the most important characteristics of play was its spacial separation from ordinary life. A closed space is marked out for it, either materially or ideally, hedged off from everyday surroundings. Inside this space the play proceeds, inside it the rules obtain. Now, the marking out of some sacred spot is also the primary characteristic of every sacred act. This requirement of isolation for ritual, including magic and law, is much more than merely spacial or temporal. Nearly all rites of consecration and initiation entail a certain artificial seclusion for the performers and those to be initiated. Whenever it is a question of taking a vow or being received into an Order or confraternity, or of oaths and secret societies, in one way or another there is always such a delimiting room for play. The magician, the augur, the sacrificer begins his work by circumscribing his sacred space. Sacrament and mystery presuppose a hallowed spot.

Not only is "Streams" by far the most successful of the group of poems assembled under the heading *Bucolics,* but it is a poem of generous gratitude and unstinting praise from a poet who was feeling the weight of years, and no longer frequently in the mood to praise. In fact the group of poems is given its own epigraph, in which Auden's personal feelings of bitterness, alienation, abandonment, are mixed with a religious sense of gratitude and an obligation to express it.

> *Fair is Middle-Earth nor changes, though to Age,*
> *Raging at his uncomeliness,*
> *Her wine turn sour, her bread tasteless.*

The tone of these three lines is remarkably complex, doubling back upon itself, filled with challenge, self-loathing, piety, stoicism. The term "Middle-Earth," as observed earlier, is more likely to derive from Langland's *Piers Ploughman,* a favorite work of Auden's, than from Tolkien (who, for that matter, was a teacher of medieval literature and may himself have borrowed the term from Langland). The acknowledgment that this world is "fair" as well as a midway point between the possible ends that await us, is to see it in traditional and pious terms as a testing ground, and also as a boon such as would elicit (as it did in "Precious

Five") the requirement "Bless what there is for being." The "fairness" of
the world is to be celebrated in *Bucolics,* as it has been by poets of all
tongues and in all ages. But before the first line is finished, a note of
qualification is introduced. The earth remains permanently fair, but man
does not; and the fact that he does not makes it difficult for him to take
pleasure in her eternal youth. The bread and wine that would normally
be sacramental, representing at the very least the gifts to man of the natural
world, no longer seem efficacious. His rage, in Age, is all directed at
himself, since she is unaltered. His situation, but for his mortality, is that
of Tithonus married to Aurora. The self-hatred of Age, denied the
satisfaction of pleasure in the world, yet commanded to praise and express
gratitude, is something close to monstrous in the sort of torture it
expresses. The pronouns, male and female, indicate a love match that has
gone wrong. And behind all this there is, despite the "raging," a stoic
acceptance that is, as it were, the syllogistic or Hegelian resolution of the
two warring impulses with which this brief poem began. The motion of
the poem is, of necessity, circular, progressing from praise to rage to
resignation which (being wholly preoccupied with the human self) must
finally return to the objective "Middle-Earth," unchanged, indifferent,
eternally youthful and fair, and requiring homage. And the stoic stance
reminds us that Auden, in a poem significantly titled "First Things First,"
concluded with the line "Thousands have lived without love, not one
without water." There have been other poets, including Yeats, who have
raged at old age. But in Auden's case, with no wife or children, always
fixated upon younger men from the time of his first interest in Kallman,
the situation is especially painful.

The poetic sequence with which the book concludes is *Horae Canonicae.*
Two of the poems in this group, "Prime" and "Nones," had already
appeared in the volume titled *Nones* and are reprinted in *The Shield of
Achilles* in their proper canonical order, though it must be pointed out
that there are two such orders. The more familiar breviary names and
orders the hours thus: matins, lauds, prime, terce, sext, nones, vespers,
and compline. Auden appears to be following the shorter breviary, or
*Horae Diurnae,* eliminating matins, which not only was celebrated as a
midnight office but was not uncommonly said on the previous afternoon
or evening. The observation of the hours derived from the Jewish practice
of praying "at the third, sixth, and ninth hours," and to these were added
midnight (when Paul sang in prison) and the beginning of day and of night.

Auden puts lauds, said at cock-crow, or dawn, at the end of his sequence for what are manifestly celebratory reasons.

"Prime," the first of the sequential poems, has already been discussed. It concerned the return of the soul or of consciousness from the realm of "nocturnal rummage" to the world, speaks of that moment of awakening as "Holy," and likens the speaker to "Adam sinless in our beginning, / Adam still previous to any act." The hour of "Prime" is six A.M. The next hour is terce, celebrated at nine A.M. The speaker of "Terce" is fully conscious by that hour, and therefore no longer the singular individual he was in "Prime," but now a member of society, and, in a sense, its spokesman. The poem exchanges the first-person singular pronoun, "I," of "Prime" for the first-person plural pronoun, "we"; and the view in "Terce" has greatly enlarged from the first poem.

"Terce" is composed of three stanzas, the first of which concerns three representative people: a hangman, a judge, and a poet. It also concerns three major concepts by which we live, and which appear in the stanza with capitalized initials: Justice, Law, and Truth. At nine in the morning each of the persons is about to begin his professional life, which means to act, as distinct from the sinless condition of being "previous to any act." The very fact of taking action involves humans in the possibilities of sin and error, and of violating Justice, Law, and Truth, of which it is said that none of the three representative humans fully understands their import. There is an echo once again of the last line of the *Divine Comedy* in "the Law that rules the stars," and when it is said of the poet, rather cunningly, that he "does not know whose Truth he will tell," a good number of things are implied. For one thing, there is a good deal of debate (in which Auden has participated on both sides) about whether poetry is truthful or a pack of lies. Secondly, the poet is always at liberty to speak in the voice of another person, so that it will not be his own, but another's, truth that he speaks. But the capital initial of the word "Truth" suggests a further reference to John 14:6—"Jesus saith unto him, I am the way, and the truth, and the life: no man cometh unto the Father, but by me." The three actors in this stanza are compelled by the routines of life and social necessity to act, but are touchingly or naively unaware of the measureless resonances and implications of their actions.

The three representatives of the first stanza stand for the collective "we" of the second, the ordinary humans who go through familiar daily routines, and are to be distinguished from "the Big Ones" who can annihilate a city and are not, because of their enormous power, subject to our daily disciplines, or, still more to the point, to our hours. We, the nameless, unimportant, average people, simply pray to "get through the coming day," which could bring any number of unforeseen mishaps, embarrassments, or pains. The powerful ones seem to us like "godlings / Of professional mysteries" because they are apparently exempt from the Kafkaesque humiliations to which ordinary life exposes us. We think, therefore, in terms not of final causes or eschatology, but merely of getting through the day till by "sundown," or the bell that liberates us from work, we will be free from compulsion and humiliation, and at our ease at home.

Being therefore a part of a vast social mechanism, we are, as the third stanza asserts, more or less interchangeable parts. "At this hour [nine A.M., the hour at which the normal routines of work begin 'with a dead sound on the final stroke of nine'] we all might be anyone." Eliot too had pointed to this uniformity: "Sighs, short and infrequent, were exhaled, / And each man fixed his eyes before his feet." As contrasted with all of us, and also with the godlings of power, all of whom have secret or public wishes of our and their own, "our victim . . . is without a wish." The "victim" is not named or identified, but he knows what will happen.

> (that is what
> We can never forgive. If he knows the answers,
> Then why are we here, why is there even dust?)

The irritability of that parenthetical outburst should remind us of the tone and the predicament of Herod in For the Time Being. Mankind finds itself involved in the insoluble paradox of being granted free will but of being part of an inexorable plan of sin and redemption. Our victim knows that "for once" things will go as routine dictates, there will be no eruptions or interruptions from the powers above or below (though this will be the only "miracle" that will happen). That is to say, he knows this will be "an ordinary" day, and that "by sundown / We shall have had a good Friday." There are a number of meanings to this conclusion. On the simplest level, if we survive the regimen of the day, and the day is the last day of the business week, our Friday will be good because it inaugurates the liberation of the weekend, as well as having somehow miraculously spared us from the dangers, humiliations, and upheavals that we feared. The word "good" is used by the church in reference to a day or a season observed as holy, and in this sense it is commonly applied to the day on which the Crucifixion is ceremonially remembered. It also has the effect of recalling some lines from Eliot's "East Coker."

The dripping blood our only drink,
The bloody flesh our only food:
In spite of which we like to think
That we are sound, substantial flesh and blood —
Again, in spite of that, we call this Friday good.

But there is beyond all this the troubling sense that we "shall have had a good Friday" because in some unwitting way we will have contributed to the sacrificial death, brought it about by our very unwittingness, represented by the three persons of the first stanza who did not know the full significance of Justice, Law, and Truth.

Like "Terce," "Sext" is divided into three sections. Sext is celebrated at high noon, inaugurates the anguish of the Passion, and anticipates the Crucifixion. The poem is composed in unrhymed distichs, and its three sections all conclude by pointing to "this death" or "this dying." Moreover, each section makes reference to a "city" or to "cities" as emblems of community and civilization of one sort or another. The poem divides all of society into three, rather than two, groups, as "Terce" had done. The three groups here are those who act as "agents" in the death, those whose authority commands the death, and the vast, faceless and nameless crowd of those who are witnesses in the literal and religious senses. The first section, concerning the "agents," is so guileful in its admiration of technical or professional competence that we are astonished to find that the very people we were invited to admire are in fact profoundly incriminated.

1

You need not see what someone is doing
to know if it is his vocation,

you have only to watch his eyes:
a cook mixing a sauce, a surgeon

making a primary incision,
a clerk completing a bill of lading,

wear the same rapt expression,
forgetting themselves in their function.

How beautiful it is,
that eye-on-the-object look.

To ignore the appetitive goddesses,
to desert the formidable shrines

of Rhea, Aphrodite, Demeter, Diana,
to pray instead to St. Phocas,

St. Barbara, San Saturnino,
or whoever one's patron saint is,

that one may be worthy of their mystery,
what a prodigious step to have taken.

There should be monuments, there should be odes,
to the nameless heroes who took it first,

to the first flaker of flints
who forgot his dinner,

the first collector of sea-shells
to remain celibate.

Where should we be but for them?
Feral still, un-housetrained, still

wandering through forests without
a consonant to our names,

slaves of Dame Kind, lacking
all notion of a city

and, at this noon, for this death,
there would be no agents.

It seems to me that the best commentary on this section of the poem is one that Auden published in an essay called "Pride and Prayer" in the March 1974 issue of *The Episcopalian*.

As an antidote to Pride, man has been endowed with the capacity for prayer, an activity which is not to be confined to prayer in the narrow religious sense of the word. To pray is to pay attention to or, shall we say, to "listen" to someone or something other than oneself.

Whenever a man so concentrates his attention—be it on a land-scape or a poem or a geometrical problem or an idol or the True God—that he completely forgets his own ego and desires in listening to what the other has to say to him, he is praying.

Choice of attention—to attend to this and ignore that—is to the inner life what choice of action is to the outer. In both cases man is responsible for his choice and must accept the consequences. As Ortega y Gasset said: "Tell me to what you pay attention, and I will tell you who you are." The primary task of the schoolteacher is to teach children, in a secular context, the technique of prayer.

Petitionary prayer is a special case and, of all kinds of prayers, I believe the least important. Our wishes and desires—to pass an exam, to marry the person we love, to sell our house at a good price—are involuntary and therefore not in themselves prayers, even if it is God whom we ask to attend to them. They only become prayers in so far as we believe that God knows better than we whether we should be granted or denied what we ask.

A petition does not become a prayer unless it ends with the words, spoken or unspoken, "Nevertheless, not as I will, but as thou wilt." Perhaps the main value of petitionary prayers is: when we consciously phrase our desires, we often discover they are really wishes that two-and-two should make three or five, as when St. Augustine realized he was praying: "Lord, make me chaste, but not yet."

Of the "agents" described in this first part, engaged as they are in a secular form of prayer, it is their *competence* to act (to make the sauce, perform the operation, complete the bill of lading, collect sea shells, or make flint tools) that at once recommends them for their disinterested skill and at the same time makes them competent to carry out the sentence of death with which each section of the poem ends. It is, perhaps, their very "selfless" concentration on detail, their professional expertise, that prevents them from seeing the full meaning and impact of their specialized tasks. They have groomed themselves to be the "hangman" of "Terce."

The second section of the poem is devoted to the authorities who command, make plans, and see themselves as incarnations of *Fortitudo, Justicia, Nous,* the last of which terms means "mind" or "intellect." Though such powerful and self-satisfied men are not much liked by anyone, it is paradoxically they who provide us with "basilicas, divas, / dictionaries, pastoral verse, / the courtesies of the city." This is not to say they are poets or lexicographers, much less singers or architects. It is instead to say that these "judicial mouths" commandeer the talents of others; they are the patrons of the arts, and though we know them to be "very great scoundrels," we also know that existence would be "squalid"

without them. Once again the city is mentioned as an emblem of civilization. Finally, if it were not for them, "there would be no authority / to
command this death." Auden's mixed attitude towards the cultural
benefits they bestow as contrasted with the brute force they exhibit is
much like that of Yeats in the section of "Meditations in Time of Civil
War" subtitled "Ancestral Houses."

The last section of "Sext" concerns the crowd. Any crowd is made up
of individuals, and individuals are at liberty to notice or not, according
to their whims, whatever events take place in the secular world. The crowd
does not see these events, for it seems to have but one eye, while at the
same time its mouths (which always are hungering) seem "infinitely
many." Again, the crowd

> is never distracted
> (as everyone is always distracted)
>
> by a barking dog, a smell of fish,
> a mosquito on a bald head:
>
> the crowd sees only one thing
> (which only the crowd can see),
>
> an epiphany of that
> which does whatever is done.

This is a curiously veiled, circumlocutious way of saying a number of
things. The crowd is a community, the community of mankind, and what
it sees here is the terrible event that will be its salvation. "That / which
does whatever is done" is not alone the earthly power of agents or
authorities, but a supernatural revelation or epiphany of a salvific death,
and of human brotherhood. It is by dint of this revelation, this acceptance
of brotherhood, this sense that belief is not private but communal, this
capacity for reverence, that mankind is superior "to the social exoskele-
tons." They (ants or bees) are also communal in their lives, and live by a
certain "governance," with their own monarchs. But we are distinguished
from them in the rhetorical question with which the poem ends. Of these
insects the poem asks,

> When
>
> have they ever ignored their queens,
> for one second stopped work

on their provincial cities, to worship
The Prince of this world like us,

at this noon, on this hill,
in the occasion of this dying?

Since the next poem will be "Nones," we may safely conjecture that the reference to "this hill" is to Golgotha; and this in turn will perhaps explain the almost embarrassed periphrasis employed when describing what it is that "only the crowd can see." It is the horror and agony from which the crowd's eyes will be still more pointedly averted in "Nones." Such averting of the eyes is commented upon in Auden's *A Certain World:* "Christmas and Easter can be subjects for poetry, but Good Friday, like Auschwitz, cannot. The reality is so horrible, it is not surprising that people should have found it a stumbling block to faith . . . Poems about Good Friday have, of course, been written, but none of them will do . . . The 'Stabat Mater' which sentimentalizes the event, is the first poem of medieval literature which can be called vulgar and 'camp' in the pejorative sense."

The poem "Nones," referring to the canonical hour observed at three P.M., has already been discussed. Nones is followed by the six P.M. service of vespers. The text in Auden's "Vespers" is a prose-poem "narrative" of the encounter, as it were, on an early evening preprandial stroll, of two men who are one another's "Anti-type." The term itself, along with Auden's statement that "Sun and Moon supply their conforming masks," suggests an indebtedness to the antithetical types of Yeats's "A Vision," though for Auden's purposes the Sun and Moon will signify little more than the complete temperamental opposition between the two types. Auden identifies himself with one of these and regards the other as his enemy, knowing full well that the other regards him in exactly the same way. They are as opposed to one another as were the embattled followers of Hermes and Apollo in "Under Which Lyre," though this is both a more serious poem and a more serious opposition.

The two sides of the irreconcilable controversy were laid out at considerable expository length in Auden's essay "Dingley Dell and The Fleet." In the text of "Vespers" Auden declares, "Both simultaneously recognize his Anti-type: that I am an Arcadian, that he is a Utopian." Of these two types Auden, in his essay, had written,

Our dream pictures of the Happy Place where suffering and evil are unknown are of two kinds, the Edens and the New Jerusalems.

Though it is possible for the same individual to imagine both, it is unlikely that his interest in both will be equal and I suspect that between the Arcadian whose favorite daydream is Eden, and the Utopian whose favorite daydream is of New Jerusalem there is a characterological gulf as unbridgeable as that between Blake's Prolifics and Devourers.

In their relation to the actual fallen world, the difference between Eden and New Jerusalem is a temporal one. Eden is a past world in which the contradictions of the present world have not yet arisen; New Jerusalem is a future world in which they have at last been resolved. Eden is a place where its inhabitants may do whatever they like to do; the motto over its gate is, "Do what thou wilt is here the Law." New Jerusalem is a place where its inhabitants like to do whatever they ought to do, and its motto is "In His will is our peace."

It is worth pausing to notice the comparative temperance and evenhandedness with which the two types are represented in the essay, for Auden will turn out in the context of "Vespers" to be the vigorous partisan of the Arcadian and the contemptuous enemy of the Utopian. But here in the essay the Utopian is given a motto from the *Paradiso* of Dante, in which a perfect *future* is envisioned, though not, of course, an earthly one. And it is perhaps not just the distinction, but the confusion, of earthly and heavenly dreams that lies at the core of the opposition of the two types. The backward-looking Arcadian is likely to have been blessed with so blissful a childhood that his life has enacted the symbolic Fall from grace in the Garden of Eden, a lapse which, by dint of his own efforts, he cannot repair. His dream is of a pastoral innocence, tinged with a gentle melancholy. The danger he is subject to is inaction, acedia, the sense of an irrecoverable happiness that has gone forever. The forward-looking Utopian may well have suffered privations in childhood or youth, which have confirmed him in his resolution to escape them if this is humanly possible. His initial impulse may have been completely a personal one, but he has quickly learned that his own sufferings are firmly linked with the sufferings of others—of his class, his race, religion, or whatever. And he has seen not only that he cannot solve his problem by himself, but that he must devote himself to the problems he shares with others. The danger he is subject to is a heedless activism, the conviction of the tyrant that ruthless power can transform society into any desired shape.

What may be most interesting in this opposition is that in the course of his life Auden was a partisan of both sides. He began as a social reformer, and was severely rebuked for writing of "the necessary murder." He certainly seriously believed that the active will could change both the individual and society for the better. He came in due course to distrust man's capacity fully to see and understand the meaning and consequences of his own acts, and his vision of happiness became in time, and as a consequence of much unhappiness, largely retrospective. By the time he came to write "Vespers" he had pretty well lost patience with what I think it is fair to call his former self. And this seems to me to be characteristically true of all "converts." Their impatience with the errors of their former ways extends almost by logical necessity to all those who still entertain those errors; and by this means the convert seems to alter self-criticism into a condemnation of all those who have not, like him, converted. One can see this contempt for his own past enlarged into a general repudiation of the Jews by St. Paul. And Auden, though he is dealing with something far less embracing or serious than religious doctrine or salvation, nevertheless allows himself to express a civilized but undisguised contempt for his Anti-type.

Consider but one example from "Vespers": "In my Eden a person who dislikes Bellini has the good manners not to get born: In his New Jerusalem a person who dislikes work will be very sorry he was born." There is a curious lack of symmetry in these paired statements, in which the tyrannous threats are deployed only on one side. It is necessary first to explain that the Bellini mentioned is not, alas, one of the great family of Venetian painters, but instead Vincenzo Bellini, composer of *Norma* and *I Puritani*. There is, admittedly, no way for the uninstructed reader to figure this out; one simply has to be acquainted with Auden's particular tastes, which in the course of time he elevated into "tests" by which he rather arbitrarily determined who was civilized. To be sure, we all locate our friends among those whose tastes and interests more or less coincide with our own; in Auden's case it simply became more doctrinaire, and more a secret code or set of standards by which any interlocutor could be judged with an alarming precision. Some were *in*, others *out*, according to decisions as severe as a Calvinist's God. It is the arcane and hierophantic character of this sort of examination, its covert and unspoken standards, that remind one immediately of the "Journal of an Airman" in Auden's first book, with its instructions about how to recognize the "enemy." And it clearly has a homosexual mystique about it.

But it is also worth noticing, in the example from "Vespers," the phrase "good manners." We have already observed in Auden an inclination to substitute rules of behavior for moral or ethical standards. Of this tendency a friend (and his collaborator on *The Viking Book of Aphorisms*), Louis Kronenberger, wrote in a memoir called "A Friendship Revisited": "To be sure, much of what I thought of as his Englishness rested on habits, injunctions and values acquired very early in life. His own personal sense of what's done or is not done smacked much more of the nursery and the schoolroom than of later, worldlier origins. As for people, he seldom wasted time dissecting or passing judgement on them; someone, to him, was either a gent or not a gent—this a judgement in terms of character, not class." The application of such standards to artistic taste is perfectly illustrated from the recollections of Orlan Fox, from the same collection of homages edited by Stephen Spender from which the Kronenberger passage is taken. Fox observes, "His collection of records of serious music was heavy on opera. *Lucia di Lammermoor* is the acid test for anyone who thinks he likes opera, he would say. Or: 'No gentleman can fail to admire Bellini.'"

In any case, the Arcadian and Utopian antagonists meet briefly at six P.M. (by chance? providentially?) and size each other up. They seem to be what they were first called, Anti-types of one another. But just as the convert was once what he now so vigorously opposes, each one of this pair recognizes something fraternal and necessary in his opposite.

Was it (as it must look to any god of cross-roads) simply a fortuitous intersection of life-paths, loyal to different fibs,

or also a rendezvous between accomplices who, in spite of themselves, cannot resist meeting

to remind the other (do both, at bottom, desire truth?) of that half of their secret which he would most like to forget,

forcing us both, for a fraction of a second, to remember our victim (but for him I could forget the blood, but for me he could forget the innocence)

on whose immolation (call him Abel, Remus, whom you will, it is one Sin Offering) arcadias, utopias, our dear old bag of a democracy, are all alike founded:

For without a cement of blood (it must be human, it must be innocent) no secular wall will safely stand.

The prose-poem "Vespers" concludes on a note of equity between the contending parties, and a shared sense of the ritual cost of the preservation of any stable society—such a forfeit as was hinted at in the address to S. Restituta in "Ischia." The social compact is sealed in human blood, as Andrew Marvell acknowledged in his "An Horatian Ode upon Cromwell's Return from Ireland," where he declares, regarding the establishment of Rome on the Capitoline Hill,

> So when they did design
> The Capitol's first line,
> A bleeding head where they begun,
> Did fright the architects to run;
> And yet in that the State
> Foresaw its happy fate.

Marvell is alluding to a passage in Livy's *Annals,* which he only slightly embellishes, and which recounts an event also mentioned by Pliny and Varro. According to Livy, when excavators were engaged in digging the foundations of the temple of Jupiter Capitolium, they encountered "a man's head, face and all, whole and sound: which sight . . . plainly foretold that [Rome] should be the chief castle of the empire and the capital place of the whole world." It may be that both Marvell and his sources are trading upon the "philological authority" for the establishment of a capital in its secular and religious governance, but such linguistic omens have always been taken seriously. For Auden, if the victim does not reconcile enemies in the course of "Vespers," he is very dimly recognized by them as both innocent and as the premise, in his sacrificial role, for all dreams of a perfect society.

"Compline"—the canonical hour is celebrated either at nine P.M. or just before repose—is suitably composed in the same sixteen-line stanzas employed for "Prime" and "Nones." Its formal link to "Prime" recalls that the first hour brought into daylight and consciousness the soul that, while the body was dormant, had been occupied with the "nocturnal rummage" of dream life, and which now returns in a state of newborn innocence to the world of the living. In "Compline," with symmetrical ceremony, the conscious mind prepares to relinquish itself to the world of sleep, to abandon "desire and the things desired," to allow the body to escape and join "the chaster peace" of plants, and, in prayer which is both penitential and hopeful, to complete the cycle of the day, which is also the cycle of life itself. Both "Prime" and "Compline" are formally linked to the pivotal poem "Nones" because the canonical hour of nones is the sacrificial center of human life, and of the whole sequence.

Once again, in "Compline," internal rhyming becomes a trifle too compulsive and noticeable, though never so harmfully as elsewhere. The first stanza is concerned with the voluntary relinquishment of the will which the speaker, like all humans, undertakes by the very fact of going to sleep. Here it is done gracefully and gratefully, the concupiscence of the eye, the lusts of the flesh, and the pride of life, surrendered in the hope that everything that has come to pass in the course of this day (a day both commonplace and extraordinary) will finally make "sense." Yet at the moment before sleep the speaker, like all of us, remembers only random and disconnected details (all of them symbolic of our fallen condition) which seem to lack relevance to any "meaning" or "narrative." There may even be a note of petulance or irritation in the first stanza's concluding lines,

> And I fail to see either plot
> Or meaning; I cannot remember
> A thing between noon and three.

Rarely in the course of his poetry has Auden punctuated with more dramatic precision. The two statements above, separated by a semicolon, seem to the speaker a disjunctive sequence; they are simply two things that irk him as he prepares to go to sleep, because they may disturb his tranquility. But we know, as he himself shall know before the poem is done, that the two are causally related; that what he cannot remember is precisely what he does not wish at the moment to remember, and what he has averted his eyes from almost throughout the poem: the Passion and the Sacrifice that took place between noon and three. And in a kind of recapitulation of a device employed in "Sext," where each section employed a modified refrain that made mention of "this noon" and "this death" or "this dying," as well as its carefully repeated mention of the "city" or "cities," in "Compline" every stanza will make mention of the central interval between noon and three.

The second stanza recalls once again the Kantian linkage of "the starry heavens above and the moral law within," as the speaker becomes aware only of the sound of the beating of his own heart and of "the stars / Leisurely walking around." The "meaning" of these two motions escapes him, though he is now prepared to admit the possibility that his heart (that is, his desires, purposes, ambitions) had something to do with what happened between noon and three. He further supposes that the constellations are not only Kant's "starry heavens" but the very orders of the angelic hosts themselves in their celestial concert of the harmonious music of the spheres, singing "of some hilarity beyond / All liking and happening," which is to say, in divine celebration. But the speaker, now in a mood of repentance, acknowledges that he does not "know what they know / Nor what I ought to know." And, refusing to make frivolous guesses at either ("scorning / All vain fornications of fancy") he prays to both outward and inward motions to accept the separations that sleep entails.

The third stanza begins with a perfect awareness that the speaker is but "a stride" from the world of dreams, the mysterious world from which he was reborn in "Prime," and to which, with its "unwashed tribes of wishes," he is about to return. There, in that primitive anthropologist's paradise of obscure cults and arcane rituals, will probably be found "odd rites" and "magic" "to propitiate / What happens from noon to three." And there follows here a brief, symbolic, deeply suggestive but at the same time obscure, dream event, more telling, perhaps more private, than any I can recall in Auden's work. He has just declared that the "unwashed tribes of wishes" have "odd rites which they hide from me," in much the same way that, in the previous stanza, the meaning of the singing angels and of his own heart is obscure to him. And then, suddenly, almost parenthetically, we glimpse a momentary, fugitive dream event:

> — should I chance,
> Say, on youths in an oak-wood
> Insulting a white deer, bribes nor threats
> Will get them to blab —

From very early in his poetic career, Auden went foraging in the buried regions of the unconscious, sometimes in a spirit of charming levity, as in these, as it must now be noted, suppressed stanzas from the poem that would in the course of time be titled "Heavy Date."

> So I pass the time, dear,
> Till I see you, writing
> Down whatever nonsense
> Comes into my head;
> Let the life that has been
> Lightly buried in my

Personal Unconscious
Rise up from the dead.

Why association
Should see fit to set a
Bull-dog by a trombone
  On a grassy plain
Littered with old letters,
Leaves me simply guessing,
I suppose it's La Con-
-dition Humaine.

As at lantern lectures
Image follows image;
Here comes a steam-roller
  Through an orange grove,
Driven by a nursemaid
As she sadly mutters:
"Zola, poor old Zola
  Murdered by a stove."

These stanzas play, in a spirit of levity, with the seemingly random—but, to psychoanalytic scrutiny, telling—collocations of images that present themselves to the "Personal Unconscious." Whether those in "Heavy Date" are a true account of the poet's mental life or merely contrived for purposes of amusement and to suit the necessities of stanzaic form we cannot determine, though in a poem of such deliberate and casual lightness it may not matter. But here in "Compline" something serious is going on. One cannot, in fact, read the enigmatic lines in "Compline" without recalling a passage from the conclusion of Eliot's *The Use of Poetry and the Use of Criticism:*

Why, for all of us, out of all that we have heard, seen, felt, in a lifetime, do certain images recur, charged with emotion, rather than others? The song of one bird, the leap of one fish, at a particular place and time, the scent of one flower, an old woman on a German mountain path, six ruffians seen through an open window playing cards at night at a small French railway junction where there was a water-mill: such memories may have symbolic value, but of what we cannot tell, for they come to represent the depths of feeling into which we cannot peer. We might just as well ask, why, when we try to recall

visually some period of the past, we find in our memory just the few
meagre arbitrarily chosen set of snapshots that we do find there, the
faded souvenirs of passionate moments.

(In a footnote to this passage, Eliot comments that "the pre-logical
mentality persists in civilized man, but becomes available only to or
through the poet.") We take Eliot's brief list as persuasively candid,
personal, and revealing partly because of its remarkable specificity;
and partly because in his own poetry he reverts to certain prized images
(like the rose garden) that bear for him a meaning still greater than any
he can communicate, simply because they are "his." Given the impressive
weight of what he has to say precisely about the obscurity of the
topic—though he is talking about memory and Auden is writing about
dreams, they are really addressing the same problem—it would be rash
of me to make any conjectures about those youths in the oak wood
"insulting a white deer," and I approach the puzzle with suitable
diffidence and trepidation.

Our dream life is under no obligation to be as literal or as accurate as
our memory tries to be; and we are not required to assume that Auden
may have had a personal confrontation with the curious scene he describes. But I will rashly venture that he has appropriated his "white deer"
from Petrarch's celebrated *candida cerva*, in the sonnet so brilliantly but
tendentiously translated by Sir Thomas Wyatt in a version that begins,
"Whoso list to hunt, I know where is an hind . . .'" Petrarch's sonnet,
which in tone and import is really quite remote from Wyatt's, is in fact
about a premonition of Laura's premature death; and in the Italian sonnet
Caesar is assimilated to God, the protector and preserver of the white
deer, which, in the dazzle and obscurity of sunset, suddenly disappears. I
wish to suggest that Auden is indicating something about the abuse and
mockery offered to something he regards with very deep and personal
reverence. I would claim no more than this, but all by itself it seems to me
suggestive enough.

After his momentary dream scene (which may in fact be the "untruth"
he speaks of, though "untruth" is an evasive word, covering any number
of disguises), a scene he had reached by a "stride," it is now "one step to
nothing,"

> For the end, for me as for cities,
> Is total absence: what comes to be
> Must go back into non-being

For the sake of the equity, the rhythm
  Past measure or comprehending.

In these lines, with an impressive humility, the poet accepts the hour of
his death as well as the obliteration of sleep.
  The final stanza, rich in further obscurities, requires quotation in toto.

Can poets (can men in television)
  Be saved? It is not easy
To believe in unknowable justice
  Or pray in the name of a love
Whose name one's forgotten: *libera*
  *Me, libera* C (dear C)
And all poor s-o-b's who never
  Do anything properly, spare
Us in the youngest day when all are
  Shaken awake, facts are facts
(And I shall know exactly
  What happened today between noon and three),
That we, too, may come to the picnic
  With nothing to hide, join the dance
As it moves in perichoresis,
  Turns about the abiding tree.

The question about whether poets can be saved cannot fail to be both
personal and serious, though its weight is greatly lightened by the parenthetical dig at "men in television," who are of necessity more corrupt than
poets simply because they earn more and must submit to the whims of
powerful advertisers and a vulgar public. The "unknowable justice" is
that inscrutable judgment that asserts itself throughout the Old Testament, and announces its definitive return "in the youngest day when all
are / Shaken awake." To "pray in the name of a love / Whose name one's
forgotten" could conceivably be a supremely personal statement about
Auden's return to a faith from which he had emphatically lapsed. It could
also refer to a worldly love, once cherished but no longer existing. The
"*libera Me, libera* C" may perhaps be an adaptation to very personal
purposes of the closing of the Pater Noster, *Et ne nos inducas in
tentationem. Sed libera nos a malo*, in which "deliver us" (from evil) is
interpolated to, first, "deliver me," and then, "deliver C," whom we may
take to be either Chester Kallman or any anonymous person, like X or Y.

In any case, when on the latter day all are "shaken awake" and "facts are facts," and there are no more "vain fornications of fancy"; when the poet shall know exactly "what happened between noon and three"; when there are no more evasions, the crime is acknowledged and the sacrifice humbly and gratefully accepted—then the god who is prayed to in the Latin phrase *libera me*, "deliver me," is asked to spare us, "That we, too, may come to the picnic / With nothing to hide," since our sins will have been forgiven. (The phrase about "nothing to hide" recalls the lines in "In Praise of Limestone": "The blessed will not care what angle they are regarded from, / Having nothing to hide.") The banquet in heaven, and its dance, with which the poem ends, is made accessible by being called a "picnic," which takes place in an open landscape or garden, while the dance is said to move "in perichoresis." This word means "rotation," but it has a special theological meaning which refers to the relationship of the persons of the Trinity. In his attempt to unravel the contesting doctrines of early Christianity, Gibbon had occasion to try to explain the Trinitarian mystery. "This pure and distinct equality [of the Three Persons] was tempered," he said, "by the internal connection and spiritual penetration which indissolubly unites the divine persons," and in a footnote he refers to this as "perhaps the deepest and darkest corner of the whole theological abyss." As for the "abiding tree" with which the poem ends, it may be Christ, to whom St. Augustine refers as the tree of Life. And it is worth noticing at this point how shy Auden was throughout his life of mentioning the name of Christ outright.

Lauds, the first office of the day in the abbreviated *Horae Diurnae*, is celebrated at cock-crow, and commonly ended with the recital of the last three psalms. Auden's poem "Lauds" is emphatically the most impersonal in the whole sequence. Though there is of necessity a voice that speaks, and this voice speaks in benediction ("God bless the Realm, God bless the People"), the poem is devoid of personal pronouns either singular or plural. There seem to be two reasons for this. The poem apparently expresses a condition of something like preconsciousness, that state preceding even the condition of "Prime," a state in which the "real" world gently asserts its existence as though without reference to any particular consciousness; it is merely and completely *there*. And the speaker is wholly aware of its alterity without, at the same time, being aware of himself as one who has just awakened into self-consciousness. The second reason for this impersonal quality concerns the poem's form which, as we learn from Monroe K. Spears, is that of the medieval Spanish *cossante*, "close to folk poetry and to music." It is composed of rhymed distichs, each followed by an unvarying refrain. The distichs alternate rhymes between odd- and even-numbered stanzas, and they also observe a strict pattern of repeating lines, as in a villanelle or pantoum. These strictures assist in the expression of the kind of innocence we associate with a nursery rhyme. And there is something almost awkwardly child-like about the poem.

For one thing, there are Auden's rhymes. One need not be particularly troubled by the rhyming of "people" and "temporal," though it is only the weak syllables that are rhymed. More disturbing is the rhyming of an accented with an unaccented syllable, as in "sing" and "awaking." Imperfect as these rhymes sound, they nevertheless play a tyrannic and coercive role in the poem, so that we are given the disfigured locution in the following couplet:

> The crow of the cock commands awaking;
> Already the mass-bell goes dong-ding.

The defiant inversion of "ding-dong," undertaken purely for the sake of the rhyme, is as disconcerting as it would be to say of a clock that it goes "tock-tick." Both expressions are conventional; and the poem is based upon conventions as well. It is disturbing to find one set of conventions violated for the sake of another.

The refrain that follows all of the seven couplets, "*In solitude, for company,*" rhymes with nothing else and exhibits a complexity that contrasts with the folk-like simplicity of the main body of the poem. It speaks of the isolation of the waking soul who, in waking, joins humanity, and thus recalls the final part of "Sext," which declared that belief is communal. It is, possibly, the covert and plaintive utterance of the lonely poet who has found a way to conceal his own anguish behind the seeming anonymity of his poetic form. It is as well a declaration that our rebirth to this world, as to the next, involves a rejoicing that cannot and should not be done alone. Finally, in a single line, it quietly unites the private and public worlds Auden had addressed more or less alternately from the beginning of his career.

The centrally placed section of the book, *In Sunshine and in Shade,* is awarded its own epigraph:

> *Guard, Civility, with guns*
> *Your modes and your declensions;*

*Any lout can spear with ease*
*Singular Archimedes.*

The little verse is pregnant with implied paradox of the very kind Yeats employed. For civilization to endure it must stoop to the methods of the barbarian (though it happened to have been a Roman lout who slew Archimedes). To adopt such methods is to expose oneself to the dangers of becoming barbaric, but not to adopt them is to be as vulnerable and extinguishable as Archimedes, who, drawing geometric designs in the sand, was slain when Syracuse was taken by Roman forces. There is, of course, no solution to this puzzle, and it reminds us of how imperiled, both from within and from without, "civility" always must be. It also partakes of the mutual and contrasted relationships of sunshine and shade.

Something of the puzzle in this epigraph is expressed in a less compact and aphoristic way in "Fleet Visit."

The sailors come ashore
Out of their hollow ships,
Mild-looking middle-class boys
Who read the comic strips;
One baseball game is more
To them than fifty Troys.

They look a bit lost, set down
In this unamerican place
Where natives pass with laws
And futures of their own;
They are not here because
But only just-in-case.

The whore and ne'er-do-well
Who pester them with junk
In their grubby ways at least
Are serving the Social Beast;
They neither make nor sell—
No wonder they get drunk.

But the ships on the dazzling blue
Of the harbor actually gain
From having nothing to do;

Without a human will
To tell them whom to kill
Their structures are humane

And, far from looking lost,
Look as if they were meant
To be pure abstract design
By some master of pattern and line,
Certainly worth every cent
Of the millions they must have cost.

The first stanza presents the shore-leave sailors as especially innocent and unaggressive. Reading the comic strips may be an index of their level of education, but it is also characteristically the medium of fairly child-like fantasy by which aggressions are sublimated; the complexities of the moral world are neatly boiled down to good guys and bad guys, and the triumph of virtue is inevitable. This innocence is further emphasized by their devotion to baseball games and their indifference to the story (or the poems) of the Trojan War. That war is either old news or literature; the ball game is an immediate part of their own world. Moreover, the game and the war are analogous in that they are two kinds of competition carried on within certain prescribed limits of time and space, and, despite appearances to the contrary, according to certain rules. But the game, in the end, is more innocent than war. The choice and mention of Troy in the first stanza is apt enough in itself, but it is preparatory for the Trojan horse–battleship analogy with which the poem will close.

The second and third stanzas are concerned with the aimlessness of these sailors in a foreign port. They are divorced from the general population by every convention, and are unable to participate in anything that pertains to the normal routines of life, including the common economic ones that are based on the laws of supply and demand and that are our accepted means of survival. Economics, too, like baseball, is a kind of game with serious consequences, though not so serious as those of war. By the time the third stanza is over, the sailors have been, as it were, quarantined within a domain of innocence, exempted even from the civil warfare of low-class economic maneuverings, to say nothing of an interest in the feats of Homeric heroes.

The last two stanzas are given up wholly to admiration of the ships. If the sailors seem "lost" in having nothing to do, the ships, by contrast, gain from their current nonutility, and, as works of complex and elaborate naval architecture, seem to be exercises in "pure abstract design," or huge works of nonrepresentational sculpture. They, too, like the sailors, seem attractive and innocent, though in their case innocence is predicated on the fact that they are "Without a human will / To tell them whom to kill." And immediately we realize that it is the innocent sailors themselves who supply that will. The battleships thereby become Trojan horses, so appealing in their outward beauty as to bedazzle and seduce, but housing a force of power and conquest. They are a species of the guns that, in the epigraph, guard the modes and declensions of "Civility." Those modes and declensions are the linguistic properties of social intercourse, but they must be protected by the very instruments that are hostile to such intercourse. Finally, and with a touching irony, the millions that the ships cost have nothing whatever to do with the innocent aesthetic value for which the poet prizes them; and none of the men who man them would imagine themselves as the guardians of "modes and declensions."

I want now to turn to a brief lyric about which I have a highly unorthodox, and possibly impermissible, view. It is called "Hunting Season."

> A shot; from crag to crag
>     The tell-tale echoes trundle;
> Some feathered he-or-she
>     Is now a lifeless bundle
> And, proud into the kitchen, some
> Example of our tribe will come.
>
> Down in the startled valley
>     Two lovers break apart;
> He hears the roaring oven
>     Of a witch's heart;
> Behind his murmurs of her name
> She sees a marksman taking aim.
>
> Reminded of the hour
>     And that his chair is hard,
> A deathless verse half done,
>     One interrupted bard
> Postpones his dying with a dish
> Of several suffocated fish.

Given Auden's characteristic formality of mind, I would conjecture that this poem was first written with the stanzas in a different sequence. Both a more logical and more dramatic order would obtain if the final stanza were placed second, and the second reserved for the end. This would put side by side the two stanzas that concern the death of a creature (a fowl and some fish) for the nourishment of one or another of the human race; and it would leave till the end the quite different murderousness that is still latent but implicit in the behavior of the two lovers towards one another. Their mutual hatred and suspicion is not, strictly speaking, carnivorous, and thus ought to be distinguished from the straightforward culinary concerns of the other two stanzas. Moreover, the stanza about the lovers is frankly dramatic, in pronounced contrast to the sardonic humor of the other two stanzas, and would best exhibit that contrast by following the other two.

The humor of the first stanza, tinged though it be with a sort of disgust, is conveyed by the humanizing "he-or-she" applied to the killed bird by the "proud" hunter, whose pride cannot be based, after all, on any equality in this duel. The human hunter, moreover, is referred to as an "example of our tribe," and we are allowed to think that he is not a pretty example. And "tribe," as it was commonly used in the eighteenth century, referred to (according to the OED) "a group in the classification of plants, animals, etc., usually forming a subdivision of an order, and containing a number of genera: sometimes used as superior and sometimes inferior to a family; also, loosely, any group of animals." This has the effect of reducing humans to an animal level, though making them more brutal by virtue of their acquired technology for killing. The stanza Auden has placed last contains the same sort of humor. The poet is not actually aware that he is hungry, but only that he is uncomfortable, and that there are conventional hours for eating. Though he writes "deathless verse," he is obliged to postpone his own dying by living cannibalistically off the slaughtered and cooked bodies of other creatures. Again, the match between them is, as always, unequal.

Auden's second stanza, however, is markedly different from the other two, and is singularly lacking in humor. The two antagonists are one another's equals, no actual murder takes place, and the stanza has nothing to do with eating. The hellishness which it describes should remind us of the closing stanza of the song "Deftly, admiral, cast your fly," with its reference to the Furies. For it is surely the Furies who possess this couple. And it is just possible that if this poem is in some way deeply personal, Auden may have thought he could conceal its horror by surrounding it with a mordant levity as exhibited in what are now the first and last stanzas.

Let us turn now to the grand and impressive "Ode to Gaea," which is, like the poem to "Ischia" among others, an elaborate and classically modeled tribute of praise to the natural world, and, like "Precious Five," an expression of deep and moving gratitude. The poem is oddly constructed in that it is written in syllabic quatrains, the first lines being composed of thirteen syllables, the second lines of twelve, the third lines of seven, and the final lines of eight; but in addition the first and second lines are rhymed throughout, while the rest are left unrhymed. This has the odd effect of letting the poem hover formally between the practice of its unrhymed classical forebears and common English verse. The poem also moves in the slow elegance of wide gesture common to some of Auden's best essay-poems; and here it is especially suitable that he should cover a lot of ground when he has the whole earth for his subject.

The tone is lush and expansive right from the first, as the earth is surveyed from a plane above it in a manner Auden has used before. Our "Mother" Earth is called, somewhat primly, the "Nicest" daughter of Chaos, and that note of fastidious, nurse-maidish judgment will reassert itself later in the poem. Given the fact that the earth's surface is largely water, it is this surface that first impresses itself upon us "With great swatches of plankton, / Delicious spreads of nourishment." That tasty note is obviously slightly mischievous, but it, too, smacks of the nursery parlance used to persuade children to eat something they are likely to resist. And after a witty claim that the world is actually stranger to us now than she was when large parts of her were unknown, her sheer abundance of water suggests that she is professing, "Of all pure things Water is the best," a claim that should remind us of the kinship of this poem to George Herbert's "Man," which first likens Man to the world and then focuses on the excellence and importance of the basic, indispensable element of water.

> Each thing is full of dutie:
> Waters united are our navigation;
>   Distinguished, our habitation;
>   Below, our drink; above our meat;
> Both are our cleanlinesse. Hath one such beautie?
>   Then how are all things neat?

There is more than a coincidental relationship between Herbert's poem and Auden's. In addition to the man/world/water relationship, it may be said that both are essay-poems, homiletic in Herbert's case, more personal but almost equally didactic in Auden's. If Gaea commends the element of water, what does she feel about the human inhabitants of her domain? Herbert was still able to think of Man as the finest work of God and the supreme achievement of Creation. In Auden's poem, the more primitive forms of natural growth, "the older lives" which "Have no wish to be stood in / Rows or at right angles" repudiate the punctilious orderliness of the latecomer, Man. Auden has pleasure inventing mock eras that presume to measure human progress, "seven gods ago" and "Before the Ninth Catastrophe." Given the dubiousness of such "progress," it is plausible for mortals to attribute their unsteady and capricious fortunes to the whims of comparatively indifferent gods (a note struck often enough in the poems of Hardy). Our predication of Olympian powers is based on pettiness and envy of strengths we do not possess: hence the "riddle," "Why are all / The rowdiest marches and the / Most venomous iambics composed / By lame clergymen?" Interestingly, it is "Good-manners" which asks this "easy" riddle, and which also favors pleasant nursery tales with happy endings.

—so we were taught

Before the Greater Engines came and the police
Who go with them, when the long rivers ran through peace
And the holy laws of Speech were
Held in awe, even by evil tongues,

And manners, maybe, will stand us in better stead,
Down there, than a kantian conscience . . .

Touchingly, the recollection of a childhood world of safety, peace, and Edenic beauty suggests a form of behavior based wholly on decorum, of arbitrarily imposed standards of conduct, as though the conscience itself were the least dependable, most corruptible, of human faculties. (This pronounced distrust of the "conscience," which appears from time to time in the later poetry, is worth notice, and seems almost like an ultramontane hedging against the dangers of antinomian heresies.) Of course, the era "before the Greater Engines came" is the time of children's toys, and, more personally in Auden's case, probably of the pumping-engine he first loved. Quite suddenly we break out of this meditation and recall that we are engaged in looking down upon the earth: "from overhead / Much harm is discernible." Not only is wreckage plainly visible, but so is the corrupt heart of man, where "the pious peasant's only son . . . Dreams of cities where his cows are whores." Given this wholesale viciousness, what hope can anyone cherish?

> When the wise
> Wilt in the glare of the Shadow, the stern advise
> Tribute and the large-hearted
> Already talk Its gibberish,
>
> Perhaps a last stand in the passes will be made
> By those whose Valhalla would be hearing verse by Praed
> Or arias by Rossini
> Between two entrees by Carême.
>
> We hope so.

There is a good deal in this passage that calls for comment. Whatever tyrannic power it is that threatens us is obscurely called "the Shadow," dimly reminiscent perhaps of comic books; but this one paradoxically emits a glare strong enough to make the wise wilt, the stern capitulate, and the large-hearted, in a misguided spirit of cooperation, to "talk Its gibberish." In the face of such complete power, the "last stand in the passes," it turns out, will be made, somewhat astonishingly, by people *with the right taste.* They will be, as it were, the defenders of civilization, but it seems that their only qualifications consist of a refined appreciation for music, poetry, and haute cuisine. Of necessity, they are not the wise, the stern, or the large-hearted. We may guess more precisely at the identities of these heroes of civilization by recalling the first few stanzas of "Footnotes to Dr. Sheldon" in *Nones.*

> Behold the manly mesomorph
> Show his splendid biceps off,
> Whom social workers love to touch,
> Though the loveliest girls do not care for him much.
>
> Pretty to watch with bat or ball,
> An Achilles, too, in a barroom brawl,
> But in the ditch of hopeless odds,
> The hour of desertion by brass and gods,
>
> Not a hero. It is the pink-and-white,
> Fastidious, slightly girlish, in the night

When the proud-arsed broad-shouldered break and run
Who covers their retreat, dies at his gun.

The reference to Carême is to Marie-Antoine Carême, dubbed "the Lamartine of the kitchen range," a protégé of Talleyrand's, who served the Prince Regent of England and Tsar Alexander I of Russia, from experience in the latter of whose realms he introduced borsch into European cuisine. He had studied architectural drawings as a boy and used them in designing his more flamboyant pastries. He is credited with originating vol-au-vent, and was the author of *L'Art de la cuisine au XIXme siècle*. In noticing his presence in this poem, it may be worth remembering a number of things. In *A Certain World* Auden reproduces two and a half pages of an account by Alexandre Dumas of the life of Carême. In the essay "Reading" in *The Dyer's Hand*, Auden outlines his own imaginary Eden, and having described its landscape, climate, language, religion, and so forth, gets around to its Public Statues, which are exclusively "confined to famous defunct chefs." This is, on the one hand, understandable in one who had for a long time the companionship of Chester Kallman, who is reputed to have been an excellent cook. It is at the same time surprising in one who smoked and drank as heavily as Auden did, and who was far from fastidious in regard to most of his personal habits. Auden saluted M. F. K. Fisher with the dedication to her of one of his poems (titled "Tonight at Seven-Thirty," the ritual hour of Auden's evening meal). Fisher, who was surely one of the greatest modern writers on food, was perfectly aware that fine cooking may take a place, in her own words, among "the benign as well as corrupt attributes of culture," a wisdom that not all writers on the subject (for example, the dandyish Lucius Beebe) have shared with her. In the same sequence from *About the House,* in a poem retitled, in a phrase of Brecht's, "Grub First, Then Ethics," Auden again imagines the defenders of the City, the citadel of civilization, enjoying "a good dinner, that we / may march in high fettle, left foot first, / to hold her Thermopylae." We will also recall that in "Vespers" it was Bellini rather than Rossini who was made the touchstone of cultivation.

Nevertheless (to return to the "Ode to Gaea"), the poet recognizes that his dream of a saving elite is in fact but a dream, that justice often deserts us, and "Earth, in the end, will be herself; she has never been moved / Except by Amphion," who is the archetypal poet, the harpist who by his music alone built the walls of Thebes. Reference is made to the futility of

the Sicilian Expedition of the Peloponnesian War, and to the crude
propaganda of orators which led to the Athenian defeat, recalling the lines
from "September 1, 1939,"

> Exiled Thucydides knew
> All that a speech can say
> About Democracy,
> And what dictators do,
> The elderly rubbish they talk
> To an apathetic grave . . .

The poem closes with an elaborate rhetorical question which in its first
appearance lacked its question mark—though there were other typographical errors in the poem as well. The question is asked, ". . . what, /
To [Gaea], the real one, can our good landscapes be but lies, / Those
woods where tigers chum with deer and no root dies, / That tideless bay
where children / Play bishop on a golden shore?" There is much courage
and gravity to this end, which acknowledges freely that the cozy images
of childhood, "our good landscapes," comforting though they may be or
have been, are nevertheless simply lies to which the real world is entirely
indifferent. The poem takes place in the spring of the year, the time of
"Cupid's Coming," and the earthly evidences of spring are seen or
imagined from the plane in which the poet travels. But neither spring nor
Cupid is guarantee of the success or triumph of love, and this poem, along
with Gaea herself, renounces the easy solutions of happy endings. It has
about it, in fact, the same dreams of the perfect landscape, undercut by a
deflating return to reality, that is to be found in the second Epode of
Horace, in which a great paean of praise is offered in behalf of the simple
pastoral life, elaborated and extended upon with relish, only to have the
reader discover at the end that all this praise has been uttered by a Roman
entrepreneur immediately before going off to collect debts and make
investments. Auden's poem, however, is the more extravagant and wide-
ranging, and probably the more personal of the two.

"Gaea" exhibits the formalities of an ode, as distinguished from the no
less demanding but different formalities of a song. Over the course of his
career Auden wrote many songs, some of which have been discussed, and
a few of which were clearly composed in admiring imitation of the
tradition of the American musical comedy. But he was also a friend of a
number of "serious" composers (Britten, Henze, Nicholas Nabokov,
Stravinsky) and wrote texts, necessarily of a different sort, for some of

their more ambitious works. In addition, he was acquainted with a wholly different song tradition—that of the Elizabethans.

The two kinds of music (the "popular" and the "serious") involve different prosodic considerations, and while there are no rules that are fixed and fast, some useful distinctions can be laid down. The "popular" song, of the kind for which Auden wrote a number of lyrics as a young man, may be conveniently exemplified by the opening lines of Cole Porter's "I've Got You Under My Skin."

> I've got you ———— under my skin;
> I've got you ———— deep in the heart of me;
> So deep in my heart ———— you're really a part of me;
> I've got you ———— under my skin.
>
> I've tried so ———— not to give in;
> I've said to myself, this affair never will go so well,
> But why should I try to resist when, darling, I know so well,
> I've got you ———— under my skin.

Porter was a composer who served as his own lyricist, and like the best of his composer colleagues (Richard Rodgers, George Gershwin) he was a meticulous respecter of the accentual values in his texts. His songs, both comic and serious, abound in the sort of triple rhymes ("go so well," "know so well") that appear above, and his music was always at the service not only of verbal but of accentual clarity. Consider only the terminal feet in the lines above. Three out of the eight lines conclude with "under my skin," which is metrically and musically matched with "not to give in." These are all choriambic feet, that is, two accented syllables with two unaccented ones between them. These choriambs conclude the first, fourth, fifth, and eighth lines. The remaining lines are concluded by paeonic feet, which, though requiring three unaccented syllables together with one accented one *in any combination,* in fact put the accent here infallibly on the second of the four syllables. This metrical tidiness is simply confirmed later in the song when Porter introduces the paeonic rhyme of "mentality" with "reality." The elaborateness of this metrical design has the attractive effect of reinforcing the obsessiveness which is the theme and mental framework of the song.

By way of contrast, consider a song by Ben Jonson, from the satiric comedy *Cynthia's Revels.*

> Slow, slow, fresh fount, keep time with my salt tears;
> Yet slower yet, oh faintly, gentle springs;

List to the heavy part the music bears,
　Woe weeps out her division when she sings.
　　Droop herbs and flowers,
　　Fall grief in showers;
　　Our beauties are not ours;
　　　Oh, I could still,
　Like melting snow upon some craggy hill,
　　Drop, drop, drop, drop,
Since nature's pride is now a withered daffodil.

The prosodic complexities and subtleties of this lyric are enormous, even when compared to the sophistication of Porter's lines. The first line is made up entirely of monosyllabic words, ten of them in all, composing what would perhaps serve as a pentameter line were it not for the fact that there are but two unaccented words in the whole of it: "with my." This remarkable and insistent piling up of strongly accented words we know to be an *equivalent* of a normal pentameter line, since its mate, the third line, is a perfect one with only a trochaic substitution in the first foot—which is a well-approved liberty. Jonson's heavy accents here are, of course, expressive of the mournful tenor of the song, the painful protractedness of the misery it describes, and the relentless dripping of the fountain and the tears. But in addition, the slow steady emphasis of syllable after syllable invites us to read and hear the line as if it were written in syllabics rather than in accentual meter. And it gives the composer a great deal of liberty with regard to musical setting, a liberty he would not enjoy in the setting of polysyllabic words. The first line, then, may be seen as a very free departure from a pentameter norm, which the ensuing three lines observe in their own idiosyncratic ways. What Jonson has done here is to provide rich opportunities for the composer by moving between syllabic and accentual patterns. The fifth and sixth lines are composed of a spondee followed by an iamb, which, again, is a singular departure from what looked like a reluctant accommodation to iambic pentameter in the opening quatrain. The seventh line is more idiosyncratic still, composed as it is of an amphibrach followed by an anapest. The brief eighth line is a simple trochee and iamb, and is followed by a fairly orthodox pentameter line, which leads directly into the four-times-repeated "drop" of the penultimate line—which, again, by its monotonous insistence expresses the slow melting and dripping of icy waters and the relentless repetitions of the pangs of grief. The final line is a hexameter, made the more noticeable in its departure from the five-foot norm by the fact that the extra foot is supplied by the adjective "withered," and that the line could have attained its perfect pentameter form if the adjective, which is not essential to the grammatical sense, had been eliminated. And the extended line once again offers the composer room for his own art.

The difference between the two kinds of lyrics may be roughly described by the claim that the "popular" one is in fact the more conservative, exact, and inelastic of the two, while the Jonsonian lyric is bolder, more unorthodox, and more expressive, leaving room for musical expressiveness and inventiveness as well. The former is firmly accentual; the latter shifts smoothly and at will between accentual and syllabic. And it is this second kind that has served as Auden's model for the "Barcarolle" he wrote for Stravinsky's *The Rake's Progress*.

Stravinsky himself, in his autobiography, made clear how important to him in the setting of words were syllabic considerations. Writing about the challenge of setting a poem by André Gide, Stravinsky declares, "With the exception of two melodies for some lines by Verlaine, this was my first experience of composing music for French words. I had always been afraid of the difficulties of French prosody. Although I had been living in France for twenty years, and had spoken the language from childhood, I had until now hesitated to use it in my music. I now decided to try my hand, and was more and more pleased as my work proceeded. What I most enjoyed was syllabifying the music to French, as I had done for Russian in *Les Noces,* and for Latin in *Oedipus Rex.*"

Here, then, is Auden's "Barcarolle."

> Gently, little boat,
> Across the waters float,
> Their crystal waves dividing;
>     The sun in the west
>     Is going to rest:
>         Glide, glide, glide,
> Towards the Islands of the Blest.
>
> Orchards greenly grace
> That undisturbèd place,
> The wearied soul recalling
>     To slumber and dream
>     While many a stream

> Falls, falls, falls,
> Descanting on a child-like theme.
>
> Lion, lamb and deer,
> Untouched by greed or fear,
> About the woods are straying,
>     And quietly now
>     The blossoming bough
>     Sways, sways, sways,
> Above the clear unclouded brow.

It can be claimed with a certain plausibility that Auden's poem owes something to Baudelaire's "L'Invitation au voyage," which, after all, also involves a journey by boat to a languorous, soothing, and almost Edenic paradise. Auden's mention of "the wearied soul" is particularly Baudelairean, and both poems are "set" in the evening, at sundown. But I think it can also be claimed that Baudelaire's poem is refulgent with an excessive luxury and has about it a note of undeniable depravity, obliquely hinted at in the phrase *tes traîtres yeux*, which suggests a peculiar and possibly disturbing relationship between the two parties. The approaching night will provide a sexual occasion for Baudelaire's couple, while it will simply be the hour of repose and sleep for the solitary soul in Auden's poem.

There are a number of ways to describe the metrical pattern of the first three lines of each stanza, but it is both simplest and most accurate to say that in all three cases the lines progress from five through six to seven syllables. In each case the third line ends in a participle, the accented syllable of which provides the rhyme for the repeated word in the sixth line; hence "divi*ding*" rhymes with "glide," "reca*lling*" with "falls," and "*stray*ing" with "sways." The fourth and fifth lines, throughout, are each composed of an iamb followed by an anapest. The sixth line seems like a conscious imitation of Jonson's tenth line, and the final lines are once again accentual tetrameter lines. The poem thus shifts back and forth freely between syllabic and accentual patterns much as Jonson's did.

But Auden's is neither grief-stricken, like Jonson's, nor involved with self-indulgent lassitudes and sexual servility, like Baudelaire's. The dream that it presents is emphatically innocent and, in Auden's own words, "child-like." There is nothing less than an Isaian beatitude and peace described in the final stanza, and if there is a "wearied soul" in the poem, he is recalled to a state of innocence betokened by the "clear unclouded brow" of the last line. To be sure, the song is part of an opera about the decline of its hero into conditions of depravity and madness, but within the confines of the text of the song itself, the vision of innocence is sanitized or, perhaps, protected by a kind of textual quarantine. In its vision of a purity and innocence associated not only with Isaiah but with childhood, it speaks of something in Auden's character and of his feelings about his own childhood.

Something of the same prosodic experimentation and innovation is to be found in another poem in the volume. It is not identified as a "song," though it seems to invite musical setting. If it isn't a song or from an opera, like the "Barcarolle," it is nevertheless about an opera, and for that reason Auden may have resorted to his metrical inventiveness. It is called "The Proof," and it concerns the testing, by fire and water, that the young hero and heroine of Mozart's *The Magic Flute,* Tamino and Pamina, must undergo (very much like the tests placed upon Ferdinand and Miranda by Prospero in *The Tempest*) by way of validating their devotion to one another. The poem is composed of two extremely complex stanzas, each of fifteen lines. They exhibit a patent symmetry and balance, the first giving voice to Fire, the second to Water; the first putting Tamino's name before Pamina's, the second reversing this order; and both stanzas containing a fourteenth line in parentheses. Such formal balances are immediately noticeable. But it is the rhythmical variations within each stanza that must have afforded Auden a special pleasure. Here is the poem's first stanza.

"When rites and melodies begin
    To alter modes and times,
And timid bar-flies boast aloud
    Of uncommitted crimes,
And leading families are proud
    To dine with their black sheep,
What promises, what discipline,
    If any, will Love keep?"
        So roared Fire on their right:
        But Tamino and Pamina
        Walked past its rage,
        Sighing O, sighing O,
In timeless fermatas of awe and delight
    (Innocent? Yes. Ignorant? No.)
        Down the grim passage.

The first eight lines of the stanza appear (purely on the basis of typographical layout) to be composed of alternate tetrameter and trimeter lines, the first trimeter rhyming with the second, and the third with the fourth. Of the tetrameter lines, the first rhymes with the fourth (the stanza's seventh line)—an unusually large rhyming interval—while the second rhymes with the third. But this illusion of alternating line lengths is created chiefly by typographical disposition. The lines are in fact two sets of couplets in "fourteeners," iambic septameter, which is the meter Chapman used for his translation of the *Iliad,* and which Golding used for his version of Ovid's *Metamorphoses.* Both these Elizabethan monuments of translation were written in fourteener rhymed couplets. (It is worth noting as well that fourteener rhymed tercets, broken typographically as Auden has done into alternating tetrameter and trimeter lines, were used by Lewis Carroll in "The Walrus and the Carpenter.")

Auden's first eight lines are enclosed in quotation marks, and spoken, in the spirit of somber and ominous warning, by Fire, symbolic of ungoverned passion. The very capacity of "rites and melodies" to alter our ways of life bespeaks precisely the tyrannic employment of the arts for political ends that Auden had long been on guard against, and which he recognized with aversion in Plato's *Republic.* The warning uttered by Fire consists of a description of a society all of whose values have been undermined or inverted. But since Love (as distinct from lust) must be based both on discipline and on promises (a word involving deep personal feelings on Auden's part), how shall it survive in a lawless and immoral society? The plain, rational answer is, it won't. But we, in this poem, are not only in the world of opera, where virtually anything is possible, but in the Mozartian world of *The Magic Flute,* where destiny, magic, and a supremely benign composer will bring about the same perfection and success of love contrived by the collaboration of Prospero and Shakespeare. There are, of course, a number of ways to feel about this, the most lighthearted perhaps being a simple pleasure in the absurdities of romance, and the equally child-like delight in seeing the hero and heroine triumph over their enemies and the obstacles thrown in their ways. But there is a serious and morose corollary to this view, or, if you prefer, an adult supplement, which is that the possibilities of true love are entirely reserved to romantic fiction and myth, and not to be expected in the ordinary course of life. Just how much of these views Auden entertained, or how he kept them in balance, the poem does not expressly say, though we may allow ourselves to speculate about it.

The next line, "So roared Fire on their right," is composed of four trochees with a catalectic closure, and the corresponding line in the second stanza ("So hissed Water on their left") is prosodically the same. The remaining lines of the stanza, beginning with the tenth line, are composed as follows: (10) two paeons, (11) a spondee and an iamb, (12) two amphimacers, (13) a virtual torrent of amphibrachs, (14) two choriambs, and (15) finally, a line which, when matched with its corresponding line in the second stanza, clearly demands to be read syllabically, both lines being composed of five syllables, though they may be described as a dactyl and a trochee.

What is striking about all this is its sheer unexpectedness; it is constantly in the process of taking us by surprise. In the second stanza, the speech of warning uttered by Water (the chaotic and undisciplined element that also corresponds to ungoverned passion) is, if anything, more ominous than the warning of Fire. It presents us with the nightmarish domain we also encountered in the penultimate stanza of "Nones." The most crucial and terrifying warning is that with which Water concludes: "What swarming hatreds then will hatch / Out of Love's riven heart?" That Love should be transformed to hate is both a complete paradox and a not uncommon experience. In the penultimate line of the second stanza, instead of the twin choriambs of the first we have two amphimacers. The two corresponding lines, both enclosed in parentheses, shift the positions of their "Yes" and "No," and play a significant "stage direction" role in the poem. The first of them—"(Innocent? Yes. Ignorant? No.)"—is descriptive of a perfect love, which is not so unworldly as to be foolish, but which remains uncontaminated by any surrounding corruption. The second—"(Frightened? No. Happy? Yes.)"—expresses an absolute confidence conferred by a love that has endured the most severe of ordeals. Auden himself could, like any of us, dream of such a love; and could also have consigned it wholly to the realm of imagination or of art.

In a spirit of mischievous levity, Auden composed a poem in rhymed couplets, dedicated to the art historian Edgar Wind (who had been a colleague of his at Smith College, where Wind taught from 1948 to 1955) and which is titled, with deliberate quotation marks, "'The Truest Poetry Is the Most Feigning.'" All by itself, the title presents a challenge, since it is a misquotation, and one does not know whether this represents carelessness or playfulness on Auden's part. He was of course capable of both. It will be worth supplying the context from which the poem's title derives, Shakespeare's *As You Like It,* III, iii.

TOUCHSTONE. I am here with thee and thy goats, as the most capricious poet, honest Ovid, was among the Goths . . . Truly, I would the gods had made thee poetical.

AUDREY. I do not know what poetical is. Is it honest in deed and word? Is it a true thing?

TOUCHSTONE. No, truly; for the truest poetry is the most faining, and lovers are given to poetry, and what they swear in poetry may be said, as lovers, they do feign.

AUDREY. Do you wish then that the gods had made me poetical?

TOUCHSTONE. I do truly; for thou swear'st to me thou art honest. Now if thou wert a poet, I might have some hope thou didst feign.

We have here a little seduction scene, laden with puns. Part of its humor lies in the fact that while Touchstone is merely a clown, one of the retinue of the banished duke, he is nevertheless, by virtue of being a member of the noble entourage, a true sophisticate, especially when compared with the pastoral innocence (and ignorance) of Audrey, "a country wench" upon whose person he has clear and carnal designs. In the dialogue between them, he is often speaking over her head to the audience in general, and more particularly to that literary segment of the audience who will catch his learned puns, and enjoy a laugh at the expense of a simple, and simple-minded, girl, whose only fortune is her looks and her simplicity. In Shakespeare's day the words "goats" and "Goths" were virtually indistinguishable, and linked by the Latin derivation of "goat" to the "capricious" Ovid. Still more subtle, the words "fain," which means desire, and "feign," which means falsify or deceive, were then, as now, identical in sound. It may plausibly be asked how an audience, without benefit of the written text, could make the distinction Shakespeare intends; and the answer is an extremely literary one—Touchstone intends an allusion to the first line of the opening sonnet of Sidney's *Astrophel and Stella,* "Loving in truth, and fain in verse my love to show . . ." There is not the least reason to suppose that Audrey is expected to grasp this; Touchstone seems simply to be muttering little jokes for his own amusement while he tries to figure out a way of achieving a seduction. What Auden has done, in altering the passage, is to narrow and confine Shakespeare's meanings. In declaring that "the truest poetry is the most faining," Touchstone was saying that it was most expressive of desire. This means a good number of things, including the general rhetorical motives of persuasion, probably, though not necessarily, in behalf of love, for the motive to persuade could belong, with various grades of legitimacy, to all the arts, and be employed for a variety of purposes. Persuasion would of necessity have to include deceit and fraud among its arsenal of devices, though it would not be confined to these alone, as Auden confines it in changing Shakespeare's wording. In any case, it seems fair to assume that when Auden writes, "Good poets have a weakness for bad puns," he is likely to have Shakespeare in mind.

It also seems likely that Auden intends an allusion not only to Shakespeare but to "the most capricious poet, honest Ovid." There is an intimate relationship between Auden's rhymed couplets and the 1661 translation of the Latin poet's *Ars amatoria, The Art of Love,* by Francis Wolferton, from which long work a few specimens may serve as illustration.

> First must a letter sealed an entrance find;
> Let your wax bear the impress of your mind.
> And let your letter love-expressions bear,
> To which you must add an imploring prayer.
>
> A promise hurts you not; then promise much;
> It makes those that are not rich seem to be such.
> Your letter wins her, if she credits it;
> Hope's a false goddess, yet for you most fit.
>
> With handsome words you must prepare her mind;
> First try if those will entertainment find.
>
> Fear not to promise—promises will move—
> And call the gods as witness to your love.
> Jove from above laughs at love's perjuries,—
> Bidding Aeolus blow away such tricks,
> For he himself to Juno swore by Styx
> Falsely, and he our great exemplar is.

Not just the pentameter couplets (from which Wolferton obviously departs from time to time) or the subject matter itself, but Ovid's sophisticated, scandalizing, and rather immoral tone seems to be part of what Auden was trying to capture.

Furthermore, the double indebtedness, to Shakespeare and Ovid, wonderfully complicates the meanings of the poem, which can be broken down into two major, and independent, claims: 1) that lovers are full of deceit, that love poems are full of falsehood, meant only to gain carnal and self-gratifying ends, and 2) that all poetry, whether love poetry or any other kind, is, of necessity, and ought to be, full of lies. These are, to be sure, related notions, but they are by no means identical. The second of these ideas is clearly the larger and more philosophical one, having to do with the very nature of art and its relation to reality. As Basil Willey explains in *The Eighteenth Century Background,* "When opening a book of poetry, wrote Jean Le Clerc in the last year of the seventeenth century, the reader should remember that he is about to peruse 'the Work of a Liar, who intends to entertain him with Fictions . . . The poets are full of false thoughts, by which if we are not deceived, yet we insensibly lose a good Taste and right judgment, which are the finest ornaments of human nature.' "

What Auden seems to do in this amusing poem is to shift back and forth between the two poles of meaning. In behalf of the second, more weighty one, he has written, in the essay called "Writing" (in *The Dyer's Hand*),

> What makes it difficult for a poet not to tell lies is that, in poetry, all facts and all beliefs cease to be true or false and become interesting possibilities. The reader does not have to share the beliefs expressed in a poem in order to enjoy it. Knowing this, a poet is constantly tempted to make use of an idea or a belief, not because he believes it to be true, but because he sees it has interesting poetic possibilities. It may not, perhaps, be absolutely necessary that he believe it, but it is certainly necessary that his emotions be deeply involved, and this they can never be unless, as a man, he takes it more seriously than as a mere poetic convenience.

It can, I think, be fairly argued that there is something equivocating about this statement, in which we are asked to make a very uncertain distinction between believing in something and not believing in it but being deeply involved emotionally in it. There are those who have taken the passage as representing Auden's embarrassed and not wholly successful defense against his shifting allegiances, from politics to heterodox psychology to orthodox religion, the defense presumably being that he never truly "believed" in any of the views he was later to repudiate, but simply entertained them as "interesting possibilities." The chief weakness of this "defense" is that it can be applied to any doctrine or ideology Auden adopted at any point in the course of his career, and thus makes his religious stance as dubious and tentative as any of those he abandoned.

This view rejoices the hearts of his vigorously secular admirers. The problems involved are, of course, far more complicated than Auden's little statement acknowledges, and are dealt with at greater length and with more subtlety by I. A. Richards and T. S. Eliot, among others.

The poem begins with the Ovidian pretense that it is offering directions not just to the lover but to the writer of love poetry, and the instructions are to avoid literalness above all: to be "subtle, various, ornamental, clever," and depart as freely as imagination permits from the bare facts of the actual situation.

> Suppose your Beatrice be, as usual, late,
> And you would tell us how it feels to wait,
> You're free to think, what may be even true,
> You're so in love that one hour seems like two,
> But write—*As I sat waiting for her call,*
> *Each second longer darker seemed than all*
> (Something like this but more elaborate still)
> *Those raining centuries it took to fill*
> *That quarry whence Endymion's love was torn;*
> From such ingenious fibs are poems born . . .

The mention of Beatrice chimes with a reference to Dante seven lines earlier, and the elaborate comparison of "seconds" to "raining centuries," embedded in a context of classical mythology, is very much in the Ovidian mode. The passage, however, should serve to remind us how often Auden has employed or departed from his own advice here. In "Heavy Date" he is precisely concerned with occupying his mind in waiting for a loved one to show up. Still more to the point, in a long series of poems, beginning perhaps with the ballad "As I Walked Out One Evening," and continuing through "Serenade" and "The Willow-Wren and the Stare," he presents lovers making extravagant and usually implausible declarations of undying devotion, for the most part in a context that ruthlessly undermines such protestations with a biting irony. Auden's prose meditation *Dichtung und Wahrheit* (a title borrowed from Goethe) begins, "Expecting your arrival tomorrow, I find myself thinking, *I love You:* then comes the thought:—*I should like to write a poem which would express exactly what I mean when I think those words.*" The rest of the meditation is devoted to the difficulty of this undertaking. (In the course of the meditation Auden again makes his characteristic association of Tristan with Don Giovanni.)

The poem continues:

> The living girl's your business (some odd sorts
> Have been an inspiration to men's thoughts):
> Yours may be old enough to be your mother,
> Or have one leg that's shorter than the other,
> Or play Lacrosse or do the Modern Dance;
> To you that's destiny, to us it's chance;
> We cannot love your love till she take on,
> Through you, the wonders of a paragon.

It would have been perhaps a trifle clearer if Auden had used italics for emphasis in the first of these lines, thus: "The living girl's *your* business," as distinct from ours, who are your readers. We as readers have no personal investment in the literal truth or falsity of the love situation you are describing; we merely wish to be titillated and entertained, and are prepared for any number and elaboration of lies from you, so long as they will satisfy our interest, prurient or otherwise.

> If half-way through such praises of your dear,
> Riot and shooting fill the streets with fear,
> And overnight, as in some terror dream,
> Poets are suspect with the New Regime,
> Stick at your desk and hold your panic in;
> What you are writing still may save your skin:
> Re-sex the pronouns, add a few details,
> And, lo, a panegyric ode which hails
> (How is the Censor, bless his heart, to know?)
> The new pot-bellied Generalissimo.

There is a lot of androgynous fun going on here, which emphasizes the deceitful and feigning quality of poetry, and which reflexively points to the fact that "The living girl's your business" may itself be a deception. As Auden said in "The Fall of Rome," "All the literati keep / An imaginary friend." Of course, the chief suggestion of these lines is that there is no real difference between flattery of a loved one and flattery of a hateful tyrant—both are crudely self-interested gestures.

> Though honest Iagos, true to form, will write
> *Shame!* in your margins, *Toady! Hypocrite!*
> True hearts, clear heads will hear the note of glory

And put inverted commas round the story,
Thinking—*Old Sly-boots! We shall never know
Her name or nature. Well, it's better so.*

We find ourselves here in the thick of Auden's not quite resolved feelings about just how much of a writer's or artist's private life his audience is entitled to know. At various times Auden took unequivocal positions against the public's right to any such knowledge, and he famously desired all his correspondents to destroy all letters of his in their possession. At the same time, he took a lively interest in gossip of all kinds, liked to read the biographies of others (including other writers), and took particular interest in the kind of material that ordinary society commonly suppresses or denies. Hence his early interest in Freud, Lane, Lawrence, Layard. "Sly-boots" is not only an especially British expression, but one normally employed "in a mild or jocular" way (according to the OED), which makes Auden's use of it rather pointed in the title of an essay about J. R. Ackerley and his father, "Papa Was a Wise Old Sly-Boots," an essay about very unorthodox sexual behavior. In any case, the curious effect of the passage quoted above is to suggest that almost any commendatory piece of writing, on whatever subject, regarding whatever person, has a hidden erotic premise and meaning; and that if the sexual implications are misaligned from a conventional point of view, this may or may not be part of the deceitfulness of poetry. We are invited to think pretty much anything we like, including all the possible sex permutations and combinations, as possibly lying behind the poet's words.

For, given Man, by birth, by education,
Imago Dei who forgot his station,
The self-made creature who himself unmakes,
The only creature ever made who fakes,
With no more nature to his loving smile
Than in his theories of a natural style,
What but tall tales, the luck of verbal playing,
Can trick his lying nature into saying
That love, or truth in any serious sense,
Like orthodoxy, is a reticence.

These concluding lines of the poem have moved a great distance from their initial relationship to Ovid or to Wolferton's version of the *Ars amatoria*. We are here much nearer to Pope, and the Pope, moreover, of the Moral Essays. There are some who have viewed these closing lines as an especially deceitful casuistry, by which the poet seems to claim that truth can be arrived at only by lying. Whether or not this is true, it can more firmly be maintained that the end of the poem appears to contradict the beginning, since the end recommends "a reticence," while the beginning urged, "By all means sing of love but, if you do, / Please make a rare old proper hullabaloo." The paradoxes can be resolved if we posit the idea that love is to be absolutely distinguished from any statement made about it, such as a poem. In this sense, the truest love is the most silent, for words themselves are altogether untrustworthy, being as they are the instruments of fallen men. We may also assume that the resolution of Auden's seeming paradox is the one Emily Dickinson suggests in the lines, "Tell all the Truth but tell it slant— / Success in Circuit lies." That is, indirection is our only recourse. Once again, it may be objected that to call Man "the only creature ever made who fakes" is to forget the exquisite gifts for fakery with which birds, beasts, and insects are endowed. Auden is at his most astute in his jests about the word "nature" and mankind's tortured relationship to its many meanings. As for the last two lines, I am able to understand orthodoxy as a "reticence" only in the sense that it is conservative and that it may be said to depend upon the tacit as well as the confessed assent of the congregation of believers. This would be a curious thing to assert about "truth," whether or not one believes it should be applied to "love."

Auden was forty-seven years old when, in 1954, he composed "A Permanent Way." He would continue to work and write until his death at the age of sixty-six in 1973. But the tone of this poem, underneath a superficial pretense of cheerfulness, is deeply and touchingly discouraged. The poem exhibits a clear and unconcealed debt to Frost in its simple allegory of travel and in its generally spare language. It bears a family resemblance to Frost's "Neither Out Far Nor In Deep," and, perhaps even more, to "The Road Not Taken." Auden's poem, however, is composed in the complicated spirit of resignation, mixed with a strong portion of determination to avoid the least suggestion of self-pity—which is to say, in a spirit of the stoic manliness that he condemned in Marcus Aurelius but enjoyed in the tragic heroes of Italian operas.

The poem is a frank acknowledgment that sexual adventure and the expectation of new erotic experience are no longer to be hoped for, presumably on grounds of age, though this is not explicitly stated. When the poet says that he is "forcibly held to [his] tracks" and speaks of the allegorical train on which he travels as held to "the dogma of its rails," we are made aware of a kind of coercion that could be either self-imposed or exacted by outside forces. The speaker of the poem adopts the attitude that the limitations imposed upon his travel—his complete inability to deviate from a fixed path—is in fact a good thing and greatly to be valued, not least for the safety it affords. There will no longer be any messy affairs; a lot of heartbreak will be avoided.

> And what could be greater fun,
> Once one has chosen and paid,
> Than the inexpensive delight
> Of a choice one might have made.

It seems clear that a lot of answers could be furnished for the rhetorical question about "what could be greater fun." The poet has decided to settle for a wholly imaginary erotic life, and affects to be quite content with this. Under the circumstances, we are allowed, I think, to suppose that he has been brought to this condition by sufficient experiences of pain, accompanied by a pronounced sense of aging. We are reminded of that Delphic, circular little poem that served as epigraph to *Bucolics: "Fair is Middle-Earth nor changes, though to Age, / Raging at his uncomeliness, / Her wine turn sour, her bread tasteless."* Auden's determination to stifle any tendency to self-pity is a characteristic to be found in other parts of his poetry, and in some of his prose as well. It suggests something of the code of the schoolboy that figured in some of his early work, and in the notion he shared with Isherwood of "the truly strong man." But it was more than a self-created or school-instilled doctrine of virtue. It was literary as well, and may indeed have been embraced because Auden found himself admiring it in many of the writers he most loved. One of the first of these was Thomas Hardy, and stoicism was Hardy's emotional last and first resort. But late in Auden's life, in fact in June 1971, roughly two years before his death, he wrote "Ode to the Medieval Poets," which begins,

> Chaucer, Langland, Douglas, Dunbar, with all your
> brother Anons, how on earth did you ever manage,
>     without anaesthetics or plumbing,
>     in daily peril from witches, warlocks,
> lepers, The Holy Office, foreign mercenaries
> burning as they came, to write so cheerfully,
>     with no grimaces of self-pathos?

It is these poet-heroes, along with Hardy, Frost, and a number of others, that hover imperceptibly behind such a poem as "A Permanent Way," in which the poet declares himself prepared to settle for nothing more than the "dream / Of a love or a livelihood" that might fit the passing scene but which is presumably never to be his. To be sure, almost all of us are given to daydreams instinct with envy or unfulfilled wishes. But there is to this poem a conscious adoption of an asceticism that is altogether alien to the poet's nature, and against which, in the epigraph quoted above, Age rages.

"The Shield of Achilles" is not only the title poem of the book but also the first of the section called *In Sunshine and in Shade,* and it may be said to represent emblematically and almost to perfection the title of its section. It is based very clearly, though only in part, on the last part of the eighteenth book of the *Iliad,* in which the making of Achilles' shield by Hephaestus, at the behest of Thetis, is described in spectacular detail. The description is monumental, grand, deeply impressive, and elaborately detailed, and in this it serves at the very least a double function. It is the description of the making of a work of art, and in its reverence for particulars it is a glorification of the artist's function as a celebrant of all existence—for the entire cosmos and its implicit order is represented on the shield. It is also a positing and what may be regarded as a philosophical acceptance of that cosmic order. This order is assumed to be eternal, and to participate in something like the paradoxical nature described by Empedocles as a constant oscillation between Love and Strife. Empedocles wrote,

There is a double becoming of perishable things and a double passing away. The coming together of all things brings one generation into being and destroys it; the other grows up and is scattered as things become divided. And these things never cease continually changing places, at one time all being united in one through Love, at another each borne in different directions by the repulsion of Strife. Thus, as far as it is in their nature to grow into one out of many, and to become many once more when the one is parted asunder, so far they come into being and their life abides not. But, inasmuch as they never cease changing places continually, so far they are ever immovable as they go round the circle of existence.

Love and Strife on the Homeric shield are represented by the embossed presentation of two cities. One showed weddings and wedding feasts, a bride and her maids in procession, with men dancing in rings and singing nuptial songs of celebration. It presented the peaceful arbitration of legal disputes, the two parties presenting their cases in public and awaiting judicial decision. The second city is under siege, and the segment of the shield devoted to it depicts all manner of slaughter, ambush, treachery, flame, plunder, and destruction. The graphic detail is made persuasive by two factors. Homer's narrative has already presented us with hideous accounts of agonizing death, so nothing on the shield is likely to come to us as a surprise. But also we are never allowed to forget that what we are "witnessing" is a work of art, and we are invited to mix our admiration for the skill of the artist (who not incidentally happens to be a god) with a solemnly meditated sense that Hephaestus represents the world as it truly is. In addition to the two cities there are rural scenes with plowed fields, harvesters, vineyards, shepherds, and flocks, and, as a concluding detail, a dancing circle. In the Robert Fagles translation, the passage about superbly worked metals (which seem through sheer artistry to produce the colors of the grape, the luminosity of stars and of torches, the very stain of blood) concludes in this way.

> Here young boys and girls, beauties courted
> with costly gifts of oxen, danced and danced,
> linking their arms, gripping each other's wrists.
> And the girls wore robes of linen light and flowing,
> the boys wore finespun tunics rubbed with a gloss of oil,
> the girls were crowned with a bloom of fresh garlands,
> the boys swung golden daggers hung on silver belts.
> And now they would run in rings on their skilled feet,
> nimbly, quick, as a crouching potter spins his wheel,
> palming it smoothly, giving it practice twirls
> to see it run, and now they would run in rows,
> in rows crisscrossing rows—rapturous dancing.
> A breathless crowd stood round them struck with joy
> and through them a pair of tumblers dashed and sprang,
> whirling in leaping handsprings, leading out the dance.
>
> And he forged the Ocean River's mighty power girdling
> round the outmost rim of the welded indestructible shield.

Auden's poem moves back and forth between two complementary or opposed stanzaic and prosodic patterns. There are four eight-line stanzas, written largely in trimeter lines, but with many substitutions and variations from a basic iambic pattern so that an elegant lyric freedom and an elaborate syncopation are obtained. These stanzas are interspersed among highly regular stanzas of rhyme royal, the seven-line pentameter stanzas Auden used in the spirit of high levity in the *Letter to Lord Byron*, but which are used here with another effect altogether. The two kinds of stanzas are not only metrically different. The song-like lyric one renders a dramatic account of the making of the shield, and has named, identifiable characters in Thetis and Hephaestus; in addition, the shield is being made specifically for Achilles, who is also named. The rhyme-royal stanzas contain no identifiable persons, and no one has a name; there are "multitudes," and "bored officials," and a nameless "urchin," but the world presented by these stanzas is a faceless and anonymous one. And there is one more distinction to be made between these different stanzas. The lyric ones present a scene that clearly derives from Homer, and all of the expectations of Thetis are based upon the beautiful and terrible balance of Love and Strife that appeared on the shield to be made for her son. The rhyme-royal stanzas, however, represent the pitiless and impersonal world of modern warfare and its unrelieved aftermath. The poem was written in 1952, when the full horror of WWII and its destructive effects were beginning to be appreciated.

Attention deserves to be paid to the prosody of the lyric stanzas, since Auden is as daring and innovative here as anywhere in his work.

> She looked over his shoulder
> For vines and olive trees,
> Marble well-governed cities,
> And ships upon untamed seas,
> But there on the shining metal
> His hand had put instead
> An artificial wilderness
> And a sky like lead.

The rhyme scheme of these lyric stanzas is simple and uniform throughout: the second line rhymes with the fourth, and the sixth with the eighth. In addition, the first three of the four such stanzas all open with the same line. Moreover, in the first three of these stanzas, all the unrhymed lines except the penultimate one have feminine endings. The penultimate lines in the stanzas are metrical deviations from the rest of the lines, being each tetrameters instead of trimeters. And perhaps most important of all, three

out of the four stanzas, this time including the final one, conclude with a
line in which the three accented syllables are crowded tightly together at
the end:

⌣ ⌣  / / /
And a sky like lead
  ⌣ ⌣   / / /
But a weed-choked field
  ⌣    ⌣   / / /
Who would not live long

(The exception to this metrical coda—"Quite another scene"—lends
gravity and weight to the others by simple contrast.) To return to the
penultimate line of the first of these lyric stanzas, "an artificial wilderness"
is a complicated phrase. For one thing, we are regularly reminded that the
images we are presented with are the creation of an artist, the smithy
Hephaestus, so that anything he creates in the way of images upon the
shield is of necessity "artificial." Secondly, the term "artificial wilderness"
is by ordinary standards an oxymoron, since the general meaning of
"wilderness" is of a natural landscape untamed, possibly not traversed or
even inhabited by humans, while "artificial" involves some conscious and
deliberate tampering. Moreover, "a sky like lead" is meant to be ominous,
but is quite in keeping with a work of art made entirely of metals. Each
of the first three lyric stanzas begins with the hopeful expectations of
Thetis, based on Homeric precedence, and on a presumed acceptance of
a world in which there was no want of horror and pain but also, and in
more or less equal degrees, joy and honor and celebration. The second
lyric stanza speaks of the space on the shield "where the altar should
have been," but which, in this "modern" version of the world, has been
usurped by our particularly modern kinds of barbarity, desolation, and
inhumanity.

The intervening, rhyme-royal stanzas are metrically impeccable, exhibiting that regularity we can easily identify with the faceless military
regimen they largely describe. The first set of these stanzas describes
something like the Nuremberg rallies of Storm Troopers, and annual
National Socialist Party conventions that began in 1933 and went on for
many years. Uniformed personnel lined up in rigid formations in incomprehensible numbers would salute and shout "Heil Hitler" on the command of loudspeakers broadcasting the voice of someone invisibly remote
and far away. But we are not entitled to suppose that such putative

patriotic rallies are purely a Nazi creation. The carefully managed control of public opinion in wartime, and the express manipulation of the sentiments and morale of combat troops, are fairly widespread practices.

The second set of these stanzas describes a grotesque public execution which, since it takes place in a wartime context, looks like the consequence of the deliberations of a kangaroo court, if any such legal niceties have been observed at all. What is described, the public killing of three men by a firing squad, is presented as a travesty of the Crucifixion. The second of the stanzas ends,

> What their foes like to do was done, their shame
> Was all the worst could wish; they lost their pride
> And died as men before their bodies died.

It is perhaps too easily supposed that the rhyme-royal stanzas are exclusively devoted to the contemporary world, as distinct from the lyric ones with their Homeric details. But matters are not so neatly divisible. Homer describes the killing of the Trojan Thestor by Patroclus in the sixteenth book, where the fully aware Thestor dies a particularly horrible death. In his introduction to Robert Fagles' translation, and in regard to this very passage, Bernard Knox describes Thestor as "gaping like a fish on the hook. The spear-thrust destroys his dignity as a human being even before it takes his life." There is, moreover, a famous commentary on the Homeric account of a "death before death" in the celebrated essay by Simone Weil called "The *Iliad*, or, The Poem of Force." It was first published in a French journal in December 1940 and January 1941. Translated by Mary McCarthy, it was published in the United States by Dwight Macdonald in the November 1945 issue of *Politics*. Formulating a definition of force as it figures in the *Iliad*, Simone Weil writes,

> Exercised to the limit, [force] turns man into a thing in the most literal sense: it makes a corpse out of him. Somebody was here, and the next minute there is nobody here at all; this is the spectacle the *Iliad* never wearies of showing us . . . From [force's] first property (the ability to turn a human being into a thing by the simple method of killing him) flows another, quite prodigious too in its own way, the ability to turn a human being into a thing while he is still alive . . . A man stands disarmed and naked with a weapon pointing at him; this person becomes a corpse before anybody or anything touches him. Just a moment ago, he was thinking, acting, hoping . . . Soon,

however, he grasps the fact that the weapon which is pointing at him will not be diverted; and now, still breathing, he is simply matter; still thinking, he can think no longer.

It is certainly possible that Auden had read this essay and had Weil in mind as he was writing his poem. But the kind of barbarity described in Homer, and commented upon by Bernard Knox and Simone Weil, was not confined to "pagan" times, and Auden was very likely to have been acquainted with published accounts of the German concentration camps. One such account, by Eugen Kogon, published in 1950 and called *The Theory and Practice of Hell,* dealt very specifically with the policied humiliation and dehumanization of camp prisoners, the purposeful removal of their last shreds of dignity before murdering them. (Subsequently, there have been even more excruciatingly detailed accounts of the same thing.)

Here is the last of the rhyme-royal stanzas.

> A ragged urchin, aimless and alone,
>   Loitered about that vacancy; a bird
> Flew up to safety from his well-aimed stone:
>   That girls are raped, that two boys knife a third,
>   Were axioms to him, who'd never heard
> Of any world where promises are kept
> Or one could weep because another wept.

The word "that" in the second line refers to the place of execution described in the previous rhyme-royal stanza, now abandoned and reduced to a "vacancy." The "civic violence," as distinguished from the "military violence," is a kind with which the urchin is numbingly familiar, and I believe that by this point in his literary career we are entitled to suppose that Auden had reserved for himself a special burden of meaning as regards the absence of "any world where promises are kept." As for the virtue of compassion alluded to in the final line above, we know it to be singularly absent from the world we inhabit, for all its Christian pretensions. In fact, it makes a more persuasive appearance in the barbarous, pagan world of Homer than in our own. In the final book of the *Iliad,* and once again in the Fagles translation, Priam comes humbly to Achilles to beg for the slain body of his son Hector. The passage deserves extended quotation.

> The majestic king of Troy slipped past the rest
> and kneeling down beside Achilles, clasped his knees

and kissed his hands, those terrible, man-killing hands
that had slaughtered Priam's many sons in battle.
Awesome—as when the grip of madness seizes one
who murders a man in his own fatherland and flees
abroad to foreign shores, to a wealthy, noble host,
and a sense of marvel runs through all who see him—
so Achilles marveled, beholding majestic Priam.
His men marveled too, trading startled glances.
But Priam prayed his heart out to Achilles:
"Remember your own father, great godlike Achilles—
as old as *I* am, past the threshold of deadly old age!
. . . . .
Fifty sons I had when the sons of Achaea came,
nineteen born to me from a single mother's womb
and the rest by other women in the palace. Many,
most of them violent Ares cut the knees from under.
But one, one was left me, to guard my walls, my people—
the one you killed the other day, defending his fatherland,
my Hector! It's all for him I've come to the ships now,
to win him back from you—I bring a priceless ransom . . ."
. . . . .
Those words stirred within Achilles a deep desire
to grieve for his own father. Taking the old man's hand
he gently moved him back. And overpowered by memory
both men gave way to grief. Priam wept freely
for man-killing Hector, throbbing, crouching
before Achilles' feet as Achilles wept himself,
now for his father, now for Patroclus once again,
and their sobbing rose and fell throughout the house.
Then when brilliant Achilles had his fill of tears
and the longing for it had left his mind and body,
he rose from his seat, raised the old man by the hand
and filled with pity now for his gray head and gray beard,
he spoke out winging words, flying straight to the heart:
"Poor man, how much you've borne—pain to break the spirit! . . ."

There can be no question but that Auden relies on our remembrance of
this scene, and the striking compassion of Achilles. And he is employing
something like Montaigne's irony in his essay "Of Cannibals," which
Shakespeare made use of in *The Tempest,* and which makes much of the

fact that pagans or primitive peoples seemed to exhibit moral excellences that were not to be found in so-called Christian societies.

It remains to examine the dramatic scansion of the last lyric stanza.

> ⌣ / /    / ⌣ ⌣
> The thin-lipped armorer
> ⌣ / ⌣   / ⌣ ⌣/
> Hephaestus, hobbled away;
> / ⌣ ⌣ ⌣ / ⌣    /
> Thetis of the shining breasts
> / / ⌣ ⌣ /
> Cried out in dismay
> ⌣ / ⌣ / ⌣    /
> At what the god had wrought
> ⌣   / ⌣ / ⌣    /
> To please her son, the strong
> / ⌣ ⌣ ⌣ / / ⌣ ⌣ / ⌣
> Iron-hearted man-slaying Achilles
> ⌣    ⌣ / / /
> Who would not live long.

The last line should remind us of another point. Achilles elected to die in battle, having been granted the choice of this fate or of living out a full term of life without dishonor. We are meant to remember his choice and its significance—that immortal fame could be attained by valor and honor in battle. And this is possible only when combat is conducted, as it was in Homer, according to what should not improperly be called "the rules of the game." On this topic Huizinga has made some pertinent observations.

> Fighting, as a cultural function, always presupposes limiting rules, and it requires, to a certain extent anyway, the recognition of its play-quality. We can speak of war as a cultural function so long as it is waged within a sphere whose members regard each other as equals or antagonists with equal rights; in other words its cultural function depends on its play-quality. This condition changes as soon as war is waged outside the sphere of equals, against groups not recognized as human beings and thus deprived of human rights— barbarians, devils, heathens, heretics and "lesser breeds without the law." [Huizinga's foreword is dated June 1938. It is difficult to

believe that he did not have the Nazis in mind as he wrote these words. They were to close the University of Leyden, where he had taught all his life, and he was banished to house arrest "in a remote parish in the eastern part" of Holland, according to G. N. Clark of Oxford. He died on February 1, 1945, only a few weeks before his country was liberated.] In such circumstances war loses its play-quality altogether and can only remain within the bounds of civilization in so far as the parties to it accept certain limitations for the sake of their own honour. Until recently the "law of nations" was generally held to constitute such a system of limitation, recognizing as it did the ideal of a community of mankind with rights and claims for all, and expressly separating the state of war—by declaring it—from peace on the one hand and criminal violence on the other. It remained for the theory of "total war" to banish war's cultural function and extinguish the last vestige of the play-element.

More than the "play-element" has been lost from war and civilization. It is no longer regarded as important that war should be conducted within "the sphere of equals," and such considerations were no bar to the American campaigns against Granada or Panama, nor to the British against the Falkland Islands. As for separating the state of war "from peace on the one hand and criminal violence on the other" by the deliberate and public act of "declaring it," we must acknowledge to our shame that the longest war in American history, the Vietnam War, was never declared.

"The warrior-hero of the Homeric epics," wrote Auden in his essay "The Greeks and Us," ". . . is an aristocratic ideal. He is what every member of the ruling class should imitate, what every member of the subject class should admire without envy and obey without resentment. The closest approximation to a god—the divine being conceived as ideally strong—possible to man." Such heroes, in their concern for values of honor, equity, fairness, maintain in the teeth of fate what Huizinga would call the rules of the game. They take personal responsibility for their fate, and often in the *Iliad* this means a personal, direct confrontation with a champion from the enemy side who is acknowledged as a peer and equal. Frequently in the course of Homer's epic all action seems to stop while two heroic contenders from the opposed camps challenge each other to single combat, the preliminary to which requires a proud and defiant boast of genealogical distinction. Such citations of ancestry are no doubt meant to be daunting and boastful; but they are more seriously a public means by which it may be established that the two contenders are precisely "equals." Honor would forbid a hero to fight with his inferior. In book three of the *Iliad* a proposal is made that the issue of the war be decided by single combat between Paris and Menelaus, as champions of their respective parties. For reasons in which the gods play a part, this does not come satisfactorily to pass, but the epic continues with such impressive one-to-one confrontations. Diomedes and Glaucus are so impressed with one another's backgrounds (their ancestors were linked by acts of bravery and kindness) that they agree not to fight one another. But there is a duel between Ajax and Hector, as there is between Patroclus and Sarpedon, and then between Hector and Patroclus. The final and conclusive confrontation of this kind is between Achilles and Hector. In every case each hero formally and elaborately identifies himself, speaking in his own person before undertaking personal action. This tradition of personal confrontation with an equal plays an enormous actual and symbolic part in Aeschylus' *Seven Against Thebes,* in which the seven attacking champions outside the city walls are ceremonially named, and seven defending champions each lauded with genealogical distinctions, appointed to oppose the attackers at the seven gates of the city. A great weight is put by Aeschylus upon the parity of the opposed champions, and the final pair are, of necessity, the two fratricidal sons of Oedipus.

This classical and heroic tradition was imitated or renewed with the medieval traditions of chivalry. Knights not only challenged one another to single combat but were meticulous in observing the practice of fighting only with their equals. For this purpose they identified themselves, raising their visors so as to be recognized. And a refusal to identify oneself constituted legitimate ground for the refusal of an opponent to fight a stranger. Just such a situation seems to imperil the dénouement of *King Lear.* Edmund is challenged to combat by his disguised and anonymous brother, Edgar. Edgar identifies himself to the herald, the arbiter of the duel, by saying,

> Know that my name is lost,
> By treason's tooth bare-gnawn and canker-bit;
> Yet I am noble as the adversary
> I come to cope.

Following this Edgar directly and defiantly challenges Edmund.

                                   I protest—
Maugre thy strength, place, youth, and eminence,
Despite thy victor sword and fire-new fortune,
Thy valor and thy heart—thou art a traitor,
False to thy gods, thy brother, and thy father,
Conspirant 'gainst this high illustrious prince,
And from th' extremest upward of thy head
To the descent and dust below thy foot
A most-toad-spotted traitor. Say thou 'no,'
This sword, this arm, and my best spirits are bent
To prove upon thy heart, whereto I speak,
Thou liest.

To this taunt, Edmund replies with a clear knowledge that the terms of
chivalric challenge would afford him perfect ground to refuse to fight.

                      In wisdom I should ask thy name.
But since thy outside looks so fair and warlike,
And that thy tongue some way of breeding breathes,
What safe and nicely I might well delay
By rule of knighthood I disdain and spurn.

It is that ineffable "way of breeding," that mark of gentility, which
persuades Edmund to fight a stranger who is in fact his own betrayed
brother.

   Clearly the notion of personal heroism expressed in terms of military
valor is a medieval and even Renaissance inheritance from classical
models. These were emblematically personified by the Nine Worthies, all
of them celebrated for their martial valor. There were three Jews (Joshua,
David, and Judas Maccabaeus), three Gentiles, that is, pagans (Hector,
Alexander, and Julius Caesar) and three Christians (Arthur, Charle-
magne, and Godfrey of Bouillon—the last being the leader of the First
Crusade). The glamor that attached to these exemplars of manly virtue
was widely acknowledged for centuries; but it began to lose its luster with
the invention of gunpowder and the development of firearms. And that,
of course, was only the beginning.

   Once heroes confronted each other face to face. Modern warfare is so
conducted as to make such confrontations virtually impossible. Bombar-
diers do not see the faces of their victims, who, in general, are as likely
to be women, children, and bedridden civilians as enemy troops. In any

case, they are unseen from the height of a plane or through the instruments for sighting artillery pieces. Even riflemen take aim at a sanitary distance from the body they intend to kill. We have "smart bombs" and a technology so advanced that equity among combatants is precisely what all armies seek to avoid. Modern weaponry can devastate whole cities, destroy an entire nation's infrastructure, leaving its population subject to starvation and rampant disease, quite apart from the killing done by bombs and by bullets. Generally speaking, governments strive to maintain a monopoly on crime, legitimizing that kind which serves to their advantage, and which they call "war," and condemning any freelance operations of the same sort when privately conducted by individuals or small groups. The very notion of a "just war," once sanctioned by the Roman Catholic Church, has by our time become so thoroughly discredited that the Vatican newspaper, *La Civiltà Cattólica,* has argued that the multinational (but chiefly American) war against Iraq brought to an end forever the possibility of a morally sanitized war. They write: "We must conclude that modern war is always immoral."

Clearly in such conditions military heroism as traditionally understood is impossible. And the dispensing of medals and military honors in modern times is little more than a political act. Auden was not the first to think so. In the course of time he came increasingly to believe that the only kind of heroism available to modern man was that of martyrdom: the selfless relinquishment of one's life for the benefit of others, or in the name of one's faith. To be sure, an ancient hero could sacrifice his life: Achilles chose his fate. But he still had worldly glory and immortal fame as his goal, whereas Auden's martyrs are a different breed. He wrote of them in an essay in *Secondary Worlds* called "The Martyr as Dramatic Hero," in which, by the way, he raises sound and powerful questions about the suitability, in Eliot's *Murder in the Cathedral,* of Thomas Becket as martyr-hero. But theatrical considerations apart, Auden would have found Dietrich Bonhoeffer greatly to be preferred as a "hero" to, say, Audie Murphy, the most decorated American soldier in WWII, whose baby-face good looks obviously played some part in the role of hero to which the army appointed him, and led to a brief and inauspicious film career from which he retired into appropriate obscurity.

It should also be added that between the diametrical opposites of "warrior-hero" and martyr lies a curious and many-peopled realm made up of quasi-legitimate troops. These would include all manner of unaffiliated ad-hoc forces, underground networks, terrorist groups, and insurrectionist gangs, not excluding the secret agents who play so important a symbolic role in Auden's early work. These are of course a strange and mixed lot, including as they must such gallant forces as the French Maquis of WWII, and other equally heroic partisan factions, along with such terrorist organizations as Abu Nidal now represents. All are dedicated, sometimes fanatic, groups or cells whose allegiance to their own causes is beyond question, and whose willingness to make the ultimate sacrifice is not in doubt. But these, whether or not we admire them, are neither the martyrs Auden came to regard as heroes nor the public and avowed warrior-heroes of tradition, since they are all secret operatives. The martyr-hero is in fact the nearest thing to what Auden first was searching for in his concept of "the truly strong man." Moreover, the martyr perfectly combines the "public" and "private" aspects of life that had obsessed Auden from the start. For a true martyr must not seek martyr-dom; he must quietly accede to its imposition, and this "act" is for him a purely private victory. But a hero is more or less by definition a very public figure, whose action alters the fate and lives of others. In this poem, the three men who are executed and the abandoned urchin are not martyrs; they are, alas, merely victims. All of this has had the effect of making traditional heroism a thing of the past and greatly diminishing the world of human possibility. Auden's "The Shield of Achilles" is about that terrible diminishment.

# IX. The Hidden Law

Everything in the previous chapters was written without any prior agenda, hidden or overt—insofar as I am qualified to speak about my own conscious and unconscious intentions. I determined to address myself to those poems, collections, essays, plays, or fragments of Auden's recorded conversations that particularly delighted, interested, or (sometimes) provoked me, but especially those works that inspired admiration or seemed to demand comment and elucidation. Not until I finished the previous chapter did I cast about for a title to this book or consider the notion of looking for some thread that might serve thematically to unite what I had written. I could almost say I resisted such an impulse, feeling that all too often critical inquiries apply Procrustean methods, lopping off something here by cunning omission, laboring a point too heavily there, all in behalf of an *a priori* thesis to which the poet and his work are tortured into conformity.

Such thematic studies have become a fashion with us. These days we are unlikely to be surprised by titles like "Milton and Misogyny," "Ralegh and 'The School of Night,'" or (with a bow of grateful acknowledgment to W. B. Scott) "The *Summa Contra Gentiles* and the Minor Poems of Chittiock Tichborne." To such invented titles could be added, with no sense that common practice was violated, two that were actually employed for papers given, heaven help us, at the 1989 meetings of the Modern Language Association in Washington, D.C.: "Desublimating the Male Sublime: Auto-erotics in Melville and William Burroughs" and "'The Pea That Duty Locks': Clitoral Imagery and Masturbation in Emily Dickinson." (By way of contrast, Auden's own forays into sexual explicitness are, with only one exception I can think of, either touchingly candid, as in his essay on J. R. Ackerley, or witty, as in the final stanza of "In Schrafft's":

> Which of the seven heavens
> Was responsible her smile

Wouldn't be sure but attested
That, whoever it was, a god
Worth kneeling-to for a while
Had tabernacled and rested.

—where it becomes clear that the posture of prayer is exactly that of oral sex.)

If we have grown used to the sort of critical titles listed above, it is partly because they try to beguile us with a presumptive modesty. The critic is insisting right from the start that he would not rashly presume to address all of Milton (or Chittiock Tichborne) and that he ventures to consider only a single aspect of the poet or novelist he is so bold as to examine. It is meant to be a stance of winning diffidence, though of course it implies at the same time that no one, however magisterial or Johnsonian his overview, has yet done justice to the true importance of the perceptions about to be presented.

So in looking over what I had considered and written through the penultimate chapter of this book, I at first wondered whether I should think of employing any other title than the plain use of the poet's name—whether or not I had, as it were despite myself, uncovered a theme or set of themes that could unify the works and attitudes of an artist so versatile, mercurial, protean as Auden, who, in his capacity for development and change, resembles Picasso and Stravinsky more than any of his literary contemporaries. And only after some reflection did I think I had located thematic strands or ideas that, though taking different shapes at different phases of his career, still figured importantly both early and late.

There are at least three such themes or characteristics that deserve more attention and space than I shall be able to give them here. One of these is language, another is the idea of the hero, and the third is the notion of the frivolity of art. I will venture a word or two on each.

I touched earlier on the scale and variety of Auden's language, and the pioneering breadth of his poetic vocabulary. It is worth adding that in this regard he moves well beyond the confines of any of his great contemporaries or predecessors, including Yeats, Frost, Eliot, and Stevens. In the reach and variety of his vocabulary the poet he most resembles—one of his literary heroes—is Rimbaud, of whom Enid Starkie wrote: "It is in the poems of this period [the period closing with *Le Bateau Ivre*], from April until his departure for Paris in September, that we find Rimbaud's daring experiment in vocabulary, in his use of words never hitherto used in poetry—trivial words, scientific words, obscene words, and colloquial expressions. It is the language of this period which influenced poets of the succeeding generation such as Laforgue, and through them, reached the modern poets of almost every country." Doubtless, Professor Starkie had Eliot chiefly in mind as the heir of this linguistic revolution, and Eliot himself has openly acknowledged his debt to Laforgue and Corbière. But those debts were, with Eliot, far more a matter of emotional stance than of language; he learned from his French mentors ways of conveying a cynical world-weariness, and a clownish self-mockery that stood him in good stead in his early poems. Auden's use of language, on the other hand, was far more experimental and exploratory than Eliot's, venturing as it does both into the hieratic and demotic and mixing the two in unusual and sometimes shocking ways.

Auden's linguistic forays start at the very beginning of his career and continue to the end. Moreover, he took a lively and continuing interest in poetry as a linguistic "game." "'Why do you want to write poetry?' If the young man answers: 'I have important things I want to say,' then he is not a poet. If he answers: 'I like hanging around words listening to what they say,' then maybe he is going to be a poet," Auden commented in "Squares and Oblongs." Yet if language is a "game," it can nevertheless be a serious one. In 1939 he boldly asserted

> Time that is intolerant
> Of the brave and innocent,
> And indifferent in a week
> To a beautiful physique,
>
> Worships language and forgives
> Everyone by whom it lives;
> Pardons cowardice, conceit,
> Lays its honours at their feet.

This is a daring, though not a novel, claim; Wilde, Shaw, and others had already declared the absolute divorce between the work of art as a perfectible artifact and the character and personality of its creator. It could even credibly be argued that Eliot's doctrine of "impersonality" is derived directly from this position which was embraced by the "decadents." In any case, Auden not only exalted the art of language (as Mallarmé, and after him, Eliot, had done: ". . . our concern was speech, and speech impelled us / To purify the dialect of the tribe . . .") but also kept himself constantly alerted to the dangers entailed by the debasement of language. One of the hermetic proscriptions in "Under Which Lyre" commands that "Thou shalt not be on friendly terms / With guys in advertising firms," since the abuse of language for commercial purposes (persuading people to buy what they don't want and don't need, or what is patently harmful to them, like cigarettes) is only another form of the abuse of language as employed for political domination, or as used by the military when they refer to buildings and human beings respectively as "hard" and "soft" targets. And the final poem ("Compline") in *The Shield of Achilles* begins its last stanza with the question, "Can poets (can men in television) / Be saved?" By the time he came to write this poem, salvation for Auden was by no means the same as the posthumous fame conferred by Time on those who used language well. And so both poets (which now means those skilled in the use of language, and therefore the guardians of civilization) and men in television (which means those concerned to draw audiences large enough to satisfy wealthy sponsors) may find themselves in, astonishingly, the same boat.

Another protracted concern of Auden's relates to the idea of the hero. In the early poetry this figure presents himself in the ambiguous guise of the spy, the solitary explorer of unfamiliar regions, the secret agent. At times he was identified with "healers," chiefly psychic healers, but also with political revolutionaries. These were identified in the course of things with "the truly strong man," who had no need to impress anyone and was therefore likely to be utterly unknown to the world at large. Avoidance of publicity was, in fact, a central part of his heroism, and he was pointedly to be distinguished from "the truly weak man," who was likely to be famous and whose daring was celebrated in the press. Such faux heroes were driven, often by the ambitions imposed upon them by their mothers, to perform astonishing feats, but always without the serenity and inward Zen-like indifference that belonged to the true hero. Auden's own pantheon of heroes went through remarkable changes, individuals being enthroned and dethroned at a fairly brisk pace, and their names (some famous, some not, including Gerhart Meyer, Freud, Lenin, T. E. Lawrence, Blake, Homer Lane, D. H. Lawrence) appear in the texts of his early poems.

At the same time, and not unconnected with these, there are the heroes of medieval romance and the Wagnerian operas. These too, through Auden's identification with the duets he sang as a child with his mother, remained so strong a focus of identification for him throughout his life played just before his burial. Carpenter reports that in 1962, dining with the Stravinskys, Auden said, "When my time is up I'll want Siegfried's Funeral Music and not a dry eye in the house." This unashamedly romantic style of hero may seem almost the reverse of "the truly strong man" and his self-effacing ways, but they all are "healers" of a kind, and connected to the deep mysteries of the unconscious. In addition, the *Ring* cycle bears striking resemblances to the sagas which Auden had cherished almost since childhood.

As a final stage in the morphological development of Auden's idea of a hero there is the figure of the saint. Clearly a kinship exists between the saint and "the truly strong man," both of them exhibiting a total indifference to the values and concerns of this world. The earlier figure was never identified with orthodox Christianity, while the latter certainly is. Both may be "healers" who serve their fellow men, but only the latter serves God, and often God alone. It is striking that Auden should, from first to last, have sought for some such heroic figure. The same cannot be said for the other great poets of his time. Eliot had *literary* heroes (as Auden did, too), while Yeats's feelings about heroism were either derived from folk tradition or were highly mixed and ironic, as, for example, in "Easter 1916." Frost evades the issue; Stevens regards it abstractly; Pound's heroes include Sigismondo Malatesta, who raped his own daughter and son. And, of course, there was Pound's admiration for *Il Duce.*

A third general topic that weaves its way through Auden's career is one that concerns his notion of the frivolity of art. There are many forms of evidence for this notion, including, of course, some of the poems themselves, beginning as early as "Uncle Henry" (dated ?1931 in the Collected Poems) and continuing through the Letter to Lord Byron to include the limericks, the many poems designated as "light verse," such as "Heavy Date," as well as the more serious and poignant "Refugee Blues" (shorn of its title in the Collected Poems, and identified only by its first line, "Say this city has ten million souls"). There were those who took Auden's frequent shifts of intellectual allegiance—the abandoning of one position in favor of another—to be itself a kind of frivolity, tainting (in the view of those who hold this attitude) all but his earliest poems. And beyond question some of his poems are openly taunting, like "Under Which Lyre," which may be thought of as a characteristic gesture of impudence. It is dated 1946. In 1969, as the epigraph to *Epistle for a Godson,* Auden wrote,

Each year brings new problems of Form and Content
new foes to tug with: at Twenty I tried to
vex my elders, past Sixty it's the young whom
    I hope to bother.

The insubordinate and cheerfully defiant bravado of such poems is in all likelihood connected with Auden's frank declaration that, as the youngest of three brothers, he became accustomed to feeling he was the youngest member of any company he was in. It is doubtless also connected with school and university games and fictions (the invention of the realm of "Mortmere," the general disposition to flout authority, and the rebellious mood of Waugh's *Brideshead*). In addition there was, if it were needed, the authority of Byron to the effect that "the end of all scribblement is to amuse," as well as what may be thought to be Byron's literary antithesis: Eliot and his definition, quoted earlier, of poetry as "entertainment."

But in the course of time Auden found what amounted to a theological foundation for what may have been his native disposition to regard art in general and poetry in particular as "frivolous," and the grounds were, whatever else they were, not Eliot's. They were Kierkegaard's. The Danish philosopher had made careful distinctions between the aesthetic, the ethical, and the religious modes of existence, the first one being the most trifling and inferior, while the last was the most perfect. To adopt so severe, and, it must be added, puritanical, a view was deliberately to contrive to forget that the Psalmist and Isaiah, St. Francis and St. John of the Cross, the Reverend George Herbert and Gerard Manley Hopkins, S.J., were poets, and that Beato Angelico and Fra Filippo Lippi were painters—all of them engaged in their artistic lives without compromising their serious devotion to religion. Auden's own "impatience" with the attitudinizing of many poets about their profession—especially the Romantic poets and their modern heirs, but others as well—can be illustrated by a statement from "Squares and Oblongs": "Milton's intuition in his *Ode on the Nativity* gives the lie to his personal over-estimation of the poet's importance. If the Fall made man conscious of the difference between good and evil, then the Incarnation made him conscious of the difference between seriousness and frivolity and exorcised the world." Kierkegaard, too, was a deliberate iconoclast, attacking with vigor and wit the bastions of complacent middle-class religious piety. He had written, "From the Christian point of view and in spite of all aesthetics, any poet's existence is a sin, viz., the sin that one is writing poetry instead of living; that one occupies oneself with God and truth only in one's imagination instead of aiming at experiencing both existentially." He had, moreover, written a "novel," called "The Diary of a Seducer" (contained in the volume titled *Either/Or*), which provides an analysis of Mozart's *Don Giovanni*, an opera with which Auden was obsessed. Kierkegaard, in other words, provided Auden with a great deal that fortified, or else transformed, ideas he had long entertained. What is remarkable in the end is that Auden was able to convert what might have been a secular prejudice into a religious conviction, maintaining the same general stance towards poetry throughout.

But now we must consider two themes or leitmotifs of Auden's poetry that are certainly distinct from one another, yet also surely related. One of them is the public/private polarity, and the other is the phrase I have taken as the title of this book, and which is borrowed from one of his poems.

As regards the first of these, the binary terms of "private" and "public," it may be said that there has long been a kind of popular literature which is anti-establishment, subversive, and which rejoices in its ability to appear perfectly innocuous to the unsuspecting majority. Some have claimed that the fulsome praise of Nero in Lucan's *Pharsalia* was precisely intended to be recognized as patently absurd by the cognoscenti. In our own times there have been songs like "Puff, the Magic Dragon," which is covertly about smoking pot, but which was broadcast and bought in recordings by unsuspecting multitudes; Bob Dylan's "Blowing in the Wind" seems to be about the same topic, while the Beatles' "Lucy in the Sky with Diamonds" is purportedly about the blisses of LSD. This witty capacity to "pass" as inoffensive would have held an appeal for any beleaguered minority, either political or sexual, and Auden both gleefully and seriously employed it in his poetry.

There is, however, another sense in which Auden deals with the confrontation of public and private worlds, and this becomes forcefully dramatic in those poems of the 1930's and '40's when the public world of national and international crisis irresistibly invaded the private world of love or dreams or hope. The poems of this period—some of his greatest and best known—include "September 1, 1939," the elegies for Yeats, Ernst Toller, and Freud, "A Summer Night," "A Bride in the 30's," the epithalamion for Giuseppe Borgese and Elisabeth Mann, and many more.

The interdependence of private and public realms was also a feature of Auden's revisionist reading of Freud. As reported earlier, in his 1929 journal Auden observed, "Freud's error is the limitation of neurosis to the individual. The neurosis involves all society." (This quotation appears in Edward Mendelson's *Early Auden*, though not in his presentation of that journal as it appears in *The English Auden*.) In any case, the collision of these two worlds, made as explicit as possible by what amounts to an unresolvable paradox, is stated in the two famous lines, "There is no such thing as the State, / And no one exists alone." The entire force of this paradox is borne by the judicial, impartial, balancing conjunction, "and."

But in the course of time Auden was to enlarge his view of the paradox by means of its religious applications. He saw in the relationship of the protestant and catholic views (regarded as impulses or tendencies, rather than as establishments, and therefore with lower-case initials) a paradigm for the predicament of the individual and the social role he is obliged to play. He wrote in "Greatness Finding Itself" that "protestantism is correct in affirming that the *We are* of society expresses a false identity unless each of its members can say *I am;* catholicism correct in affirming that the individual who will not or cannot join with others in saying *We* does not know the meaning of *I*." And the poetic sequence *Horae Canonicae* is a brilliant exfoliation of these ideas, concluding as it does with "Lauds" and the simple refrain "In solitude, for company."

The polarities (sometimes, though not always, expressed as conflict) take the shapes of mixed feelings, of private desires entertained in the midst of social gregariousness, of selfishness mortified by magnanimity. Consider a brief prose commentary from *The Age of Anxiety:* "Had they been perfectly honest with themselves, they would have had to admit that they were tired and wanted to go home alone to bed. That they were not [perfectly honest] was in part due, of course, to vanity, the fear of getting too old to want fun or too ugly to get it, but also to unselfishness, the fear of spoiling the fun for others" ("fun" in this context is virtually a synonym for "sex"). And this sexual anxiety can be traced through a good deal of Auden's poetry. Consider "Every young man fears that / He is not worth loving," from "Heavy Date," and the poignant conclusion of "First Things First": "Thousands have lived without love, not one without water," not to mention that poem of putatively "cheerful" renunciation, "A Permanent Way." This anxiety, this sense of the possibility or growing likelihood of being exiled from the domain of love (as, for example, in the early lyric "Dear, though the night is gone") might perhaps explain

his interest in, and sense of fraternity with, some celebrated cripples. But
if any such association was made even unconsciously by him, Auden was
far too acute to not have been aware that deformity generates resentment
which multiplies deformity—a terrible truth registered in "O for the doors
to open." Indeed, physical deformity was for him often the external sign
of an inward condition, Miss Gee's cancer being nothing less than "the
distortions of ingrown virginity." Still, there is no denying that Auden felt
a kinship with Pope, and Byron, and Kierkegaard. If he did not literally
share their physical malformations, he must at times have regarded his
homosexuality as a grave blemish in the eyes of society at large. If he did
not quite "descant" upon his own deformity in the manner of Richard III,
he was nevertheless conscious of the danger of growing too old or too
ugly to win love, and his poems represent a steady progress of stoic
resignation to his condition of exile.

And now, the Hidden Law. In accordance with its name, it adopts many
forms and countless disguises. It is at least implicit in some of the
heterodox psychosomatic theories Auden favored early in his life, and
expresses itself especially in their doctrines about the dangers and penal-
ties of suppression. In the early poems it appears as an inexorable doom,
portended by the smallest, most innocuous of omens—the "crack in the
teacup" that "opens / A lane to the land of the dead." It prophesies the
death of "the old gang," both individuals and whole societies. It was
poked fun at by William Empson in his tour de force smack at Auden,
with its refrain, "Waiting for the end, boys, waiting for the end." It
surfaced as personal illness, as well as in nightmares or prophetic dreams.
It leaves its signature in such lines as "There is always a wicked secret, a
private reason for this" (from "At last the secret is out"), "Doom is dark
and deeper than any sea-dingle" ("The Wanderer"), "In the burrows of
the Nightmare / Where Justice naked is . . ." ("As I walked out one
evening"), and "Here are all the captivities" ("Schoolchildren"), and it is
developed more fully in such early poems as "Consider this and in our
time," "Oxford," "Detective Story," "Song of the Beggars," and some
other of the poems just discussed under the rubric of the public/private
polarities.

The Hidden Law expresses itself in what we loosely call "Poetic
Justice," for which children often have what appears to be an unappeas-
able appetite, satisfied momentarily by certain kinds of folk-tales and fairy
tales. It is a strict and retaliatory force, perfect and impersonal in its
mercilessness, and therefore all the more attractive to children who can

so plausibly regard themselves as helpless and victimized. But it is by no means childish. It appeases our artistic craving for dénouement in both the most sophisticated classical drama and in farce and fiction as well; and it even figures in our ways of reading history itself. We are familiar with one of its classical manifestations in the figures of the Furies, who raise their sinister heads now and again in Auden's poetry. In classical times their propitiatory names were the Eumenides (the Kindly Ones), an appellation that might have been privately ironic, but never openly or consciously uttered in that tone, and was certainly supplicatory. They are absolute in their power and inscrutable justice, the "rightness" of which we become aware only after the fact, when it is too late. Their appearance is always wholly unexpected, and was probably no less than a total surprise to the first-night audience that glanced through its program to acquaint itself with the *dramatis personae* of T. S. Eliot's *The Family Reunion*.

Amy, Dowager Lady Mochensey

Ivy, Violet, *and* Agatha, *her younger sisters*

Col. the Hon. Gerald Piper, *and* the Hon. Charles Piper, *brothers of her deceased husband*

Mary, *daughter of a deceased cousin of Lady Monchensey*

Denman, *a parlourmaid*

Harry, Lord Monchensey, *Amy's eldest son*

Downing, *his servant and chauffeur*

Dr. Warburton

Sergeant Winchell

The Eumenides

The "judgment" represented by these ancient powers is referred to both directly and obliquely in an astonishing number of Auden's poems. It may be that they deck themselves out as "the witnesses" in a variety of poems. They are surely the ones to whom the poet addresses his question when he asks "what judgement waits / My person, all my friends, / And these United States." There are the judgments before which Auden arraigns himself in the *New Year Letter*, where his judges are three in number, corresponding to the classical Furies who are named Tisiphone, Megaera, and Alecto. They lurk behind all of Auden's impulses for moral stock-taking, as they appear, for example, in the final part of *Letter to Lord Byron*. And not only does this "judicial" element belong to the imaginative world of children, to folk and fairy lore, to classical drama, to various varieties of fiction and history, but it is central to much Jewish theology, and plays a powerful part in that part of the Holy Scripture of the Jews that Christians designate as the Old Testament.

The books of Job and Jonah may be cited for their awesome accounts of divine justice and mercy as altogether mysterious and incomprehensible. They are among the most persuasive and bewildering texts in Holy Scripture, and they discovered their modern analogue in Kierkegaard's sustained meditation on the sacrifice of Isaac and Abraham. They reduce us, as they once reduced Job himself, to speechlessness, awe, reverence, and resignation. They ruthlessly sever the realms of our normal ethical judgments from the absolute realm of divine justice, and show us how feeble and trivial are those instincts as well as those deeply considered meditations we regard (privately or publicly) as our best. They expose the unbridgeable gulf between our own values and those of God, and assert that there is no comprehending the latter. To this dilemma, Kierkegaard's solution is the "leap of faith." But the dilemma itself, unpalliated by any putative remedy, is starkly presented again and again in the fictions of Franz Kafka, whose evocation of the Hidden Law is terrible in its force and authority.

The Law figures in Auden's work as the *deus absconditus* (mentioned early in the sonnet sequence *The Quest* of 1940, and later in "Hands" of 1959). This evasive Godhead is supremely the God of the Old Testament, who declared unequivocally, "There shall no man see me and live" (Exodus 33:20). But this sense of human bereavement can also be found in other parts of Scripture: "We see not our signs: there is no more any prophet; neither is there among us any that knoweth how long" (Psalms 74:9), and the terrible cry of Psalm 22 (made familiar as the cry from the Cross), " 'Eli! Eli! lama sabachthani?' which is to say, 'My God! My God! why hast thou forsaken me?' " There are, of course, many other such texts that might be cited, but these alone would have provided a precedent and foundation for George Herbert's magnificent poem on this subject, "Decay."

> Sweet were the dayes, when thou didst lodge with Lot,
> Struggle with Jacob, sit with Gideon,

Advise with Abraham, when thy power could not
Encounter Moses strong complaints and mone:
     Thy words were then, *Let me alone.*

One might have sought and found thee presently
At some fair oak, or bush, or cave, or well:
Is my God this way? No, they would reply:
He is to Sinai gone, as we heard tell:
     List, ye may heare great Aarons bell.

But now thou dost thy self immure and close
In some one corner of a feeble heart:
Where yet both Sinne and Satan, thy old foes,
Do pinch and straiten thee, and use much art
     To gain thy thirds and little part.

I see the world grows old, as when the heat
Of thy great love, once spread, as in an urn
Doth closet up it self, and still retreat,
Cold Sinne still forcing it, till it return,
     And calling *Justice,* all things burn.

This leads us directly to a consideration of theodicy, defined in the OED as "the vindication of the divine attributes, esp. justice and holiness, in respect to the existence of evil; a writing, doctrine, or theory intended to 'justify the ways of god to men.' " The very fact that such a theory is called for is itself an index of our general perplexity about the Hidden Law, signifying our desperate belief that it must exist, as well as our no less desperate frustration at our inability to make it out. Theologians of various persuasions have, of course, offered us any number of theodicies. And so have poets. Milton may perhaps be the most celebrated of these, but Hopkins' "The Wreck of the Deutschland" is equally a vision of the meaning of the divine purpose in what seems like the senseless suffering and death of the innocent and blameless—and we have seen that not only were many of Auden's poems framed as prayer, but the prologue to *On This Island,* "O love, the interest itself in thoughtless Heaven," was explicitly indebted to Hopkins' great poetic plea for a redeemed and sanctified England, a poem that very deliberately offers a straightforward theodicy, which, once again, is expressed as the Hidden Law: "(And here the faithful waver, the faithless fable and miss)."

None of Auden's contemporaries dealt with the problems of a theodicy more directly than Frost did in *A Masque of Reason.* It is, no doubt, an impudent work, markedly devoid of the usual forms of reverence, not only for God but for Yeats.

MAN.    You're not asleep?
WIFE.                                                No, I can hear you. Why?
MAN.    I said the incense tree's on fire again.
WIFE.   You mean the Burning Bush?
MAN.                                                        The Christmas Tree.
WIFE.   I shouldn't be surprised.
MAN.                                                                The strangest light!
WIFE.   There's a strange light on everything today.
MAN.    The myrrh tree gives it. Smell the rosin burning?
            The ornaments the Greek artificers
            Made for the Emperor Alexius,
            The Star of Bethlehem, the pomegranates,
            The birds, all seem on fire with Paradise.
            And hark, the gold enameled nightingales
            Are singing. Yes, and look, the Tree is troubled.
            Someone's caught in the branches.
WIFE.                                                        So there is.
            He can't get out.
MAN.                                    He's loose! He's out!
WIFE.                                                                It's God.
            I'd know him by Blake's picture anywhere.
            Now what's He doing?
MAN.                                            Pitching throne, I guess,
            Here by our atoll.
WIFE.                                    Something Byzantine.
            (*The throne's a plywood flat, prefabricated,*
            *That God pulls lightly upright on its hinges*
            *And stands beside, supporting it in place.*)

This is the opening of Frost's *Masque,* and it gets its digs in at Yeats by way of allusions to the Greek artificers, the pomegranates, birds, and gold enameled nightingales, but most pointedly to the Byzantine contraption of a throne that cannot stand on its own (it collapses shortly after the *Masque* begins) and that obviously represents for Frost the (from his point of view) jerrybuilt contrivance of Yeats's entire theory of historical necessity. And, by implication, it mocks (mistakenly, as I think) that aspect of Yeats's theory that seems to allow no place for God. In this sense, despite the air of comradely and undignified banter with God, and at His august expense, there is true seriousness and reverence for the inexplicable in Frost's dramatic poem, in which, of course, the MAN and WIFE turn out to be Job and his wife, who, in their interview with divinity, are left just as baffled by the puzzle of theodicy as they were originally.

It is true, of course, that Yeats did reject the entire Judeo-Christian tradition, not excluding its God. In its place he erected the extraordinary "machinery" elaborated and explained in his momentous prose work, *A Vision*, in which the civilization of Byzantium plays a pivotal role. Near the close of that strange work he wrote:

> I think if I could be given a month of Antiquity and leave to spend it where I chose, I would spend it in Byzantium a little before Justinian opened St. Sophia and closed the Academy of Plato. I think I could find in some little wine-shop some philosophical worker in mosaic who could answer all my questions, the supernatural descending nearer to him than to Plotinus even, for the pride of his delicate skill would make what was an instrument of power to princes and clerics, a murderous madness in the mob, show as a lovely flexible presence like that of a perfect human body.
>
> I think that in early Byzantium, maybe never before or since in recorded history, religious, aesthetic and practical life were one, that architect and artificers—though not, it may be, poets, for language had been the instrument of controversy and must have grown abstract—spoke to the multitude and the few alike. The painter, the mosaic worker, the worker in gold and silver, the illuminator of sacred books, were almost impersonal, almost perhaps without the consciousness of individual design, absorbed in their subject matter and that the vision of a whole people.

This notion of "unity of being," determined by the cyclical mechanism of historical process, was central to Yeats's *Vision* and the butt of Frost's joke; but I cite them both here for another reason as well. The passage of Yeats just quoted should not mislead an uninstructed reader into supposing that the poet found Christianity appealing, or persuasive, or true, in its Byzantine phase. It was "unity of being" alone that he found attractive. His historical machinery determined that Christianity was now obsolete, and that we were about to enter an era of which the symbol would be the Sphinx of "The Second Coming," a defiantly anti-Christian poem. Yet in spite of his firm and elaborate repudiation of the Christian religion, Yeats, in the final analysis, was after what amounts to a theodicy without a God. He comes close to admitting as much in the slightly embarrassed as well as haughty words that close his introduction.

> Some will ask whether I believe in the actual existence of my circuits of sun and moon . . . To such a question I can but answer that if sometimes, overwhelmed by miracle as all men must be when in the midst of it, I have taken such periods literally, my reason soon has recovered; and now that the system stands out clearly in my imagination I regard them as stylistic arrangements of experience comparable to the cubes in the drawing of Wyndham Lewis and to the ovoids in the sculpture of Brancusi. They have helped me to hold in a single thought reality and justice.

The reconciliation of "reality" and "justice" is nothing less than what a theodicy presents. But Yeats (and Frost) lead to a further point. *A Vision* closes with an epilogue, a poem which has suffered a severe rebuke from no less a judge than R. P. Blackmur, who writes,

> There is another defect of Yeats' magical system which is especially apparent to the reader but which may not have been apparent at all to Yeats. Magic promises precisely matters which it cannot perform—at least in poetry. It promises, as in "The Second Coming," exact prediction of events in the natural world; and it promises again and again, in different poems, exact revelations of the supernatural, and of this we have an example in what to many has seemed a great poem, "All Souls' Night," which had its first publication as an epilogue to *A Vision*. Near the beginning of the poem we have the explicit declaration: "I have a marvelous thing to say"; and near the end another: "I have mummy truths to tell." "Mummy truths" is an admirable phrase, suggestive as it is of the truths in which the dead are wrapped, ancient truths as old as Egypt perhaps, whence mummies commonly come, and truths, too, that may be unwound. But there, with the suggestion, the truths stop short; there is, for the reader, no unwinding, no revelation of the dead. What Yeats actually does is to summon into the poem various of his dead friends as "characters"—and this is the greatness, and only this, of the poem: the summary, excited, even exalted presentation of character. Perhaps the rhetoric is the marvel and the evasion the truth. We get an impact as from behind, from the speed and weight of the words, and

are left with an ominous and terrified frame of mind, the revelation still to come. The revelation, the magic, was in Yeats's mind; hence the exaltation of his language; but it was not and could not be given in the words of the poem.

It seems to me that Blackmur has found this poem as blameworthy as he does only because he has curiously neglected two aspects of its proper context. The first is indicated by its title, "All Souls' Night," which is traditionally the festival when ghosts walked abroad; hence the summoning of what Blackmur patronizingly calls "characters." On this night, the spirit world, in which Yeats appeared to believe, was potentially accessible to the world of the living. And what Yeats sought in his *Vision* was scarcely less than what Dante found in *his,* which is nothing less than a theodicy. The following lines, in all their visionary expectation, were quoted earlier (in Chapter 3) and are worth repeating here, as an illustration of Yeats's ambition and audacity.

> Such thought—such thought have I that hold it tight
> Till meditation master all its parts,
> Nothing can stay my glance
> Until that glance run in the world's despite
> To where the damned have howled away their hearts,
> And where the blessed dance . . .

This "glance" is a Dantean glimpse of Eternity, embellished with its absolute "judgments" of the damned and the blessed. And the poem, as the epilogue to *A Vision,* has that extraordinary historico-philosophic text to ratify its claim to be able now, after much study and meditation, to view the whole human panorama, both of the living and the dead, and to do so moreover while holding in a single thought "reality and justice." The claim is, admittedly, audacious, but it had been performed by other poets in the past, and Yeats was counting upon the elaborate meditation of *A Vision* itself to buttress his claim. The poem is, to be sure, an epilogue. But it nevertheless points forward to the use of visionary powers granted by the discipline that went into the composition of the book which preceded it. It announces its newly found capacity to "say marvelous things" and utter "mummy truths." Dante did nothing less when he visited the dead.

"All Souls' Night," the epilogue to *A Vision,* may be compared in at least one respect to an epilogue of Auden's: the one he wrote for *The*

*Orators,* and which begins "'O where are you going?' said reader to
rider." Auden's poem has suffered the same kind of rebuke that Blackmur
leveled at Yeats's epilogue: that it excites us to unfulfilled expectations.
Of Auden's poem it is objected that it is putatively a summons to action,
a rallying cry in behalf of a new and better life; but since it offers no explicit
program, no definitive ways of change, it is as feeble an appeal as Harry
Emerson Fosdick's *The Power of Positive Thinking,* which, however
popular it may once have been, was never thought serviceable as the
grounds for political or societal renovation—which is obviously Auden's
goal. As was the case with Blackmur, critics who take this line about
Auden's poem contrive to overlook its context as epilogue—an oversight
made much easier for them by Auden's republishing the poem without
title and grouped under the heading "Songs" both in his *Collected Poetry*
(1945) and in his *Collected Shorter Poems* (1957). But the poem seems
far less enfeebled when viewed as the culmination of that strange, diagnostic examination of English malaise and social morbidity that constitutes the main body of *The Orators.* The very name of that work is itself
a repudiation of those who merely *talk,* "lecturing on navigation while
the ship is going down." Auden's epilogue, though a poem, and therefore
of necessity couched in words, is a rejection of such "talk," and the
Hamlet-like hesitations that go with it as unsuitable in a crisis when
immediate action, as vigorous and unmeditated as an *impulse,* must be
counted upon as the only way to avoid catastrophe—and the poem dates
from a period in Auden's life when, in admiration of theories of Lane and
Lawrence, Auden put great stock in the sanctity and *health* of impulses.
While the poem does not provide any specific program to cure the English
of their ills, it implicitly recommends the instinct to vacate the scene of
the crime, the realm of hesitation, dalliance, and delay. It needs quotation
here, both for its own sake and because I want to compare it to another
poem, this one by T. S. Eliot, as a way of suggesting that both poems, in
their different ways, convey something of the Hidden Law.

> "O where are you going?" said reader to rider,
> "That valley is fatal where furnaces burn,
> Yonder's the midden whose odours will madden,
> That gap is the grave where the tall return."
>
> "O do you imagine," said fearer to farer,
> "That dusk will delay on your path to the pass,
> Your diligent looking discover the lacking,
> Your footsteps feel from granite to grass?"

"O what was that bird," said horror to hearer,
"Did you see that shape in the twisted trees?
Behind you swiftly the figure comes softly,
The spot on your skin is a shocking disease."

"Out of this house"—said rider to reader,
"Yours never will"—said farer to fearer,
"They're looking for you"—said hearer to horror,
As he left them there, as he left them there.

I think it could be claimed that there is at least one technical fault to be found with this poem, and it has to do with pronouns. We may read the poem as presenting either six characters or two who play multiple roles; which is to say that "rider," "farer," and "hearer" may be the same active figure or three distinct and individual personages, and the same could be said of the passive figures of "reader," "fearer," and "horror." The problem arises only in the final line, which involves both singular and plural pronouns. My guess is that Auden was caught short at discovering that he had more or less boxed himself into writing "As they left them there, as they left them there," in which the repetition of third-person plural pronouns would leave everyone grammatically bewildered. His not entirely satisfactory solution was to incorporate "rider," "farer," and "hearer" into one symbolic hero-escapee while leaving the impotent and terrified enemy divided and plural.

But before any further comment on this poem I must present the poem of Eliot's, "Journey of the Magi," to which I wish to compare it.

'A cold coming we had of it,
Just the worst time of the year
For a journey, and such a long journey:
The ways deep and the weather sharp,
The very dead of winter.'
And the camels galled, sore-footed, refractory,
Lying down in the melting snow.
There were times we regretted
The summer palaces on slopes, the terraces,
And the silken girls bringing sherbet.
Then the camel men cursing and grumbling
And running away, and wanting their liquor and women,
And the night-fires going out, and the lack of shelters,
And the cities hostile and the towns unfriendly

And the villages dirty and charging high prices:
A hard time we had of it.
At the end we preferred to travel all night,
Sleeping in snatches,
With the voices singing in our ears, saying
That this was all folly.

Then at dawn we came down to a temperate valley,
Wet, below the snow line, smelling of vegetation;
With a running stream and a water-mill beating the darkness,
And three trees on a low sky,
And an old white horse galloped away in the meadow.
Then we came to a tavern with vine-leaves over the lintel,
Six hands at an open door dicing for pieces of silver,
And feet kicking the empty wine-skins.
But there was no information, so we continued
And arrived at evening, not a moment too soon
Finding the place; it was (you may say) satisfactory.

All this was a long time ago, I remember,
And I would do it again, but set down
This set down
This: were we led all that way for
Birth or Death? There was a birth, certainly,
We had evidence and no doubt. I had seen birth and death,
But had thought they were different; this Birth was
Hard and bitter agony for us, like Death, our death.
We returned to our places, these Kingdoms,
But no longer at ease here, in the old dispensation,
With an alien people clutching their gods.
I should be glad of another death.

Much of great subtlety and insight has been written about this poem, which I shall not trouble the reader by rehearsing here: the debt to Lancelot Andrewes, the proleptic significance of the three trees, the wine-skins, presumably matters of which the Magus himself is strikingly unaware. It is this sense of the speaker's ignorance of the full meaning of his own words in which the Hidden Law of this poem partly inheres. There are, nevertheless, a few other items I think worth further notice. The first of these concerns the claim of the Magus that simple prudence dictated the choice of traveling by night, a means of avoiding the hostility and depredations of the cities, towns, and villages through which the caravan was obliged to pass. In other words, this was not done in order to follow a star, of which no mention is made. I must return to this point later. Secondly, among the proleptic scenes or events we are given glimpses of extremities (hands dicing, feet kicking) divorced entirely from the bodies to which they belong; and these extremities are associated with Christ's betrayal and derision (the thirty pieces of silver that was Judas' fee, the kicked wine-skin a sign of contempt for the sacrificed blood), and they may be seen in their strangely amputated states in Beato Angelico's fresco *The Mocking of Christ,* in cell 7 at the monastery of San Marco in Florence, and it seems to me at least possible that Eliot might have had in mind these hands and heads divorced from any identifiable persons, the symbolic tormentors of the Passion.

Similarly, much is concealed from us by the declaration, "so we continued / And arrived at evening, not a moment too soon / Finding the place; it was (you may say) satisfactory." These last words are usually read as ironic (and unwitting) understatement, perhaps expressing the not altogether easy noblesse oblige of kings in a manger, consorting with beasts and shepherds. But as Eliot surely knew, the ecclesiastical and theological definition of "satisfactory" is "serving to make satisfaction or atonement for sin." Eliot might have expected that not all of his readers would know this. The more pressing question is, did he wish us to believe that the Magus himself knew this? I suspect that the Magus does not. Most of the signs of future events have been couched in ambiguous terms that might appear to bear no special meaning or weight. But the question becomes important to the poem's final strophe.

There seems to be something like a consensus of critical feeling about the tone of the conclusion of this poem, which, it is said, appears to border on despair and exhaustion of hope. The longed-for death in the final line is usually construed as the yearning for annihilation that seems also to close another of Eliot's Ariel poems, "A Song for Simeon," a feeling with which we became acquainted in *The Waste Land.* It is reflected in the curious anecdote retailed to Peter Ackroyd in regard to Eliot's fondness for playing patience: "When W. H. Auden once found him playing that game and asked him why he seemed to relish it, he reflected gravely and then replied, 'Well, I suppose it's the nearest thing to being dead.' " Moreover, in his review of Eliot's book of essays *For Lancelot Andrewes,* Edmund Wilson, in 1929, wrote: "One recognizes a point of view which is by way of

becoming fashionable among certain sorts of literary people, yet this usually presents itself merely as a sentiment that it would be a good thing to
believe rather than as a real and living belief. And, though Eliot lets us know
that he does believe, his faith, in so far as we find it expressed in these
essays and in his recent poems [the date of "The Journey of the Magi" is
1927], seems entirely uninspired by hope, entirely unequipped with
force—a faith which, to quote his own epigraph, is merely 'ready to die.' "

However well or ill those words may apply to *For Lancelot Andrewes,*
I shall try to make a case for the claim that they do not properly apply to
"Journey of the Magi." If I am right, much of the meaning of the
poem—both its meaning for the reader, and its more intimate meaning
for Eliot himself—hinges on the crucially ambiguous line, "All this was a
long time ago, I remember." We are not told, and are never to learn, *how*
long. Most paintings of the Epiphany represent the Three Kings not merely
as fully grown men but often as, in at least one case, elderly, white-bearded
or gray-haired. There would, in any case, be an interval of thirty-three
years between the scene of the Nativity and the sacramental Death on the
Cross that would be required to bring into all its force and authority the
New Dispensation. Before the Crucifixion the salvific effects of the new
faith are still no more than a promise. The Magus, remembering the Birth
as having taken place "a long time ago," could not in any way become
the beneficiary of the New Dispensation until thirty-three years had
passed, by which time we may imagine him to have become an old man.
Again, perhaps proleptically, he knows this, because the other death for
which he yearns is not the annihilation of the self but the redemptive
Death, the *consummatum est,* for which the Birth was only a preparation.
Yet his present incapacity to understand the Birth as wholly miraculous
and a ratification in itself of the New Dispensation should explain the
express omission of any mention of the Star of Bethlehem, and even of
the name of the place itself. It is, for him, at this point, no more than "the
place," and the Star merits, in his mind, less notice than, for example, the
"three trees on a low sky."

Again, if I am right about this, the poem might well have had a deeply
personal meaning for Eliot himself, and might represent a kind of "confession," his acknowledgment that he had not yet perfectly embraced the
faith to which he nominally adhered, that his imperfect spiritual status
was, like the Magus's, that of a person whose faith was incomplete, and
still awaited the acceptance of the full burden and benefit of the sacrificial
Death. Such a "confession" as I construe here would have been made

quite consciously by the poet, though without full comprehension by the Magus. The Hidden Law would, nevertheless, be detectable in both cases.

As for the analogue between this poem, so clearly religious in its theme irrespective of any conflicting interpretations, and Auden's " 'O where are you going?' said reader to rider," which seems resolutely secular—a call to action virtually for its own sake, a repudiation of the past rather than a clear vision of a future—the proposal may seem ludicrously far-fetched. And I would have to acknowledge that the connection is not self-evident; but then, the Hidden Law would scarcely be hidden if it were instantly detectable.

A number of commentators have informed us that Auden's poem is "modeled" on a folk ballad called "The Cutty Wren." This ballad was, so far as I am able to discover, virtually unknown until Auden himself brought it to light by including it in his 1938 *Oxford Book of Light Verse.* It is not to be found in Child's famous collection of ballads, nor in any other such collection that I know of. Monroe Spears claims that Auden may first have encountered it in Walter de la Mare's wonderful anthology, *Come Hither,* a favorite book of Auden's childhood. But only two stanzas of the ballad, and in a form significantly varied from the one Auden would quote in his own anthology, are to be found, not in the body of de la Mare's collection, but buried as a snippet among the notes. There can be no question, of course, of the immediately detectable formal relationship and auditory resemblance between "The Cutty Wren" and Auden's poem, but I would claim a more pressing and important relationship, which will require quotation of the whole ballad.

> O, where are you going, says Milder to Malder,
> O, I cannot tell, says Festel to Fose,
> We're going to the woods, says John the Red Nose,
> We're going to the woods, says John the Red Nose.
>
> O, what will you do there, says Milder to Malder,
> O, I cannot tell, says Festel to Fose,
> We'll shoot the Cutty Wren, says John the Red Nose,
> We'll shoot the Cutty Wren, says John the Red Nose.
>
> O, how will you shoot her, says Milder to Malder,
> O, I cannot tell, says Festel to Fose,
> With arrows and bows, says John the Red Nose.
> With arrows and bows, says John the Red Nose.

O, that will not do, says Milder to Malder,
O, what will do then, says Festel to Fose,
Big guns and cannons, says John the Red Nose.
Big guns and cannons, says John the Red Nose.

O, how will you bring her home, says Milder to Malder,
O, I cannot tell, says Festel to Fose,
On four strong men's shoulders, says John the Red Nose,
On four strong men's shoulders, says John the Red Nose.

O, that will not do, says Milder to Malder,
O, what will do then, says Festel to Fose,
Big carts and wagons, says John the Red Nose,
Big carts and wagons, says John the Red Nose.

O, what will you cut her up with, says Milder to Malder,
O, I cannot tell, says Festel to Fose,
With knives and forks, says John the Red Nose,
With knives and forks, says John the Red Nose.

O, that will not do, says Milder to Malder,
O, what will do then, says Festel to Fose,
Hatchets and cleavers, says John the Red Nose,
Hatchets and cleavers, says John the Red Nose.

O, how will you boil her, says Milder to Malder,
O, I cannot tell, says Festel to Fose,
In pots and in kettles, says John the Red Nose,
In pots and in kettles, says John the Red Nose.

O, that will not do, says Milder to Malder,
O, what will do then, says Festel to Fose,
Brass pans and cauldrons, says John the Red Nose,
Brass pans and cauldrons, says John the Red Nose.

O, who'll have the spare ribs, says Milder to Malder,
O, I cannot tell, says Festel to Fose,
We'll give them to the poor, says John the Red Nose,
We'll give them to the poor, says John the Red Nose.

A word or two about the poem's title and putative subject seems in
order. "Cutty" means small, short, abbreviated, and is also a vernacular

word for the wren itself. ("Sark" is a shirt or undergarment, and the Cutty Sark is a clipper ship with short sails.) There is, consequently, a patent and comic irony in the poem as it regards a specifically *small wren* that would need to be borne home not on the shoulders of "four strong men" but in "big carts and wagons"; against whom bows and arrows are impotent weaponry, and for the killing of which "big guns and cannons" are required; that cannot be eaten with ordinary knives and forks but would require "hatchets and cleavers," and which finally could not be cooked in "pots and kettles" but would instead demand "brass pans and cauldrons." This seems very much like the nonsensical hyperbole we frequently find in folk songs and children's literature.

But I want to propose a more serious explanation for this hyperbolic enlargement of the nominally small wren. I suggest that this curious poem, like much folk literature, has a source in ancient and complex folk custom. I am untroubled about the mention in the poem of "big guns and cannons" as signifying a specifically modern era, because whatever the date of the poem (I can discover no provenance for it), I am convinced that it echoes a tradition older than it may fully be aware of. In this it would resemble the pagan fertility rituals Jessie Weston found encrusted with religious gemmation in medieval quest romances. And like her, I turn for confirmation of my supposition to anthropology, and more specifically to James Frazer, who has this to say in *The Golden Bough:*

Ceremonies closely analogous to . . . Indian worship of the snake have survived in Europe into recent times, and doubtless date from a very primitive paganism. The best-known example is the "hunting of the wren." By many European peoples—the ancient Greeks and Romans, the modern Italians, Spaniards, French, Germans, Dutch, Danes, Swedes, English and Welsh—the wren has been designated the king, the little king, the king of the birds, the hedge king, and so forth, and has been reckoned amongst those birds which it is extremely unlucky to kill. In England it is supposed that if any one kills a wren or harries its nest, he will infallibly break a bone or meet with some dreadful misfortune within the year; sometimes it is thought that cows will give bloody milk . . .

Notwithstanding such beliefs, the custom of annually killing the wren has prevailed both in this country [England] and in France. In the Isle of Man down to the eighteenth century the custom was observed on Christmas Eve, or rather Christmas morning. On the twenty-fourth of December, towards evening, all the servants got a holiday; they did not go to bed all night, but rambled about till the bells rang in all the churches at midnight. When prayers were over, they went to hunt the wren, and having found one of these birds they killed it and fastened it to the top of a long pole with its wings extended. Thus they carried it in procession to every house chanting the following rhyme:

> We hunted the wren for Robin the Bobbin,
> We hunted the wren for Jack of the Can,
> We hunted the wren for Robin the Bobbin,
> We hunted the wren for every one.

[In Ireland] on Christmas Day or St. Stephen's Day [which is the day after Christmas] the boys hunt and kill the wren, fasten it to the middle of a mass of holly and ivy on the top of a broomstick, and on St. Stephen's Day go about with it from house to house, singing,

> The wren, the wren, the king of all birds,
> St. Stephen's Day was caught in the furze;
> Although he is little, his family's great,
> I pray you, good landlady, give us a treat.

Whatever Frazer's account may signify as regards ancient pagan customs, its Christian relevance cannot be doubted, and it clears up many puzzles about the ballad. Surely the wren, identified as "king," fixed to the top of a pole "with extended wings," must be a symbol of Christ. Though he is little (especially at his birth at Christmas), his family is great, traceable after all to Jesse, David, and Solomon (to speak only of the less distinguished branch of the family). Though little, he cannot even be borne by four strong men but needs big carts and wagons to convey him, just as the infant Christ was nearly too heavy to be borne by St. Christopher (characterized by hagiographers as "a man of gigantic stature"). It furthermore explains the paradox that it is considered bad luck as well as wicked to kill the wren, and at the same time a ritual requisite, so that every year, just at the Christmas season, the wren is killed "for every one," and his "spare ribs" are given "to the poor." This paradox accords furthermore with the curiously ambivalent responses of Festel in the second line of each stanza. When he repeatedly says "O, I cannot tell," we are left uncertain whether this means he doesn't know or that he is unwilling to tell. If he doesn't know, the "mystery" of the ritual (its

Hidden Law) is being kept from him, just as the secret meaning of the ritual itself is couched in terms that are not easily accessible. If he does know but is reluctant to say, this may be because of his understandable discomfort about violating the taboo against killing the wren. Yet for all his reluctance, whenever Milder says "O, that will not do," he immediately asks "O, what will do then?" as though acceding to the ritual slaughter.

And what is the relevance of all this? We have heard Isherwood declare that Auden "enjoyed a high Anglican upbringing . . . The Anglicanism evaporated, leaving only the height: he is still much preoccupied with ritual, in all its forms." That was written in 1937. We have heard Auden himself, in an essay of 1964, say, in regard to the important "vision of agape" he experienced in 1933, "Among the various factors that brought me back to the Christian faith in which I had been brought up, the memory of this experience and asking myself what it could mean was one of the most crucial, though, at the time it occurred, I thought I had done with Christianity for good." What I am trying to suggest is that Auden modeled his epilogue to *The Orators,* a nominally secular poem that concluded a genuinely secular work, on a poem whose Christian import cannot be doubted. He did this at a period of his life when he was at least unconscious of any Christian belief, so that the Hidden Law was, as far as we can, or he could, judge, truly hidden from him. By the time he assembled the *Oxford Book of Light Verse* he was at least prepared to let perceptive readers discover a source of his epilogue, and thereby to acknowledge the Hidden Law within it. In contradistinction to Eliot, whose revelation about the condition of his faith was intended to be understood, first of all by God, and then by such of the initiate as knew the travail of his doubts and yearnings, it seems quite possible that Auden himself may have been initially unaware of the relevance to his own spiritual life of the old poem upon which he had modeled his own.

> The Hidden Law does not deny
> Our laws of probability,
> But takes the atom and the star
> And human beings as they are,
> And answers nothing when we lie.

# Acknowledgments

The author wishes to acknowledge the sources of works quoted in this book, and to thank the parties listed below for permission to reprint them.

W. H. Auden: Collected Poems, edited by Edward Mendelson. Copyright © 1976 by Edward Mendelson, William Meredith, and Monroe K. Spears, Executors of the Estate of W. H. Auden. Reprinted by permission of Random House, Inc., and Faber and Faber Ltd.

W. H. Auden, *The Dog Beneath the Skin*, in *W. H. Auden: Plays and Other Dramatic Writings*, edited by Edward Mendelson (Princeton University Press, 1989). Copyright 1930, 1933, 1940, 1966 by W. H. Auden; copyright renewed 1962, 1968. Copyright 1935 by the Modern Library, Inc. Copyright 1935, 1937, 1938, 1939 by W. H. Auden and Christopher Isherwood. Copyright renewed 1963, 1965. Copyright 1988 by the Estate of W. H. Auden. Reprinted by permission of Curtis Brown, Ltd.

W. H. Auden, poem-letter to Chester Kallman, Christmas Day, 1941; "The Traction Engine"; and "In the Year of My Youth," copyright 1978 by the Estate of W. H. Auden. By permission of the Estate of W. H. Auden.

Elizabeth Bishop, "A Miracle for Breakfast," from *The Complete Poems: 1927–1979*. Copyright © 1979, 1983 by Alice Helen Methfessel. Reprinted by permission of Farrar, Straus & Giroux, Inc.

Joseph P. Clancy, translator, *The Odes and Epodes of Horace*. Copyright 1960 by the University of Chicago.

T. S. Eliot, *Murder in the Cathedral*. Copyright 1935 by Harcourt Brace Jovanovich, Inc. Renewed 1963 by T. S. Eliot. Reprinted by permission of Harcourt Brace Jovanovich, Inc., and Faber and Faber Ltd.

T. S. Eliot, "Burnt Norton" and "East Coker," from *Four Quartets*. Copyright 1943 by T. S. Eliot. Renewed 1971 by Esme Valerie Eliot. Reprinted by permission of Harcourt Brace Jovanovich, Inc., and Faber and Faber Ltd.

T. S. Eliot, "Mr. Eliot's Sunday Morning Service" and "Journey of the Magi," from *Collected Poems 1909–1962*. Copyright 1936 by Harcourt Brace Jovanovich, Inc. Copyright © 1964, 1963 by T. S. Eliot. Reprinted by permission of Harcourt Brace Jovanovich, Inc., and Faber and Faber Ltd.

William Empson,"Just a Smack at Auden," from *Collected Poems of William Empson*. Copyright 1949, renewed 1977 by William Empson. Reprinted by permission of Harcourt Brace Jovanovich, Inc., and by permission of The Hogarth Press and Lady Empson.

Robert Fagles, translator, *The Iliad*. Translation copyright © 1990 by Robert Fagles. Introduction and Notes copyright © 1990 by Bernard Knox. By permission of Viking Penguin, a division of Penguin Books USA Inc.

Robert Fitzgerald, translator, *The Odyssey* (Garden City, N.Y.: Anchor/Doubleday, 1961).

Robert Frost, "A Masque of Reason" and "The Lesson for Today," from *The Poetry of Robert Frost*, edited by Edward Connery Lathem. Copyright 1942, 1945 by Robert Frost. Copyright © 1970, 1973 by Lesley Frost Ballantine. Copyright © 1969 by Holt, Rinehart and Winston. Reprinted by permission of Henry Holt and Company, Inc., and by permission of Jonathan Cape and the Estate of Robert Frost.

Rolfe Humphries, translator, *The Aeneid of Virgil: A Verse Translation*, edited and with notes by Brian Wilkie. Copyright © 1987 by Macmillan Publishing Company, a division of Macmillan, Inc. Copyright 1951 by Charles Scribner's Sons. Reprinted with the permission of Macmillan Publishing Company.

Alvin Kernan, *The Death of Literature* (Yale University Press, 1990). Copyright 1990 by Yale University.

Charles Martin, translator, *The Poems of Catullus*. Copyright 1979 by Charles Martin. Copyright 1990 by The Johns Hopkins University Press.

Howard Nemerov, "On Being Asked for a Peace Poem," from *The Collected Poems of Howard Nemerov* (University of Chicago Press, 1977). By permission of Margaret Nemerov.

*The Diary of Vaslav Nijinsky*, edited by Romola Nijinsky (New York: Simon and Schuster, 1936). By permission of Eric Glass Ltd. on behalf of the Estate of Vaslav Nijinsky.

# Index of Auden's Works

# General Index